...to e zucha chopagni ... ...ho
...o le feste ..ora ser... ...m
...ve que p certe sua... ...
...cho inpisa so rimasto daspecta...
...nir mene Costa e p ch mo ue sto
...o pel sopra dicto zucha cho...
...gi accio ch se fussi tempo da...
... e fromo p ui ma promesso ...
...di quali marmi uoi incho durr...
...rro cho frac e faro ho to a...
...ui e danarj ch uoi uorreto...
...la dipisa chome mauisousti e...
...Cosa espero auere risposta
...fati ch uostre io me sono ul...
...be ch prima lo sapeuo e
...stoui ubrigatissimo e so cer
...sta opa abbia aessere buon
...ho Cagniolo schultore

MICHELANGELO

pani dua
ū bochal di vino
una aringa
tortegli

una salata
quatro pani
ū bochal di tondo
ū quartuccio di bruscho
ū piattello di spinaci
quatro alice
tortelli

sei pani
dua minestre di finochio
una aringa
ū bochal di tondo

MICHELANGELO

VOLUME I

THE ACHIEVEMENT OF FAME

1475–1534

MICHAEL HIRST

YALE UNIVERSITY PRESS

NEW HAVEN AND LONDON

Designed by Gillian Malpass

Printed in China

LIBRARY OF CONGRESS CATALOGING-IN-PUBLICATION DATA

Hirst, Michael.
Michelangelo. The achievement of fame, 1475–1534 / Michael Hirst.
p. cm.
Includes bibliographical references and index.
ISBN 978-0-300-11861-2 (cloth : alk. paper)
1. Michelangelo Buonarroti, 1475–1564. 2. Artists–Italy–Biography.
I. Michelangelo Buonarroti, 1475–1564. II. Title.
III. Title: Achievement of fame, 1475–1534.
N6923.B9H55 2012
709.2–dc23
[B]
2011042294

Frontispiece: Lists of food made by Michelangelo,
Casa Buonarroti, Florence, Archivio Buonarroti, vol. x, fol. 578*v*

Endpaper illustrations: Letter from Michelangelo to Donato Benti,
Casa Buonarroti, Florence, Archivio Buonarroti, vol. v, 20, fol. 195, 57*r*

CONTENTS

PREFACE

The impetus to write a new biography of Michelangelo is directly related to the emergence of much revised and new material concerning the artist, his life and his work. The most notable event has been the publication of five volumes of his correspondence (1965–83), which includes not only letters written by him but also those addressed to him. Their publication owed much to the energy and dedication of Paola Barocchi and Renzo Ristori.[1] This corpus was supplemented by the publication of a further two volumes, generally referred as the *Carteggio indiretto* (1988 and 1995), which contain valuable material previously scattered and difficult to locate.[2] A final invaluable book, containing the artist's contracts, appeared in 2005.[3]

However, biographical material concerning the artist had begun to attract editorial attention a number of years earlier. Already in 1970 there had appeared the complete publication of Michelangelo's *Ricordi*, a book of more than four hundred pages, many of which, following a well-established Florentine tradition, are concerned with the details of his financial life.[4] A further invaluable resource is the collection of Giovanni Poggi's papers, at present housed in the Istituto Nazionale di Studi sul Rinascimento in Florence.[5]

The researches of the past, not least those of Gaetano Milanesi and Karl Frey, will undoubtedly remain outstanding contributions to the study of the artist's life and work, and recent decades have witnessed many significant additions to the subject. The challenge to any twenty-first-century biographer of Michelangelo is to integrate relevant new material with the old, in order to enhance our understanding of the artist's biography and achievements.

The story of Michelangelo's life has here been concluded in 1534, when the artist would move definitively to Rome. Thirty years of activity still remained and it is hoped that an account of these later decades can be returned to.

I should like to express my gratitude to all those institutions that have facilitated access to the original works and to those colleagues who have aided me in confronting the challenge of the bibliographical resources, which are almost inexhaustible. Particular thanks are owed to the libraries of the Warburg Institute in London, the Kunsthistorisches Institute and Istituto Nazionale di Studi sul Rinascimento at Palazzo Strozzi in Florence and the Bibliotheca Hertziana in Rome. Without their facilities, and a grant from the Leverhulme Foundation, this book would have remained unwritten. The Conway Library of the Courtauld Institute of Art has assisted with photographs, and Irene Brooke has collected the photographs and has helped with proof-reading. Arnold Nesselrath of the Vatican Galleries provided generous assistance when most needed, and Gillian Malpass of Yale University Press has been a constant support. Finally, my greatest debt is to my wife, Diane Zervas, for her unfailing advice and encouragement.

Michael Hirst
London, May 2010

I

FLORENTINE ORIGINS

THE BUONARROTI FAMILY

In his later years, one of Michelangelo's most active concerns was to emphasize the noble origins of his family. As early as 1520, he had formed a belief that the Buonarroti family were descended from a noble family, the counts of Canossa. A long-standing associate of the artist visited Count Alessandro da Canossa in the summer of that year, undoubtedly at the artist's instance. As a consequence, the count wrote to Michelangelo in October in the warmest terms, addressing him as 'honoured kinsman', and claiming that an ancestor, Simone da Canossa, had served as *podestà* in Florence in the past.[1]

If a letter by Michelangelo, written in 1548 to his nephew Leonardo, is to be believed, Count Alessandro had even visited him in Rome, an event the artist would dwell on with pride.[2] His gratification over the alleged connection is confirmed by the fact that, at some point in the 1520s, he executed a large drawing of a legendary count of Canossa, which now survives in a copy. The subject of the connection is alluded to at some length in the opening sentences of Condivi's Life of 1553, where an explanation is added of how the family name was changed to Buonarroti Simoni.[3]

If, however, on the one hand the old artist's letters emphasize the family's distinguished lineage, on the other they refer repeatedly to its decline, a fact reflected in the diminution in the number of significant public offices held by members of the family. Of greater moment is Michelangelo's awareness of a decline in its economic prosperity. The decline in office-holding has been outlined a number of times and not every detail need be examined here.[4] Michelangelo's own great-grandfather, Buonarrota, had enjoyed notable public success. He had served as a prior no less than three times, in 1390, 1397 and 1404.[5] His eldest son was almost as successful. The second son, Leonardo, Michelangelo's grandfather, served as a prior in 1456 and his uncle Michele in 1469. After this, there was a long pause; we have to wait until November 1515 for a member of the family to serve the two-month term as prior, the artist's own younger brother, Buonarroto.[6]

Michelangelo's references to the decline in the family's fortunes are a recurrent theme in the letters written to his nephew Leonardo, son of Buonarroto, in the late 1540s. In one of December 1546, while reminding him that the family sprang from a noble line, he went on to explain that, although he himself had always striven to restore the fortunes of their house, he had been let down by his brothers.[7] In a subsequent letter of June 1551, written when he has reached the age of seventy-six, he explains that he does not wish to dwell on the misery in which he found the family; it would require more than a book to describe. He has received only ingratitude for his efforts.[8]

Economic adversity involving the family seems to have set in during the earlier years of the fifteenth century. If one report can be depended on, one of the more successful family members left all his wealth to a confraternity at his death in 1428.[9]

Michelangelo's paternal grandfather, Leonardo, born in 1399, seems to have engaged in some form of banking. Marrying for the second time in 1432, he had seven children. No less than four of these were daughters, and one of these died young. But it was the marriage of his daughter Lisa in 1449 that provoked an acute financial crisis.

Her husband was a notary from Anghiari, Giusto Giusti, who would play a significant part in the affairs of the Florentine government; a remarkable series of his *ricordi*, vividly noting his very active life, survives.[10] Leonardo Buonarroti was unable to raise the money required to pay the dowry of 300 florins and was compelled to cede his house on the Piazza de' Peruzzi to his prospective son-in-law until the

money could be raised. These events show that he had made no provision for such an eventuality by investing in the Monte delle Doti,
or Dowry Fund, created to preclude such adversities. Leonardo's tax
return of 1458 shows that his property had not been recovered; listing
the dependants ('bocche') in his household, apart from his wife and
his two sons, Francesco and Lodovico, he refers to daughters still
unmarried.[11]

In their joint tax declaration of 1470, Francesco and Lodovico state
that 1,000 shares in the Monte Commune had been sold to meet the
problem of Lisa's marriage. The house that had been handed over to
her husband had not been retrieved, and the two brothers were living
in rented accommodation. Their financial constraints seem to have
been real, even if the sum that they reckoned they owed the commune
of 13 soldi seems exceptionally low.[12]

The positive feature of the Buonarroti family's fortunes was their
ownership of the house and land at Settignano, a property that would
play a constant role in the life of the family. The property is already
listed in the *catasto* return of 1477 of Leonardo and his brother Michele.
The house is described as that of a gentleman, *signorile*; there was land
and a workman's dwelling attached. When the property had been
acquired has not been established, but it had probably been bought in
the period of the greatest prosperity of the family in the previous
century. Despite future vicissitudes, the family held on to the property
for centuries and, in radically altered form, the house still exists.[13]

Two years after their declarations of 1470, both Francesco, born in
1434, and Lodovico, born ten years later in June 1444, married. The
marriage of Francesco was brief, for his wife died a year later. In the
following year, he married again; his second wife was Cassandra di
Cosimo Bartoli, who would create problems for the family on Francesco's death in 1508. Lodovico married Francesca, daughter of Neri
de Miniato del Sera and Bonda Rucellai, who brought with her a
dowry of a little over 400 florins.[14]

In their joint *catasto* declaration of 1480 the economic condition of
the two brothers appears to have improved. They had inherited a small

property from their uncle Michele, who had died in 1471; they declared they were renting it. Francesco appears to have dabbled in some modest banking activity, renting a 'banco' outside Or San Michele; the fact suggests that he was a member of the bankers' guild, the Arte del Cambio.[15]

The two brothers and their dependants were living together in a fraternal household. It comprised no less than nine members, including their still living mother. Four of Lodovico's sons are listed, for the fifth, Sigismondo, would be born in the following year. The house was being rented for a relatively modest sum from Filippo di Tommaso Narducci, who may have been a distant relative. The house in question, however, has been consistently misidentified. The correct property is the large house situated on the corner of Via Bentaccordi and Via Borgognone, some metres distant from the house traditionally identified as the family home, which bears a commemorative plaque and remains an 'object' of respect for tourist parties.[16]

How long the Buonarroti remained there is not known. When the two brothers filed their tax return for the Decima of 1498, they had moved. Still renting, they were situated close to San Pier Maggiore, faithful, as always, to the quarter of Santa Croce.[17] Conditions may have been easier by 1498. Their paternal grandmother had died in 1494. Lodovico's eldest son, named Leonardo after his grandfather, had become a Dominican brother in the summer of 1492. In the year of the Decima, Michelangelo, aged twenty-three, was in Rome, about to begin work on the marble *Pietà* that would establish his fame.

When Michelangelo, in his letter to his nephew, had referred to the miserable state of the Buonarroti family in his youth, he was accusing his brothers of their failure to contribute to the family's recovery. He had remained silent over his father's failure to alleviate its decline. Indeed, in a passage in Condivi's biography, which undoubtedly reflects Michelangelo's own words, we find Lodovico, in a reported exchange with Lorenzo de' Medici, conceding his failure to pursue a career.[18] His attempts to better the condition of the family seem to have been modest, and although he married a second time in 1485, his second wife, about whom little is known and who produced no children, would die in the summer of 1497.[19] Lodovico's letters, a substantial number of which survive, reveal an ageing man who seems to have been a constant prey to anxieties. Familiar is his complaint in a letter of 1500 to Michelangelo in Rome that he has five sons and has reached the age of fifty-six, yet there is no one to offer him a glass of water.[20]

In his passage describing Michelangelo's later entry into the Medici household, Condivi recounts how, at Lodovico's request, Lorenzo de' Medici had granted him a post in the Florence customs house, the Dogana. In a revisionist attempt to discredit the information, it has been claimed that Lodovico had already held a post there in 1479. The surviving documentation of 1479 refers to Lodovico having been drawn for office in the Dogana but records that he had declined the assignment. The fact suggests a disinclination to improve his circumstances.[21]

One office that he would accept would acquire subsequent fame, for it was during his six-month term as *podestà* of Caprese and Chiusi that Michelangelo was born. Lodovico had been drawn for the office in September 1474, which would last until late March 1475.[22] Subsequent confusion over the date of Michelangelo's birth would spring from the fact that the Florentine year began on 25 March, the Feast of the Annunciation. Hence, Vasari would write that the birth date was 6 March 1474.

In this he was followed by Condivi who, there can be no doubt, was depending on information received from the artist. Michelangelo had written to his nephew in Florence in April 1548, asking him to forward information about his birth, and informing him that he would find it in a 'libro di ricordi' that had been kept by Lodovico.[23] Lodovico's book is lost, as is the letter that Leonardo must have sent in response. However, a later text of the passage about the birth survives, giving the hour and day of birth, the year calculated in Florentine style.[24]

Had Lodovico's book survived, we might have learnt more about the episode of Michelangelo being sent to a wet-nurse, a *balìa*. The evidence for this is a familiar passage in Condivi's biography, where he refers to the episode. Lodovico had sent his son to a wet-nurse at Settignano, the daughter of a stone cutter and the wife of another. Condivi relates that Michelangelo, partly in jest but perhaps also in earnest, had said that it was no cause for surprise that he so delighted in the use of a chisel, knowing that the wet-nurse's milk has such force that it can often change the child's disposition. In referring to this fact, the artist was echoing a long-standing Tuscan belief.[25]

In keeping his *ricordi*, Lodovico had been following a widespread and deeply rooted Florentine practice, one that has been much studied in recent years.[26] The loss is irreparable, for his *libro* must have contained precious material relating to the family, not least information about the artist's childhood and emerging career. It would also, perhaps, have provided information about his wife, Francesca del Sera, mother of five sons, who would die in December 1481 at the age of thirty. Only a single reference to her survives in the artist's letters, and she is nowhere recorded in his poetry or in Condivi's biography.

One aspect of her role, however, does emerge. While Lodovico's book of *ricordi* is lost, copies of a few pages of an informal account-book, a *libro di spese*, have survived. They offer some glimpses of events between 1477 and 1480. They contain, for example, a few references to Michelangelo as a child. We learn that, in early August 1478, Lodovico paid 7 soldi for a pair of shoes for the infant Michelangelo, followed, in the same month, by a payment of 10 soldi for a lace dress.[27]

More significant are references to hospitality extended to the family by Francesca Buonarroti's mother, Michelangelo's maternal grandmother, Bonda Rucellai. Now widowed, she still lived in the villa at Fiesole that had been acquired by her deceased husband, Neri de Sera, in 1467. One such visit to the villa is recorded in October 1478, when Lodovico, Francesca and their three sons, Leonardo, Michelangelo and the recently born Buonarroto, went to stay with her to escape what

would be the last serious outbreak of plague in Florence in the fifteenth century.[28]

It has been suggested that a distant connection through marriage
between Bonda and the Medici could have led to the introduction of
Michelangelo into the circle of Lorenzo de' Medici.[29] Perhaps a more
tangible connection may be found in the close proximity of Bonda's
villa at Fiesole to another, the one that had been built by Cosimo de'
Medici's younger son, Giovanni, who had died in 1469. Inventories
reveal that a room at the villa was designated as that of Lorenzo.[30]

The fragmentary evidence for Michelangelo's childhood can be supplemented by evidence of a different kind. A close friend of Vasari,
Don Miniato Pitti, when in Rome in 1563, had visited the old
Michelangelo, who had less than a year to live. Pitti had asked the
old artist his age and had received the reply that he was eighty-eight.
He had gone on to refer to an event in 1478. He recounted how he
had been carried on his father's shoulders to witness the public execution of leaders of the Pazzi conspiracy, the plot that had led to the
murder of Giuliano, brother of Lorenzo de' Medici, in Florence cathedral. Michelangelo had referred specifically to Jacopo Pazzi, one of the
leaders who were publicly hanged from a window of Palazzo Vecchio
on 28 April 1478. One can only speculate as to whether this precocious
exposure to violent death may have contributed to the mature
Michelangelo's apprehensive nature, one that would lead to his repeated
flights from perceived danger.[31]

FROM SCHOOLROOM TO WORKSHOP

While references to the three-year-old Michelangelo are modest,
information about the subsequent years scarcely exists. The only statement to shed some light on his early upbringing is one to be found
in Condivi's biography. He writes that Lodovico recognized his second
son's abilities and sent him to school with Francesco da Urbino.[32]

Lodovico had sent his eldest son, Leonardo, to learn to read with
the local priest at Settignano in 1477 when he was four years old.
Whether he followed a similar course with Michelangelo is unknown.
The pattern of education of the period would suggest that, after mas-
tering reading and writing in Italian, he would have proceeded to
study under an abacus teaching and, only after this, would have gone
to study Latin under Francesco da Urbino, perhaps at the age of
eleven, which takes us to 1486.[33] Evidence has survived that shows
that Leonardo had been the pupil of an abacus teacher when aged a
little over nine.[34]

The name of Francesco da Urbino indicates that Lodovico attached
importance to Michelangelo's education. He is documented as a teacher
no later than 1483 and, by this date, had probably drawn up his own
Latin grammar, the *Regole*. The book is now lost but it makes an
appearance in an inventory of his books that Leonardo da Vinci drew
up in 1503, suggesting that at that date the older artist was still concerned to acquire Latin.[35]

How long Michelangelo remained with Francesco da Urbino is
unknown, although the period must have been brief, prior to his
involvement in the workshop of Domenico Ghirlandaio. In his old
age he confessed his lack of Latin to his friend Donato Giannotti and
expressed his wish to acquire it. There is some evidence that, earlier
in life, he had avoided the use of Latin. He did not add Latin inscriptions, as did Raphael, when representing the sibyls of antiquity. He
was one of the signatories who signed the petition in 1519 requesting
the return of Dante's bones to Florence and was unique among those
involved in expressing his wish in Italian rather than Latin.[36] And on
at least two occasions he appeared to have required that the Latin text
of important contracts be translated into the vernacular.[37]

Condivi's passage describing Michelangelo's early wish to be an artist
is a familiar one. The emphasis on Lodovico's opposition to his son's
aspirations may have been exaggerated by the old artist, anxious to
dwell on his early struggles. His emphasis, however, on the role played
by Francesco Granacci in supporting his wishes is likely to be deserved.

Granacci is credited, not once but twice, with having contributed to his career at this point.

The Granacci family were of no great social distinction; indeed, the artist's grandfather had been a baker. They had lived in the quarter of Santa Croce since at least 1427; in the family's *catasto* return of that year, they declare a house they owned in Via Ghibellina, the street in which Michelangelo would make his first purchase of property in 1508. In a *catasto* return of 1479–80, Francesco is described as eleven years old, implying a birth date of 1469 or 1470. He was, therefore, Michelangelo's senior by five or six years. It has been persuasively suggested that he entered the Ghirlandaio workshop in the mid-1480s.[38]

Condivi, in a familiar passage, states that Granacci provided Michelangelo with drawings from the Ghirlandaio workshop and that he passed on to him an example of Martin Schongauer's engraving of the *Temptation of St Anthony*. The young Michelangelo is reported to have painted a copy on panel of such distinction that rumour had spread that it had aroused Ghirlandaio's jealousy.[39]

Condivi does not explicitly deny that Michelangelo had been a mentor of the Ghirlandaio workshop. His remark that he had learnt nothing from him might be regarded as implicit confirmation of the fact; the statement was probably prompted by the alleged behaviour of Domenico's son, Ridolfo, who is reported to have claimed that the subsequent greatness of the artist owed to what he had learnt from his father.[40]

Vasari, however, understood Condivi's passage as an attempted rebuttal of what he had written in his Life of 1550, where he had referred to a document confirming the fact. In his massively revised Life of 1568, published four years after the artist's death, Vasari returned to the issue. Referring to Condivi's statement while avoiding naming him, he now went to the length of printing the text of the indenture, which he had copied from a book of *ricordi* of the two Ghirlandaio brothers, Domenico and Davide. The text had been written by Lodovico. Dated 1 April 1488, it states that Michelangelo is to remain with them for three years in order to learn to paint and to provide whatever assistance they may require. In an entry written below, Lodovico stated that he had received 2 florins. Vasari added a mistaken statement that Michelangelo had been fourteen when he entered the workshop.[41]

Michelangelo's admittance to Ghirlandaio's workshop at the age of thirteen was a contravention of the rules of the guild to which painters belonged, the Arte de' Medici e Speziali, which laid down fourteen as the minimum age for the enrolment of an apprentice.[42] In fact, he had already been associated with the Ghirlandaio workshop nine months before his formal enrolment in April 1488. A recently discovered payment to Domenico for his work in progress on the altarpiece that he had undertaken for the Ospedale degli Innocenti in Piazza Santissima Annunziata reveals that credit was collected on 28 June 1487 by Michelangelo. In performing the task, he was acting in a traditional role assigned to junior but trusted assistants in the workshop.[43]

Ghirlandaio's *Adoration of the Magi*, still in the museum of the Ospedale, is one of his finest panel paintings, carried out with consummate care and still in excellent condition. The twelve-year-old Michelangelo could have witnessed the master at work on it and learnt from his example an ideal of finish in panel painting that he would not forget. His involvement in the shop could also have led him, at this early age, to encounter others who would later play a significant part in his career. One of these could have been Giuliano da Sangallo; he appears in the surviving accounts for work on the frame of the altarpiece and on the tabernacle that crowned it.[44] He was destined to come to Michelangelo's aid just twenty years later in devising the scaffolding for the Sistine Chapel ceiling.

How long Michelangelo remained in the Ghirlandaio workshop is not known. He cannot have stayed for the term of three years prescribed in his indenture; subsequent developments suggest that his presence there did not exceed eighteen months at most. There seems little doubt, however, that he was in the workshop at the time when Ghirlandaio was occupied with completing one of the most taxing assignments of his career, the fresco decoration of the Tornabuoni Chapel in Santa Maria Novella. Begun earlier, it seems probable that the most intense activity there, which involved no less than two of the chapel's three walls, extended from 1488 to 1490.[45] Attempts to see Michelangelo's hand in the murals are naive. But he must have been an acute observer of how Ghirlandaio ran his workshop and was probably involved in the mechanical tasks that fresco painting entailed, such as grinding colours and preparing lime.

It is perhaps no coincidence that Michelangelo himself would initially engage a team of assistants of about the number adopted by Ghirlandaio when he came to plan the mural decoration of the Sistine Chapel ceiling. But Ghirlandaio's example as both a painter on panel and, most obviously, as a draughtsman left a profound mark on his future work, a gift from the master to whom, in old age, he would deny any valued role in his professional upbringing.[46]

MICHELANGELO, LORENZO AND BERTOLDO

In the second letter of Michelangelo to have survived, addressed to his father from Rome on 1 July 1497, he would sign himself Michelangelo sculptor, 'Michelangelo scultore'.[47] He would continue to adopt the practice for many years, even in those written when he was at work painting the ceiling of the Sistine Chapel. The latest example of this form of signature that now survives is of 1526.[48] A little more than twenty years later, he would write that he no longer wished to be addressed as 'sculptor'.[49]

Nevertheless, despite the artist's own early emphasis on his calling as a sculptor, the circumstances in which he became one have occasioned differences among his biographers. In both editions of his Life, Vasari would state that it was no less than Ghirlandaio himself who was involved in introducing him to the Medici garden at San Marco, accompanied by Francesco Granacci. Condivi confines himself to the statement that it was Granacci who introduced him to the garden, thereby denying any significant role on the part of Ghirlandaio.[50]

As has been seen, it remains a matter of speculation when Michelangelo left the Ghirlandaio workshop. Vasari states that he spent no longer than a year there, thereby freeing the young man to have passed no less than four years in the circle of Lorenzo. Where we might hope for exactitude on the part of Condivi, we find him less explicit than we might wish. He writes, certainly at the artist's instance, that Michelangelo entered the Medicean circle when he was aged between fifteen and sixteen. The statement implies that this happened at some point in 1490 or 1491; the earlier year is the more probable.[51] It is worth adding here that neither writer makes any reference to an apprenticeship of Michelangelo with Benedetto da Maiano, with whom it has been implausibly proposed that he underwent an early training as a marble sculptor.[52]

Influential doubts have been expressed in recent times about the sculpture garden on the *piazza*, even extending to scepticism about its very existence.[53] That it did exist has been conclusively demonstrated and it has been established that Lorenzo acquired the property in the 1470s.[54]

The date might suggest that, in instituting a garden of sculpture, Lorenzo was inspired by what he saw on a visit to Rome with his brother-in-law Bernardo Rucellai, prompted by the election and subsequent coronation of Pope Sixtus IV in 1471. No less than Alberti guided them round the city. Rome would become celebrated for its sculpture gardens, but it should be noted that most of these were formed at a time following Lorenzo's visit.[55] And sculpture had already been a feature of the garden of Palazzo Medici on the Via Larga, open to select visitors. One reference to the reality of the San Marco garden mentions the presence of Leonardo da Vinci there.[56] Still more striking, and relevant for an assessment of what went on there, is the information that Michelangelo, two years following Lorenzo's death, left the garden in the early autumn of 1494 in circumstances that will be described below.

More problematic is the issue of a school for sculptors in the garden, supervised by Donatello's former assistant Bertoldo di Giovanni. Vasari already refers to the garden in the edition of 1550, and Torrigiano is there noted as a frequenter. The topic is greatly elaborated on in the revised edition of 1568, where he names no less than nine artists and the alleged membership listed raises serious problems of chronology.[57]

There is undoubtedly a good deal of anachronistic embellishment in Vasari's list of those involved. Some, however, can be shown to have had dealings with Michelangelo, not least the modestly endowed Giuliano Bugiardini, an almost exact contemporary who would prove a staunch friend and who is documented as a dining companion of Michelangelo decades later. Pietro Torrigiano's relations with Michelangelo would achieve notoriety. We are told that the two used to copy Masaccio's frescos in the Carmine together. This would lead to a notorious episode when, incensed by Michelangelo's comments on his work, Torrigiano struck his companion and broke his nose. The episode was well known in Florence and the truth of the story is confirmed by dependable portraits of the artist.[58]

Vasari may have exaggerated when he wrote that it was Lorenzo's aim to create a school of native sculptors under the direction of Bertoldo di Giovanni. Nevertheless, there could have been an element of truth in what he wrote. In the decade of the 1480s Florence would be deprived of two of its most celebrated sculptors, Andrea Verrocchio, who had won the competition to carry out the equestrian statue of Bartolommeo Colleoni in Venice, and Antonio Pollaiuolo, who left to go to Rome to undertake the tomb of Pope Sixtus IV, following his death in August 1489.

There is explicit evidence of Lorenzo's own awareness of a lack of native talent in a letter written on 8 August 1489, a reply to a request from his ambassador in Milan, Pietro Alamanni. Alamanni had passed on a request that help be sent from Florence to Milan to collaborate on the huge undertaking of the equestrian bronze statue of Francesco Sforza, a taxing project given to Leonardo by Francesco's son, Lodovico il Moro. In his letter, Lorenzo explains that he has given thought to the request but cannot offer help. He explicitly voices a regret over a lack of sculptors in the city.[59] The request related to the task of casting on a monumental scale, and Lorenzo's own favoured sculptor, Bertoldo di Giovanni, although a master of small bronzes, cannot have been regarded as an appropriate candidate.[60]

Vasari did not see fit to award Bertoldo with a biography in his *Vite*, but he refers to him in the Lives of both Donatello and Michelangelo. In both of these texts, he states that Bertoldo completed work on the two bronze pulpits undertaken by Donatello for San Lorenzo. A recently discovered document of March 1466 actually refers to the possibility of an impending collaboration of Bertoldo with Donatello, hence confirming the association with the old master, who would die nine months later in December.[61] There seems, therefore, little room for doubt that Bertoldo was associated with Donatello on his last works. What remains unknown is when Bertoldo was born, although it should be noted that, when discussing his involvement in the garden when Michelangelo was there, Vasari explicitly writes that he was too old to work.[62]

Whether it is appropriate to characterize Bertoldo as a court artist is a matter for debate. The closeness of his relations with Lorenzo is confirmed by a letter he wrote to his patron in 1479.[63] There is evidence, for example, that he was expected to give Lorenzo advice on his acquisitions.[64] The inventory of Palazzo Medici drawn up following Lorenzo's death in 1492 shows that Bertoldo had a room provided for him. It explicitly refers to a work of his now lost and mentions three others that can be securely assigned to him and which survive. One of the latter is the celebrated *Battle* relief placed over a fireplace in a small room facing the *sala grande*.[65] Such domesticity granted to Bertoldo was not without Medicean precedent. A rather inconspicuous sculptor, Andrea dell'Aquila, is reported to have lived for many years in Palazzo Medici, the beneficiary of the hospitality of Lorenzo's grandfather Cosimo.[66]

Condivi's total silence with regard to Bertoldo would seem to reflect Michelangelo's marginalizing in old age those who had contributed to his artistic upbringing. He could have entered the Medicean circle in time to learn from Bertoldo; indeed, it may have been Bertoldo who arranged for the young man's move to Palazzo Medici and enjoyment of the same privilege of a room that he had done. Bertoldo would die at Poggio a Caiano in December 1491, just four months before Lorenzo's own death in the following April.

That the young Michelangelo studied Bertoldo's work has been recognized for more than a hundred years. Bertoldo's bronze *Battle* relief exercised an enduring influence.[67] Another work of Bertoldo's, his bronze *Orpheus*, which may have been accessible to him, and may date from as early as 1471, presages the *figura serpentinata* of the following century.[68] Memories of Bertoldo's inventions would endure and need not be dwelt on here.[69] However, his chosen material of bronze did not, it would seem, weaken the young man's dedication to marble.

Condivi's account of Michelangelo's introduction to Lorenzo de' Medici is among the liveliest passages in his book, making much of the young man's carving of a faun, Lorenzo's praise of the work and his criticism that the sculptor had erred in leaving the head with all the teeth intact. Lorenzo, we are told, overcame the opposition of Lodovico, who could not distinguish between a sculptor and a stonemason. There followed Michelangelo's move to Palazzo Medici and the hospitality extended to him, Lorenzo frequently summoning the young man to inspect his collection of jewels, cameos, medals and other precious objects.[70] This account has been declared a myth by some recent sceptics. Yet we should recall a later comment of Pope Leo X to Sebastiano del Piombo, recorded in a letter of the latter of October 1520. Leo, second son of Lorenzo and exactly the same age as the artist, had explained to Sebastiano how he and Michelangelo had grown up together.[71]

Lorenzo's favour, we are told, also extended to Lodovico, meeting his request that he be granted an office that had become vacant in the

Florence customs house, the Dogana. This has also been dismissed as a fiction. But its truth is confirmed by an episode of 1513, following the Medicean restoration. Early in that year, Lodovico wrote to Lorenzo's son, Giuliano de' Medici, following the family's return to power, asking for the restitution of the office he had lost with the fall of the Medici in 1494.[72]

Michelangelo worked on two carvings in Lorenzo's lifetime. The earlier, now generally referred to as the *Madonna of the Stairs*, is a still slightly tentative but very personal exercise in low relief, *rilievo schiacciato*, which had been employed on a number of occasions by Donatello many decades earlier and adopted by a later generation of sculptors, among them Desiderio da Settignano. The marble block that the young artist employed is no more than 3.5 centimetres deep (pl. 1). Had Michelangelo died after working on it, the relief would probably have come to be assigned to an unknown follower of Donatello. Its lack of concessions to decorative ornament is striking. The invention is one of exceptional austerity and, despite the background *putti*, of striking melancholy. It may well have been undertaken in an early moment following the young man's introduction to the garden, prior to his entry into the household of Palazzo Medici.[73]

The *Madonna of the Stairs* was not brought to complete finish. It would remain what could be called a 'lost' work for decades. Vasari knew nothing about it when he wrote his account of the artist in his book of 1550 and Michelangelo himself evidently felt it required no mention when describing his early life to Condivi. Its whereabouts prior to his death are unknown. Described for the first time in print in Vasari's biography of 1568, it would be presented as a gift to Duke Cosimo de' Medici by the artist's nephew, Leonardo.

Michelangelo's subsequent work, the marble relief of the *Battle of the Centaurs and Lapiths* (pl. 2), is carving of a very different character by an artist who has put behind him the tentativeness of the *Madonna of the Stairs*. It too had been unknown to Vasari when he published his *Lives* in 1550 and seems to have been first recorded in print in Condivi's biography of three years later. Its history is, however, not so completely lacking in incident as that of the earlier work. In 1528 surviving letters record that, at that moment, an attempt to acquire it was made on behalf of Federico Gonzaga, Marquis of Mantua. The episode is of great interest and will be returned to at a later point in this book. Here, however, it is important to note that the artist is reported to have declared that he had undertaken the work for 'a great lord'. This leaves no doubt that the *Battle* had been conceived and undertaken for Lorenzo himself and it is well-nigh certain that the young artist broke off work on it when Lorenzo died in April 1492.

The *Battle* relief, which reveals great ambition and a familiarity with the antique far removed from his earlier relief, was a sculpture that Michelangelo was prepared to refer to in his exchanges with Condivi. Indeed, it is discussed at some length, although only in a later comment on Condivi's passage did the artist indicate that it had been left unfinished.[74]

The evocation of violence in the relief does not facilitate the exact identification of the figures. Whereas for some, the figure on the left represents Theseus, for others he is Hercules. In remarking on the relief to Condivi, Michelangelo refers both to the Rape of Deianira and the Battle of the Centaurs. The latter subject was one described at great length by Ovid in his *Metamorphoses*; he devoted no less than 325 verses to the episode, and a number of features in the work reflect his text. The battle between Lapiths and Centaurs was certainly one that can be found elsewhere in the period that concerns us.[75]

Michelangelo confided to Condivi the striking fact that, in com- posing the relief, he had been helped and encouraged by Angelo Poliziano. Poliziano had gone through the story, part by part, explaining everything to him.

Poliziano is the only member of the Medicean circle to be expressly named in Condivi's book. Born in Montepulciano, he seems to have entered the household around 1472 and he would be entrusted with the education of Lorenzo's eldest son, Piero; he was still active in this role in the early 1480s. He would be portrayed twice by Domenico Ghirlandaio, once in the Sassetti Chapel in Santa Trinita in the

company of Lorenzo's sons and again in the Tornabuoni Chapel in
Santa Maria Novella. He was an astonishing polymath, and a review
of his many activities cannot be undertaken here. A few years before
Michelangelo had entered the circle of Palazzo Medici, he had supervised the publication of the first printed edition of Alberti's *De Re
Aedificatoria*, which appeared in 1485 with Poliziano's personal dedication to Lorenzo.[76]

In what ways the young artist profited from Poliziano's friendship
cannot be established. It may have been Poliziano who introduced him
to the works of Alberti and, perhaps, as he had done with Ovid, examined the texts with him. While the *De Pictura* had been translated into
the vernacular, the *De Statua* had not. In the *De Statua*, Alberti contended that the sculptor carves the block of stone to reveal the pre-
existing figure within. It was a concept that would appeal deeply to
Michelangelo and would appear in poems written many years later.[77]

IN THE SERVICE OF PIERO

Lorenzo died at the Medici villa at Careggi before daybreak on 8 April
1492. It was where his grandfather, Cosimo, had died in 1464. Cosimo
had achieved the age of seventy-five; Lorenzo, for a long time suffering from declining health, was forty-three.

A description of his last hours was written by Piero Parenti, no lover
of the Medici family. He recounts that, conscious of his impending
death, Lorenzo expressed three wishes. One was to have seen his son
Giovanni, recently created a cardinal. The second was that the building
of the villa at Poggio a Caiano be completed. And the third wish was
that provision be made for his cherished collection of Greek and Latin
manuscripts. Parenti named those who visited him as he lay dying, who
included Poliziano, Piero della Mirandola and Girolamo Savonarola.
Lorenzo had summoned his eldest son, Piero, to whom he gave advice
about his future. His body was first taken to San Marco and subsequently moved to San Lorenzo.[78]

The many expressions of grief at Lorenzo's death cannot be reviewed here at length. One of the most eloquent was that contained in a letter of Poliziano of 18 May, addressed to his friend Jacopo Antiquario in Milan. He wrote: 'With the demise of him, the sole instigator of my scholarship, my passion for writing has perished too, and almost all my enthusiasm for my past studies has faded away.'[79] The note of grief, however, was not confined to close Medicean circles. Praise of Lorenzo was widespread and extended to such relatively modest figures as the coppersmith Bartolommeo Masi.[80] A remarkable passage about Lorenzo was written into his diary by Luca Landucci, laying emphasis, among other tributes, on his success in obtaining the cardinal's hat for his second son, Giovanni, the future Pope Leo x.[81]

Condivi relates that Michelangelo returned to live with Lodovico after Lorenzo's death, demoralized by the loss of his patron. Then, recovering, he turned to work. He acquired a block of marble that had lain neglected, unprotected from wind and rain. From it, he carved a statue of Hercules measuring over two metres high.[82]

Only following the passage about the *Hercules* does Condivi turn to Michelangelo's return to the service of Piero de' Medici, as if implicitly dissociating the two events. He relates that he was summoned by Piero to make a snowman in the courtyard of Palazzo Medici and was awarded the hospitality that he had enjoyed under Lorenzo, given the same room and accorded an honoured place at his table. We are told that he was treated on the same footing as a Spanish groom who could run as fast as Piero rode, a scarcely flattering comment.[83]

It can, in fact, be shown that the artist's hostility to Piero evident in Condivi's account involved a wilful manipulation of events. If what he writes is accepted, it must be concluded that the *Hercules* was undertaken for his own private satisfaction. That the statue was, on the contrary, made for Piero was proposed a number of years ago, and this suspicion has been confirmed by the recent publication of documents relating to the sale of Medici property that took place after Piero had fled the city. We are presented, in other words, with a flagrant *damnatio memoriae*.[84]

Later events are here worth noting. Letters written by Michelangelo when he had arrived in Rome in 1496 reveal that he was prepared to undertake work for the exiled Piero, although these indicate that the artist was let down. The indictment of Piero in Condivi's text is that Lorenzo's eldest son was proud and overbearing, possessing neither the goodness of Giovanni nor the humanity of Giuliano.[85]

Michelangelo's *Hercules*, given its scale and subject, could have been his first heroically conceived sculpture. Its disappearance is grievous. Circumstantial evidence points to the probability that he gave it as a present to the Strozzi family, perhaps in 1506.[86] It was exported to France in circumstances referred to in a subsequent chapter. The evidence of its appearance is, unfortunately, not dependable.[87]

One further work of sculpture is associated by Condivi with this period, a wooden crucifix, which Michelangelo undertook for the prior of Santo Spirito. Described as a little under life-size, we are told that the artist made it as a form of thanks to the prior, who had facilitated his undertaking anatomical studies, providing him with a room and with corpses.[88]

Piero may have played a decisive part in introducing his young protégé to the Santo Spirito community. Like his father before him, Piero became an *operaio*, elected to the office in March 1493.[89] While Piero was on familiar terms with the Augustinians, it is improbable that Michelangelo had many contacts within a relatively distant *quartiere*. The availability of corpses can be explained by the adjoining infirmary or hospital, its existence confirmed by contemporary documents.[90] A comparable case is provided by Leonardo's well-known dissection of the corpse of an old man at the hospital of Santa Maria Nuova some fifteen years later. How far this activity of Michelangelo was an isolated episode is difficult to determine. It appears not to have been his last, for a rather bizarre episode indicates his making a dissection following his return from Rome and after Piero Soderini had been elected to the office of *gonfaloniere* for life in 1502.[91]

The crucifix would subsequently prove to be an elusive work. After major changes in Santo Spirito from 1600, it seems to have disappeared.

Its recovery is a relatively recent one, in 1963 (pl. 3). Although its original situation over the high altar must have been the choice of Prior Niccolò di Bichiellini, it can never have exercised a great effect because of the slenderness of the form. Its current display in Giuliano da Sangallo's sacristy shows it to good advantage.[92]

Such a stable environment suggested by the activities at Santo Spirito would not endure. The decision of Charles VIII of France to invade Italy in pursuit of his claim to the kingdom of Naples was followed by a successful invasion and steady progress south. In late October 1493, with the situation ever more threatening, Piero left Florence to treat with the French king. Negotiations that followed led to Piero's notorious surrender of the fortresses of Pisa, Livorno, Pietrasanta and Sarzana to the French. The climax precipitated by Piero's actions occurred on 9 November, when, on returning from a futile further visit, Piero was refused access to the Palazzo della Signoria.[93] Accompanied by his two brothers, Giuliano and Cardinal Giovanni, Piero fled to Bologna. Charles entered a Florence no longer under the control of the Medici regime on 17 November.[94] The Medici brothers, given a cool reception by the Bentivoglio, proceeded to Venice.

One of the most bizarre episodes in Michelangelo's life, however, if Condivi is accepted, is that surrounding the young man's flight from Florence. This took place many weeks before the Medici collapse of November. We are plunged into the events with great abruptness. If what he writes is dependable, the chief protagonist in the drama was a fellow member of Piero's household, identified in his account as Cardiere.

Cardiere is no phantom figure, even if the unfolding events seem scarcely credible. We are told that his skills as an improviser on the lyre had been greatly valued by Lorenzo. His significance in the Medicean circle is indicated by the fact that he was one of the privileged group who had accompanied Piero to Rome in December 1492 to congratulate Alexander VI on his election as pope.[95] Condivi's Cardiere is an Italianization. He can be identified as Johannes Cordier, a Netherlandish master of the viola who had been born in Bruges.[96]

Good friends, Cardiere would confide in Michelangelo a dream, in which the dead Lorenzo had appeared clad only in a tattered gown. He had ordered Cardiere to tell Piero that he would shortly be driven out of Florence and would never return. Cardiere had refused Michelangelo's pressure to follow the dead man's instructions and inform Piero of his experience. On a subsequent morning, Michelangelo had encountered a terrified Cardiere. Lorenzo had reappeared in a second dream and struck him for refusing to speak to Piero. Yielding to Michelangelo's insistence, Cardiere had started out for Poggio a Caiano. He had met his patron on the road, accompanied by Piero Dovizi da Bibbiena, one of Piero's closest confidants, who had greeted his story with derision.[97] We are told that Michelangelo left Florence two days later, accompanied by two companions who are not named. They took the road to Venice but lack of money compelled them to retrace their steps. Michelangelo, however, blessed by the providential appearance of a protector when they reached Bologna, remained there. As proposed below, one of his companions was probably a fellow sculptor, Baccio da Montelupo.

The events as narrated by Condivi have an almost apocalyptic character. Nevertheless, the young artist's abandonment of the garden at San Marco is confirmed by a contemporary letter. It was written by a member of Piero's household, Ser Amedeo, on 14 October, and was addressed to his brother Adriano, the man who had cast Bertoldo's bronze *Bellerophon* group and who was now working Naples. Amedeo reports that Michelangelo has left the garden to go to Venice. He had not informed Piero, who has taken his behaviour much amiss.[98]

Although Amedeo does not give the exact date of Michelangelo's abrupt departure, he is clearly referring to a very recent event. Alarm in Florence about the proximity of the French had begun to spread, and was greatly increased by the departure of the French envoys empty-handed on 10 October.[99] It would be characteristic of the artist to act precipitately. In a later crisis that threatened Florence in 1512, he would write to his family from Rome urging them to be the first to flee.

BOLOGNA AND AFTER

Recounting events to Condivi, Michelangelo reported that he had left Florence with two companions. After a pause in Bologna they had gone on to Venice, but lack of money compelled them to return to Bologna. That he remained there rather than returning to Florence like his companions was due, we are told, to a curious accident.

Condivi explains that those entering the city who were not native Bolognese had to submit to a particular requirement: they were obliged to have a thumb-nail impressed with red sealing wax. Inadvertently failing to comply, Michelangelo was led to what he refers to as the Ufficio delle Bullette, a form of customs house, and fined. Unable to pay, he was saved by the presence there of a distinguished Bolognese, Giovan Francesco Aldrovandi, who paid the fine and invited him to enjoy the hospitality of his house. Fortune had not deserted him.[100]

Aldrovandi was a significant figure in the Bologna of Giovanni II Bentivoglio. He had served on many diplomatic missions and had, indeed, been *podestà* in Florence in 1488. His public career survived the vagaries of political change in Bologna, for his abilities were employed not only by the Bentivoglio but also, subsequently, by Pope Julius II. Condivi's reference to his membership of the governing body of the city, the Sedici Riformatori, was correct. But other aspects of his personality, perhaps not least his material prosperity, must also have recommended him to the young artist, so recently deprived of his Florentine patron. Aldrovandi's house in the Via Galliera contained a remarkable library, and his literary tastes lend substance to the account in Condivi of patron and artist passing the evening together, the young man invited by his host to read Dante, Petrarch and, occasionally, Boccaccio. The role assigned to Aldrovandi in introducing Michelangelo to San Domenico is entirely credible, for he himself had supervised the restoration of an earlier monument in the church.[101]

Condivi states that both of Michelangelo's companions returned to Florence while he stayed on in Bologna, enjoying the patronage of Aldrovandi and enlisted to provide marble statues still lacking on the

Arca in San Domenico. It is probable that one of these companions was his fellow Florentine sculptor, Baccio da Montelupo. This belief is supported by the fact that Baccio, some months later, would deliver a terracotta group of the *Lamentation* to San Domenico, which was put in place, following its painting, between January and April 1495. Both sculptors were, therefore, active in the church in these early months of the new year.[102]

In taking up work on the sculptural programme of the Arca, Michelangelo was following in the footsteps of a sculptor whose very name associated him with the project, Niccolò dell'Arca, who had died only recently, in early March 1494.[103] The extent of Michelangelo's contribution has, however, actuated much debate. Condivi states that the artist contributed two statues, the *St Petronius* and a kneeling angel. Early and dependable evidence, on the other hand, claims that he was involved in three. This source is a manuscript of *ricordi* of a man involved with San Domenico for many decades, Fra Lodovico da Prelormo. He states that Michelangelo carved a large part of the *St Petronius*, all the *St Proculus*, and a kneeling angel.[104] Despite many differences of opinion expressed about the statues in recent times, Fra Lodovico's information is compatible with the appearance of the figures (pls 4, 5).[105]

The order in which the artist worked on the three figures has been much discussed. Perhaps he was first handed the *St Petronius* to complete and his two independent carvings followed. Condivi relates that his stay in Bologna was cut short by threats from an unidentified rival artist, and there can be no doubt that work on the sculptural decoration of the Arca remained unfinished and was resumed by Antonio Lombardo after 1530.[106]

When Michelangelo left Bologna seems not to have been recorded. The Florentine government had granted an amnesty to followers of the exiled Medici in March 1495, but work on the Arca figures can scarcely have been finished much earlier than the summer.

If, in leaving Bologna, Michelangelo lost a patron in Giovan Francesco Aldrovandi, he gained a new one on his return to Florence,

Lorenzo di Pierfrancesco de' Medici, born in 1463. He and his brother, Giovanni di Pierfrancesco, were youthful cousins of Lorenzo il Magnifico, who had extended help to them after their father's death in 1476. Lorenzo di Pierfrancesco came from a highly cultivated background. Years later, in 1498, Botticelli's *Primavera* would feature among the contents of the brothers' house in the Via Larga.[107]

How Michelangelo came to enjoy Lorenzo's patronage is not known; the suggestion that he actually lived in the house of the two brothers in Florence is unconfirmed but not impossible. All that is reported is Condivi's statement that he carved for Lorenzo di Pierfrancesco a statue of a youthful St John the Baptist; the information appears to be confirmed by such a figure listed in the inventory of their house in the Via Larga.[108] Lorenzo di Pierfrancesco's importance for the artist was not limited to his commissioning of a sculpture; he would play a part in Michelangelo's move from Florence to Rome in the summer of 1496.

A remarkable feature of life in Florence in the months preceding this move to Rome should not escape mention: the role of Girolamo Savonarola. The friar's authority had reached a point in the midsummer of 1495 where Landucci would remark that his followers implicitly obeyed him.[109] His series of sermons in the early months of 1496 would achieve extraordinary authority; they also involved unprecedented attacks on the Roman Curia.[110]

It is noteworthy that the artist refers to Savonarola only briefly in Condivi's book; he states that he has studied his writings and has always held him in grand affection, still recalling the preacher's voice.[111] Other evidence is difficult to come by, but what exists points to a marked lack of sympathy for the Frate and his followers on the part of other members of the Buonarroti family.

One piece of evidence dates from Savonarola's own lifetime. Piero d'Argenta, a faithful assistant of the artist who was with him in Rome, would write to Buonarroto in March 1497. He gives news about events in Rome and refers to Savonarola with sharp irony. In the event, the Frate was excommunicated by Pope Alexander VI just two months later. The tone of Piero d'Argenta's remarks effectively excludes any great sympathy for Savonarola in the family circle.[112]

A few further scattered references to Savonarola's followers contained in the family correspondence, some made well after the Frate's death in 1498, seem to confirm a lack of sympathy with the *piagnoni*. When, for example, Michelangelo felt obliged to dismiss one of the assistants he had summoned to help him with the painting of the Sistine Chapel ceiling, his father Lodovico wrote in response that he warned his son that the *piagnoni* were a source of trouble.[113]

A more striking episode dates from many years later. Writing to his father about the troubles he was having with one of his senior assistants, Stefano Lunetti, over work in the New Sacristy at San Lorenzo, Michelangelo confirms his willingness to sack him but observes that were he to do so, all the *piagnoni* in the city would fall upon him.[114] Only in some of his earlier poems can one detect echoes of the dead Frate's indictment of the abuses of papal Rome. But the influence, if there, does not require our accepting that he was a *piagnone*; many of the same criticisms he could have found in Petrarch's poetry.

II

THE FIRST ROMAN ENCOUNTER

The twenty-one-year-old Michelangelo left Florence for Rome in the early summer of 1496. His first surviving letter was written on 2 July, at the end of his first week in the city, addressed to his Florentine patron, Lorenzo di Pierfrancesco.[1]

He first turns to his initial encounter with Cardinal Raffaele Riario, to whom Lorenzo di Pierfrancesco had written an introductory letter on his behalf. The cardinal had readily welcomed him and had shown him what Michelangelo describes as 'certe figure', undoubtedly referring to sculpture in the great man's collection. On the following day, he had requested that Michelangelo come to what is described as the 'chasa nuova', signifying the great palace on the construction of which Riario was engaged, the Palazzo della Cancelleria. Overcoming Michelangelo's reported modesty, the cardinal ordered from him a life-size statue, the *Bacchus*, for which a block of marble was at once acquired. The artist reports to his father that he will set to work.

Michelangelo turns to the reason for his journey to Rome in the second part of his letter, his aim to regain a statue he had recently completed. He refers to it as 'el bambino'. What he writes has to be read in the light of information provided decades later by his biographers. A passage of Condivi's explains that after the artist had finished the work, his Florentine patron, Lorenzo di Pierfrancesco de' Medici, had suggested to him that it should be passed off as an antique, thereby greatly enhancing its value. We are told that a fellow

Florentine with Roman connections, whom Condivi does not name
but who is identified by Vasari as Baldassare del Milanese, paid 30 ducats
for the carving, took it to Rome and subsequently sold it to Cardinal
Riario for 200 ducats.[2]

Condivi adds that Riario, subsequently concerned that he had been
deceived, sent a close associate to Florence, who, after many enquiries,
met Michelangelo and learnt that the *Cupid* was his work. Unidentified
by Condivi, the circumstantial evidence suggests that he was Jacopo
Gallo, the artist's future friend, who, with Florentine partners, acted
as Riario's banker. An entry in Riario's account that has survived
shows that, on 5 May, weeks before the artist's arrival in the city, he
was credited with 200 ducats, the sum he had paid for the rejected
Cupid.[3]

In this first letter of 2 July, Michelangelo expresses his determination
to regain the sculpture, but reports that Baldassare del Milanese, who
had evidently regained it after Riario had relinquished it, had threatened to cut it into a hundred pieces and flatly refused to surrender it.
Michelangelo was destined never to retrieve it.

Nevertheless, the *Cupid* would achieve a certain fame in Rome.
The interest that it aroused in the city is borne out by two letters
written to Isabella d'Este, Marchioness of Mantua. In the earlier, of
27 June 1496, her correspondent, mindful of her unflagging pursuit of
antiquities, reports that he has just seen a carving of Cupid offered for
sale to no less than Cardinal Ascanio Sforza, the Vice-Chancellor of
the Church. The *Cupid* is described as recumbent and asleep; it is
considered by some to be antique and by others as modern. Which-
ever is the case, it is absolutely perfect. He would not part with it for
400 ducats; the owner, unidentified but probably Baldassare, is asking
200.[4]

Another letter to Isabella followed nearly a month later, on 23 July.
Her correspondent reports that the work is modern and that the master
who has made it has arrived in Rome. It is so perfect that everyone
had believed it to be antique. Now that it has been established as
modern, he believes that it will be offered for a low price. However,

if the *marchesa* does not want it because it is not antique, he will say no more.[5]

Isabella, single-minded in her search for ancient art, did not pursue the *Cupid* further in 1496. Even if she had learnt the identity of the sculptor, his name would probably have meant little to her at this date. By a number of vicissitudes, she would be presented with Michelangelo's sculpture as a present in 1502 by Cesare Borgia, the son of Pope Alexander vi. Isabella would report that, for a modern work, the *Cupid* has no equal: 'el Cupido per cosa moderna non ha pari'.[6]

If the artist's endeavour to retrieve his statue ended in failure, his decision to remain in Rome and undertake work for Cardinal Riario must have seemed one offering opportunities on a scale difficult to find in a Florence in economic difficulties and divided by political differences. Raffaele Riario, born in Savona in 1460 and related to Pope Sixtus iv through the female side of the family, was, in the 1490s, one of the most prestigious members of the Curia. He had been created cardinal, with the title of San Giorgio al Velabro, in late 1477, when he was only seventeen years old. He would become head of the Camera Apostolica in 1483.[7]

Work on his new palace, later known as the Cancelleria, probably began in 1489. The importance given to the *cortile* was a consequence of Riario's passionate devotion to theatrical life and to his interest in Vitruvius.[8] He was a significant collector of antique sculpture, and one of his first steps on meeting the young artist was, as has been seen, to introduce him to some of his pieces. Two of the most impressive of these were colossal statues of the *Muse Melpomene* and of *Juno*, which probably belonged to him by this date. A later drawing records the *Melpomene* in the courtyard of the cardinal's palace.[9]

Whereas Riario lived at some distance from his building site, close to the church of Sant'Agostino while construction went forward, the Gallo family had lived near the site of the new building for many years, close to the old church of San Lorenzo in Damaso, in the area of the city known as the *rione* Parione. The early church would be destroyed during the construction of the new palace. Their property seems to have been quite extensive, perhaps constituting more than a single building, situated in the vicinity of Via Leutari. It appears to have suffered grave damage during the sack of Rome in 1527.[10]

The Gallo family had been engaged in banking during the second half of the fifteenth century, conspicuously so by Jacopo's father, Giuliano, who had died in 1488. His tomb would be erected in the new church, which had been begun at the latest in the summer of 1489, and which would be incorporated into the fabric of Riario's palace.[11]

While the identification of Jacopo Gallo with the representative whom Riario had dispatched to Florence must remain conjectural, there can be no doubt of the importance he had for Michelangelo once he had arrived in Rome. The partnership of Gallo with the Florentine banker Baldassare Balducci was a fact by 1488 and it was their joint bank that handled much of Riario's business, including the financing of the palace, from 1489.[12] That Gallo actually extended hospitality to Michelangelo in the early period of his stay in Rome is implicitly suggested in Condivi's text and is supported by a reference in the Balducci bank books to a payment made by Cardinal Riario for wine to be delivered to Michelangelo in Jacopo Gallo's house shortly after the carving of the *Bacchus* for Riario was under way (pl. 6).[13]

Michelangelo's progress with the *Bacchus* can be followed in payments made to him from Riario, recorded in the Balducci account-books. The initial outlay was 10 ducats for the cost of the marble. Successive payments to the artist of 50 ducats were recorded on 23 August 1496, 8 April 1497 and 3 July 1497. The final one explicitly refers to the *Bacchus*.[14] What these brief references do not tell us is that the statue provoked a falling-out between patron and artist. Just two days before the final payment, Michelangelo had written to his father, Lodovico, explaining that he could not leave Rome until his affairs with the cardinal had been straightened out and he had been paid for his work.[15]

These circumstances suggest that Cardinal Riario was not happy with the *Bacchus* and the supposition appears to be confirmed by the fact that the sculpture was acquired by Jacopo Gallo. Such a sequence of events would explain a silence about the true identity of the patron who had commissioned it, which endured for centuries, and Michelangelo's old-age disparaging comments about the cardinal.[16] Michelangelo would, in fact, scarcely surpass passages of virtuosity in the execution of the group, but its brutal realism in the depiction of drunkenness has frequently disturbed even informed critics.

Clearly, however, in acquiring the *Bacchus*, Jacopo Gallo was displaying not only loyalty to the young artist but also a discerning judgement that would lead him to acquire a further work from his guest, a statue of Cupid. The Gallo *Cupid* has disappeared; a later sixteenth-century description dependably informs us that the figure was full-length and standing, his quiver and arrows at his side and a vase at his feet.[17] While the *Bacchus* is recorded in the Gallo family garden in a celebrated drawing made by Martin van Heemskerck in the early 1530s, no dependable record of the *Cupid* survives; it remains one of Michelangelo's truly lost creations.[18]

THE PIETÀ

If, as circumstances suggest, Cardinal Riario had declined to accept the *Bacchus*, this would not be the only setback experienced by Michelangelo. In a letter of 19 August 1497, addressed to his father, he reports that he has undertaken a sculpture, 'una figura', for the exiled Piero de' Medici and has purchased the marble to execute it. The information is at odds with his declaration in a previous letter to Lodovico that he hoped soon to be back in Florence. He goes on to explain that Piero has let him down. He has suffered a further setback in purchasing a piece of marble that had proved defective. He is now at work on a new block for his own satisfaction. No more is heard of the undertaking, but the chronology suggests that this could have been the *Cupid* acquired by Gallo.[19]

The artist's admission to his father that he had undertaken a work for Piero excludes the assumption that, at this point, he had abandoned all dealings with his former patron, now an exiled and much-discredited figure. Contemporary accounts indicate that Piero led a life of reckless dissipation in the city. His shortage of money would lead to his pawning of jewellery to obtain credit from no less than Agostino Chigi.[20]

The early letters exchanged with Lodovico, few in number as they are, contain a premonition that it would be to Michelangelo that members of the family would turn when in financial need. In the very first that survives, of July 1495, the artist reports the arrival in Rome of his elder brother, Leonardo. Born in November 1473, Leonardo entered the Dominican convent of Santa Caterina in Pisa in July 1491 and made his profession the following year. It seems that he was subsequently exiled to the convent of Santa Maria della Quercia in Viterbo and, from what Michelangelo writes, had been robbed on his way to Rome. The artist states that he has given his brother money to pay for his return to Florence.[21]

A more substantial financial problem would arise in the summer of 1497. Lodovico's second wife, Lucrezia da Gagliano, whom he had married in May 1485, died in July, involving Lodovico in expenses. At the same time, he was caught up in a lawsuit to settle a debt with the husband of his sister, Brigida. Michelangelo writes that he will help his father if Lodovico cannot find the money, a presage of situations that would arise in the future.[22]

In the letter of 19 August in which he recounted his setback with Piero de' Medici, he reports that Buonarroto has arrived in Rome. He writes that he has no space to put his brother up, suggesting that he was still living with Gallo.

A few months later, his situation would be dramatically changed by the commission to undertake the marble group of the *Pietà* for an eminent French member of the Curia, Cardinal Jean de Bilhères de

Lagraulas (pl. 7). Less flamboyant a figure than Riario, he had lived uninterruptedly in Rome since he had been sent there, many years earlier, to negotiate with Pope Innocent VIII by Charles VIII of France. It appears that Innocent had wished to make him a cardinal but had died before carrying out his intention, a step taken by Innocent's successor, Alexander VI, in September 1493. De Bilhères would take the title of Santa Sabina, but he would remain most frequently referred to as the Cardinal of Saint-Denis, where he had been abbot since 1474.[23]

In the funeral oration that would follow the cardinal's death in August 1499 we learn that, at that date, he was seventy-one years old. Clearly, his advancing years must have led de Bilhères to make provision for his final resting place. The site that he chose was one replete with French royal associations, Santa Petronilla, one of two late antique mausoleums attached to the south side of the old basilica of St Peter's. Petronilla had become the object of particular devotion on the part of King Louis XI and his son, Charles VIII, and their patronage of Santa Petronilla received official recognition by Pope Innocent VIII. As a consequence, the building came to be called the Cappella del Re di Francia.

In choosing to be buried in Santa Petronilla, Cardinal de Bilhères was, therefore, aiming to commemorate many decades of service to the French crown. It has been established that the mausoleum housed six radiating chapels. One of these was dedicated to the saint herself, situated opposite the entrance leading from the basilica.[24] In his one recorded reference to his future resting place, returned to below, the cardinal does not define its exact location in Santa Petronilla. The proposal, however, that Michelangelo's group was planned for a side wall of one of the chapels is not credible.[25]

In what way the cardinal approached Michelangelo remains unknown. Once more, Jacopo Gallo could have been involved. It is his name that would appear on the contract drawn up many months later as the artist's guarantor, his role evidently acceptable to the cardinal. There is no evidence that he acted as banker to de Bilhères as he had done for Riario. Nevertheless, it is probable that their paths had crossed; it is worth recalling that Gallo had had a papal office as *scrittore apostolico* years earlier.[26]

Following events bear out the relationship of trust established between artist and patron. De Bilhères himself wrote to the Anziani of Lucca, the city's administrative body most involved with diplomatic correspondence, on 18 November. He states that Michelangelo will deliver the letter and explains that he is to carry out a *Pietà* in marble, representing a clothed Virgin Mary, with Christ nude in her arms, which is to be placed in a certain chapel he intends to found in Santa Petronilla in St Peter's in Rome. He requests the Lucchesi to grant the artist every help in his task of quarrying and transporting the marble necessary for the project.[27]

It seems clear that Michelangelo failed to find in Rome a block of marble of the scale required for the two-figure group that satisfied him; it is worth noting that the breadth of the *Pietà* block is approximately that of the blocks for the *Allegories* in the Medici Chapel at San Lorenzo in Florence. Quality, however, may also have been a consideration. Imperfections are clearly visible in the marble he had adopted for the *Bacchus* and, as already noted, a block he had acquired following the statue's completion had proved defective and had to be abandoned.

In November 1497 the artist deposited in his account with the Balducci, which he had opened no later than 23 March 1497, the substantial sum of 100 cameral ducats, a down payment from Cardinal de Bilhères.[28] And on 18 November he drew money to acquire a dappled grey horse for the journey to Carrara and a smaller sum to meet expenses on the way. These payments could imply that he was anticipating travelling alone, an occurrence he seems to have avoided whenever he could.[29]

Details of Michelangelo's subsequent movements are scarce. But a letter from a dependable assistant he had recently acquired, Piero d'Argenta, who had remained in Rome, addressed to Buonarroto in Florence on 13 January 1498, shows that he had spent Christmas with

his family. Piero expresses his amazement that none of the artist's
friends in Rome has had a word from him since he left.[30]

There are no records of Michelangelo's initial stay in Carrara in the
autumn of 1497; indeed, his presence there in this period has even
been questioned.[31] But there can be little doubt that it was in this
period, undocumented as it is, that he sought and found the marble
of the quality he required and, before leaving for Florence, made
arrangements for its quarrying. The memory of where he had found
the marble of the quality he demanded was not forgotten. For, many
years later, in August 1524, one of his most dependable assistants would
write to him that a fellow quarryman had found good marble just
below the place where the stone for the *Pietà* had been quarried. The
information shows that the site was at Polvaccio, some way above
Carrara.[32]

When the artist returned to the quarries is not recorded. His presence there in February 1498 is confirmed by his payment for the
harness of the horse that would pull the cart traditionally employed to
transport marble.[33] Perhaps, therefore, at least some of the marble that
he had ordered had now reached the foot of the quarries. Michelangelo
had returned to Rome by March 1498; he had been absent for
approximately four months. The pattern of such intense personal
involvement in his supply of marble seems to have been without
precedent and would remain a life-long one.

The arrival of the marble in Rome, however, would be subject to
significant delays. We learn of these in a letter of an associate of the
French cardinal in Rome to the Florentine Signoria, requesting the
Florentines to intervene with the Marquis of Massa, Alberico
Malaspina.[34] The unidentified man whom Michelangelo had entrusted
with the dispatch of the marble had been held up in his work. The
letter conveys the willingness on the part of the cardinal to pay
the appropriate sum of money to allow the operation to proceed.
The problem seems to have arisen over the *marchese's* insistence on the
payment of a tax or *gabella* relating to marble exported from his
territory, a recurrent problem encountered by those involved in the

marble trade in the area. The Signoria complied with the cardinal's
request. They wrote to Alberico Malaspina on 18 April, requesting his
collaboration, and replied to the cardinal on the same day, reporting
on their action.[35]

A letter from his dependable assistant, Piero d'Argenta, addressed to
Buonarroto in Florence, shows that Michelangelo was back in Rome
by 10 March 1498.[36] His first journey to supervise the selection of his
material as a sculptor was concluded. Many more would follow, and
although the presence of sculptors at the quarries was not without
precedent, the number of his visits would be difficult to match in any
period.[37]

The delivery of his marble, transported by sea and disembarked at
a point of the Tiber known as the Ripa, began in June, as is clear
from payments made by the artist for the unloading. These were substantial, and it has been persuasively proposed that he had ordered
more marble at Carrara than was required for the cardinal's commission; at least two shipments were involved, implying a number of
blocks. Perhaps, impressed by the quality of the material he had
encountered for the first time, he invested in stone that he may have
calculated that he would employ in the future.[38] When he precipitately
left Rome for Florence in 1501 to secure the commission for the
David, he would leave a stock of marble behind. On 30 August he is
found paying for the transportation of the marble to his living quarters.
These are referred to only as his *chasa*, and no details survive recording
where, and on what scale, he had secured spaces large enough to house
the stone and provide the working area to carry out the monumental
two-figure group.[39]

Michelangelo received a payment of 50 ducats from the cardinal on
27 August. And on the same day a written agreement was drawn up
and signed by the patron and Jacopo Gallo. It is the first contractual
document involving the artist to have survived. He is to receive in
all 450 papal ducats for the undertaking, 150 to precede the start of
work. Gallo pledges that the sculptor will complete the sculpture

within a year and that it will be the most beautiful work in marble in Rome.[40]

Cardinal de Bilhères would die in early August 1499, a year after the agreement had been drawn up. The term allowed the artist for the execution of the *Pietà* has, for the most part, been judged impossibly brief and no certain information exists regarding the date of its completion. If this extended beyond the contractual deadline, it follows that the patron never saw the finished work.[41]

The *Pietà* displays a number of features that may have owed, in part, to the wishes of his French patron, not least the anachronistically youthful aspect of the Virgin.[42] Another feature of the sculpture is the prominence of the signature that Michelangelo chose to introduce, no doubt conscious of the future public display of the work in Santa Petronilla. It was a feature that would lend itself to anecdote in the later sixteenth century and one to which he would not return. In his idiosyncratic adoption of the imperfect, *facebat*, in place of the more traditional *fecit*, it may be possible to see a reflection of what he had picked up from Poliziano in his early years.[43]

MICHELANGELO PAINTER

In his letter to the authorities in Lucca of 1497, Cardinal de Bilhères had characterized Michelangelo as the Florentine sculptor, 'statuario fiorentino'. While accurate, the description was too exclusive. The former member of Domenico Ghirlandaio's workshop was also involved in painting during these years spent in Rome.

Evidence of this fact exists in one of the bank books of the Balducci. On 27 June 1497, when his work on the *Bacchus* must have been completed, there occurs an entry that shows that the artist drew a small sum to pay for a panel on which to paint. The sum, of 3 carlini, is a very modest one.[44] The purchase has been tentatively associated with the painting now in the National Gallery in London, commonly

referred to as the *Manchester Madonna* (pl. 8).[45] However, there is much
to favour associating it with a now lost painting made for San Pietro
in Montorio.[46]

This work, passed over in silence by Condivi, would be referred to
by Vasari in his second edition. He writes that Michelangelo made a
cartoon for a small panel painting, carried out by a man he fails to
name but who, he states, had been Cardinal Riario's barber. The
subject of the work was the Stigmatization of St Francis; it was situated
in the first chapel on the left of the church as one entered. His passage
implicitly suggests that the episode took place at the end of Michelangelo's first year in Rome. The date agrees with that of the payment for
the wood.[47]

This appears to be the first known episode of Michelangelo the
painter providing a design that would be transcribed in a painting by
another artist. Who was this painter? A very dependable later sixteenth-century writer, well informed and a friend of Tommaso de'
Cavalieri, referred to the painting as by Michelangelo but qualified his
information by adding that some say that it is by the hand of a pupil
of his, 'Pedro de Argento'. He added that the work had been painted
in old-fashioned tempera and was not greatly admired.

The writer in question was Pablo de Céspedes, whose first stay in
Rome ended in 1577 and who had enjoyed a privileged position in
Roman circles of the 1570s. The element of doubt in his account of
the painting, as to whether Michelangelo had himself carried out its
execution or whether, 'as some say, it is by a certain Pedro de
Argento', can scarcely be the consequence of some sacristan's gossip.
It should also be remembered that San Pietro in Montorio was under
Spanish patronage.[48]

By chance, a later sketch of the painting, by the noted collector and
antiquarian Sebastiano Resta, has survived. It indicates that the picture
was horizontal in form and, therefore, probably not large in scale. The
lively action of the saint distinguishes the image from the traditionally
more passive representations of the scene.[49]

The 'Pedro de Argenta' to whom Céspedes would refer many decades later is Piero d'Argenta. His first appearance is constituted by two letters he wrote, in Michelangelo's absence at Carrara, to Buonarroto in Florence. In the earlier, of 13 January 1498, he complains, as noted earlier, of Michelangelo's neglect of his Roman friends and expresses his anxiety for news. A further letter, of 10 March, is again addressed to Buonarroto, with whom he clearly established close terms when the latter had been in Rome in the previous year. His warmth towards the Buonarroti, however, extends also to Lodovico, whom he regards as his father.[50] It is frustrating that we catch no more than glimpses of Piero. He would return to Rome to help Michelangelo in the early stages of preparation to paint the Sistine Chapel ceiling. As late as 1529 he would offer to shelter Michelangelo in a period of adversity. It has been cautiously proposed that he may have been the executant of a small group of modest paintings.[51]

Michelangelo's own early activity as a painter is obscure. While the unfinished painting now commonly referred to as the *Manchester Madonna* is generally, although not unanimously, accepted as his, it is not known at what point he was engaged on it.[52] What is certain is that he was asked to paint an altarpiece for the church of Sant'Agostino in Rome in his last eight months in the city.

Documentary evidence demonstrates that by early September 1500 he had undertaken to carry out the painting. It was destined for a chapel that had recently been endowed with the sum of 500 ducats, although the patron had died in November 1496. Legal problems relating to the will had been resolved only in 1499. It had fallen to Cardinal Riario to supervise the sale of the dead man's property in the summer of 1500. Since Riario had become Protector General of the Augustinian Order, it may have been he who had encouraged the patron, Bishop Ebu, to choose Sant'Agostino as the site of his funerary chapel.[53]

On 2 September Michelangelo was paid 60 ducats to undertake a panel painting for the church; the fact is recorded in his account with

the Balducci bank.[54] More extensive documentation relating to the
project survives in the account-books of the church. One of the
entries, dated 1501, records that Michelangelo's payment had been
made by two men who were closely involved with the furnishing of
the chapel, Bartolommeo de Dossis and Jacopo Gallo. The former,
closely connected with Cardinal Riario, lived in a house with a sculpture garden not far from the church. The retrospective character of this
information, recording that the artist had received 60 ducats, would
seem to exclude the possibility that this was no more than an initial
payment, with others to follow. No further ones are listed.[55]

Michelangelo's willingness to take on the project points to his reluctance to leave Rome and return to Florence, despite assurances in his
letters that he planned to do so. It is an obscure moment in his life.
Buonarroto had visited him in the autumn of 1500, one of the many
pilgrims who flocked to Rome for the Anno Santo. It appears that he
had reported to Lodovico, on his return to Florence, that Michelangelo
was living in miserable conditions.[56]

What became of the project? That so intimate an associate as Jacopo
Gallo was involved would encourage the belief that the artist began
work on it and we know of no other commitment in the winter
months of 1500–01 to distract him from the commission. Although
the connection has been doubted, it seems well-nigh certain that the
large panel painting now in the National Gallery in London, representing the dead Christ being carried to the tomb, was the artist's response
to the undertaking (pl. 9). The panel had a Roman provenance,
recorded in no less a collection than that of the Farnese in Rome in
1644; the description of the work is exact and it is unequivocally
ascribed to Michelangelo.[57]

The artist broke off work on the panel at a late point in its execution. His reasons for leaving Rome can be turned to later; it may well
have been the case that the decision was precipitate. Michelangelo
would take steps to return the money he had received for undertaking
the painting only as late as November 1501.[58] And, from the evidence
that survives, it appears that another painter was approached to carry

out the work. He is laconically identified as 'Maestro Andrea' in the documents. Payments to him seem to have begun in this same month of November; but the total sum he would receive – his final surviving payment is dated June 1502 – would be less than that agreed for Michelangelo. 'Maestro Andrea' is a figure of some interest, but no description of what he supplied appears to have survived; his contribution, if completed, seems to be irretrievably lost.[59]

The London painting is an astonishing invention for a twenty-five-year-old artist. Nevertheless, its incomplete state might be regarded as a threatening portent. The previous works, carried out in the time-consuming medium of marble, constitute a striking record of achievement. The long series of major unfinished works still, at this point, lay in the future.

III

RETURN TO FLORENCE

THE MARBLE *DAVID*

Michelangelo's stay in Rome came to an end in the spring of 1501. It had lasted nearly five years, and despite promises to Lodovico that he would soon return to Florence, the earliest made in July 1497, he had repeatedly postponed the move. A letter of Lodovico's of mid-December 1500 had been especially pressing and he had assured his son that, once back in Florence, he would have work to do. If he cannot complete work on the marble in his possession, he should leave it with one of his Roman friends and return to it when back in Rome.[1]

Michelangelo was rarely responsive to his father's injunctions but, on this occasion, he would accept his advice. In late February he received a loan of 80 ducats from Jacopo Gallo and, as surety, left with him an unspecified amount of marble. On 18 March he had transferred to the bank of Bonifazio Fazi in Florence no less than 260 ducats, a clear indication that his move was imminent.[2]

Michelangelo's return to Florence came very shortly after Leonardo's return to the city in the previous year. Vasari would claim that his homecoming was prompted by the urging of his family and friends, in order that he could secure for himself a huge block of marble belonging to the Opera of Florence cathedral. His information agrees with the contents of Lodovico's letter. Perhaps, therefore, Michelangelo was one of the many who, Vasari would report, went to see Leonardo's cartoon of the *Virgin and Child and St Anne* exhibited at Santissima

Annunziata, circumstantially described in a letter of 3 April 1501 to Isabella d'Este.[3]

The marble had been in the quarters of the Opera for many decades. It had been ordered as long ago as 1464 by the Wool Guild, the Arte della Lana, charged with administering the affairs of the cathedral.[4] The block is reported to have been 9 *braccia* tall, approximately 18 feet or 5.5 metres. The huge monolithic block had been quarried at Carrara on behalf of the sculptor Agostino di Duccio. In the later deliberations that took place prior to Michelangelo's involvement in 1501, we are told that Agostino had started work and had worked badly. In fact, he had been paid off by the Opera in December 1466. The project had concerned a statue to decorate one of the buttresses of the cathedral, but none of these earlier documents cites the identity of the projected statue.[5]

A subsequent attempt to revive the project was undertaken in May 1476, when the Opera consigned the marble to Antonio Rossellino, one of the leading Florentine sculptors of his generation. But nothing came of this step.[6]

The decision of the Opera, at the start of the new century, to turn its attention once more to the huge block in its possession, came at a rather quiet period in activity of the cathedral. Nevertheless, at a time when stocks of marble at the Opera were low and when stone expropriated from the property of the dead Lorenzo de' Medici was being pressed into service, it seems that there was no intention to sacrifice the block quarried nearly forty years earlier for other uses. At a time of political and economic adversity, the decision to revive the statue project was a relatively cheap one; the material was at hand, its scale a painful reminder of earlier and unfulfilled ambitions.

The identities of the consuls and *operai* at the time that concerns us are recorded, but these do not resolve the question of the timing of the renewed enterprise. A man certainly involved was the architect Cronaca, at this point *capomaestro* of the works at the cathedral. Vasari's insistence on ascribing a leading role in the renewal of the project to Piero Soderini is doubtful.[7]

The earliest surviving evidence for the final chapter in the story of the block is a well-known *deliberazione* of the *operai* of the cathedral of 2 July 1501; two new ones had been elected on the previous day. From its text we learn that the block is in the courtyard of the Opera. The three *operai*, following instruction from the consuls, decide that the badly roughed out man of marble, called David, lying flat in the courtyard, should be raised up to stand on his feet, so that qualified experts can resolve whether it can be finished. Neither the experts nor any prospective sculptor are named.[8]

Sufficient progress was made to enable the contract with Michelangelo to be drawn up on 16 August, the day immediately following the Feast of the Assumption. Consuls and *operai*, gathered together, mindful of the honour of the Opera, chose Michelangelo to carve and finish the man called the *Gigante*, previously badly roughed out by Agostino di Duccio. Michelangelo is allowed two years to carry out the work, beginning in the following month of September, and his payment is established as 6 large gold florins a month, making a total remuneration of 144 florins. However, it is added that when the statue is completed, the consuls and *operai* then in office are to judge whether the sculptor deserves a larger sum.[9]

Events proceeded rapidly. In the following February the consuls then in office decided to pay Michelangelo no less than 400 florins. Three days later, the *operai* referred to the statue as already well advanced, 'iam semi-factum'.[10]

A further event, revealed only recently, shows that Michelangelo had come close to completing the *David* by the midsummer of 1503 (pls 10–11). This is disclosed in a brief *deliberazione* of the *operai* dated 16 June 1503. They make provision for a public viewing of the statue one week later, on 23 June, the eve of Florence's important feast-day of the Birth of St John the Baptist. On that day, the door of the protective structure housing the statue, built in the late summer of 1501, is to be opened and all who wish to see the statue may do so. The event recalls the public showing of Leonardo's cartoon two years earlier; works of art had now assumed a striking notoriety. By this date, Soderini had been elected *gonfaloniere di giustizia* for life, and could well have contributed to the decision.[11]

The celebrated meeting of January 1504 was convened to discuss a particular issue: the future site of the *David*. Although it is clear that Michelangelo was not present, the preamble to the *deliberazione* of the *operai* who called the meeting shows that they were acting in response to an official report from Michelangelo, 'master of the said Giant', and the consuls of the Wool Guild. The *operai* express the wish to place the statue in an appropriate place, which must be firm and solid; in order to pursue this aim, they have resolved to call the meeting. Implicit, therefore, is the willingness to consider a site differing from that of the cathedral buttress envisaged earlier. The choice of January anticipated by one month the artist's deadline of February.[12]

The preamble is followed by the list of those who were present; but the scribe who wrote the surviving text was clearly making a copy from a summary record of what had been expressed at the meeting and the results are, at times, confused. A lengthy analysis of the document would be out of place here. The list gives thirty-one names but is not dependable: while Andrea Sansovino is listed, a marginal note records that he is absent in Genoa. At the end of the transcript, it is reported that not all who spoke have been recorded. Most of those listed are painters, architects, wood-workers and goldsmiths. Two important exceptions were the First and Second Herald of the Signoria, Francesco di Lorenzo Filarete and his son-in-law, later a friend of Michelangelo, Angelo Manfidi. A substantial number, including the artist's friend Giuliano da Sangallo, proposed a site in the Loggia dei Lanzi on the Piazza della Signoria, on the grounds that the marble was fragile because of long exposure and required a covered location.

One of the most memorable of the contributions was that of the First Herald of the Signoria, Francesco Filarete, who was the first to speak. He favoured one of two sites: either on the raised *ringhiera* to the left of the door of the palace or, alternatively, the palace courtyard within. His remarks in favour of the former, which would involve displacing Donatello's bronze group of *Judith and Holofernes*, have achieved some notoriety. He refers to the group as a deadly sign. The image of a woman killing a man is not fitting. Furthermore, the group had been placed there under an evil constellation. From that time, things had gone from bad to worse and Pisa had been lost. Turning to the alternative of the palace courtyard, he states that the *David* at present there is an imperfect figure for the retracted leg of the statue is 'sciocha', or imperfect. Of his two options, he favours the site on the *piazza*.[13]

Many of those who spoke favoured the Loggia dei Lanzi, in part concerned by the vulnerable condition of the marble. There is no explicit evidence of Michelangelo's own preferred choice. The issue of the statue's location is nowhere referred to in Condivi's Life. Piero Parenti, however, a very dependable source, would write that the statue was taken to the *piazza* on Michelangelo's advice. He added that the carving was not approved by all, but that the sculptor was excused by the pre-existing defects of his marble.[14]

Nevertheless, events surrounding the moving of the statue had progressed extremely slowly. The silence would be effectively broken on 1 April, when the cathedral consuls and *operai* directed Cronaca and Michelangelo to transport the statue to the Piazza della Signoria. But serious delays would follow, and the government was compelled to intervene. The diarist Landucci reported that the statue reached the *piazza* on 18 May, but only on 28 May did the Signoria that had assumed office on 1 May decree that the statue should replace the *Judith* before the palace. Nothing could be further from the courtly decision-making projected decades later by Vasari. The journey of the statue to the *piazza*, if we may believe Landucci, took four days, and it suffered stoning on its journey.[15]

The sources confirm that the formal unveiling of the statue took place on 8 September 1504, the day when a new Signoria assumed office, affirming that the statue belonged to the Florentine state. It now enjoyed possession of no less than four statues of the young hero, two by Donatello, one by Verrocchio and one by Michelangelo. No longer banished to a buttress of the cathedral, Michelangelo's *David*, now placed before the seat of government, assumed the role of an exemplum of heroic victory, one much needed in the context of the protracted struggle to regain Pisa.

As already noted, Parenti refers to criticism on the part of qualified observers when the statue was unveiled. The exaggerated scale of the head and the over-emphatic hands have disturbed viewers over the centuries (pl. 11). The large hands, however, may well have been prompted by a tradition that David was *fortis manu*, an aspect of the boy hero referred to by no less than Savonarola.[16]

In Condivi's book the emphasis is not so much a triumphalistic one as a recital of the huge problems that the artist had overcome. We have only one comment of Michelangelo's own made while at work on the statue, the celebrated inscription set down on a sheet containing a sketch for the bronze *David*, probably dating from 1502. It is an endecasyllabic message of supreme confidence:

> Davicte cholla Fromba
> E io collarcho
> Michelagnolo.

The sculptor's self-identification with David is therefore complete; the issue of a successful outcome is not in doubt and the 9 *braccia* block will be subdued as Goliath had been.[17]

The subsequent fortunes of Michelangelo's statue would begin with the gilding of the sling and tree stump and the more substantial change of the addition of a garland of twenty-eight gilded leaves to cover *David*'s genitals.[18] This could have been a response to Savonarolan objections, but a different explanation may lie in the fact that, with Soderini's election to life office and his move into the Palazzo della Signoria, women, for the first time, gained a place in the heart of the city's government. The overt display of *David*'s genitals may have proved too much for Argentina Soderini and her retinue to accept.[19]

An extensive account of subsequent political attitudes to the statue cannot be attempted here. It would be appropriated by conflicting parties in the troubled later history of the republic. Thus, writing years

later, Jacopo Nardi, reflecting on events in 1511, when the base of the
statue was struck by lightning, saw in the event an ill omen for the
republic, which was, in fact, destined to fall in the following year.[20]

When, however, *David*'s left arm was shattered in late April 1527
in the 'Tumulto del Venerdi', it was reported by a Medicean adherent
that even the *Gigante* had suffered on behalf of the house of Medici.[21]
Perhaps no other work of Michelangelo's would be subjected to such
conflicting interpretations.

A SECOND *DAVID*

The contract drawn up for the marble *David* had not expressly forbidden the artist's involvement in other projects. And it is striking to
recall that, even before the formal document was signed, Michelangelo
had already entered into a contractual agreement in the summer of
1501 to execute no less than fifteen marble statues for the altar of
Francesco Piccolomini in the cathedral of Siena.

He seems to have actively confronted this task only as late as 1503.
At this point, it is more appropriate to turn to a project taken on in
August 1502, just a year after the contract for the marble *David* had
been signed. The commission came from the Florentine Signoria itself
and involved a statue to be presented to an important Frenchman,
Pierre de Rohan, Maréchal de Gié.

Born in 1450 into a highly distinguished family, de Rohan would
become a professional soldier and a trusted servant of both Charles VIII
and Louis XI. He had become familiar with the outstanding works of
art he had seen in Florence, and in November 1499 the Florentine
Signoria had bestowed on him a present of seven marble and two
bronze heads.[22] The need to ingratiate French allies was, at this point
and, indeed, for years to come, of prime importance if the republic
was ever to succeed in regaining Pisa, an event achieved only in 1509.
In any account of the employment of art as a tool of political ingra-
tiation, that of the bronze *David* occupies a special case, perhaps not

least in the many vicissitudes to which the undertaking would be subject.[23]

Our first notice of the project is contained in a letter of 22 June 1501. Writing from Lyons to the Dieci di Balìa, the two envoys, Pierfrancesco Tosinghi and Michelangelo's own former patron, Lorenzo di Pierfrancesco de' Medici, explain that de Rohan wishes to receive a bronze statue like that in the courtyard of the Palazzo della Signoria. They explain that although he has professed his willingness to pay for the work, they believe that he hopes to receive it as a gift. Given the services that de Rohan had done on behalf of the post-Medicean regime in the summer of 1495, such an expectation was not unrealistic. The work he wishes to acquire is a figure of the bronze *David* like that in the courtyard of Palazzo Vecchio, 'chome quello ch'è nella chorte della Signoria Vostra'.[24]

The Dieci replied on 2 July. They expressed their sympathy with the request but point to problems. They have looked for a master capable of producing the sculpture requested but confess to difficulties, because of a lack of good masters.[25] They were not to be left in peace. On 17 July 1501 Tosinghi wrote again, informing the Dieci that de Rohan had pressed him to repeat his wish to have the work.[26]

A striking document of 26 August 1501 shows that the Florentine government had taken the request seriously. On that day, a year before any contract would be drawn up, the Signoria directed the Parte Guelfa to provide a quantity of bronze sufficient for the casting of a *David* similar to that near the head of the staircase in the palace, close to their quarters on the second floor. This was Donatello's *David*, which had changed places with Verrocchio's in late December 1495; the latter's *David* had been placed in the courtyard in place of the earlier work.[27]

How far the lack of sculptors referred to by the Dieci was a dependable indication of the situation is open to question. Nevertheless, it is worth noting that the contract for the desired work would be drawn up only a year later. Dated 12 August 1502, the Signoria commission Michelangelo, 'magistro sculture', to undertake a figure of David. The work is to be carried out in bronze and is to measure 2¼ *braccia* high, a little over 135 centimetres. The text explicitly refers to the fact that the Signoria wishes to make a gift of the statue to the Maréchal de Gié when completed. Michelangelo is to finish the work in six months and the Signoria promises to pay him an initial sum of 50 florins. A striking detail of the contract is their assurance that they will supply him with the bronze required for the future casting of the work.[28]

Michelangelo may have tacitly accepted the commission a year before he signed the contract, despite his undertaking of the *Gigante*. It must be recalled that the Signoria wielded authority incomparably greater than the Opera of the cathedral, as their future appropriation of the marble *David* makes clear. We may also now be concerned with an artist whose self-confidence could have led him to treat formal agreements with a certain licence. While the statue described in the contract is smaller than Donatello's, perhaps because it was destined to travel, the artist may well have exceeded his brief. Although the wishes of the French patron must have been familiar to all concerned, the text of the contract makes no mention of a requirement that the sculptor follow an already existing work. It has been plausibly suggested that the weight of the completed statue, as given in a letter of Piero Soderini of October 1508 prior to the dispatch of the work to Livorno, implies that Michelangelo's statue was larger than Donatello's.[29]

The series of delays in the delivery of the *David* to de Rohan would prove remarkable, provoking an exceptional correspondence. The failure to expedite the gift meant that the Frenchman never acquired it. His friendly attitude to the city would be emphasized in a letter of late December 1502 to the Dieci and the need to complete the work is urged.[30] The question would be raised in subsequent correspondence. And in a letter of 30 April 1503, the Dieci would promise the completion of the statue by the Feast of St John the Baptist, 24 June, only to add that even this is not certain. It depends on the artist holding to his promise and this is not secure, given the nature of such people.[31] In fact, on the previous day, the Signoria had decided to raise

Michelangelo's payment to 70 florins in place of the 50 stipulated in the contract.[32]

Six months later, Pierre de Rohan would suffer disgrace at the French court and his career would be irreparably destroyed. Nevertheless, the crisis would be resolved. Writing from Florence to the Dieci on 1 April 1504, the Florentine envoy, Niccolò Valori, recommended that, in this radically changed situation, the statue should be presented to the royal treasurer, Florimond Robertet.[33] His career had much in common with that of de Rohan. He also had accompanied Charles VIII to Italy in 1494 and had become a keen admirer of Italian art. His acuity as a patron had led him to commission a small devotional painting from Leonardo da Vinci, the work that would come to be known as the *Madonna of the Yarnwinder*.[34]

Years would pass before Robertet would gain possession of the statue; he is recorded as having commented that, given the incompetence of the Florentines, it was little wonder that they had failed to regain Pisa.[35] Another fact contributing to the delay in the completion of the *David* would be Michelangelo's move to Rome in 1505.

A consequence of the delay in delivering the sculpture would be the artist's registration as a debtor to the commune, a situation known as being *a specchio*, which could have disqualified him from holding any government office. The loss of documentation relating to office-holding between 1506 and 1510 makes a picture of his situation unclear, although he could have been exonerated by 1511. As late as 1519, however, his brother Buonarroto, a dependable witness, would refer to Michelangelo's having been *a specchio* and would explicitly relate his situation to his failure to deliver the *David*.[36]

The surviving documentation relating to Robertet and the statue resumes only in 1508. At this point, with Michelangelo once again absent, Piero Soderini, *gonfaloniere* for life, would assume an active role. Writing to the Florentine envoy in France on 30 June 1508, he reports that the statue has remained unfinished because Michelangelo has been called to Rome.[37]

Soderini would fail in his attempt to persuade Pope Julius to relinquish Michelangelo; at this point, the artist was taking his initial steps to paint the Sistine Chapel ceiling. The choice of the man to chase the bronze fell on Benedetto da Rovezzano; although Michelangelo had been approached to select a sculptor for the task, it is not clear that Benedetto was his choice, although he would pay him for his work.[38]

The statue, finally chased, would be sent to Livorno in early November, prior to its shipment to France. It would be Michelangelo's first work recorded to have left Italy (pl. 12). Many years later, his marble *Hercules*, followed by his panel painting of *Leda*, would travel to France. None of the three works now survives.

STATUES FOR SIENA

As suggested earlier, there are grounds for believing that Michelangelo left Rome for Florence as early as mid-March 1501. There are, however, indications that, while still in Rome, he had developed an interest in a new project for a distinguished Sienese patron, Cardinal Francesco Piccolomini. This involved the carving of marble statues to decorate the cardinal's altar in Siena cathedral.

A brief text in Michelangelo's own hand, dated 22 May 1501, indicates that he was already aware of the prospective commission.[39] The patron is referred to only as 'esso Reverendissimo Monsignore', but future events revealed his identity as Cardinal Francesco Piccolomini. Born as long ago as May 1439, he was the nephew of the celebrated Pope Pius II who had created him archbishop of Siena and who would make him a cardinal in his first consistory of March 1460. He took the title of Sant'Eustachio.

The contract that followed, concerned with the provision of no less than fifteen statues for the Cappella Piccolomini, is one of the most detailed that ever involved the artist, its numerous clauses indicative of the close personal participation of the patron. It bears three signatures: that of the cardinal, dated 5 June 1501, in Rome; that of Michelangelo, with no location indicated, on 19 June, and that of the dependable Jacopo Gallo, in Rome, on 25 June. This succession of events suggests that the document was sent to Michelangelo in Florence for his signature, and then returned to Rome.[40]

Details concerning the origins of the assignment are lost. But it is probable that the paths of patron and artist had recently crossed. For Cardinal Piccolomini had acted as one of the three executors entrusted to supervise the execution of the will of the deceased Cardinal de Bilhères, patron of the marble *Pietà*. He had died less than two years earlier, in 1499.[41]

The length of the contract is quite exceptional and displays an unflagging attention to detail, indicative of the cardinal's involvement in his project. He must also have been deeply concerned about the striking delays it had already encountered, one originally envisaged to incorporate his tomb. Work on the commission had been begun as long ago as 1481, if not earlier. The undertaking had been entrusted to one of the leading marble sculptors active in Rome at that time, Andrea Bregno.

The original contract has not survived, but an ancillary agreement relating to Bregno's transportation of marble to Siena has done so, dated 23 May 1481, precisely twenty years before the developments that concern us here. It shows that Bregno had undertaken to carry out the making of the monument *in situ*. He may have remained in Siena until the winter of 1486; the monument bears the date 1485.[42] His advancing years may have prevented his completing what was a massive task.

As drawn up in the summer of 1501, the new contract with Michelangelo involved the provision of no less than fifteen marble statues, each a little over 120 centimetres in height. To these was added a stipulation that he should complete a statue of St Francis, the patron's own name saint, already begun by Pietro Torrigiano in Rome. The cardinal sought to keep a close control over the future work. He is to decide on the identities of the statues. The artist is requested to visit Siena, familiarize himself with the altar and to take measurements. He is allowed to carve the statues in Florence, but they are to be worked on in pairs, each pair to be assessed on completion. The overall payment is to be 500 ducats and the entire project to be completed within three years.[43]

The contract also contained a clause that Michelangelo should take on no other work while engaged on the cardinal's project. And it is at this point that we encounter an artist who would be ready to ignore constraints that he had only recently promised to observe. The Piccolomini contract is dated 25 June. He would undertake the giant marble *David* on 16 August.

Cardinal Piccolomini, now aged sixty-four and in declining health, would make a second and final will on 30 April 1503. He refers to the undertaking he has assigned to Michelangelo, emphasizing the importance of his project and the requirement that the statues be carried out 'cum omni pulchritudine et perfetione'. There is no express statement that any had been begun. His insistent wish is that in the event of his death, his two brothers, Jacopo and Andrea Piccolomini, should see to the completion of the project and the placement of the statues on his altar.[44]

In failing health, the cardinal would be elected pope on 22 September 1503, taking the name of Pius in memory of his celebrated uncle. But his pontificate would last only a few weeks. He would die on 18 October and would be succeeded by Giuliano della Rovere, who took the title of Julius II.

Negotiations between the artist and the Piccolomini heirs would conclude with a new contract drawn up on 11 October 1504. Its text shows that, at this point, he has delivered four statues, those seen today in Siena cathedral. They are not identified by name (pl. 13).[45] The new agreement requires the provision of the rest of the statues already ordered. But the expectations of the heirs seem scarcely realistic. For they demand that the eleven statues still awaited from Michelangelo are to be completed within the next two years: 'ad faciendas dictas XI figures adhuc per duos annos predictos ab hodie proxime futuros'.[46]

More immediately, the artist is to proceed with a further three statues, and the payment for these will now be met by the 100 ducats originally planned for the final figures. The terms here agreed, never respected, for no further statues would ever be made, would create extraordinary problems as late as 1561, when Michelangelo had reached the age of eighty-six.

The four statues consigned before the signing of the new contract in the autumn of 1504 would be followed by no more. When Michelangelo made his decision to abandon the enterprise is not recorded. That he had contemplated pursuing it is shown by a letter to him from Lodovico of late June 1510, which indicates that the artist had ordered further marble some time before. In a letter of the summer of 1511, abandonment is expressly referred to in a letter to his father. Writing at a moment of pause in his work in the Sistine Chapel, he refers to his obligations to the Piccolomini heirs and explains that he intends to return to them the 100 ducats that they had advanced to him at the time of the new contract of 1504. Later events show that this never happened.[47]

A prolonged silence concerning the project in surviving sources would be broken in 1537, at a point when Michelangelo was deeply involved with the commission to paint the *Last Judgement* in the Sistine Chapel. A contract had been drawn up in Siena in December 1537, whereby the still outstanding credit of 100 ducats had been transferred from Antonio Maria Piccolomini to an old servant of the dead cardinal, Paolo Panciatichi of Pistoia. The latter would himself write to Michelangelo in Rome on 11 December, informing him of the event. He still urges the artist to provide drawings for the Siena project.[48]

The issue would reappear in 1561. In the spring of that year Michelangelo himself wrote to Paolo Panciatichi, expressing a wish to see once more the text of the contract of 1504 and bring the issue to a close. The letter is lost but there exists Panciatichi's reply of 1 May 1561.[49]

A further letter of the artist of 20 September 1561 has survived. It is addressed to his devoted nephew Leonardo and in it he requests

him to search for a copy of the contract in Florence that had been
drawn up in 1504 with Pope Pius's heirs.[50] Those still familiar with
the protracted issue must have been few. He refers to his own great
age and his wish to settle the matter, so that Leonardo will not be
troubled by the problem after his death, 'a ciò che dopo me
l'ingiustamento non fussi dato noia a voi'. Old as he is, he states that
he can still recall that the papers relating to the issue ended up in the
hands of the prominent Florentine notary Lorenzo Violi. Unable to
locate his own copies, he urges Leonardo to spare no expense in procuring one.[51]

It had taken the artist close to forty years to attempt to resolve the
issue, perhaps finally impelled by pressures that are not recorded. On
21 April 1564, a few weeks after the old man's death, Leonardo would
deposit 100 ducats from his uncle's estate in the Monte della Fede in
favour of the Piccolomini family.[52] Some form of restitution had been
finally achieved. But most of the niches in Cardinal Piccolomini's altar
would remain empty, recording one of the most protracted and least
engaging episodes in the artist's life.

THE HALL OF THE GREAT COUNCIL

The admiration aroused by the public showing of the marble *David*
before the Palazzo della Signoria on 8 September 1504 could be
regarded as a vindication of the decision, discussed earlier, to deprive
the Opera del Duomo of their statue and place it before the seat of
the Florentine government.[53] It confirmed the remarkable standing of
Michelangelo, already indicated by the commissioning of the bronze
David in 1502 and the ordering of no less than twelve marble statues
by the cathedral *operai* in April 1503. Further testimony to the artist's
reputation would follow: the commission to contribute to mural decoration in the newly constructed Sala del Maggior Consiglio in Palazzo
Vecchio. This monumental addition to the earlier building was now
urgently required to accommodate the meetings of the republican

government established following the flight of Piero de' Medici in November 1494. Building began in July 1495 and construction was carried out with great rapidity. Much influenced by the example of the great Council Hall in Venice, the Florentine Council held its first meeting in the scarcely completed room as early as February 1496, a striking testimony to the energy of the new regime so dominated by Savonarola.[54]

Steps to decorate the new hall would follow, but this subsequent phase in its history would be marked by setbacks. The commission to provide a panel altarpiece was awarded to Filippino Lippi in May 1498, but he seems to have made little progress with the project before his death in 1504. The commission would be reassigned to Fra Bartolommeo, but he failed to complete the painting, now housed in the Museo di San Marco.

A further step was the commission, in June 1502, of a marble statue of *Christ* from Andrea Sansovino, one of the city's most experienced sculptors, planned for the *residentia*, the place occupied by the *gonfaloniere* himself, but this work also never reached its planned place in the Sala.[55]

The most prestigious achievement of the government was to obtain the services of Leonardo. Now aged just over fifty, the Signoria, in approaching him, was taking a step not free from risk. He had, for example, failed to meet an obligation to paint an altarpiece for the chapel of the Signoria in Palazzo Vecchio as long ago as 1478. It may well be that, in approaching him, Piero Soderini, elected to life office as *gonfaloniere* of the city in November 1502, played a significant part. The government was also prepared to employ Leonardo in other roles.[56]

Leonardo's initial contract, if there was one, has not survived. Nor has one relating to Michelangelo's subsequent involvement. Even had they been drawn up, it is unlikely that they would have clarified the issue that has exercised many historians and art historians, the precise location envisaged for their paintings in the new Sala. Vasari's later silence on this issue is particularly frustrating in the light of his own complete remodelling of the space for Cosimo I. He does refer to the room's original fenestration in his Life of Cronaca, co-architect of the Sala. He states that the room was lit by two windows on the east wall and four on the west.[57] This information, despite latter-day sceptics, is likely to be correct. It would encourage the belief that the murals were planned for the east wall where the ceremonial seat of the *gonfaloniere* seems to have been located, and that they were envisaged to flank his *residenza* on either side. To judge from dependable copies of Leonardo's and Michelangelo's inventions, it is clear that in Leonardo's *Battle of Anghiari* the figures are lit from the right, while Michelangelo's bathing figures are lit from the left, reflecting the light sources closest to them (pls 14, 15).[58]

That the Signoria first approached Leonardo seems clear from the documents that survive, although we are denied the certainty of contracts. Already in October 1503, while Michelangelo was still occupied with the marble *David*, payment was made to provide Leonardo with a space adequate to house him in preparing a full-scale cartoon. The space chosen was the Sala del Papa, adjoining the church of Santa Maria Novella. He was consigned the keys to the Sala on 24 October 1503. Scaffolding to enable him to work on the cartoon was being prepared by early 1504.

As not infrequently the case with Leonardo, however, problems would emerge. By May 1504 delays are referred to in the documents. A *deliberazione* of the Signoria of 7 May would attempt to impose a deadline on the artist, requesting him to complete the cartoon by February 1505. He was, however, granted an important concession. Were he to begin painting that part of his composition for which the cartoon was already made, such a provisional agreement would be accepted.[59] Payments of March 1505 refer to outgoings for the scaffolding of Leonardo. A Florentine diarist would record that among events of October 1505 Leonardo began to paint the wall of the council hall above the place of the twelve *Buoni Uomini*.[60]

What of Michelangelo? Already in the first edition of his *Lives* of 1550, Vasari would report that the artist had been granted space to execute his cartoon in the Ospedale de' Tintori, the Hospital of the Dyers, at the church of Sant'Onofrio, close to Santa Croce.[61] Recently discovered documents confirm what Vasari wrote about the location where Michelangelo carried out the cartoon. On 22 September 1504, shortly following the public showing of the *David*, he would be granted permission to use the *sala grande* of the hospital to carry out his work for the Palazzo della Signoria.[62]

The subjects selected for the murals were both battle scenes and clearly had great significance for the Florentine Signoria and Piero Soderini. That assigned to Leonardo represented the victory of the Florentines over the Milanese at Anghiari in 1440. It could be described as the last major military victory of the Florentines.[63]

The choice of subject for Michelangelo involved an episode in the struggle with Pisa, one that would have had, therefore, a greater contemporary resonance. Michelangelo's response to his commission was described at great length by Vasari in his biography of the artist.[64] Michelangelo's composition, frequently referred to as the *Bathers*, and recorded in many copies – the best the grisaille rendering at Holkham Hall – was, however, only a part of his planned mural. It represented a particular episode that had taken place on 28 July 1364, when Florentine soldiers, their weapons put aside, had taken to bathing in the Arno to escape the heat and were taken unawares by the hostile Pisans. The source for the painting, traditionally regarded as a passage of the Florentine historian Filippo Villani, has now been identified in Leonardo Bruni's *History of the Florentine People*, translated into Italian in 1473.[65]

Michelangelo, celebrated as the artist of the *David*, seems to have wasted no time in engaging with his new commission. Already at the end of October there survives a payment to a *cartolaio*, a paper merchant, for paper for his cartoon, 'per il cartone di Michelagnolo'.[66] Further payments to him would follow, a substantial one at the end of February 1505.[67]

When Michelangelo completed the part of the cartoon familiar to us today from the grisaille copy at Holkham is not documented. It is important to recall that drawings indicate that this scene was only a part of his overall project (pls 14–15). Nor is it known when he completed this episode. The artist broke off work on the project for Soderini when he left Florence for Rome in the spring of 1505, an episode to be returned to. It would be one of the many setbacks that the *gonfaloniere* suffered at the hands of his cherished artist. It has been proposed that Michelangelo returned to complete the cartoon only when he fled from Rome in April 1506, and it is also worth recording the relevance of a letter that his friend in Rome, Giovanni Balducci, wrote to him in Florence on 9 May, following the artist's precipitate flight from the papal court. He refers to the artist's work going forward, on what must certainly have been the cartoon.[68] What happened to the work following Michelangelo's decision to make peace with Pope Julius at Bologna in the autumn of 1506 is unknown. At some point, not recorded, it must have been taken from Sant'Onofrio and put on view in the Sala del Gran Consiglio, where it is recorded by the dependable Albertini in 1510.[69] Already in 1508, Michelangelo, once more in Rome, had attempted to arrange a visit for an unidentified young Spaniard to see the cartoon, now in the Sala, but was unsuccessful.[70]

The battle scene, had it been completed, would have been one of the youthful Michelangelo's most extraordinary works. The competition with Leonardo lent a unique character to the circumstances. An anecdote concerning the two artists, recorded by the author of the Codice Magliabechiano, describes a confrontation between the two, which, if true, must have occurred during this period. Meeting close to Palazzo Spini, the writer credits Michelangelo with taunting the older artist over his failure to carry out the Sforza monument in Milan, and ascribes to Leonardo an embarrassed reaction to the jibe.[71]

IV

THE ARTIST AND POPE JULIUS

IN THE SERVICE OF THE POPE

Michelangelo's commitment to his Florentine undertakings following the completion of the marble *David* was not sufficient to resist the prospect of working for Pope Julius in Rome (pl. 16). The circumstances in which he entered the pope's employment cannot be established in great detail, but he was not the only artist who would abandon Florentine commitments in order to serve him. A few months after Michelangelo's journey to Rome in the early spring of 1505, he would be followed by Andrea Sansovino, called to Rome in the autumn, whose first work for the pope would be the tomb of Cardinal Ascanio Sforza in Santa Maria del Popolo.[1]

No evidence has survived to indicate that, his decision made to serve the pope, Michelangelo attempted to mollify his Florentine patrons, the most significant of whom was, of course, the *gonfaloniere a vita*, Piero Soderini. Preparations to paint his battle scene in the Sala del Maggior Consiglio would come to a halt. Not even the first of the twelve marble apostles destined for the cathedral seems to have been begun at this point. While Andrea Sansovino sought permission from his patrons, the Calimala guild, to leave his work in Florence unfinished, no evidence exists to indicate that Michelangelo negotiated his leave-taking with the Signoria, although he may have attempted to gain the sanction of Piero Soderini.

Evidence does suggest that Pope Julius was anxious to obtain the artist's services no later than the early months of 1505. A hundred florins was paid to him by the pope as early as February 1505, as a surviving record of the Salviati bank in Florence shows. The sum may have been the first he ever received from a pope. By 27 March Michelangelo had arrived in Rome.[2]

Agreement on the project of the pope's tomb seems to have been reached very rapidly. A letter addressed to Alamanno Salviati by Francesco Alidosi, dated 28 April, was concerned with arranging credit of no less than 1,000 ducats in favour of the artist. He explains that the payment is to facilitate the start of the acquisition of marble. He adds that the artist could be trusted with a larger sum and that Pope Julius is happy with the dispositions that have been made; he remains 'contento e riposato'.[3]

Julius's decision to place management of the undertaking in the hands of Francesco Alidosi is telling. He would be created a cardinal by the pope in December 1505. But he had long exercised great authority in the Curia. Visiting Rome in 1503 for the celebrations marking Julius's election, Machiavelli observed that Alidosi enjoyed a unique position at the papal court.[4]

It seems probable that Giuliano da Sangallo played a part in the assignment of the project to Michelangelo. As noted earlier, Giuliano's path had crossed that of the youthful Michelangelo and, more significantly, Vasari explicitly associated Giuliano with the papal commission.[5] At this point, Giuliano had been in Rome for nearly a year, leaving Florence only a few months after his appearance at the meeting called to discuss the future of the marble *David*. His association with Julius was long-standing, for he had faithfully served him during the years of the cardinal's exile in France.

Vasari could have gained his information from Giuliano's son, Francesco, who was a close associate. Years later, in a much-noted letter of 1567 written by Francesco da Sangallo to Vasari's friend and mentor, Vincenzo Borghini, he would explicitly associate his father with Michelangelo's move to Rome.[6] The letter, celebrated for Francesco's account of the discovery of the *Laocoön* group in January 1506, would state that Michelangelo, early in the year, was a constant visitor to Giuliano's house; at that point, Francesco was twelve years old. Giuliano's attempt to make peace between Michelangelo and Pope Julius in the following year will be returned to.

The part played by Alamanno Salviati in facilitating the employment of Michelangelo by Pope Julius is striking. Although not acting as a legally bound guarantor of the artist, his role was a significant one. Alamanno, together with his cousin Jacopo, had been among the most influential figures in the early years of the Soderini republic; both had supported Piero in his election to life office as *gonfaloniere* in 1502. Nevertheless, by 1504 their support had turned to hostility and the part that Alamanno played in helping woo Michelangelo from his Florentine commitments must raise suspicion about his role.[7]

THE RETURN TO CARRARA

Michelangelo drew 60 ducats from his Roman account on 28 April 1505; this suggests that he left the city to return to Florence soon after. During his stay in Rome, he had successfully negotiated the project to carry out Pope Julius's tomb, one that would come to haunt his life. And, as noted, it was also on 28 April that Alidosi wrote his letter to Alamanno Salviati concerning the advance of 1,000 ducats. The payment was a detail Michelangelo would see that Condivi would include in his biography.

The artist was still in Florence at the end of June, when he deposited 600 ducats in the account at Santa Maria Nuova. The sum would ultimately contribute to the artist's first investment in property, a farm outside the city near the village of Pozzolatico.[8] Whether he resumed work on the projects he had abandoned on leaving for Rome is not documented. In June, while Michelangelo was still in the city, Leonardo was actively at work on the *Battle of Anghiari*, but there is no clear evidence that he himself returned to his preparations for the *Battle of Cascina*. Other obligations he seems also to have neglected, such as the demanding task of the chasing of the bronze *David*.

Looking back, the artist was uncertain about the extent of his impending journey to Carrara in search of marble. He was still in Florence in late June; exactly when he left for the quarries is not recorded. There is little information to shed light on this visit, the artist's second to the quarries. That work had progressed is nevertheless indicated by a document of November. On the twelfth of the month, a contract was drawn up between Michelangelo and two natives of Lavagna who would agree to deliver to Rome 34 *carrate* of marble. These would include two blocks of 15 *carrate* each. Since one *carrata* was the equivalent of 1,000 kilograms, the pieces were of an impressive scale.[9]

Condivi would state that Michelangelo had had two assistants to help him with his work at Carrara, but he does not name them. We learn more from a second contract, however, drawn up on 10 December in Carrara, concerned with future quarrying. One of the men concerned was Matteo di Cucarello, one of the artist's most trusted assistants, who would still be active in his service, involved with quarrying material for the façade of San Lorenzo, as late as 1517.[10] One of the two witnesses was Baccio di Giovanni, described as 'scultore fiorentino', who, there can be little doubt, was Baccio da Montelupo, who had been with Michelangelo at Bologna in the winter of 1494–5. This contract of December is one of the few pieces of evidence relating to the artist's prolonged presence at the quarries.

Alongside such sparse indications of his life at Carrara there can be mentioned what is one of the most extraordinary passages in Condivi's biography. He relates how, living in the harsh environment of the Apuan Alps, Michelangelo was one day seized by the wish to carve a colossus from one of the mountains that overlooked the sea, which could serve as a landmark for sailors. Condivi writes, surely repeating what he had been told by the old artist, that he was prompted by the material to hand and by a wish to emulate the ancients. He would have put his wish into effect if time and the demands of his assignment had allowed it. In one of his rare self-references, Condivi writes that he heard the artist speak of the subject with great regret.

The passage prompted in the old artist one of the comments on Condivi's text that was recorded by Tiberio Calcagni. The idea was a madness that had come to him, 'una pazzia venutami'. But, he adds, if he had been certain of living four times as long as he had lived, he would have gone ahead. Evidently recalling antique examples, his obsession with releasing the form from the material never found an expression more fantastic than this.[11]

A more sober world awaited him in Florence. His failure to attend to one of his earlier commissions, the twelve marble apostles for the cathedral, contracted for with the Opera in April 1503, would lead to the artist's relinquishment of the house explicitly given to him to facilitate his work on the project. On 18 December 1505 the *operai* recorded their decision that the house should be let, persuading Michelangelo to relinquish any claim on the property, built on the corner of Via Pinti and Via della Colonna, designed by his close friend Cronaca.[12]

Michelangelo had returned to Rome by 29 December. He may have co-opted a marble worker to travel with him. During his absence from the city, Pope Julius had created Francesco Alidosi a cardinal, a step bitterly contested in the consistory.

THE SECOND FLIGHT

A letter of Michelangelo to his father of 31 January 1506 contains information about the artist's situation in Rome following his return from Florence. He expresses his frustration over delays in the arrival of his marble from Liguria. There have been only two days of good weather since he came back.[13]

In fact, he reports that one shipload of stone has arrived a few days previously. He had drawn money to deal with its arrival on 21 January. The boat had incurred great danger from the stormy conditions: after the marble had been unloaded, at the Ripa, the disembarkation point on the Tiber beneath the Aventine Hill, the river had risen and submerged the blocks.

Other information emerges from the letter, especially his concern for a work in Florence that is discussed below, the group of *Virgin and Child* destined for Bruges (pl. 17). It must be shown to no one. A later reference of the artist's expressly states that, at this date in 1506, he had accommodation behind Santa Caterina delle Cavallerotte, a church destroyed in the seventeenth century. The information is repeated in Condivi's biography, who adds that Pope Julius, to facilitate his visits to the artist's workshop, provided a bridge from the corridor that ran from the Vatican Palace to Castel Sant'Angelo.[14]

The letter to Lodovico of January 1506 is the only one to have survived before the crisis in Michelangelo's relations with Pope Julius would erupt in April. The loss of correspondence is a grievous one. Its absence means, for example, that there is no recorded personal reaction to an event of a sensational character, the discovery of the *Laocoön* group in mid-January on the Esquiline Hill. If the later evidence of Francesco da Sangallo is dependable, Giuliano, his father, had been dispatched to the site by Julius, and Michelangelo had accompanied him.[15]

For the crisis of April, the most immediate account exists in Michelangelo's own letter to Giuliano of 2 May 1506, one of the most discussed of his entire correspondence, written after his flight to Florence.[16] It is free of the accretions encountered in his subsequent recital of events. It was written in reply to a now lost letter from Giuliano, acting on the pope's behalf. It is evident that Giuliano had reported that Pope Julius had taken Michelangelo's abrupt departure badly, but had said that he would respect what had been agreed between them.

The artist seems to have attempted to maintain a relatively controlled tone; he wishes his Florentine friend to read it to the pope. He reports that on Saturday, 11 April, the day preceding Easter Sunday, he had heard the pope, at table with a jeweller and the master of ceremonies, declare that he did not intend to spend anything further, not a single *baiocho* more, on small or large stones. Taken aback, he had, nevertheless, prior to leaving, asked for further money to continue his work. The pope had told him to return on Monday. He had returned on the Monday, then the following Tuesday, Wednesday and Thursday. Finally on Friday, 17 April he had been turned away, or, as he himself writes, thrown out, 'cacciato via'. The man responsible had said that he knew him but was obeying orders. Receiving the same response on Saturday, he grew desperate.

He adds that there was a further reason, apart from the rebuffs that he had undergone, that prompted his leaving. Adopting a cryptic form of expression, he writes: 'This [the papal rejection] was not the only reason for my departure; there was also something which I do not wish to write about. It is enough that it led me to think that, if I remained in Rome, my own tomb would have been made sooner than that of the pope. And this was the reason I left immediately.' He does not specify on which day he left, probably on the Saturday, 18 April. The latter day was the one that had been chosen for the ceremonial laying of the foundation stone of the new St Peter's.

Michelangelo assures Giuliano that he wishes to proceed with the project. In five years' time, the period he evidently estimated required for its completion, the tomb can be erected in St Peter's, wherever the pope wishes. But, the chief feature of his later remarks is his declared wish that the work should be carried out in Florence, where he will work better and with more dedication, 'farò meglio e chon piu amore'. He allows himself the prediction that the work will have no equal in the world.

The artist would return to the crisis of 1506 in the drafts of two subsequent letters addressed to his dependable friend Giovan Francesco Fattucci, dated in late 1523.[17] He writes that Julius has changed his mind about proceeding with the tomb but he, Michelangelo, did not realize this, and, as a consequence, has been shown the door. Michelangelo's complaint that funds from Julius II had dried up is, in fact, confirmed by other evidence. Documentation shows that he had been paid 500 ducats on 24 January 1506 and it seems that he had not received, as had been agreed, any further payment at the end of

February. There seem, therefore, to have been grounds for his impatience and disappointment in April.[18]

The artist's remark that Julius had changed his mind is a reminder
that he had been absent from Rome for eight months and may not
have kept abreast of events in the comparative isolation of Carrara. At
this point, he does not appear to have regarded Bramante as the creator
of his difficulties. Indeed, to judge from later letters, it seems that it
was only with the passage of time that Michelangelo came to identify
him as the man who had ruined him. The hatred would emerge
unforgettably in Condivi's book of 1553. Nevertheless, the adverse
events of the spring of 1506 remained in his memory. For example,
he refers to a man who had attempted to remonstrate with the obdu-
rate papal *palafreniere* who had barred his access to the pope as 'uno
vescovo luchese', who can have been no other than Pope Julius's
much-loved nephew, Cardinal Galeotto Franciotti, destined to die
young in 1508.

The most dramatized account of the events of April 1506 is encountered in Condivi's book. The artist, for whom no door had ever been
closed, had responded to the papal usher who blocked his way that
the pope would have to look for him elsewhere. He took the rapid
post north, telling two companions to follow. In a later *postilla* to
Condivi's text, the old man added that he reached the security of
Florentine territory in twenty hours of riding. At Poggibonsi, he had
been overtaken by horsemen sent in pursuit by Pope Julius, bearing a
letter demanding his immediate return. He replied that, since the tomb
had been abandoned, he was no longer under obligation to the pope
and would never return. Then he went on to Florence.[19]

Two of his Roman friends would write letters to him that have
survived. One of these was from Giovanni Balducci of the Rome
bank, replying to a lost letter of the artist.[20] He explains that he has
read a now lost letter to Giuliano da Sangallo. He presses him to return
to Rome once commitments in Florence have been met. The calming
tone of Balducci's letter is a reminder that, had Jacopo Gallo still been
alive in 1506, events might have assumed a less dramatic turn.

A day later, on 10 May, Piero Rosselli wrote to the artist in Florence.[21] A man whose position at the papal court was increasingly
jeopardized by Bramante, he had, as Cronaca's brother-in-law, known
Michelangelo well in the period of the marble *David* in Florence. His
letter is a remarkable one, even recounting events at the pope's supper
table. On the previous evening, the pope had summoned Bramante
to examine some drawings. He had expressed his belief that Giuliano
da Sangallo would succeed in bringing Michelangelo back to Rome.
Bramante had replied: 'Holy Father, nothing will come of it, because
I have talked with Michelangelo many times and he has repeatedly
told me that he does not wish to attend to the [Sistine] chapel.' He
states that Michelangelo wishes to work on the tomb 'e none a la
pittura'. Bramante is reported to have told the pope that he does not
believe Michelangelo has the courage to confront the painting of the
chapel ceiling. He points out that Michelangelo has not painted many
figures, and that these would be high and in foreshortening. Bramante's reference to Michelangelo's misgivings could well have been
true.

Rosselli had then reported the pope as saying: 'If he does not come
he does me wrong and therefore I believe he will, in any event,
return.' At this point, Rosselli writes, he himself broke in and addressed
Bramante with bad language in the pope's presence. His outburst
silenced Bramante and led him to regret what he had said. Addressing
himself to the pope, Rosselli denied that Bramante had ever spoken
to Michelangelo and expresses his belief that Michelangelo will return
when His Holiness wishes.

The references to the decoration of the chapel were consistent with
events. From the spring of 1504 the fabric of the Sistine Chapel had
been threatened by movement of the south wall. Services had been
suspended for a time. Both the initial damage and steps taken to
strengthen the building constituted a threat to the existing decoration
of the ceiling.

The reluctance ascribed to Michelangelo to intervene, conveyed in
Rosselli's letter, rings true. In 1506 Michelangelo could have had little

or no experience in painting on plaster, and it is circumstantially plausible that Bramante, the 'gran prospettivo', should have assumed that the projected decoration would be in foreshortening. When Michelangelo wrote to Giuliano da Sangallo that, had he stayed in Rome, it would have been his own tomb rather than the pope's that would be in question, it was not a fear of assassination that took hold of him, but rather a dread that the ceiling undertaking would be the end of him. It would require further pressure, some no doubt adopted in the months that would be spent in Bologna where he had gone as the pope's 'prisoner', that would be required to get him back to Rome.

A FEARFUL ARTIST

If, as seems to be true, Michelangelo achieved less in the period in Florence extending from April to November than he had in the comparable period of 1504, it should be recalled that his situation was much less secure. If the pope had, in reality, sent horsemen in pursuit of him in April, it had been to no avail. Many years later, in his familiar retrospective letter of 1542, he would claim that the pope had addressed no less than three briefs to the Florentine Signoria demanding his return, a statement repeated in Condivi's biography.

Nevertheless, a papal brief dated 8 July survives. Addressed to the priors and the *gonfaloniere*, it recalls that Michelangelo had left without permission. It calls for his return and pledges that he will come to no harm. Rather, he will enjoy the favour of the pope as he had done before his leaving Rome.[22]

No doubt the Signoria replied formally, but no such letter has survived. But one from Piero Soderini, *gonfaloniere a vita*, has done so. The recipient is unidentified but was probably his brother Francesco, cardinal at the Curia. Piero would have recourse to him again at later stages in the crisis. The letter is undated, but, from its location in Soderini's minutes, it would seem to have been written between 5 and 14 July.[23]

Soderini writes that:

Michelangelo the sculptor is so terrified that, notwithstanding the brief of Our Lord [i.e., the pope], it would be necessary for the Cardinal of Pavia, that is Francesco Alidosi, to write a letter to us, signed by himself, which will guarantee his safety...We have used and will continue to use all our means to make him return. We assure Your Lordship that if gentleness is not adopted, he will flee with God from here, as he has already twice wished to do...I will adopt every means, having learnt how much it is desired by His Holiness and by the Cardinal of Pavia.[24]

Soderini's description of Michelangelo's apprehensive state rings true; he refers to him as 'impaurito', and more or less in hiding, 'quasi aschoso per paura', although, when referring to the episode later, the artist went so far as to claim, with gross exaggeration, that he remained for almost seven or eight months in hiding. In Condivi's *Vita*, however, the old artist had stated that, because of his fear of Pope Julius, he had contemplated accepting an invitation to go to the Levant to work for the Ottoman sultan, at that point Bajazet II, who lived until 1512. It had reached him through the mediation of Franciscan friars, but Soderini had dissuaded him, declaring that it was better to choose death by going to the pope rather than life by serving the Turk.

Michelangelo confirmed the truth of the episode when he commented on Condivi's passage, even adding that he had made a model of a projected bridge that was to connect Pera with Galata. Further confirmation can be found in a much later letter written to him in April 1519 when a renewed opportunity of going to Constantinople occurred. His correspondent, Tommaso da Tolfo, recalled discussions with the artist fifteen years earlier about the possibility of making the journey, in the house of Giannozzo Salviati.[25]

Michelangelo did not leave Florence for either Turkey or Rome. But success in establishing peace would prove elusive. In late July Soderini would write to his brother, Cardinal Francesco, reporting that the Signoria had failed to persuade the artist to return to Rome; he is doubtful whether he can be made to change his mind.[26]

Only in late August was a little progress achieved. On the last day of the month, the Signoria wrote to Cardinal Alidosi, still expressing their devotion to the artist.[27] The letter was written only after the pope had left Rome on 26 August; his intention was to proceed first against the Baglione of Perugia and then Giovanni Bentivoglio of Bologna. The progress of the papal force, which included both Alidosi and Francesco Soderini, was recorded by Machiavelli, who had been dispatched as Florentine envoy to the Curia on 25 August. Julius had been at Orvieto from 5 to 8 September and then proceeded north. At Orvieto he had halted to venerate the relic of Corpus Domini and had even sailed on Lake Trasimeno.

The campaign of 1506 by Julius to recover Perugia and Bologna for the Holy See was probably the greatest of his military triumphs, all the more remarkable for its lack of bloodshed. He himself entered Bologna on 10 November. Giovanni Bentivoglio had already fled. On the following day he made a triumphal visit to San Petronio, which prompted Erasmus, a witness of the event, to report that he was acting like Julius Caesar.[28]

The Michelangelo 'case' was reopened no later than the following week. Francesco Alidosi had written to the Florentine Signoria from Bologna on 21 November, conveying the pope's wish to have the artist in Bologna; he wishes him to carry out work that Alidosi does not specify. The tone of his request is polite but firm.[29]

Both the Florentine government and Soderini responded a few days later. The former addressed their letter to Alidosi. To satisfy His Holiness they have persuaded Michelangelo to go to Bologna. They have put aside their own concerns about the works on which he is engaged in Florence. Recommending the artist to Alidosi, they express their regard for his gifts. If a remark recorded by Condivi is to be believed, Soderini had stated that the artist had tried the pope more than the king of France and that the quarrel had threatened to place the republic in jeopardy. The *gonfaloniere* was, at this time, confronted by a further

problem, Leonardo's progressive abandonment of his Florentine obligations, in favour of serving the French in Milan.

Many years later, Michelangelo would refer in candid terms to his
enforced move to Bologna. He had been compelled to act against his
own wishes, with a halter round his neck, to seek pardon from the
pope.[30]

FLORENTINE RENEWALS

Despite the precipitate nature of Michelangelo's flight from Rome in
April 1506, a letter of Giovanni Balducci of the Rome bank, dated 9
May, confirms that the artist is at work in Florence. He interprets the
news as indicating that he will not remain there for very long.[31] He
does not specify what the artist is engaged with, but is probably referring to his renewed involvement with his projected mural of the *Battle
of Cascina* for Palazzo Vecchio. He had completed his preparatory
cartoon for the group of *Bathers* in the spring of 1505, but there are
indications of his now resuming work on other aspects of the
painting.

There survives, for example, a drawing of conflict between infantry
and cavalry, and Vasari would subsequently write that the artist had
planned the introduction of cavalry in his mural.[32] Another, rarely
discussed, contains studies of a horse in profile made from life, a further
step in the preparation of the composition.[33]

The verso of this drawing contains poetry in which the artist laments
his ill treatment at the hands of Pope Julius. The date of the verse is
controversial. An influential commentator proposed one several years
later than that of the drawings on the recto, of no earlier than 1511.
Michelangelo refers to himself in the poem as the pope's 'servo antico',
a self-description claimed to be at odds with a date of 1506, but which
is more easily reconcilable with the later date. But the stark bitterness
of tone points to the earlier one, a consequence of the artist's dramatic
reaction to his sense of injustice, which forced him to flee the papal

court.[34] Some of the poem's imagery is very striking. Julius is likened to the sun. But he is also described as the barren tree, a savage conceit based on the familiar imagery of the della Rovere family oak.

Freed from his immediate duties in Rome, Michelangelo's presence in Florence would lead to his involvement with a project he had previously neglected, the obligation to carve no less than twelve over-life-size marble statues of apostles for the cathedral. The original contract with the Arte della Lana and the cathedral *operai* had been drawn up in April 1503, timing that suggested that those involved were anxious to retain his services after the *Gigante* had been finished. The statues were to replace outmoded murals painted by Bicci di Lorenzo during 1439–40. Michelangelo is to deliver one statue each year, receive a salary of two gold florins a month and personally supervise the quality of marble quarried at Carrara.[35]

A further feature of the contract was that he would be provided with a house by the *operai*. It is to be completed within three years at their expense. Its cost is established as 600 florins. Among other interesting clauses, it is established that the artist, together with his close friend Cronaca, *capomaestro* of the Opera, are allowed a consultative role. Its location was close to the corner formed by Via Colonna and Borgo Pinti.

The subsequent history of the house would prove a troubled one. The *operai* decided to rent out the property in mid-December 1505 because of the artist's neglect of his assignment. Later, following his return to Florence after he had completed his task for Pope Julius in Bologna, he himself would rent it for a year in March 1508. However, after his precipitate move to Rome to undertake the painting of the Sistine Chapel ceiling, the Opera, in June, would repossess the property.[36]

Nearly four years earlier, in late December 1504, the first marble block destined for the project of the apostles, after being unloaded at Signa on the Arno, had arrived in Florence. Further deliveries would follow, including three blocks delivered in March 1506. And it was probably one of these that the artist employed to carve the *St Matthew* following his dramatic flight from the papal court in mid-April 1506 (pl. 18).[37]

The *St Matthew* would be left unfinished, probably untouched by the artist after his period serving Pope Julius in Bologna and his brief return to Florence in the spring of 1508. It would remain in the Opera until the nineteenth century. Copied by Raphael in a drawing probably made in 1507, it exercised an influence still inadequately discussed. It inspired Vasari's remarkable passage on how the sculptor approached the block that he added in his revised Life of 1568.[38]

The early drawings relating to the apostles project, which number only two, indicate a modest aim, giving no hint of the solution arrived at in 1506. They are, in some ways, retrospective, deriving inspiration from fifteenth-century sculpture at the cathedral, portraying the apostle with right leg raised on a block and his head propped on his right hand. And it cannot escape notice that between these early ideas for the statue and the dynamic invention of 1506 there had intervened the artist's personal experience of the *Laocoön*.[39]

The months that Michelangelo spent in Florence between April and his reluctant departure for Bologna in November must have been dedicated to intensive work. His presence in Florence, however, has the consequence that much of the information that we can glean from his letters is lacking. It may have been in this period following the flight from Rome that he received the invitation (referred to above) to travel to Constantinople to serve the sultan. The episode is mentioned by Condivi in a passage in which he lists the illustrious patrons who had approached the artist.[40]

One subject that emerges in the late summer of 1506 is the requirement to dispatch to Bruges the marble group of *Virgin and Child*, still today in the church there of Notre Dame (pl. 17). The carving was commissioned by prominent members of the Mouscheron family of Bruges. They employed the Balducci as their bankers in both Rome and Florence, and it may have been through them that they met the artist.[41]

The project can be dated no later than December 1503, when Michelangelo was paid 50 ducats by the Mouscheron for a statue, 'per 1ª statua'.[42] A second payment of 50 ducats would follow in October 1504, probably also for the execution of the sculpture.[43] Further payments from the Mouscheron may also be remuneration for the carving, but details in the accounts are lacking. In August 1505 payment would be made for the packing of the sculpture, its 'inchassatura', which would appear to signal that the work had been completed some time before.[44] Nevertheless, its dispatch to the Netherlands was still under discussion in August 1506.[45]

The group is a tightly knit one, offering no vulnerable projecting surface that could have been endangered by the forthcoming journey to the Netherlands. Vasari makes no reference to the sculpture in the Michelangelo *Vita* of 1550. The omission would be made good by Condivi three years later, but his brief reference is a curious mixture of precision and error. He refers to the group as a work in bronze. He does, nevertheless, refer to the 'Moscheroni' as the patrons and states that the artist received payment of 100 ducats, information he must have had from Michelangelo and which is not at odds with the surviving documentary evidence.[46] Vasari would add nothing of substance in his second edition of 1568. The few sketches associated with the sculpture are chronologically compatible with a date of late 1504, when Michelangelo was engaged on the cartoon for the mural in Palazzo Vecchio.[47]

If some information relating to the group destined for Bruges exists, no such evidence has survived to establish the dates of the two marble *tondi* undertaken for Taddeo Taddei and Bartolommeo Pitti, neither of which the artist completed. Vasari would refer to them in both editions of his Life of Michelangelo, but gives no details, simply assigning them to the period following the completion of the marble *David* and prior to the work on the *St Matthew*. Condivi makes no reference to either *tondo*, the omission another indication of the old artist's inclination to exclude the works that he never finished.

In these years Michelangelo took on work for private patrons. Taddeo Taddei had been born in January 1470 and was, therefore, just over five years Michelangelo's senior. The member of a relatively distinguished family whose city property was situated on the Via de' Ginori and who was a long-standing member of the Arte della Lana, he would, in the near future, become a noted patron of Raphael; Vasari states that Taddeo owned two paintings by the artist. In fact, a pen drawing by Raphael of the Virgin in Michelangelo's relief survives.[48]

Taddei's tondo raises the issue of the notoriously unfinished works begun by the artist (pl. 19). Each case of the *non-finito* may present its own features. Here, it cannot be excluded that Taddei took possession of the relief after Michelangelo left for Rome to serve the pope in May 1505, on the assumption that it would be finished on his return. In this case, a further issue may have been the artist's dissatisfaction with the quality of the material after he had begun work on the block.[49]

The other marble *tondo* of this period is that referred to by Vasari as undertaken for Bartolommeo Pitti. It has remained in Florence (pl. 20). Smaller than Taddeo's, its date has been much debated. Nevertheless, the arguments of those who have seen in it a work following that for Taddei are convincing.

Michelangelo may well have been on familiar terms with Pitti, for he had been one of the *operai* of the cathedral, as a member of the Lana guild, from July 1503 to the summer of the following year. He must, therefore, have been involved with the project of the marble *David* during the period of its completion and decision over its site. From the evidence of his father's *catasto* return of 1480, Bartolommeo was twenty-seven-years old in that year; he was, therefore, substantially older than Taddeo Taddei.[50]

Whether specific circumstances promoted the commissioning of the two marble *tondi* for Taddeo Taddei and Bartolommeo Pitti has not been established. The context of marriage has, however, been associated with Michelangelo's painted *tondo* commissioned by Agnolo Doni (pl. 21). Doni had been born in August 1474, six months before the birth of the artist. He had married Maddalena Strozzi in January 1504, and their appearance would be immortalized in Raphael's portraits of the couple now in the Uffizi. Doni was a prominent wool merchant, and his house following his marriage was in the Corso de' Tintori, close to Piazza Santa Croce.[51] Allusions to both the Strozzi and Doni families have been identified in the decoration of the monumental surviving frame of the *tondo*, one of the most extraordinary of the period and convincingly ascribed in its design to Michelangelo himself.[52]

Such a proposed chronology suggests that the undertaking of the *tondo* for Doni had undergone substantial delays. Nevertheless, once begun, the artist worked with great rapidity, a fact clearly revealed during its close examination undertaken in 1985 during its cleaning. He adopted an approach of painting 'wet on wet', which certainly speeded its execution, and his careful preparation led to an absolute minimum of *pentimenti*.

Before leaving the topic of Michelangelo's stay in Florence in this period, it should be recorded that his presence there strengthened a further resolve of Soderini, to persuade the artist to undertake a second statue, a pendant to the *David*, to take its place alongside the earlier work before the Palazzo della Signoria. Just a few days after Michelangelo had left Florence for Rome, the *gonfaloniere* wrote to the Marquis of Massa, Alberico Malaspina, on 10 May, asking him to hold in safe-keeping a large block of marble that was to be employed for a second statue on the Piazza della Signoria in Florence.[53] In a further letter of December he would return to the subject, in which he explains that Michelangelo had not been granted leave by Pope Julius to leave Rome even for a period of twenty-five days. He states that there is no one else in Italy who can take on the task of preparing the block.[54] This project of providing a second statue before the palace would encounter extraordinary vicissitudes in the future.

A further episode would involve the artist at this time, the request that he would express his views on the projected construction of the *ballatoio*, or covered way, at the foot of the Florentine cathedral cupola. The authorities would write to him in Bologna on 31 July 1507.[55] At this moment, Michelangelo was deeply involved in carrying out the bronze statue of Pope Julius for the façade of San Petronio in Bologna, and no reply seems to have survived. It was a project he was called on to carry out a number of years later, testimony to the multiplicity of demands that would involve him in the future.

RETURN TO BOLOGNA

Michelangelo set out for Bologna at the end of November 1506. Francesco Alidosi had written from the papal court there on 21 November to the Florentine government, explaining that Pope Julius required the artist's presence in Bologna in order to carry out work for him.[56] Soderini would reply on 27 November; he writes that Michelangelo will be the bearer of the letter. Soderini bestows extraordinary praise on the artist, declaring him to be unique in his profession in Italy. If treated well, he will accomplish things that will be the wonder of all.[57]

Armed with his letters, the artist met his patron in the Palazzo de' Sedici. Condivi's account is full of incident. The pope greeted him with the words that it had been his duty to seek out his patron and that he had delayed until the pope had come to him. He was saved from a threatening silence by the ill-judged intervention of one of the courtiers, sent in by Alidosi. Julius then proceeded to pardon the artist and directed him to await his wishes.[58]

Perhaps even before his triumphant entry into Bologna on 11 November, Julius had made the decision to commission no less than two statues of himself. Already by 17 December a provisional one had been placed on the façade of the palace where he resided. It was apparently over life-size and made of painted wood or stucco.[59]

The commissioning of such papal statues had become traditional; on his way north, Julius could have seen the statue of one of his predecessors, Paul II, placed in a niche of the cathedral of Perugia. But the ordering of two statues on the same *piazza* indicates his aim to celebrate his remarkable political success. His pride in the effigy he would order from Michelangelo is indicated by his remarkable decision to pay for the artist's work himself, rather than the Bolognese commune, as tradition warranted.[60]

Michelangelo may not have been aware of the nature of the project that awaited him in Bologna. The letter that Alidosi had written to the Florentine Signoria had been studiously vague on the nature of the task that awaited the artist. Neither the involvement of portraiture nor the choice of bronze could have held much appeal for him. In one of the draft letters addressed to Fattucci of late December 1523, he would report that the sum required to undertake the statue he had reckoned as 1,000 ducats. But he added that he had not welcomed the choice of bronze, claiming that it was not his calling, 'non era mia arte'. However, the circumstances in which he found himself left him no opportunity to resist.[61]

He wasted no time in seeking assistants from Florence. On 10 December 1506 the Opera of the cathedral granted Lapo d'Antonio Lapo permission to leave Florence for Bologna. A decade older than Michelangelo, he had been on the payroll of the cathedral as a sculptor since 1491. The other Florentine to be summoned was Lodovico del Buono, known as Lotti. A skilled metal caster, he had served the Florentine government as a founder of artillery. Michelangelo's choice, however, would prove to be a grave mistake.

The situation in which Michelangelo found himself was an ungrateful one. The city was desperately overcrowded. His protector of twelve years earlier, Giovan Francesco Aldrovandi, was still alive. One of the leading supporters of the Bentivoglio regime, he had received a pardon from Pope Julius, who would make him a member of the newly created Council of Forty. Compelled to provide accommodation for members of the pope's party, he was in no position to repeat the hospitality he had extended to the artist twelve years earlier.

Writing to his brother Buonarroto on 19 December, Michelangelo states that he cannot offer any lodging for members of his family. He has only one room and bed to accommodate his party of four. He expresses doubts about the undertaking and fears that events could destroy him.[62] In the letters addressed to his family from Bologna, there emerges his hope to regain the pope's favour. At critical moments, he requests his family's prayers.

These letters to the family are numerous, allowing us to follow the vicissitudes of his life in Bologna quite closely. On 22 January 1507 he expresses his hope that the statue can be cast in Lent and that he can be home by Easter, which in 1507 fell on 4 April.[63] In a subsequent one, however, he reports that he has been compelled to dismiss Lapo and Lodovico. He would describe the former as cunning and deceitful and given to swindling him financially. Lodovico had been pressed by Lapo to leave with him. Subsequent letters show Michelangelo's concern about mischievous reports the two would spread once back in Florence, one that impelled him to write to the Florentine herald, Angelo Manfidi, a man he could trust.

A letter to his brother Buonarroti, dated 1 February 1507, recounts how on the previous Friday Pope Julius visited him in his workshop. He had stayed for half an hour and expressed his satisfaction with the artist's work.[64] The visit was deemed of sufficient moment to be reported back to the Florentine government by their envoy, Francesco Pepi.[65] If the anecdotes of Vasari and Condivi about the exchanges between patron and artist have any truth, these must have taken place on such an occasion.

Pope Julius left Bologna on 22 February 1507, but the situation in the city would remain volatile. At the end of April the Bentivoglio attempted to regain it, prompting the artist to report to his brother Giovan Simone that the city drowned in cuirasses: 'qua s'afoga nelle coraze'.[66] He also refers to a letter he had sent to Manfidi, asking permission from the Florentine government that a caster be sent from the city. Permission was granted on 15 May 'pro gittando imaginem eream Summi Pontifici'. Bernardo d'Antonio da Ponte was given freedom to travel to assist with the casting.

When the time-consuming process of chasing the bronze was completed is not recorded; the statue may have left the workshop around the middle of February 1508. Initially taken to San Petronio, after three days it left the interior of the church to be erected on the façade, above the statues of Jacopo della Quercia, within a specially constructed tabernacle; the event took place on the Feast of the Cathedra Petri. Julius had been portrayed seated, his right hand raised in blessing. Estimates of the scale of the figure would vary, but it was probably about 7 *braccia* in height, a little over 4 metres.

Later commentators noted a menacing aspect in the pope's gesture and the artist himself is alleged to have stated that it threatened the Bolognese if they failed to act with prudence. The minatory character of the statue prompted one of the most striking contemporary allusions to a work by Michelangelo, by Piero Valeriano. He would write:

> From whom do you flee, frightened traveller,
> As if the Furies or Gorgons
> Or the piercing Basilisk pursued you?
> Julius is not here, but only the image of Julius.[67]

Michelangelo's letters convey an antipathy to the Bolognese and his anxiety to leave the city, but it appears that the pope had forbidden his departure before the statue was installed. Other interests that cannot be defined are briefly suggested. Already in late December 1507 he had written a now lost letter to Cardinal Alidosi through his brother Buonarroto, one to which he assigned great importance. It would be followed by another, similarly addressed through his brother and sent in mid-February, which had explained his delay in leaving Bologna. In the earlier one, he had expressed his hope to be in Rome by Lent 1508.[68]

The wish is difficult to reconcile with an event on his return to Florence in mid-March 1508, when the cathedral Opera re-let to him the house on Borgo Pinti constructed to facilitate work on the twelve marble apostles. Perhaps, at some point, he still nursed the idea of working on the tomb of Julius in Florence, the plan that he had outlined in his letter to Giuliano da Sangallo in April 1506 after the break with the pope. But the call to Rome would not be resisted. When Piero Soderini wrote to the French patron of the bronze *David* on 30 June 1508 about the delays in the completion of the sculpture, he would explain that Michelangelo had been summoned to Rome by a brief of Pope Julius.[69]

The bronze *Julius* must have been one of the most remarkable images ever created by the artist. A correspondent of Isabella d'Este would write that the pope was portrayed 'in cathedra', and that the statue was more than 9 feet high and weighed 14,000 pounds.[70]

The survival of the statue was brief. The Bentivoglio would regain Bologna in late May 1511 and the sculpture would be destroyed on 13 December. Much of the material would be acquired by Duke Alfonso d'Este and transported to Ferrara, part of the bronze to be melted down to enhance his collection of artillery.

Exactly when Michelangelo returned to Florence from Bologna is not known, but it is probable that he made the move at the end of February or the early days of March 1508; a letter addressed to him by a Bolognese friend indicates that it preceded 11 March. The *operai* of Florence cathedral would rent out to him on 18 March the house that had been expressly constructed for him prior to his move to Bologna, with the intention that he would proceed with the project of the marble apostles for the cathedral, one interrupted by the wishes of the pope. He would be charged a rental of 10 large florins a year.[71] But already on 9 March he had taken the bold step of acquiring property for himself, buying three adjacent houses on the corner of Via Ghibellina and the present Via Michelangelo Buonarroti. The cost was 1,050 large florins.[72]

Some days later, on 13 March, a notable event took place in the artist's life, his formal emancipation by his father, Lodovico.[73] There seem to have been no established rules governing the age at which such a step could take place. While Michelangelo was thirty-three, there are instances of emancipation being granted at quite disparate ages. His former teacher, Domenico Ghirlandaio, had been emancipated at the age of thirty-five, other artists on occasion achieving their full legal independence much later. And it is noteworthy that Lodovico emancipated his younger son, Buonarroto Buonarroti, when the latter was substantially older than the artist had been.[74]

V

THE SISTINE CHAPEL CEILING

THE FIRST STEPS

Michelangelo, newly granted legal independence by Lodovico, had arrived in Rome by 27 March 1508. On that day, he reopened his bank account with the Balducci and deposited just under 480 gold ducats. The entry states that he has declared that the money has come from the pope.[1] This deposit would be followed by another on 10 May. This second sum was for 400 ducats and it is explicitly described in the entry that it is payment for the impending work in the Sistine Chapel, 'per conto de la chappella'.[2]

More light is shed on these laconic bank entries by the memoranda of the artist, the earliest two of his *ricordi* to have survived. The earlier of the two is not dated, but may have been written in late March or early April. In the first lines of the sheet, Michelangelo jotted down his financial requirements concerning future work on Pope Julius's tomb. He requires an immediate payment of 400 ducats and, following this initial disbursement, he requires 100 ducats a month as prescribed in earlier agreements. Lower down on the same sheet, he turns to his need of money to pay for assistants to work in the Sistine Chapel. This first *ricordo* clearly relates to his credit payment of 27 March.[3]

The second *ricordo* is dated 10 May and explicitly refers to the projected work in the Sistine Chapel. On this day he has received 500 cameral ducats from the pope in order to proceed with painting the vault of Pope Sixtus's chapel. He is to start work forthwith, following the terms of an agreement that has been drawn up by Cardinal

Francesco Alidosi and signed by himself. The *ricordo* directly relates to the credit deposited on 10 May, and shows that the artist kept 100 ducats for anticipated expenses relating to the chapel project.[4]

Since these are the two earliest of the artist's *ricordi* to have survived, it is worth noting that, despite a great many losses, Michelangelo's surviving *ricordi* run to more than 300 printed pages; the latest to have survived dates from just two years before his death. His most immediate exemplar was his own father, Lodovico, whose *ricordanze* once existed and are now lost.[5] Father and son were doing no more than adhering to a profoundly tenacious Florentine tradition; as has been seen, Vasari himself would confirm the truth of the young artist's apprenticeship with the Ghirlandaio brothers by consulting their *ricordi*.[6]

Michelangelo's own *ricordi* are almost invariably terse; although referring to a great range of transactions, they rarely spell out the purposes behind them. Compared, for example, to Leonardo, Michelangelo, as a compiler of *ricordi*, was something of a minimalist.[7]

Nevertheless, the *ricordi* that here concern us reveal the extraordinary implication that he was, in 1508, planning to proceed with both papal tomb and fresco painting in the chapel at the same time. They also confirm that he had successfully persuaded his patron of the practicality of his intentions. But before we indict the artist of a renewal of the *pazzia* that had led to the vision of the Ligurian colossus, we must recall that, for the painting of the ceiling, he envisaged a group of assistants.

Before turning to these collaborators, it is worth noting that the financial arrangements for the painting of the ceiling had been drawn up by Francesco Alidosi. Once again, therefore, Pope Julius had entrusted matters to the man who had written in such remarkable terms to Alamanno Salviati in 1505 and who would emerge, a year later, as the one member of the Curia on whose safe conduct the artist would insist before going to Bologna. In fact, Alidosi was no longer papal treasurer as he had been in 1505 when dealing with financing of the projected tomb, but it seems clear that Julius wished to entrust matters to the man who supremely enjoyed Michelangelo's confidence.

Great as Alidosi's authority was, it is unlikely that he had much more to do with the project. Only a few days after the agreement with Michelangelo had been drawn up, the pope had appointed Alidosi papal legate to Bologna and he subsequently left Rome, remaining absent until provisionally recalled in November 1508. Back in Bologna from April 1509, he would pursue the policy of brutality towards the Bolognese that would make his name one of the most hated in Italy.[8]

Away from Rome, Michelangelo remained in Alidosi's mind. He wrote to him from Ravenna in May 1510, asking him to paint a fresco in the chapel of the papal villa at La Magliana outside Rome.[9] Having been involved in renovating and amplifying the villa, he now asks the artist to paint a small-scale fresco of the *Baptism of Christ* in the chapel. Alidosi's timing could scarcely have been worse and the nature of his request says little for his perspicacity as a patron.[10]

Michelangelo made no reference to Alidosi when he looked back on his life for the benefit of Condivi. His reticence may have been prompted by his protector's ill fame, an almost universal *damnatio memoriae*. But the nature of Alidosi's end, stabbed to death in the street in Ravenna in May 1511 by Duke Francesco Maria della Rovere, may also have contributed to his elimination from the record.[11]

PREPARING FOR THE PROJECT

The first tangible step towards the painting (or, more strictly, repainting) of the chapel ceiling took place on 11 May 1508. On that day, Piero Rosselli, familiar to us from the letter that he had written during the crisis between patron and artist in 1506, confirmed that he had received 10 ducats from Michelangelo for work to remove the existing surface from the ceiling. In its place, he would apply his own rough plaster, in Italian called the *arriccio*, which would, in turn, serve as the

ground for the fine *intonaco* or plaster on which painting would
proceed. Five further payments to him are recorded. Three of these
were made by Francesco Granacci, who, after his arrival in Rome,
evidently took on a number of administrative tasks for Michelangelo
just as he had already served him in arranging the recruitment of assistants, a role discussed below. The latest payment is dated 27 July. It is
much the largest and the wording implies that it was the last in the
series for the work in hand.[12]

What cannot be resolved from these payments is whether this work
extended the whole length of the chapel or only for the first part, that
described by Condivi as extending halfway along the vault, 'della porta
fin a mezzo la volta'.[13] His words do not define where this first campaign halted. But changes in pictorial style and scale, above all the
remarkable increase in size of the figures of sibyls and prophets in the
area towards the altar, indicate that the earlier phase of painting broke
off at a point between the *Creation of Adam* and the *Creation of Eve*
(pl. 23).[14]

From what Michelangelo would write in September 1510, it might
be assumed that Rosselli's work had extended no further than halfway
down the chapel, for, the first part of the campaign of painting completed in the summer, the artist was now declaring that he required
further funds for the construction of the second part of the scaffolding.
Such claims cannot be taken at face value, however, and, in any event,
could be explained by the fact that the structure was in part a perma-
nently fixed one, in part comprising sections that could be moved.
Evidence in favour of the conclusion that the work undertaken by
Rosselli extended the whole length of the chapel is provided by Paris
de Grassis, papal master of ceremonies, in his diary, where, writing on
10 June 1508, he refers to the noise and dust that the ongoing work
was creating, impeding Vespers in the area of the presbytery.[15]

What cannot be resolved is the issue of whether ideas about the
pictorial content of the project, as well as its physical scale, were
already under discussion at this point. So early a date for the planning
of the programme cannot be excluded. Michelangelo's patron was not

a man who wasted time and it must be kept in mind that the artist had already arrived in Rome in the last days of March.[16]

Michelangelo's later comments about the planning of the decoration do not establish the moment when the programme as painted was agreed. His remarks do, nevertheless, confirm that a fundamental change took place, evinced by the two well-known and much-discussed preparatory sketches in London and Detroit, drawings that have been repeatedly analysed. Neither design bears any relation to current Florentine decorative practice; rather, a provision for many painted compartments reflects contemporary taste in Rome. It seems true to propose that they show Michelangelo responding to the expectations of his patron.[17]

The artist's later claim that, after his own complaint about the 'poverty' of the initial plans, his patron gave him a free hand to paint what he himself wanted has been rightly judged incredible. He states that the programme he now undertook extended down to the fifteenth-century narratives below, painted for Julius's uncle, Sixtus IV, a gross mis-statement. The error was, perhaps, a consequence of memory failure or carelessness. Given the tenor of the letter, however, it could have been deliberate. Michelangelo had every reason to aggrandize the physical extent of his achievement in order to strengthen his claim that he was never properly paid.[18]

It has been argued that the 3,000 ducats agreed on was a very large sum, but this is a judgement based on what had recently been paid for projects in Florence.[19] The only valid comparisons are those that relate to Roman projects of the period. Thus, it is more relevant to note that, six years later, Raphael was expecting Pope Leo to pay him 1,200 ducats for the four walls of the Stanza dell'Incendio, a much more modest undertaking in physical terms.[20]

Even a brief survey of events would be incomplete without some reference to the much-debated issue of Michelangelo's scaffolding. It was an aspect of the enterprise to which Vasari paid no attention in his Life of 1550. In Condivi's biography of three years later, it assumes a prominent and polemical character. We are told that the pope

himself invited Bramante to provide the scaffolding and that he devised
one of platforms suspended by ropes, a system that, in a different
context, Vasari refers to as 'hanging bridges', or *ponti impiccati*. The
solution required making holes in the vault itself, and Condivi relates
that Michelangelo's exposure of the impracticality of the solution led
to Bramante's public humiliation before Pope Julius. Removing
Bramante's suspended system, Condivi states that Michelangelo devised
one of his own, which required no ropes, and this solution would be
adopted by Bramante himself in the building of St Peter's.[21]

This remarkable disparagement of Bramante was not disclaimed by
the artist when he commented on Condivi's text in old age, and Vasari
himself would adopt the story almost word for word in his second
edition of 1568.[22] Yet when could Bramante's scaffolding have been
put in place? Already in the nineteenth century, a few writers saw that
the recorded events leave inadequate time for Bramante's alleged intervention and were driven to propose that his *ponti* were hung and then
removed in April. But his platforms could have been hung to any
purpose only after the old surface of the ceiling had been removed,
the task undertaken by Rosselli from 11 May. If, as seems probable,
Michelangelo took over Rosselli's scaffolding, making adjustments
where they were required, the account loses still further credibility.
It can only be concluded that the story is one aspect of the artist's
enduring rancour where Bramante was concerned.[23]

The character of the scaffolding that Michelangelo employed has
provoked discussion and dispute over many years, but the restoration
of the chapel's ceiling in the latter years of the twentieth century has
laid the debate to rest. Hitherto unrecorded, holes in the wall surfaces
at the base of the lunettes were revealed during the restoration that
had served to accommodate the diagonal wooden supports on which
the scaffolding proper rested.[24] The discovery shows that Vasari was
well informed in his Life of 1568 when he wrote of *sorgozzone*, diagonal props, which were employed in such a way that the scaffolding
itself did not touch the wall.[25] The claim advanced by Condivi,
however, and subsequently accepted by Vasari, that the solution

adopted was the artist's own invention, is not believable. It is probable that the practicality of the scaffolding as erected owed most to trained architects, not least Giuliano da Sangallo and Rosselli.[26]

Nevertheless, Michelangelo, always attentive to details, must have taken pains to see that no errors were made. This can be demonstrated by the evidence of one of his most spirited pen sketches.[27] He drew it to indicate to those involved with the erection of the second part of the scaffolding in 1511 what he was anxious to avoid: a situation where he would find himself reduced to lying in a prone position just beneath the surface of the vault.[28]

ASSISTANTS

There can be no doubt that, during his brief stay in Florence after his return from Bologna, Michelangelo had begun to seek out assistants who could come to Rome to help him in the undertaking for the pope. Although lost, his correspondence with Alidosi must have signi-fied his willingness to accept the project.[29] His steps to assemble a small team of qualified assistants show that his initial approach to undertaking the commission was governed by tradition and, most crucially, his familiarity with what had taken place when Domenico Ghirlandaio had put together his group of assistants to fresco the choir of Santa Maria Novella, the Tornabuoni Chapel. That project had been pro-ceeding in the years when the young man was in the Ghirlandaio workshop.[30] The team that Ghirlandaio had put together for his great-est enterprise in fresco painting had been one of the most efficient of its time, reflecting his quite exceptional organizational skills, which the young man had personally observed. Even the number of assistants he himself now sought was probably about the number who had operated under Ghirlandaio's direction and on his designs at Santa Maria Novella.[31]

In his first surviving *ricordo*, already referred to, after setting out his financial needs for proceeding with Pope Julius's tomb, he set down his intentions with regard to assistants. They were to come from Florence and were to number five. He is to pay each of them 20 cameral ducats. If they are prepared to accept the work, the 20 ducats will form part of their salaries. If agreement is not reached, they are to retain 10 ducats to cover the expenses of travel from Florence and for time expended.[32]

The man to whom he entrusted the practicalities of assembling his team of helpers was his long-standing friend, Francesco Granacci. This emerges from a letter of Granacci's, written in Florence and addressed to Michelangelo in Rome, datable before 23 April 1508. As often noted, Granacci's letter indicates that Michelangelo had already set enquiries afoot before leaving Florence. Granacci reports that he has approached Giuliano Bugiardini and Jacopo di Sandro, the latter a pupil of Ghirlandaio alleged by Vasari to have had a part in the painting of the high altar of Santa Maria Novella in the Tornabuoni Chapel. Jacopo had asked Granacci about his prospective salary and is reported to have said that he had had no time to discuss the issue with Michelangelo before he left. Granacci writes that he has not yet spoken with others but adds that he thinks it would be useful to have on board Agnolo di Donnino, who had trained with Cosimo Rosselli, because he had experience of fresco painting. He himself is ready to leave for Rome, along with Bastiano, that is Aristotile da Sangallo. Including himself, Granacci indicates that the prospective helpers were five in number, agreeing with that in Michelangelo's own *ricordo* of late March.[33]

Vasari evidently went to some lengths to get the details of Michelangelo's team correct when preparing the Life in his first edition of 1550. He lists Granacci's five and adds a sixth, Indaco Vecchio, a good friend of Michelangelo and who, it has been proposed, replaced the troublesome Jacopo di Sandro in January 1509, who had been creating problems since the previous October. Vasari's informant could have been the youngest member of the group, Aristotile da Sangallo, who would die in 1551, a year after the publication of Vasari's book. Vasari knew him well and introduced an informative account of his career in his second edition, stating that Aristotile had been one of his closest friends. The two had been especially close in the late 1540s in Rome when Vasari could have been actively seeking information for his project.[34]

The issue of assistants would provoke one of the many dissensions that arose between Vasari and Condivi. Vasari in 1550 had correctly noted Michelangelo's inexperience with mural painting, but his remarks seem to have aroused the old master's anger. Not only would Condivi subsequently omit any reference to the summoning of assistants; he would go much further and deny that Michelangelo had any helpers at all when he painted the ceiling, not even a *garzone* to grind his colours. And this account was even embellished by Benedetto Varchi when he came to compose his funeral oration in 1564. But Vasari stuck to his story in 1568.

A number of the assistants may have been slow to arrive. But Granacci wasted no time. He had reached Rome by 13 May 1508. On that day both he and Michelangelo addressed letters to a friar at the convent of the Gesuati in Florence; they were the most established and dependable suppliers of painting materials in the city. Michelangelo, anxious about his painting materials as he was about the quality of his marble, reported his need of good quality blues, 'azzuri begli', to Frate Jacopo di Francesco. He explains that he requires them for impending work although he gives no details, describing his prospective assignment with characteristic obliquity as painting 'certain things'. He asks that the material be sent by way of his fellow Gesuati in Rome. The tone is one of haste and it seems that no price has been fixed. In his accompanying letter, Granacci, probably more familiar with the Gesuati because of his many assignments for paintings, presses Fra Jacopo to respond and assures him that a fair price will be paid. Whereas Granacci signs himself 'pittore', Michelangelo, despite the nature of his request, signs himself 'scultore'.[35]

Where was Michelangelo now based in Rome? It is almost certain that, back in the city after an absence of two years, he once more took up living in the house near Santa Caterina delle Cavallerotte, the space he had been given by the pope in 1505. That he was living there in late 1510 is shown by a document that records that a canon of St Peter's confirms that the artist may continue to occupy the house near the *piazza* of St Peter's, granted him by Pope Julius in 1505, without the obligation to payment.[36] Various disbursements of April 1508 suggest that he needed cloth for a sheet and required a mattress. There is mention also of a Lucia who may have served as some form of housekeeper.[37] A correspondent would address him as living in the neighbourhood of St Peter's by 22 July 1508.[38] There is nothing to indicate where the assistants were housed.

AT WORK IN THE CHAPEL

The summer months of 1508 would not proceed smoothly for Michelangelo. His brother Giovan Simone came to visit him in Rome but by early July had fallen seriously ill. The artist had always been attached to him; he had repeatedly sent greetings to him through Buonarroto even when desperately overworked in Bologna. And, as recorded earlier, he had extended a helping hand to facilitate Giovan Simone's assuming a modest role in the wool business in the Via Porta Rossa. Writing to Buonarroto on 2 July, the artist reports that Giovan Simone had fallen ill the previous week and the event has added to his current preoccupations. By mid-July he had returned safely to Florence, as Lodovico reported in a letter of 21 July.[39] But the same letter indicates that Michelangelo himself is unwell and unhappy. In an anxious passage, Lodovico even goes so far as to urge the artist to abandon his new enterprise.[40]

The Roman summer would soon strike down another victim, Piero Basso. Piero seems to have travelled to Rome with Granacci in May, his assignment to be that of handyman to the artist. Michelangelo reports that he is concerned that Piero, weakened by the Roman air, could even die during the journey back to Florence. That Piero's role had been an essentially domestic one is suggested by the fact that

Michelangelo declares that he is now alone. He asks Buonarroto to request that another Florentine, Giovanni Michi, come to Rome to help him.[41]

Michi had only recently written to the artist. Signing himself his eternal servant, he informs Michelangelo that he has run into the painter Raffaellino del Garbo. He had worked with Pier Matteo d'Amelia in the past and declares that he is willing to work for Michelangelo for the same salary he had received from Pier Matteo, of 10 ducats a month. Michi's remarks show that Michelangelo's new Roman undertaking was a topic of public discussion in his native Florence.[42]

Problems in Florence would dog the artist in Rome. The gravest of these was prompted by the death of Lodovico's brother, Francesco Buonarroti, in the summer of 1508. Cassandra Bartoli, his widow, would proceed to demand the return of her dowry, as she was entitled to do. The crisis will be discussed later; but it is worth noting that Michelangelo was involved in the affair, and the desperate letters of Lodovico to him make sad reading. The outcome would also seriously affect Michelangelo's own relations with his father.[43]

Information about events in the chapel is lacking for the later months of 1508. No letters from the artist survive between late August, when he wrote to Lodovico requesting a small amount of good-quality varnish, and January 1509. That it was during this autumn that the Florentine government came to realize that they had lost their chosen artist is borne out by two letters. One of early September asks him to recommend a sculptor who could complete the bronze *David*. And Soderini's hopes to have him back to undertake the rough-hewing of the marble block for the second statue for the *piazza* were dashed. He reported in a letter to Alberico Malaspina of 16 December that Pope Julius has refused the artist permission to come to Florence even for the brief period of twenty-five days.[44]

In early October Lodovico refers to the fact that one of the assistants whom the artist had summoned from Florence, Jacopo di Sandro, has let him down. A former aide of Domenico Ghirlandaio, the reference confirms the identity of one of the assistants listed by Vasari. Lodovico comments on Jacopo's promising appearance. But he reminds his son of what he has repeatedly warned him about in the past, that all these followers of Savonarola, *piagnoni*, are a bad lot.[45] It does not follow from what he writes that Jacopo had been incompetent as an assistant, proving that painting had begun; the letter suggests some other source of Michelangelo's dissatisfaction. Jacopo would hang around in Rome for some time before returning to Florence.

The first certain indication that work had begun emerges from a letter of Lodovico's of 18 January 1509, in which he refers to his son's intense activity.[46] Confirmation is provided by a letter of Michelangelo's own of the twenty-seventh. It is a much-discussed text. In it, the artist complains of lack of money from the pope. He is reluctant to ask for funds because things are not going well. He refers to the difficulty of the work and his own inexperience. Employing a word that he uses elsewhere, he explains that what he is trying to do is still not his 'professione'.[47] What these letters do indicate is that work was under way in deep midwinter, when conditions for mural painting were not ideal.[48]

The artist's depressed tone in his letter to Lodovico reflected a serious initial setback. It was one to which Condivi would devote a well-known passage in his biography. Modern examination has conclusively shown that, of the narratives, work began on the *Flood*. Condivi writes that, after the beginning of work on the scene, mould began to appear and threatened to destroy the very visibility of the figures. As reported by Condivi, Michelangelo told his patron that painting in fresco was not his calling. But his attempt to abandon the enterprise was not successful. Pope Julius summoned Giuliano da Sangallo to confront the problem, who recognized what had gone wrong with the preparation of the plaster.[49] In fact, the composition of the plaster that the artist elected to use for the project was very different from that traditionally employed in Florence, but Giuliano had a long experience of Roman conditions.[50]

The assistants, whose presence is clearly evident in the fresco of the *Flood*, would not remain for long. Already in the early summer of 1509 Michelangelo explains to his father that he is unhappy, unwell and overburdened with work. He has learnt from one of his father's letters that the news has spread in Florence that he is dead.[51] Writing to Buonarroto in mid-November, he complains that he is suffering greatly and is physically exhausted. He continues that he has no friends and wants none. The tenor of his remarks suggests that the assistants have left.[52]

It could well have been at this time that he wrote one of his most extraordinary poems, a sonnet that describes the physical privations that he has to endure in order to pursue his work. He has already grown a goitre. His stomach is close to his chin, his beard turns towards heaven. His breast bone resembles that of a harpy and his brush, always above his face, by dribbling down, changes it into a decorated pavement. His loins have entered his belly; his bottom, to compensate, has become a crupper. He is bent like a Syrian bow – one that forms a half-circle. His reasoning has become wild and confused. In the second of the two three-line tercets that conclude the poem, he addresses a 'Giovanni' to come to his aid, to defend his dead painting and his honour, for he is not in a good place and he is no painter. To the right of the poem, the artist drew a brief autobiographical pen sketch of a figure reaching up to paint a devil-like image (pl. 24).[53]

This despair about his task did not persist. Nor did he lack some assistance even after the departure of his associates. While he no longer was either helped or impeded by fellow painters, he did not lack helpers who, while not wielding a brush, took on indispensable tasks. When, for example, he came to paint the double scene of the *Fall and Expulsion*, he had the services of a man whose identity can never be captured but who was a master in the preparation of fresh plaster. While he left the areas of landscape quite coarse, he would prepare for the nude figures an *intonaco* almost matching porcelain.

This double scene was the penultimate narrative Michelangelo would carry out before work in the chapel came to a halt. It demonstrates a mastery of invention and technical skills far removed from the earlier uncertainty. The figure of Eve in the *Expulsion* is 2 metres in height and was painted in a single session.[54] His approach to narrative displays his growing freedom from traditional iconography. Unlike, for example, Masaccio's Adam and Eve in the *Expulsion* in the Brancacci Chapel in Florence, Michelangelo's figures are completely naked, deprived of protective leaves, which indicate the circumstances of their expulsion from Eden.[55]

Nowhere is the artist's command of fresco technique more assured than in the series of the lunettes, painted without preparatory cartoons and with a virtuosity of technique scarcely rivalled in the period. This series of the *Ancestors of Christ* was probably of great importance to his patron. The dedication of the chapel to the Assumption of the Virgin, prescribed by his uncle Sixtus, had been reflected in Perugino's altarpiece on the altar wall.[56] The choice of the Ancestors for inclusion could well have been a further tribute to the Virgin by his nephew. For the genealogy of Christ, set out in the first sixteen verses of the first chapter of St Matthew, was the Gospel text read on another of her feast-days, that of her Nativity, celebrated on 8 September. There can be no doubt that Julius had a particular veneration for this feast, one that would find a last expression in his declared wish that his projected funerary chapel in the new St Peter's should be dedicated to this Nativity.[57]

AN ABSENT PATRON

The late summer of 1510 would bring troubles for the artist very different from those of undependable assistants and unsatisfactory plaster: he would lose the sustaining presence of his patron.

For many months, Julius had contemplated a new military campaign, to establish himself as the arbiter of Italian affairs and to destroy the threat of French power. Most urgent was his determination to recover Ferrara for the Church and, to this end, the step of

excommunicating Alfonso d'Este and declaring all his dignities confiscated was taken on 9 August.[58] The actual decision to go north seems
to have been made relatively quickly, as a letter of Michelangelo would
imply. Leaving Rome on 1 September, the pope travelled with great
speed and an urgency very different from the relatively leisurely pace
of the journey of 1506. No longer was there time for boating trips on
Lake Trasimeno. Whereas the earlier journey to attack Bologna had
taken more than two and a half months, this one was accomplished in
three weeks, the pope entering Bologna in triumphant fashion on 22
September, recalling events of four years earlier.

Perhaps weakened by the exhausting journey in adverse weather,
Julius fell ill. He was reported to be in bed with fever as early as 26
September. Attacks would continue throughout the autumn. One
observer reported that he was feverish every day and by 20 October
there were fears that he was dying. But his powerful constitution
would resist, a wonder to those around him. Nevertheless, he was
declared to have fully recovered only as late as 22 December.[59] Yet,
as early as 2 January 1511, now a bearded pontiff, he set out in appalling weather to join the troops besieging Mirandola. It was hoped that
its surrender would lead to the capture of Ferrara.[60]

Weeks earlier, in an undated letter to Buonarroto, Michelangelo
informs his brother that the first campaign of painting in the chapel is
close to completion; he will have finished this part of the ceiling
within a week. Once it is publicly unveiled, he expects to receive
money from the pope and to have permission to leave for a month
in Florence, something he much desires because he is not very well.
The letter was probably written in July or August, and gives no inti-
mation that the artist expected his patron to desert him.[61]

Michelangelo's expectation of a further payment from the pope,
now that the first part of his task was completed, was fully justified.
His initial payment of 500 ducats on 10 May 1508 had been followed
by another of 500 ducats in late June 1509.[62] Given the overall remuneration of 3,000 ducats that had been agreed, he was justified in
expecting at this point a further 500 to mark completion of the first

half of his assignment, a payment not in anticipation of future work but a remuneration for the work he had already achieved.

But his expectation of a public showing of his work and of his further payment would be dashed. Julius had issues of greater urgency on his mind in the summer of 1510. The coming weeks would be a period of anxiety for the artist. Two letters of early September, written by Michelangelo just after Pope Julius had left the city, graphically testify to his concerns. He has just had a letter from his father and, on the day of its arrival, 5 September, he instantly replies, expressing his deep concern over news that Buonarroto is ill.[63] He writes that he is ready to come to Florence at once, although this will jeopardize his chances of being paid. He adds that the pope has left Rome without giving him any instructions and he is at a loss as to what to do. Nevertheless, his concern for Buonarroto is paramount. He attempts to console Lodovico, assuring him that God has not created them in order to abandon them.[64]

He wrote again to Lodovico two days later. He should draw money from his account at Santa Maria Nuova if it is needed for Buonarroto's needs. He once again reviews his own predicament, once more reporting that he is owed 500 ducats and as much again to erect the scaffolding for the other half of the work and to continue with his project. He repeats that the pope has left, leaving no instructions, and that he has written to him. He is in an apprehensive state with regard to Julius, fearful that his patron will be furious if he leaves without permission. Nevertheless, he will come to Florence and be there in two days if needed; men are worth more than money.[65] The text of this letter testified to the apprehension that Pope Julius could inspire, fear not confined to his chosen artist.[66]

The adverse situation revealed in these letters could have inspired Michelangelo to compose what is one of his most problematic sonnets. There is no critical unanimity as to its date; it has been associated with his first residence in Rome and to a period as late as 1512. The sonnet is a passionate indictment of the venality and immorality of papal Rome. At one point, its language echoes Petrarch, while the text as a whole, in its denunciation of Rome, has a strongly Savonarolan ring. Helmets and swords are made from chalices and the blood of Christ is widely sold. The last six lines strike a deeply personal note. Here he has no more work, and the pope, described as 'he in the mantle', can turn him into stone as Medusa petrified Atlas. The poem is signed 'Your Michelangelo in Turkey'.[67]

The sequence of events would have allowed for the possibility that his letter to the pope was acknowledged and that he was granted leave to set out. On 12 September, a week after the second of his two letters to Lodovico, he drew 14 ducats from his account with the Balducci for his journey.[68] He would reach Florence on the seventeenth. Having left with his habitual precipitancy, he found himself without appropriate clothing and would order a belted gown and a large cloak, items required for his meeting with his patron. The payment was recorded by Buonarroto in his own account-book, a fact suggesting that his health had improved.[69] Michelangelo must also have hastened his leaving Rome in order to see Lodovico in Florence before he would leave to assume the office of *podestà* at San Casciano, a post that would involve his absence for six months. In the event, he did not arrive in time. The unexpected speed of his arrival, however, would expose Lodovico's lack of rectitude in handling money that his son had sent from Rome, an episode that is best discussed at a later point.

Michelangelo probably arrived in Bologna towards the end of September, before Julius's health broke down. Although circumstances were different from those in late November 1506, and although he was not appearing 'with a halter around his neck', his appearance could have recalled his earlier arrival in the city. Even in the changed circumstances of 1510, he could still have been perceived as a petitioner. Perhaps he once again found a supporter in Francesco Alidosi. Despite Alidosi's tyrannical behaviour as governor of the city, he still enjoyed the pope's confidence.

How long he remained in the city, which was once more on a war footing, is unknown. He would write to Buonarroto from Rome on 26 October, reporting that on the previous day he had been paid 500

ducats by the pope's datary, Lorenzo Pucci, a man with whom he
would have to deal in the future. He informs his brother that he is
sending 450 ducats to Florence, to be deposited in his Santa Maria
Nuova account.[70] In the light of his complaints of a month earlier, his
behaviour may seem paradoxical. But the decision almost certainly
implies that he had been promised further money by Julius; the sum
he received from Pucci matched what he was owed for the work
completed, but did not provide for the expenses of pursuing further
work in the chapel, the most immediate being that for preparing scaffolding. Building up his account in Florence was, of course, actuated
by his strategy to invest in property around the city.[71] But the transfer
also can be related to his distrust of all things Roman. When he came
to send a further sum to Florence in the following year, he explains
that the money is safer there.[72]

     That he had received what was owed to him for work accomplished
is confirmed by a remarkable letter addressed to him in Rome. It was
written on 2 November by no less than his old friend Angelo Manfidi,
herald of the Florentine government, who has been encountered
earlier. He has learnt from a letter of the artist that he has received
part of the money he has earned. He urges Michelangelo not to be
backward in claiming what is due to him in the future. The letter
suggests that the artist had discussed his financial problems with Manfidi
while he was in Florence and his friend seems to have taken on the
role of strengthening his resolve.[73] His worries about his finances at
this time are shown by the step he took to preserve his claim to his
workshop behind Santa Catarina delle Cavallerotte.

     But his concern would express itself in his undertaking a second
journey to Bologna. The date of his leaving Rome is not known, but
the artist was once again in Florence on 14 December and had
returned to Rome by 7 January 1511.[74] This time, money came more
slowly and in smaller sums. His discontent with his treatment is
expressed in a letter to Buonarroto of 23 February; he writes that he
may have to return to Bologna yet again. He had travelled back to
Rome in the company of Lorenzo Pucci, who had assured him that

when he himself returned to Bologna, he would see to it that he had the means he needed to continue his work. Now, weeks later, he has heard nothing.[75]

The following months of 1511 are some of the most obscure in Michelangelo's life. In one letter, he writes that he is forwarding 100 ducats to Florence to satisfy the heirs of his dead Piccolomini patron whose altar in the cathedral of Siena still awaited most of the statues he had promised to undertake in 1501. He adds that he can expect nothing from the pope in the next six months, a prediction not borne out by the evidence.[76]

What the artist was engaged in before Julius re-entered Rome in late June 1511 is unknown. It has been proposed that, with the undertaking in the chapel at a standstill, he turned to work on the pope's tomb.[77] But there is no evidence to support the conjecture. If he had turned to the tomb project, it is scarcely possible that he would not have referred to so significant a fact in the text he prepared to send to Fattucci in December 1523; the letter was a response to information required in Rome precisely relating to his failure to fulfil his obligations. In the text, he explicitly states that his time was wasted before Julius returned from Bologna. Only on his arrival did he resume work, preparing cartoons for the second part of the chapel decoration.[78]

THE LAST TWELVE MONTHS

The sixty-eight-year-old pope was back in Rome in late June 1511. He stayed the night of 26 June at Santa Maria del Popolo, the church built by his uncle, and left for the Vatican Palace on the following day. Although the route was marked by triumphal arches, there was nothing to celebrate, for this second expedition had ended in total failure. The French had re-entered Bologna on 23 May and would restore the Bentivoglio family. The following day, Alidosi, Julius's most cherished adviser, had been murdered in the street in Ravenna by the pope's own nephew, Francesco Maria della Rovere. It was an event celebrated by many, although leaving the pope distraught with grief.[79] After describing the papal return through the city, Paris de Grassis, who had accompanied the pope throughout the journey, committed to paper his judgement that the enterprise had been burdensome and futile.[80]

Michelangelo's reaction to the pope's return is unrecorded. But the events of the last ten months must have brought home to him the extent of his dependence on his patron. Indeed, writing to Lodovico a few weeks before Julius's return, he asks his father to pray for the pope, for his well-being and their own.[81] Prayers for Pope Julius would soon be urgently required.

The unveiling of what the artist had referred to as 'the part that I began', the event that had not taken place in the late summer of 1510, finally occurred on 14 August 1511, the vigil of the Feast of the Assumption of the Virgin, chosen to celebrate the chapel's dedication. Paris de Grassis would record the event in his diary, stating that the pope was present.[82]

It is rarely noted how close Julius came to death before Michelangelo resumed work in the chapel. Three days after his attendance at Vespers, he suffered a resumption of a fever that had already troubled him in early August. His weakness worsened and the prospect of his death seemed imminent. After resisting seeing Francesco Maria della Rovere, he finally consented. On 24 August he made a will, distributing to Francesco Maria, his daughter Felice, and Niccolò della Rovere more than 30,000 ducats. Once more, as in Bologna, he would recover.[83]

Writing to his father on 4 October, Michelangelo reports that he has had two audiences with the pope, the first on Tuesday, the last day of September, and a second one the following day. As a consequence of the latter, he has received 400 ducats, 300 of which he is forwarding to Florence. He asks Lodovico to pray for him, that he may acquit himself well and satisfy the pope. In that event, he predicts that he will be well rewarded. Perhaps Julius's most recent brush with death directed his thoughts once more to the issue of his final resting place.[84]

When the artist began to prepare for the resumption of his work is unrecorded; but evidence provided by some of his drawings suggests that he began to plan the last Creation scene of *God Dividing Light from Darkness* at some point in September (pl. 25).[85] In a brief note to Lodovico of 11 October, he explains that he has no time to write at length. Painting may have resumed in the chapel in early October. Once more, the artist set out to work in the season approaching winter, as he had done three years earlier.

The exhaustive restoration reports following the recent cleaning of the ceiling show that, in this second campaign, Michelangelo adopted a number of devices to speed his work, perhaps at least in part complying with the pressures from a patron whose hold on life was insecure. One indication of the pressure is the way in which the designs of the preparatory cartoons were transferred to the plaster. The time-consuming technique of transference by what in Italian is known as *spolvero*, where coloured powder would be dusted through the laboriously perforated holes of the cartoon, a technique predominantly adopted in the first campaign (including the lunettes), was, to a significant degree, abandoned. It was replaced by the adoption of *incisione indiretta*, indirect incision, the lines now incised through the paper on to the plaster. The change, clearly adopted to save time, is most clearly evident in the Creation scenes of the second part. After the *Creation of Adam*, the first of the narratives to be painted after the resumption of work, where both techniques were employed, the subsequent three Creation scenes were all carried out by means of indirect incision.[86]

The intensity of the work demanded by the need for speed is vividly conveyed in a note that Michelangelo wrote to Buonarroto months later, on 24 July 1512. It is night and he has no time for correspondence. He predicts that he will be in Florence by the coming September and can help his brother then. He is suffering hardships greater than any man has had before; he is unwell and overburdened with work. Nevertheless, he has the patience to endure until his desired conclusion is reached. He urges Buonarroto to be patient for a further two months; he is ten thousand times better off than himself.[87]

In this same month of July, an episode took place that is both familiar and noteworthy. Alfonso d'Este, his situation now gravely compromised by the retreat of the French after the battle of Ravenna, had been granted a safe conduct to come to Rome on 11 June. He left Ferrara on 23 June and arrived in Rome on 4 July. A few days later, on Sunday, 11 July, after visiting the apartments of Alexander VI, Alfonso expressed his wish to see the ceiling of the Sistine Chapel, and through the offices of the youthful Federico Gonzaga, who obtained the pope's permission, this was arranged. The duke ascended the scaffolding with a considerable number of attendants, and remained there in Michelangelo's company, unable to take his eyes off the figures. Michelangelo acceded to his request to carry out a painting for him; the duke even offered him money. Michelangelo's next recorded meeting with Duke Alfonso would take place in very different circumstances seventeen years later.[88]

Adverse news would persist during this second campaign of painting. A particularly bitter event for Pope Julius was the destruction of Michelangelo's bronze statue in Bologna on 30 December 1511. With French backing, the Bentivoglio had resumed control of Bologna on 21 May 1511. The statue would remain intact until the end of the year when, to gratify their French allies, the city council ordered its destruction. The inner façade of San Petronio was opened and the statue pulled down within the church. It was set on fire on 2 January 1512 and the head of the effigy rolled around the *piazza*. In a notorious postscript, the bronze would be presented to Duke Alfonso, most of the material employed to cast a huge cannon that would be named 'La Giulia'. Vasari claimed to have seen the head in Alfonso's *guardaroba* in 1540.[89] The pope's fury over the behaviour of the Bolognese was vented on their deputation that came to Rome to seek peace in June 1512, months after the city had been abandoned by the French.[90]

In Condivi's Life, the artist refers to the destruction of his statue with a certain passivity. But the fate of the work remained alive, and Michelangelo's future patron, Pope Clement VII, would recall its destruction as late as 1525, when concerned about the choice of bronze for one of his own projects at San Lorenzo.[91]

The French retreat from Italy would have another consequence that would touch the artist far more closely, the fall of the Soderini republic in Florence. The Florentine government's refusal to join the pope's Holy League because of long-standing loyalty to the French crown was agreed in late July 1512.[92] Relations between the Signoria and Julius had always been difficult, and in 1511 its consent to allow a schismatic council to be held on Florentine territory at Pisa had led to the repeated imposition of an Interdict by Julius.[93] At a council in Mantua held by the members of the league in August 1512, it was decided that military operations should begin against Florence and that the Medici should be re-established in the city.

The adherence of the Florentine government to the French alliance would rapidly lead to disaster. Steps to attack the city were agreed on by members of the league and on 29 August Prato was subjected to a fearsome sack.[94] The Florentine Signoria would be forced to yield. Soderini was expelled from the Palazzo della Signoria on 31 August, and his subsequent exile would take him as far as Ragusa. On 16 September Giuliano de' Medici entered the palace.[95]

Writing to Buonarroto, the member of the family whom he could trust, on 5 September, after he had heard the news of Prato, Michelangelo urges the whole family to flee to some place of safety, even if such a step involved abandoning everything that they possessed: 'life is more important than possessions'. He counsels his brother to remove all the money deposited at Santa Maria Nuova and move to Siena, remaining there until things become settled. He urges the family to take no part in public affairs, in deed or word. They should act as they would in the event of plague and be the first to flee. The letter is an astonishingly telling indication of Michelangelo's impulse to fly in the face of perceived dangers.[96]

A further letter to Buonarroto has survived, dated 18 September. Michelangelo has had the news that the Medici have been restored, and voices further fears. The family should remain quiet and shun all

friends save God. They should speak well or badly of no one, because
the future is uncertain, concerning themselves only with their own
affairs. In case of danger, they can use the money at Santa Maria
Nuova. He complains that he has no money and not even a pair of
stockings. He cannot expect the rest of his earnings before he has
finished his work, but he expects to be back in Florence by All Saints.
In the meantime, he is experiencing great difficulties and hardship.[97]

Two letters of some weeks later can be referred to at this point.
Both are addressed to Lodovico. In what is probably the earlier, he
writes in agitated terms, for his father has informed him that word has
got around in Florence that he has spoken ill of the Medici. He denies
the charge; if he has said anything, it was only what had been expressed
by many, as had happened over the sack of Prato. Even the stones
would have spoken, had they been able. He wants Buonarroto to find
out who has spread the report.[98]

His anxiety was not entirely groundless. Florentines had long memories. Raffaele Riario had been his first Roman patron in 1496.
Riario's suspected involvement in the Pazzi conspiracy of 1478 had
left a legacy of Medicean distrust, not least with Cardinal Giovanni
de' Medici, soon to be elected pope.[99] More recently, Michelangelo
had been the favoured artist of Piero Soderini, which was no recommendation in Medicean circles.

The other letter to Lodovico, undated but probably written in
October, would concern Lodovico's situation provoked by the fiscal
policy of the heavily indebted new regime.[100] Forced to raise money,
the imposition of a forced loan, an *accatto*, was decreed on 21 September. From what the artist writes, it appears that his father had been
assessed to pay 120 ducats, half to be paid in October.[101]

The news of the levy infuriated Michelangelo. Indeed, it provoked
an astonishing epistolary outburst against his fellow Florentines. Never
has he had to deal with a more arrogant and ungrateful people. The
words he employs are redolent of passages in Dante's *Inferno*. But,
although he assures Lodovico he will continue to help, he concludes
on a hostile note, including his own family among those he denounces.

He has laboured for fifteen years on their behalf, all without a word of acknowledgement.[102] Nevertheless, he includes in the letter a note to Giuliano de' Medici on behalf of his father. Lodovico was seeking to regain the office in the Florentine customs, the Dogana, which he had enjoyed under Lorenzo the Magnificent. Michelangelo's note seems not to have survived. But Lodovico's own brief letter has. It is noteworthy that, to strengthen his case, he signs the letter Lodovico Buonarroti, father of Michelangelo the sculptor.[103]

The artist wrote to Lodovico in the first days of October, reporting that he had completed his task in the chapel. The pope is very satisfied, but other things are not proceeding as he had expected. He adds, without explaining his statement, that the times are unfavourable to 'our art'. He will not, after all, be back in Florence for All Saints.[104] The unveiling of the completed work would, in fact, take place on the eve of the feast, 31 October, as Paris de Grassis records in his diary. Julius came to Vespers after his habitual afternoon sleep. Seventeen cardinals were present. Today, writes the master of ceremonies, the work of painting the chapel is finished. He adds that for three or four years the vault has been hidden from view by wooden scaffolding or some other form of covering attached to it.[105]

With the unveiling, Michelangelo had achieved a feat difficult to match in the history of painting; he had completed the second half of the undertaking in about twelve months. Experience gained in the earlier campaign of work had played a part in the achievement. Yet, in the last stages of the work, the artist had set himself tasks unmatched in the first part of the decoration. The figure of Haman would become a paradigm of foreshortening (pl. 26). And to compare the huge figure of Jonah, above the altar wall, with the corresponding figure of Zechariah above the entrance is to recognize a development over four years unequalled in the working life of most sixteenth-century painters. Aggrandizement of scale and a greater complexity of movement were accompanied by an enhanced attention to detail, as the weeping companion introduced behind the mourning Jeremiah shows.[106]

Nevertheless, the letter to Lodovico announcing the completion of his task is conspicuous for its lack of any elation. And, as has been seen, the letters that follow are marked by doubts and anxieties, compounded by the death of his patron a few months later. Julius's death in early 1513 found Michelangelo still in Rome, despite a recent remark that it seemed a thousand years since he had last seen his native city.[107]

VI

AFTER POPE JULIUS

THE DEAD POPE'S TOMB

Pope Julius died in the night of 20–21 February 1513. His health had been failing for several months. On 10 December of the previous year, he had been carried in a litter to the fourth session of the Lateran Council. On the eve of Christmas he had been too ill to attend Vespers and did not attend Mass on Christmas Day. His lucidity of mind was, however, complete until the end.[1]

His final resting place was one of his last concerns. Summoning Paris de Grassis, master of ceremonies, to his bedside on 4 February, he gave him instructions; he wished to be provisionally laid to rest in the chapel of his uncle, Sixtus IV, in Old St Peter's until his tomb, which he had already ordered to be begun, should be completed.[2]

The pope's failing health explains an event regarding Michelangelo that took place in January 1513. From the Rome branch of the Fugger bank he received 2,000 cameral ducats, 200 of which he retained for his own needs. There can be no doubt that this large payment had been made on Julius's own instructions, for he had been making use of the Fugger in the latter years of his pontificate.[3]

That this impressive sum was paid out for future work on the tomb is borne out by the fact that the money is explicitly referred to in the revised contract for the work drawn up in May, three months after the pope's death. In the text, the artist formally acknowledges the money he has already received for the project: 1,500 ducats directly received from Julius himself and a further 2,000 ducats that had been paid to him through Bernardo Bini, the man in charge of cameral disbursements.[4]

Despite this, years later Michelangelo would attempt to alter the record. In one of the drafts of the letter for Fattucci that had been explicitly prompted by Fattucci's demand, in 1523, for details about how much money had been spent on the tomb, the artist would write that, prior to the death of Julius, he had appealed to Bernardo Bibbiena and a man whom he refers to as 'Actalante' for much-needed money.[5] In response, they had arranged payment to him of 2,000 ducats. But Michelangelo implies that this money was payment still outstanding for the Sistine Chapel ceiling and that he, out of good will, had put it toward the cost of the tomb project.[6]

The two executors chosen by the dying Julius testify to his perspicacity. One was Leonardo Grosso della Rovere, another nephew of Sixtus IV. Of all those who had received preferment, he, more than any other member of the family, deserved it. He had been made bishop of Agen by Pope Innocent VIII in 1491, and was, as a consequence, inaccurately referred to by many, including Michelangelo, as 'Cardinale Aginensis', although he was, in fact, created a cardinal by Julius in December 1505. He acquired the important office of Grand Penitentiary in 1511. His learning, humanity and exemplary way of life were widely recognized. The grudging papal master of ceremonies, Paris de Grassis, described him as 'laudabiliter in omnibus et per omnia'.[7]

The other was the Florentine Lorenzo Pucci. He had been given the influential office of datary by Julius and, a fervent Medicean, would be made a cardinal by Leo X in his first creation of September 1513. His title was Santi Quattro Coronati and he was generally referred to by this description. He had been one of the formal witnesses of the dying pope's last wishes and had personally helped to lay the coffin to rest behind the altar in the chapel of Sixtus IV.[8]

The contract was signed on 6 May 1513. It provided for a total expenditure of 16,500 cameral ducats. It is declared that, of these, 3,500 ducats have been received by the artist. The sum is a very large one but needs to be viewed in historical perspective. For example, financial provision for the funeral of Alexander VI and the conclave to follow had amounted to no less than 15,000 ducats in August 1503.[9] The overall cost is, nevertheless, significantly larger than that agreed in 1505 for the earlier project. This could well mean that the new one was more ambitious; unfortunately, Michelangelo's own later statements about the respective scale of the two undertakings are hopelessly contradictory.[10]

An orderly procedure for paying the artist was set out. The responsibility for regular monthly payments fell first to Lorenzo Pucci. He was to pay the artist 7,000 ducats over the following two years. The money was to be disbursed by Bernardo Bini.[11] The outstanding 6,000 ducats were to be the responsibility of Cardinal Leonardo, who would arrange for payment through a Genoese banker. The project was to be completed by 1520, and during these seven years Michelangelo was to take on no other work that would impede progress on the tomb. Undoubtedly at the artist's insistence, given his incapacity to read the Latin text, the same notary prepared one in the vernacular, and he himself prepared a brief and summary description of the project that was to be carried out.[12]

Yet this description of the planned monument was not his last word. Only two months later, on 9 July, he drew up an agreement with a fellow Tuscan, Antonio da Pontassieve, concerning the decorative carving of the front façade of the lower storey of the monument. In contrast with his text of May, it has become half as broad again, the width increased from 20 to 30 *palmi*, more than 6.5 metres.[13]

This subcontract with Antonio da Pontassieve was concerned with the decorative carving of the lower front face of the tomb; it was witnessed by Piero Rosselli, who had prepared the chapel vault in 1508, and the artist's current *garzone*, Silvio Falcone. Although it has been frequently argued that this work had been begun during the initial period of the tomb's history, the troubled circumstances of the early months of 1506 can never have permitted serious work to be undertaken and this contract contains no hint of any work started

earlier.[14] The number of assistants is not specified in the text, but that
Antonio had a number of them is borne out in a letter of Falcone to
Michelangelo of August 1514, where Antonio is designated 'maestro',
and where the arrival of Bernardino Basso is reported to be
imminent.[15]

No site for the tomb is referred to either in the contract or in the
text of the Bull that Julius was still able to sign on 19 February, just
before his death. This laid down elaborate provision for his resting
place, the projected Cappella Giulia, which he probably envisaged for
the choir arm of the new basilica.[16] Yet with his death, there was little
chance of his plan surviving. It would have required the election of
another della Rovere pope, with a devotion to the memory of Julius
equal to that he himself had always shown for his uncle's, to safeguard
the scheme.[17]

As often observed, the project of 1513 was not a satisfactory one
(pl. 27). Although a wall tomb, it was to be attached to the wall by
side elevations that were planned to be longer than the front one,
creating a structure deeper than it was wide, and this rather anomalous
solution was not completely rectified by the increase in scale of the
front face introduced in the subsequent agreement with Antonio da
Pontassieve of July. Nor was the programme of decoration very coher-
ent, with its mixture of all'antica and Christian elements. In proposing
a crowning mandorla-like relief, with the Virgin represented standing,
holding the Child in her arms, the artist had returned to an idea he
had entertained in the New York drawing of 1505 and at that time had
discarded.[18]

Completion of the project now agreed could never have been
achieved in the time laid down, however single-mindedly the artist
might devote himself to it. The number of statues, many on an heroic
scale, came to around forty, and to these there were to be added nine
reliefs. Not even a highly organized workshop could have met the
conditions set down in May 1513. As has been seen, the artist at one
point claimed that Cardinal Leonardo had wanted a tomb larger than
that envisaged in 1505, at another that he had wished for a reduction

in scale. The greatly increased cost prescribed in 1513 would seem to substantiate that this project was indeed an amplified one. In any event, the scheme now agreed leads to the conclusion that, not for the last time, Michelangelo dazzled his patrons with an alluring and unrealizable project.

THE MINERVA *CHRIST*

The contract of the tomb of the dead pope to which the artist had put his name on 6 May 1513 forbids him to undertake any other work that would impede progress with the project. Yet, despite this injunction, we find him accepting a new commission for private patrons only two weeks later. With the ink scarcely dry on the contract, he undertakes to carve a life-size marble statue for patrons who had never been mentioned in his previous surviving correspondence. The event brings to mind the reckless disregard for existing obligations that had marked his behaviour after his return to Florence in 1501.

The contract for this new commission is dated 14 June 1514. Account-books of the Balducci bank, however, show that the project had been agreed more than a year earlier, in May 1513. An account was opened at the bank specifically to deal with payments for the new project.[19]

This new assignment to undertake a statue was the consequence of events in 1512. In February that year Marta Porcari, member of an extensive patrician Roman family, had drawn up her will. In it, she expressed the wish to be buried in the Dominican church of Santa Maria sopra Minerva, close to where she had lived and where her forebears had been laid to rest. She expressed the further wish to found what is referred to as a chapel, 'unam capellam', which, however, was probably not planned to be more than an altar where Masses could be said. To this end, she left 200 ducats, as well as bequeathing money for rites to be carried out in her memory.[20] Three men, two of them nephews, were to supervise the implementation of her wishes, but only one of them, Metello Vari, would see the project through to its conclusion. They were not to delay in carrying out the provisions of her will. If nothing had been achieved after six months following her death, the money was to go to two confraternities instead.[21]

Marta Porcari died in June 1512, but only in November is there evidence of serious discussion on the part of the two nephews. Nevertheless, a record of the proceedings reveals that some form of sculptural decoration was already envisaged by that date. By May 1513, soon after he had completed work in the Sistine Chapel, Michelangelo was approached, as the Balducci records show. But the formal contract was drawn up only in the summer of 1514, as has been seen. In the contract, payment for the statue is set at 200 ducats, the entire sum that had been left by Marta Porcari for her altar. Michelangelo is allowed four years to complete the work. No dedication had been prescribed by Marta Porcari. Now, it is laid down in the contract that the statue is to be a figure of Christ, which is to be life-size, naked, upright and holding the cross, in whatever attitude the artist chooses (pl. 28).[22]

The project was one that would cost Michelangelo dearly in time and effort; he would be subjected to a succession of setbacks. The first and most damaging was the emergence of a dark vein in the marble, an event any marble sculptor dreaded and one unforeseeable when the block was chosen. A later letter of Vari indicates the worst of all possible contingencies, a dark flaw in the face.[23]

After the second version of the statue had been installed in 1521, the artist gave the abandoned work to Vari, and it remained in the courtyard of his Roman house, where it was described by Aldrovandi.[24] It was for sale in Rome in 1607, and recent research has led to its identification with a statue once in the Giustiniani collection and now in a church north of Rome, entirely reworked and brought to completion. The dark vein is very evident.[25]

More immediately, the abandoned block, together with the two *Slaves* and the *Moses*, would remain at Macel de' Corvi when the artist went to Florence in the summer of 1516. He left Rome with the obligation to begin the work all over again.

A ROMAN HOUSE

During the years spent in Rome working for Pope Julius from 1508 to 1512, Michelangelo had had the benefit of rent-free accommodation, where he seems to have both lived and worked. The quarters had belonged to the Chapter of St Peter's and, as has been seen, the artist had felt sufficiently concerned about his security there to have his right to them confirmed in a document drawn up on 4 December 1510. Described as granted to him in order to serve Pope Julius, his claim to them could have ended with Julius's death in February 1513 and the subsequent election of Giovanni de' Medici as Pope Leo x in March 1513. In his letter to a cleric of 1542, the artist would state that, because Cardinal Leonardo Grosso della Rovere wished to increase the scale of the tomb, he had been compelled to move his marble to a new site, the house at Macel de' Corvi.[26] That this statement was a true one (among many that were not) is supported by what he had written to Fattucci in late 1523, informing him that marble he had ordered for the first project that had arrived in Rome had lain neglected on the *piazza* of St Peter's right up to Leo's election.[27] The two reasons for the move are, in any event, not incompatible.

No reference to a need for new accommodation is referred to in the contract drawn up in May 1513. That it had been Cardinal Leonardo who had seen to the matter is, however, implicitly referred to in a letter of Sebastiano del Piombo to the artist many years later, dated July 1531.[28] The house is mentioned in the revised, third, contract for the monument of 1516. It is declared that the artist may live there rent-free for the period allowed for the completion of the tomb. Its description shows that it was an extensive property with large and smaller rooms, a well, a garden, and ancillary structures that almost certainly included a stable, for the old Michelangelo kept his pony there.[29]

The contract of 1516 confirms that Michelangelo has worked on sculpture for the tomb at the house for many months. It is now laid down that the period of Michelangelo's free tenure of the property for nine years is to be computed from May 1514. In fact, the year 1514 had seen problems with regard to the artist's occupancy. In a number of letters to Lodovico, his son had referred to difficulties over terms for his use of the house; these, he complains, had even distracted him from getting on with his work.[30] In early 1515, however, he had written that the house would be his and that he would have full security. If this is a claim to ownership, the contract of 1516 implicitly denies it.

The artist's later behaviour over his claims to the house reveals a protracted obduracy, but he had some reason to expect that it would some day become his own. For in late December 1517 one of his most dependable Roman correspondents would write to him that Cardinal Leonardo had renewed a promise that, on the tomb's completion, he would receive not only the house as a gift but also a papal office.[31]

The property at Macel de' Corvi was in the Via dei Fornari in the area of Rome, long since demolished, situated between Piazza Santi Apostoli and Trajan's Forum. It was close to the church of Santa Maria di Loreto, which was still under construction at this time. The area was not a prestigious one and there seems to have been a long-established custom of treating the Forum as a rubbish dump. Many years later, in 1558, Michelangelo would be asked by the civic authorities to provide a drawing for the reordering of the area around Trajan's Column, but nothing came of the initiative.[32] In a letter of the 1540s the artist would refer sardonically to his address as Macel de' Poveri.[33] After his move in 1513, he persistently complains that he has problems in collecting his letters in the Via de' Banchi, now much further away.

1 *Madonna of the Stairs*, marble relief, Casa Buonarroti, Florence

2   *Battle of the Centaurs and Lapiths*, marble relief, Casa Buonarroti, Florence

3   Wooden Crucifix, Santa Maria del Santo Spirito, Florence

4   *St Proculus* (detail), Arca di San Domenico, San Domenico, Bologna

5 *Angel*, Arca di San Domenico, San Domenico, Bologna

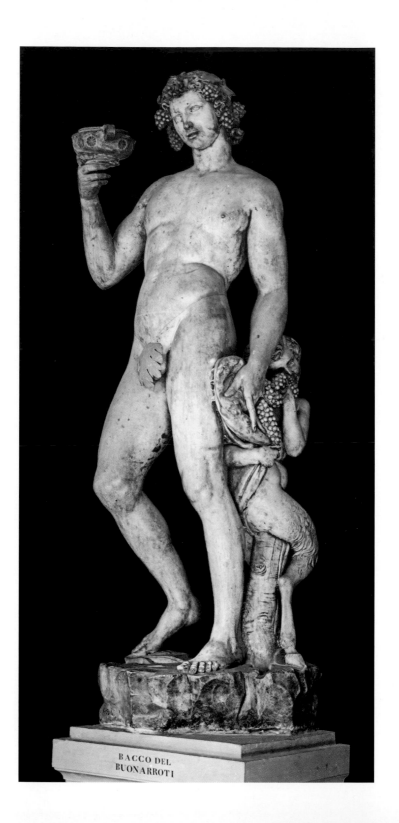

BACCO DEL
BUONARROTI

7   *Pietà*, St Peter's, Rome

6 (*facing page*)   *Bacchus*, Museo Nazionale del Bargello, Florence

8   *Virgin and Child with Saint John and Angels (Manchester Madonna)*,
National Gallery, London

9   *Entombment*, National Gallery, London

10 (*facing page*) and 11 (*above*)   Marble *David*, Galleria dell'Accademia, Florence

12   Studies for the bronze *David* and the marble *David*, with verse fragments,
Louvre, Paris, Cabinet des Dessins, inv. no. 714r

13   *St Paul*, Piccolomini altar, cathedral, Siena

15 (*above*)   Preparatory drawing for the *Battle of Cascina* cartoon

14 (*facing page*)   Cartoon for the *Battle of Cascina*, copy

16   Raphael, *Pope Julius II*, National Gallery, London

17   *Bruges Virgin and Child*, Onze Lieve Vrouwkerk (Notre Dame), Bruges

19   *Virgin and Child with the Infant Baptist* (Taddei Tondo),
Royal Academy of Arts, London

18 *(facing page)*   *St Matthew*, Galleria dell'Accademia, Florence

20   *Virgin and Child with the Infant Baptist* (Pitti Tondo),
Museo Nazionale del Bargello, Florence

21 *Holy Famly with St John the Baptist* (Doni Tondo),
Galleria degli Uffizi, Florence

I o gia facto ṅgozo i̅mq̃o stēco
chome fa lacqua agacti i̅ lonbardia
over dalero paese ch'essi chesisia
ch'aforza luetre apicha socto mēto

L abarba alcielo ellamemoria sero
i̅sullo scrignio spocto fo darpia
e l pennel sopraluiso tuctauia
me lfa gocciando u̅ richo pauimeto

E lobi entrati misō nella peccia
e fo delcul p̃ chetrapeso groppa
e passi seza glochi muouo i̅uano

D i̅azi misallugo lachortoccia
e p̃ piegarsi adietro siragroppa
e tēdomi comarcho soriano

Po fallace e strano
surgie iludicio ch lamēte porta
ch mal sitra p̃ cerboctana torta

l amia pictura morta
difedi orma giouanni elmio onore
nō sēdo i̅llogo bō ne io pictore

23 (above)   A scheme for the decoration of the vault of the Sistine Chapel, and studies of arms and hands, British Museum, London, Department of Prints and Drawings, 1859,0625.567

24 (left)   Sonnet with sketch of the artist painting the Sistine Chapel ceiling. Casa Buonarroti, Florence, Archivio Buonarroti, vol. XIII, fol. 111r

22 (facing page)   The vault of the Sistine Chapel, Vatican, Rome

26 (*above*)   *The Punishment of Haman*, Sistine Chapel ceiling

25 (*facing page*)   *God Dividing Light from Darkness*, Sistine Chapel ceiling

27   Copy after Michelangelo, *Project of Julius II Tomb*, 1513, Kupferstichkabinett, Berlin

28   *Christ Carrying the Cross*, Santa Maria sopra Minerva, Rome

29 *(following page)*   *Dying Slave*, Louvre, Paris

31   *Moses*, San Pietro in Vincoli, Rome

30 (*previous page*)   *Rebellious Slave*, Louvre, Paris

43

32 (*above*)   Drawing for the façade of San Lorenzo, Casa Buonarroti, Florence, inv. no. 43A*r*

33 (*left*)   Michelangelo's *segno*, detail of *Atlas*, Accademia, Florence

34   *Slave*, Galleria dell'Accademia, Florence   35   *Slave*, Galleria dell'Accademia, Florence

36   *Finestra inginocchiata*, Palazzo Medici, Florence

37   Tomb of Giuliano de' Medici, New Sacristy, San Lorenzo, Florence

38   Tomb of Lorenzo de' Medici, New Sacristy, San Lorenzo, Florence

39   Corner bay, New
Sacristy, San Lorenzo,
Florence

40 (*below*)   Vestibule,
Laurentian Library,
San Lorenzo, Florence

41   Study for a door in the Laurentian Library, San Lorenzo, Florence,
Casa Buonarroti, Florence, inv. no. IIIAr

42 (*facing page*) *Genius of Victory*, Palazzo
Vecchio, Florence

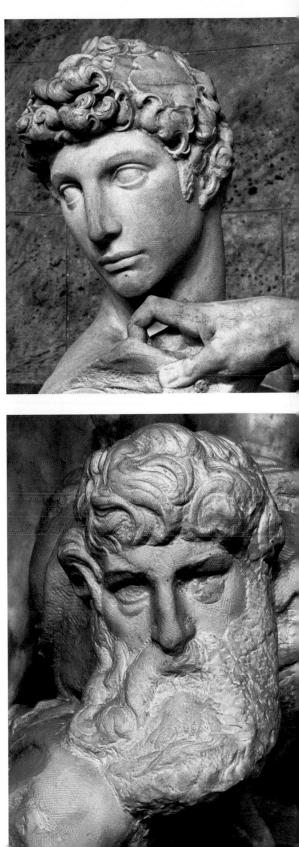

43 (*above*)   Bandinelli, *Hercules and Cacus*,
Piazza della Signoria, Florence

44a and b (*right and above right*)   *Genius of
Victory*, detail, Palazzo Vecchio, Florence

45   *Leda*, engraving after Michelangelo (reversed), British Museum, London,
Department of Prints and Drawings, 1874,0711.1791

46 *Tommaso de' Cavalieri*, Musée Bonnat, Bayonne

47   *Rape of Ganymede*, Harvard Art Museums/Fogg Museum, Cambridge, Mass. Gifts for Special Uses Fund, 1955.75

48   *Punishment of Tityus*, Royal Library, Windsor

49   Studies of heads, Uffizi Gallery, Florence

50   *Cleopatra*, Casa Buonarroti, Florence, inv. no. 2Fr

51 *Fall of Phaeton*, Royal Library, Windsor

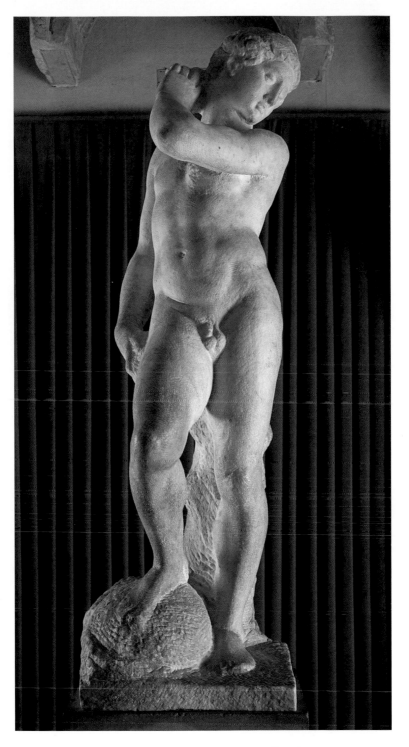

52 *Apollo*, Museo Nazionale del Bargello, Florence

Giovanni mio charo p ch lapenna e sempre piu animosa ch lalingua mi schrivo quello ch
piu volte aquesti di nomi sono ardito p rispecto ch e tempi dien a bo ch se questo e ch
vi sto etempi chome o decto cho trar alarte mia no so sero mo dasperavo piu promigione
quadio Fussi certo no la vevo piu avere no resterei p questo che io no lanovassi effacessi p el
papa tubto quello ch io potessi mai mo terrei gia chasa apta p rispecto deldebito ch voi sa
pete che io o avedo dove tornarmi cho molto macho spesa e avoi d chora si leverebe
lanoia de lla pigione e quado lamia promigione p seguiti io staro qui chome sono sta
to e ingegneromi fare e ldebito mio p ro vi prego ch voi mi dicate quello ch voi ne
mia dote accio ch io possa p sare affacti mia re sta do vi o brigatissimo io vir
ne dro queste Feste insata maria de florej

Vostro Michelagniolo a salore zo

Nevertheless, the spaces the property afforded must have been impressive, one of them large enough to accommodate a group of assistants working on the grotesque decoration of the lower front face of the monument under Antonio da Pontassieve's supervision.[34] There must also have been areas large enough to house very large blocks of marble of a scale rarely seen in the sculptural workshops of late fifteenth-century Rome. In the three years between 1513 and 1516, the artist was at work on the two *Slaves* now in the Louvre, the *Moses* and the statue of *Christ* (pls 28–31). It may have been in an area referred to by Sebastiano in 1531 as the 'botega grande' that work on these four statues was going on.[35]

Two incidents point to Michelangelo's occupation of the Macel de' Corvi house in 1513. The earlier concerns the familiar episode involving Luca Signorelli of Cortona, some twenty-five years Michelangelo's senior and probably an acquaintance of the 1490s in Florence; his greatest achievements now lay in the past.[36] In May 1518 Michelangelo wrote to the Florentine official in charge of Cortona, after attempts in Rome had failed, to have returned to him money he had lent to Signorelli.[37] Now in Florence, he gives a circumstantial account of what had happened. He describes how he and Signorelli had met by chance in Rome in the first year of Leo x's pontificate, in 1513. Signorelli had explained that he had come to see the pope and had complained that his past service to the house of Medici had gone unrewarded, although he had risked his life for them. The older artist had then asked him for a loan and told him where to send it, and in response Michelangelo had sent to him the 40 giuli requested through his *garzone*, Silvio Falcone. Some days later, perhaps his hopes of papal beneficence disappointed, Signorelli had come to the house at Macel de' Corvi and, requesting a further loan, had received another 40 giuli, which Michelangelo had gone upstairs to fetch. The end of the artist's letter is damaged, but in its final lines he strongly repudiates the claim that he had been repaid. A later *ricordo* of his shows that steps towards repaying him had been put in hand in response to his letter.[38]

Michelangelo's letter is uncharacteristically discursive. He recounts how, at the time of Signorelli's visit to the house, he was at work on a statue four *braccia* high, with the hands behind the figure's back; he was, in other words, at work on the so-called *Rebellious Slave* now in the Louvre (pl. 30). Before Signorelli took his leave, he had explained that he was not well, 'allora mal sano', and had lamented to him that he could not work. Signorelli had replied that he should not doubt that angels from heaven would take up his arms and help him.[39] With this astonishing reference to the providential status of the artist, the encounter evidently ended, the older man destined to be awarded an honoured place by Giorgio Vasari at the culmination of the Second Part of the *Lives* of 1550, the younger to crown the triumphant conclusion of the Third.

The other reference to the artist at Macel de' Corvi in 1513 occurs in a passage in Fra Benedetto Luschino's *Vulnera Diligentis*, where a nocturnal apparition is described. The circumstances are rather carefully noted; the apparition in the sky had been seen by Michelangelo in the garden of his residence, undoubtedly the *orto* of Macel de' Corvi. Fra Benedetto states that the event occurred in 1513, in the first year of Leo x's pontificate.[40]

On 21 April 1516 the della Rovere executor, Cardinal Leonardo, wrote to Michelangelo asking for his consent to a visit to the house at Macel de' Corvi. His request is on behalf of 'la Excellentia de Madama Duchessa d'Urbino'. If denied the chance to see the works there while in Rome, he reports that she will be greatly disappointed. The title that Cardinal Leonardo employs and the timing of the visit in the spring of 1516 indicate that the distinguished lady for whom he writes was not, as generally assumed, Eleonora Gonzaga, the wife of Duke Francesco Maria, but Elisabetta Gonzaga, the cultured widow of his predecessor.[41] That the visit did take place is suggested by a later sketch by Michelangelo which records a provisional assembly of those parts of the tomb's fabric already completed.[42]

The della Rovere family must have been eager to learn what Michelangelo had accomplished in the preceding three years. Indeed, the visit took place just three months before a new contract for the tomb would be drawn up. Nevertheless, the family was in a weak position to bring pressure to bear on the artist at this moment. Spurred on by members of his family, especially his widowed sister-in-law, Alfonsina, Pope Leo, in retribution for the Duke of Urbino's failure in the previous year to provide aid against the French, had decided to strip Francesco Maria of his duchy and replace him with a Medici. The Bull depriving him of his lands in the patrimony of the Church was published in March. Now, in April, the dowager duchess was in Rome to intercede on his behalf. Her plea was rejected by the pope, and the duchy would subsequently be granted to Lorenzo, Alfonsina's son and the pope's nephew.[43] The power of the della Rovere had been, for the moment, extinguished, a fact of which Michelangelo was certainly aware in the eventful months ahead.

FRIENDS IN ROME

Writing to Buonarroto in November 1509, while sorely taxed by the early stages of work on the Sistine ceiling, Michelangelo had told him that he had no friends and did not want them: 'io ò amici di nessuna sorte, e no' ne voglio'.[44] While the first part of his statement may have been true, the second was certainly not. For Michelangelo was a solitary who needed company.

Expressions of friendship rarely appear in the artist's own letters because they are so frequently actuated by pressing concerns. On the other hand, his absences would often provoke expressions of attachment and devotion in the letters of correspondents about whom we would otherwise, for the most part, know almost nothing. This is clear from the correspondence that followed his move to Florence in 1516.

But Michelangelo had travelled to Florence twice before his move there in 1516, once in August 1514, the occasion of Silvio Falcone's letter reporting on the progress of work on the marble decoration of the tomb, and again in April 1515. During this second absence, Giovanni Gellesi, a native of Prato, wrote engagingly to the artist, complaining that he felt almost an orphan without him in the great Babylon of Rome. To make good his deeply felt absence in the circle of friends, he explains that they have co-opted into the group another fellow Tuscan, Domenico Buoninsegni, who would soon come to play an exceptionally important role in Michelangelo's life.[45]

Greetings like these modify the picture of near isolation that the artist was always inclined to project. It is, for example, clear that he had resumed his friendship with Piero Soderini after the former *gonfaloniere* had been granted permission to retire to Rome by Pope Leo x. Shortly following Michelangelo's move, Soderini wrote to him in warm terms on 7 August 1516; the old ties had been restored. Even more noteworthy is the text of a letter of a month earlier written by his wife, Argentina Malaspina, addressed to one of her brothers. Michelangelo's trip to Carrara was imminent and she asks Lorenzo Malaspina to take care of him and invite him to stay. Her praise of the artist recalls that of her husband when addressing the papal court ten years earlier in the autumn of 1506. Michelangelo is much loved by her husband and is a person they believe to have few, if any, rivals anywhere.[46] There is no hint here of the *terribilità* imputed to the artist a few years later by Pope Leo.

Another friend who emerges in the correspondence of this period is Pierfrancesco Borgherini, whose Florentine banking family had had a branch in Rome since at least 1497.[47] Letters from Michelangelo of the summer of 1515 show that he had decided to move his financial dealings away from the Balducci bank to place them with the Borgherini. Only a few years younger than Michelangelo, Pierfrancesco had a keen predilection for art, and by October 1515 it appears that, despite his massive obligations elsewhere, the artist had promised to carry out a painting for his fellow Florentine, 'una certa cosa di pictura'. He writes of Borgherini in terms of deep attachment and states that he wishes to serve him. He remarks that, if he is not mistaken, Pierfrancesco has no equal among the Florentines who frequent Rome.[48]

Michelangelo would be reminded of the promised painting nearly a year later, after he had moved to Florence; after delays and vicissitudes, it seems probable that the work was painted by a friend soon to be discussed, Sebastiano Luciani.[49] The reminder had been conveyed by another Rome-based friend, a man who has enjoyed no enduring fame but who would prove of inestimable help to the master in the years ahead. For the most part he signs himself Lionardo Sellaio, Lionardo the Saddler, although in some letters he uses the form Lionardo ne' Borgherini or Lionardo Selaio ne' Borgherini, indicating that he had some role in the Rome bank. However, the real name of this crucial figure, although undetected, has survived. He is found acting as a witness when the third contract for the tomb of Pope Julius was drawn up in July 1516 and is there identified as 'Leonardo Francisci sellario florentino'.[50] From the years between 1516 and 1526 no less than seventy-six of his letters to Michelangelo have survived, but unfortunately none of Michelangelo's to him seems to have been preserved.[51]

Sellaio performed a whole range of services for the absent master. One of these was to close the house at Macel de' Corvi in August 1516 after Michelangelo had left, moving marble blocks that had remained in the garden into the house.[52] He wrote a further reassuring letter to the artist in October, followed by a similar message in the following spring, in which he reports that he has straightened up the garden, which is now yielding beans, peas and salads. But the artist seems to have been uneasy about the state of the house and, above all, the security of its contents; apart from the tomb *quadro* and unworked blocks, they included the *Rebellious* and *Dying Slaves*, the *Moses* and the first version of the *Christ*. Briefly in Rome in December 1516, he must have remained concerned, and in late 1517, when his assistant Pietro Urbano left for Rome, he gave him detailed instructions about establishing better order.[53]

Michelangelo was once more in Rome in January 1518 in order to finalize with Pope Leo the agreement to undertake the façade of San Lorenzo. And it was at this moment that he decided on the destruction of his cartoons kept in the house, which must have been those that he had made for the Sistine ceiling. On 5 February 1519 Sellaio reported that almost all of them had been burnt; he expresses his grief over the decision, while confirming that he has devotedly carried it out.[54]

But Sellaio's value for Michelangelo extended far beyond his duties as guardian of Macel de' Corvi. He is the source of a great deal of information of crucial importance to the artist. Especially significant in this regard were his excellent relations with Cardinal Leonardo Grosso della Rovere and his closest associate, Francesco Pallavicini, for this was a delicate moment in the drama of the tomb project. He passes on to them the letters that he has received from the artist in Florence, and reports back on their reactions to what they have read.[55]

On another occasion, in late 1517, Sellaio reports to the master that marble of his at the Ripa had been taken to what he refers to as 'al Popolo'.[56] It has been removed on behalf of Agostino Chigi, probably to be used for the decoration of his burial chapel in Santa Maria del Popolo, designed and carried a good way towards completion by Raphael before the deaths of both artist and patron in the spring of 1520. Sellaio writes that Chigi has disclaimed knowledge of the affair and has offered either to return the marble or to pay for it. It is, however, reported that one of the blocks has been broken.[57]

It appears that the promised restitution was never made. For the issue re-emerged in 1523, three years after Chigi's death. Michelangelo, ever retentive of memory, especially where an injury was concerned, would inform Fattucci of the two blocks taken by Chigi, give him the measurements and state that they had cost him 50 ducats.[58]

Yet it was the patronage of the wealthy Agostino Chigi that led to a friendship of far greater consequence than those just described: that with the Venetian Sebastiano Luciani, more commonly known as Sebastiano del Piombo. After several months in Venice, Chigi left for Rome in August 1511, bringing Sebastiano with him; his purpose was to employ him in painting frescos in his newly completed villa, the Farnesina.[59] In terms of artistic events, it was an exceptional moment; coincidental with the timing of the journey was the unveiling of the first part of the Sistine Chapel ceiling on 15 August, rapidly followed by the completion by Raphael of the decoration of the Stanza della Segnatura.

While Michelangelo did not shun the company of fellow artists, it may be that he was attracted chiefly to men of modest attainments, whose company at dinner would help dispel what, many years later, he would refer to as his melancholy, or rather his madness.[60] This is certainly the impression left by Vasari's anecdotes about Michelangelo and the idle Iacopo Torni, known as Indaco; if the passage is true, it seems that the master delighted in Iacopo's conviviality and jokes and, although he was one of the team assembled at the start of work on the Sistine Chapel ceiling, cannot have had great respect for his potentialities as a painter.[61]

The situation with regard to Sebastiano could not be more different. Sebastiano left Venice an already established master, a painter of both innovative public works and engaging intimate pictures.[62] For the circumstances in which the friendship was formed there is little to go on except Vasari's remarkable passage in his first edition of the *Lives*, one scarcely altered in the second. Part of Vasari's account has a slightly programmatic character, but this does not require rejecting his information, even if his source or sources remain unknown. He states that Michelangelo admired Sebastiano's early Roman works and that he adopted him as a *compagno* in an environment in which he felt increasingly threatened by the astonishing achievements of Raphael.[63]

Vasari carefully describes three occasions on which Michelangelo intervened to help his recently acquired friend. The earliest assistance was the most elaborate. On Sebastiano undertaking to paint a monumental *Pietà* on panel, at the insistence of a cleric well known to Agostino Chigi for a church in Viterbo, Michelangelo prepared the cartoon for the two figures of mourning Mary and her dead Son. The cartoon has perished, but a preliminary drawing for the Virgin on a sheet that survives confirms Vasari's story.[64]

Further collaboration would follow after Pierfrancesco Borgherini had assumed the patronage of a chapel in the Franciscan church of San Pietro in Montorio in Rome. This probably happened shortly before Michelangelo left Rome for Florence in late July 1516. Borgherini, we are told, had been assured that Michelangelo would assist Sebastiano and he did provide a small drawing for the chapel's altarpiece of *Christ at the Column*; Sellaio, now on intimate terms with Sebastiano, confirmed that it had been received in Rome in a letter of 16 August.[65]

A third occasion when Michelangelo came to his friend's assistance was one where there was much at stake. In undertaking to paint a huge altarpiece for Cardinal Giulio de' Medici's archiepiscopal church at Narbonne, Sebastiano was involving himself in competition with Raphael, who may have been approached for an altarpiece for the same destination by the cardinal some months earlier. Sellaio wrote to Michelangelo at Carrara on 19 January 1517, telling him that Sebastiano had resolved to undertake what he refers to as 'quella tavola', implying that Michelangelo was well aware of what was afoot.[66] In fact, he himself had been in Rome in the previous month of December, a visit he had made to discuss the project of the San Lorenzo façade with Pope Leo and Cardinal Giulio. He may well have played a part in securing the commission for Sebastiano from the cardinal, with whom he was now on excellent terms.[67] Whereas it would be many months before Raphael would turn to the *Transfiguration*, Sebastiano, putting on one side his work in Borgherini's chapel, turned to the *Raising of Lazarus*, the greatest challenge of his life.

The competitive situation that now prevailed in Rome would lead to extraordinary expressions of enmity on the part of Sellaio and Sebastiano. Already in his letter of January 1517, Sellaio writes that Raphael will do his utmost to thwart Sebastiano's commission in order to have no competitor.[68] In a letter of September, he reports that Sebastiano, working on his altarpiece, has performed miracles and that he can be regarded as the victor, a wildly premature judgement.[69] In a letter of July of the following year, commenting on paintings of Raphael's that have been sent to France, Sebastiano notoriously refers to the artist as 'prince of the synagogue'.[70]

Such rancour was the least attractive of the consequences of
Michelangelo's friendship. His hatred of Raphael, still exposed in
Condivi's biography of 1553, may have developed a number of years
earlier, and Raphael would seem to have become the chief object of
his enmity after Bramante's death in March 1514. It is telling that,
even before the atmosphere generated by the rival commissions had
developed, Sellaio felt the need to keep Michelangelo informed of
what Raphael was doing; it was important that the news that Raphael
had turned to sculpture should reach the absent master in Carrara.[71]

Michelangelo, as has been seen, was again in Rome in January 1518
for the ratification of the contract for the façade of San Lorenzo. He
probably visited Sebastiano's studio on that occasion to see his progress
with the altarpiece.[72] Then, with the exception of a rapid visit in 1523
after Cardinal Giulio's election as pope, he was absent from the city
for more than a decade.

The loyalty of his Roman friends survived Michelangelo's prolonged
absence. But while the ties were very valuable for him, they could
also promote demands on his time. Piero Rosselli, defender of the
artist before Pope Julius in 1506, and the man to whom he had
entrusted the preparation of the Sistine Chapel vault in 1508, wrote
to him in May 1518. He informs him that Piero Soderini, friend from
the years in Florence, has decided to commission a project in the
Roman church of San Silvestro in Capite. Soderini had taken refuge
at Ragusa after the fall of the Florentine republic. After Giovanni de'
Medici's election as pope in 1513, he had pardoned Piero and other
members of his family and the ex-*gonfaloniere* lived a quiet, now digni-
fied, life in Rome.[73] He now wishes to fund the making of a new
reliquary altar to house the relic of the head of the Baptist, patron
saint of Florence, and has turned to a fellow Florentine, Piero Rosselli,
to undertake it.[74]

A good number of letters about the project survive, although, as so
often, we do not have Michelangelo's share of the correspondence.
They begin with Rosselli's modest request that the absent master

should look at his design and offer his comments but, with near inevitability, he became involved in providing two designs himself. Soderini, in fact, wished for a reliquary altar with two tombs, presumably for Argentina and himself, to be included.[75] He was deeply disappointed that the artist could not personally superintend things in Rome, scarcely able to understand his problems in what was to prove one of the most taxing years of his life. Michelangelo's final and now lost drawn offering for the project was too large for the space available for it in San Silvestro, and the altar that exists there now is a dry and stylistically retrospective work that can scarcely reflect any intervention of his own.[76]

It is astonishing, and a striking token of the generosity of the artist, that he concerned himself with the project at all, given his almost ceaseless travel to and from the quarries at Pietrasanta, to be described shortly. It was appropriate that Soderini, in a letter of 24 July, addressed it not to Michelangelo in Florence but to wherever he is to be found: 'ubicumque sit'.[77]

THE FAMILY PROVIDER

One of the least fortunate aspects of Michelangelo's destiny was to belong to a family of failures. Lodovico was forever lamenting the wretched state of the family's fortunes, but was incapable of making any serious contribution to their improvement. Already, in 1500, he was deploring his situation; he has reached the age of fifty-six; none of his five sons is any help to him, indeed he has no one to turn to.[78] As has been seen, it appears to have been the case that it had been the young Michelangelo's association with Lorenzo the Magnificent that had led to Lodovico obtaining a modest post in the Florentine customs office, the Dogana. This employment almost certainly ended with the fall of Piero in the autumn of 1494, although he was still signing his letters 'ragioniere in dogana' as late as December 1499.[79] His petition to have the office returned to him after the Medicean restoration in 1512 has already been noted. Recalling early events for his biographer Condivi, Michelangelo reported what his father had said of himself when in the presence of Lorenzo. He had never followed a profession but had lived on his meagre income, striving, at the same time, to maintain and increase what he had inherited.[80]

Even as early as his first stay in Rome, it was to Michelangelo that his brothers began to turn for assistance, even if the sums were, as yet, trifling. Driven from his convent in Viterbo in 1497 in obscure circumstances, Leonardo, the artist's senior, would be given money to allow him the means to return to Florence.[81] Only a month later, with Buonarroto in Rome, the artist again has to come to the rescue and help Lodovico meet his debts and avoid selling Monte shares.[82] A few months later, he would send a small sum to Buonarroto, now back in Florence, for what reason is undisclosed. But already by late in the following year, a letter from Lodovico shows that Michelangelo was contemplating help for Buonarroto and Giovan Simone to set up some form of business, probably a wool concern. But at this point, the scheme did not go ahead. Lodovico rarely confessed to being consoled, but was cheered by this evidence of the artist's love for his brothers.[83]

The total gap in Michelangelo's correspondence between December 1500 and January 1506 makes following the family's business activities difficult. From a different source, however, we learn that, from September 1502 to January 1504, Buonarroto, in 1502 aged twenty-five, would enter the employment of Selvaggia, widow of the renowned Filippo Strozzi the Elder, in order to care for her sons, Lorenzo and Filippo the Younger, and also to help supervise the completing of the great family palace.[84] This connection led to Buonarroto's employment, from 1 January 1504, as an assistant in the wool business founded a year earlier by Lorenzo Strozzi and two partners. The business would operate until April 1508.[85]

Of his brothers, it was Buonarroto, just two years his junior, who inspired in Michelangelo the hope of improving the economic fortunes of the family. To help him, he made payment of 100 gold florins to

the partners of the firm on Buonarroto's behalf, with the condition
that the capital should not be removed without his, Michelangelo's
consent.[86] As has been seen, in Bologna in 1506, Michelangelo was
anxious for the dagger, declined by Aldobrandini, to be given to
Filippo Strozzi as a present. And there is some indication that in the
same year his marble *Hercules*, made for Piero de' Medici, was in the
possession of the two brothers. He surely saw them as powerful poten-
tial friends.[87]

In August 1507 Lodovico took a step to further the careers of Buonarroto and Giovan Simone by matriculating in the Wool Guild, the
Arte della Lana, an event recorded by Buonarroto himself, who referred
to the past standing of the family and the fact that an earlier Lodovico
Buonarroti had served as consul of the Wool Guild in November
1388.[88]

Buonarroto reached a new level of advancement when he became
a partner of equal standing with Lorenzo Strozzi in a new wool business, formed in May 1508.[89] Giovan Simone was also involved, although
undoubtedly in a subordinate role, as later correspondence shows.
Buonarroto himself contributed 500 gold florins to the capital of the
new company. This new enterprise was set up to run for five years,
until 1513.[90]

Despite initial optimism, this new business does not seem to have
performed very well. Then, in midsummer of 1509, Michelangelo, hard
at work on the chapel, received a now lost letter of Lodovico's that
recounted behaviour on Giovan Simone's part that threatened them
with ruin. In his reply, the artist reiterated his long-standing wish to
help the brothers to establish their own business. But the report of
Giovan Simone has compelled him to contemplate transferring the
money invested in the current business to Gismondo, the youngest of
the brothers, born in 1481. The remark could imply that he himself
had contributed money to the sum that Buonarroto had invested in
the new company, that he had retained rights over his investment, and
that Giovan Simone threatened to jeopardize the capital.[91]

Subsequently, Michelangelo undertook to write a letter to Giovan Simone that can count as the most violent in his entire surviving correspondence. Enraged by the news that his brother had even threatened their father, he himself writes of coming to Florence to show him the error of his ways, although once more offering to help Buonarroto and himself. In an extraordinary postscript, he points out that he has been going around Italy for the past twelve years, leading a wretched life, enduring every humiliation, suffering every privation, exhausting his body with every kind of toil, subjecting his own life to a thousand dangers, solely to help his family, and all he has accomplished is threatened with destruction in a single hour.[92]

This crisis provoked by Giovan Simone was not the only one to trouble the artist as he embarked on painting in the Sistine Chapel. Francesco, Lodovico's older brother, died in June 1508. It seems that he had endeavoured to pursue some kind of career in banking, to no good effect. At his death, he left no children and many debts. The crisis was twofold. Lodovico and his sons ran the risk of being responsible for Francesco's debts, and his widow, Cassandra di Cosimo Bartoli, could exercise her right to demand the return of her dowry. A further problem lay in the fact that Francesco and Lodovico had jointly owned the oldest and most prestigious family property at Settignano.

The problem of the debts could be met by Lodovico and his family acting rapidly to reject any part of Francesco's inheritance. Since he had been emancipated by his father in 1507, Michelangelo was able to have the needed document swiftly sent from Rome without an unwelcome return to Florence; he was about to begin work in the chapel.

The issue of Cassandra's dowry was more intractable. She was entitled to regain a sum of more than 500 gold florins. Michelangelo was informed of her growing threats as he struggled to overcome unfamiliar problems caused by his inexperience with fresco painting. He gave Lodovico some latitude to draw on his account at Santa Maria Nuova.

Cassandra sued Lodovico in February 1509. Lodovico's desperate
state was reported to his son in Rome; it appeared that he could be
faced with surrendering the villa at Settignano or selling most of his
shares in the Monte. In the end, such a disaster was avoided: the issue
was settled out of court in late September.[93] But Lodovico himself
emerged very badly from the affair. He held on to a substantial amount
of money that Michelangelo had sent from Rome to assist him. As
events turned out, this was not required to pay off Cassandra. He failed
to act to reimburse Michelangelo's account, only to be taken by surprise by his son's arrival, without prior warning, in Florence in late
September 1510, on his way to his first interview with Pope Julius in
Bologna.[94]

The idea already entertained as long ago as 1500, of creating a family
wool business, came to fruition in 1514. Already, in a letter of January
1512, Michelangelo wrote of his intention to fund it.[95] In a subsequent
one of July 1513, he bitterly attacked Buonarroto over his careless use
of money and his lack of gratitude, but went on to express his intention of providing 1,000 florins to launch the undertaking. He states
that he has no wish to receive any return in the way of income. But
he stipulates that, at the end of ten years, if he so requests, the 1,000
florins will be returned to him.[96] The money was paid in January 1514
and the contract for the establishment of the company immediately
drawn up; it was formed in the names of Lodovico and all three
brothers.[97] The sum of 400 ducats that he had already lent Buonarroto
earlier he had declared that the family could keep; Lodovico and his
three sons are to have 100 ducats each. In October 1514 Michelangelo
contributed another 100 ducats to the company.[98] A year later, in 1515,
Buonarroto matriculated in the Arte della Lana.

In November of the previous year Michelangelo had received a
letter warning him against investing in the business, addressed to
'Michelangelo carissimo' and signed 'Tuo amicho charo in Firenze'.
The writer explains that he has been in contact with Buonarroto and
his other brothers and has heard it said that the artist will never see
income or capital from the venture. He does not wish to promote

ill-will, but recommends Michelangelo to invest his money in some other way, on behalf of his father.[99]

Michelangelo kept the letter, although disregarding the advice. But the business seems to have been struggling from the start. By September 1515 Buonarroto was complaining that things were not going well. Michelangelo replied that he had always held that the time had not been a good one for launching the business.[100]

How far its lack of success could be attributed to the very real adverse economic conditions in Florence and how far to poor management is difficult to judge. It seems to have been the far from brilliant condition of the family that prompted the artist's disapproval of Buonarroto's marriage in 1516.[101] The precariousness of the family's finances is evident from the problems provoked by the imposition of an *accatto*, or forced loan, passed by the government in May 1517.[102] Decades later, Michelangelo would explain to his nephew Leonardo that he had always tried to restore the family's fortunes, but he had not had brothers equal to the task.[103]

POPE LEO AND FLORENCE

MARBLE SUPPLIES

The re-establishment of French authority in north Italy, achieved by Francis I on the battlefield at Marignano in September 1515, was an event with which Pope Leo, like many others, had to come to terms. The need was urgent, since there were even fears that the French might move against Florence.[1] After deliberating at Viterbo in October, he decided to meet Francis at Bologna in November. Michelangelo, so sparing in his references to current events in his letters, had informed Buonarroto as early as 6 October that the pope had left Rome and that it was rumoured that he would come to Florence.[2]

Leo had last entered the city as a cardinal in September 1512, after the collapse of Soderini's regime following the sack of Prato. They were events that, as has been seen, provoked Michelangelo's desperate letters to his family as he strove to complete his work in the Sistine Chapel. When he left the city in November 1512, Leo entrusted its government to his brother Giuliano. The political situation was not stable, and would remain one dogged by problems even after his election in the conclave of the following February.[3]

He now re-entered Florence on 30 November 1515 to scenes of extraordinary acclamation. The extent of public preparations for the *entrata* eclipsed anything previously witnessed in the city and they, in turn, provoked an unparalleled number of contemporary accounts.[4] One of the most striking of these tributes was an ephemeral wooden façade for the cathedral, designed by Jacopo Sansovino with the help of Andrea del Sarto. Vasari stated that Sansovino's façade was much admired by the pope.[5]

The claims of family *pietas* were not neglected. On 2 December, the first Sunday in Advent, the pope went to San Lorenzo, accompanied by seventeen cardinals. San Lorenzo had been chosen as the church to host the 'Cappella Papalis', a fitting tribute to Medicean associations; modifications to its interior, to allow more space, had been supervised by Leo's sister-in-law, Alfonsina Orsini, widow of Piero de' Medici. After Mass was concluded, the pope entered the sacristy and knelt in prayer before the resting place of his father, Lorenzo the Magnificent.[6] Outside, a life-size wooden statue of St Lawrence, made for the occasion, had been placed over the central door. It was accompanied by a tablet more than two metres long bearing an inscription composed by the chancellor of the republic: the saint exhorts the pope to recall the works in San Lorenzo achieved by his forebears and to complete the church.[7]

Such circumstances have come to be regarded as decisive in Leo's decision to initiate the façade that the basilica still lacked. But at least one earlier historian of San Lorenzo, commenting on the statue and inscription placed on the blank façade, struck a note of caution over assuming that features such as these were decisive in determining his behaviour as a patron.[8] The church had always been in Leo's mind. Over a year earlier, on 3 August 1514, he had issued a Bull in favour of San Lorenzo. Its text dwells on the roles of his forebears in rebuilding and embellishing the church. Plenary indulgencies are to be granted on the feast-days of St Lawrence and the patron saints of the Medici, Cosmas and Damian.[9]

On at least two earlier occasions, Leo had shown his care for façades for churches to which he was personally attached. One was the façade that he had had built for Santa Cristina at Bolsena while he had been cardinal legate to the Patrimony of St Peter. A more recent example was the restoration of the façade of his own Roman titular church, Santa Maria in Domnica, work that he set in motion immediately after his election in 1513.[10]

Odd details could point to a decision about San Lorenzo prior to the journey to Florence in November. As early as July 1515, a Florentine document refers to the possibility to resystematize the *piazza* in front of the church, an idea again discussed during the pope's visit to the city.[11] A more significant consideration arises when we turn to a letter of Michelangelo to Buonarroto dated 16 June 1515. The relevant remark is prefaced by the artist's request for 1,400 ducats to be transferred to him in Rome. He explains that he needs them for a purchase of copper and expands on the circumstances. He needs to press ahead with the tomb because he anticipates that he will, in the future, have to enter the service of the pope.[12] The copper must have been destined for work on the tomb, almost certainly the nine reliefs (or some of them) that were required in the contract of 1513; the decision whether to adopt marble or bronze had been left open for the executors to decide. In opting for the more expensive medium, he was, nevertheless, choosing the one where more of the labour involved could be undertaken by assistants.[13]

The first editor of Michelangelo's letters saw in the reference to the artist's impending service with the pope evidence that Leo was contemplating the façade project before his journey to Florence in November. Confined to a footnote, his proposal has rarely been noticed.[14] The artist's comment, as so often, is elusive. But a convincing alternative explanation for what he writes is hard to find.[15]

No further word about Michelangelo's role in the future project emerged in his correspondence until September 1516.[16] But too much can be made of this. Not a single letter of the artist's survives from November 1515 to September of the following year, a gap that explains much of the mystery surrounding the early stages of the project. A rather similar silence occurs in the history of a subsequent Medici undertaking, the building of the library at San Lorenzo. A recently discovered memorandum of 1519 refers to it, but there is no further surviving word about it until late in 1523.[17]

Michelangelo's new sense of urgency about the tomb project, voiced in the letter of June, re-emerges in one of 11 August. He informs

Buonarroto that since his return from Florence in April he has done no work, a phrase perhaps best interpreted as meaning that he has not done any carving. Instead, he explains that he has been putting everything in order and has been making models. He again refers to the need to make a great effort and the need to complete the project in two or three years, 'per forza d'uomini', a striking allusion to the collaboration he so rarely contemplates.[18]

This need of help seems to have become public knowledge, for in a letter of September, a month later, we learn that Benedetto da Rovezzano, a respected figure in Florence, is ready to come to his aid. Michelangelo writes to Buonarroto that he would gladly have accepted the offer but he has no marble available for him to work on.[19]

The issue of marble supplies repeatedly recurs in Michelangelo's letters of the summer of 1515. The artist, however, is no longer single-minded about his course of action. His uncertainty reflects the emergence of a new state of affairs achieved by papal policy; both Pope Leo and Cardinal Giulio were by this date increasingly insistent that marble should be taken not from the quarries at Carrara but from those at Seravezza, situated just a little inland and above Pietrasanta. Pietrasanta and its neighbourhood had been ceded to the French by Piero de' Medici in the autumn of 1494 and the French had subsequently sold it to independent Lucca. Following the establishment of the Medicean regime in Florence in 1512 and the subsequent election of the first Medici pope in February 1513, the Florentines had pressed the pope to restore it to Florence; no one had urged its return more strongly than Leo's brother, Giuliano. Initially hesitant, Leo finally ruled in favour of Florence in October 1513.[20]

The Florentine recovery of the quarries at Seravezza had important implications. The quality of the marble had never been considered the equal of that from Carrara, but the retrieval of Seravezza spelt the end of a near monopoly of supplies from a source outside Florentine control. A second significant step came in May 1515 when the commune of Seravezza, acting under pressure, ceded to Florence the ownership of all the marble quarries of Monte Altissimo and Monte Ceresola.[21]

One of the handicaps of Seravezza was its distance from the sea; it did not enjoy easy access to the coast as did Carrara. It appears that attention to the problem of access occupied the Curia quite early, for a payment from Cardinal Bibbiena to one of the overseers of St Peter's of 12 March 1514 was made to allow him to go to Pietrasanta to make improvements to the road.[22]

In his letters of the summer of 1515, Michelangelo appears to have wished to keep his options open. He was aware of the road project and, in fact, reports to Buonarroto in a letter of 6 July that Domenico Buoninsegni, the right-hand man of Cardinal Giulio, has assured him that the road is almost finished.[23] Nevertheless, subsequent letters to his brother indicate uneasiness about the issue. Throughout the summer he strives to get news of the true state of affairs, writing repeatedly to the *scarpellino* now employed by the Florentine Opera del Duomo, Michele di Pippo, who had helped him quarry the marble block for the Rome *Pietà* as long ago as 1498. Getting news from him proved difficult and the artist's letters are querulous.[24] But he also continued to keep in touch with Carrara. On 1 September he sent a letter, now lost, to Messer Antonio da Massa, Alberico Malaspina's chancellor.[25] A month later, he had a letter from Domenico Fancelli, familiarly known as il Zara, offering to rough hew marble for him at Carrara, but he needs the master's measurements.[26] But before the letters break off in the autumn, his problem does not appear to have been resolved, although by August he seems to have learnt that the road is not ready.[27]

Michelangelo's caution over what he had heard from Buoninsegni in July regarding the Seravezza road had been justified. It emerges that it had not even been begun in July, to judge from a letter of Buoninsegni of 4 August to Lorenzo de' Medici in Florence, nephew of the pope and, with Giuliano in worsening health, de facto ruler of the city. Buoninsegni writes that the pope is prepared to pay half the cost once expenses have been incurred but insists, with a firm grasp of building realities, that construction must begin at the coast, for, with the onset of the rains, work will become impossible in the marshes.[28] That the road had to be built on piles because of the marshes towards the sea was one of the many laments Michelangelo expressed to Condivi in old age about the project.[29] It is difficult to find an explanation of Buoninsegni's misinformation of July other than that he felt he was best serving his superiors by misrepresenting the situation to the artist and thereby discouraging his loyalty to Carrara.

For Buonarroto, the year had been one of economic difficulties, but it would end on a more cheerful note. He was elected one of the priors of the two-month Signoria elected in November, an indication that the Buonarroti were acceptable to the regime.[30] And it would fall to the priors to play a significant part in the extensive government ceremonies accompanying the pope's arrival and stay in the city. Buonarroto described some of these activities in a letter of late December to Michelangelo, prefacing his account with his belief that it would not greatly interest his brother.[31] For example, he had played a particular role in the Mass celebrated by Pope Leo himself in the cathedral on Christmas Day. A further honour would be extended to the *gonfaloniere*, the priors and their descendants in perpetuity; Pope Leo would issue a Bull creating them counts of the Lateran Palace with the right to add to their arms the Medici *palla*, lilies, and the addition of the letters Leo P.P.X.[32]

Pope Leo left Florence on 19 February 1516 in circumstances less propitious than those in which he had arrived. The prolonged presence of the papal court and its huge number of dependants had created acute inflation in the city. In his diary, Luca Landucci carefully recorded the accelerating price of food and noted the bad impression that this had made on the departing pope.[33]

Of more immediate concern was the condition in which he left Giuliano, since the death many years earlier of Piero his one surviving brother. A prey to constant ill health, Giuliano had married Philiberte of Savoy in the summer of 1515 but had been too unwell to take command of the papal troops as his role as Captain-General required.

Even before Leo left Florence, it was evident that Giuliano did not have long to live and just under a month later, on 17 March 1516, he died at the Badia of Fiesole, aged thirty-seven. His nephew Lorenzo now remained the only lay member of the line on whom Medicean aspirations depended.[34]

A THIRD CONTRACT

In his last surviving letter before the long interruption in his correspondence that has already been referred to, Michelangelo would make an astonishing admission to Buonarroto. He can do nothing about money at this juncture in November 1515. He needs to do another two years' work before he is square with 'those people' because he has received so much money. Those people, 'costoro', are undoubtedly the executors of Pope Julius, Leonardo Grosso della Rovere and Lorenzo Pucci.[35]

It is a rare moment of candour. The artist is conceding that his remuneration has not been matched by results. Since May 1513, when the contract had been drawn up with the executors, Michelangelo had received a great deal of money for work on the tomb project on top of what he had had earlier. His own *ricordi* show that at this point he had received no less than 4,200 cameral ducats since May 1513; another payment of a further 400 ducats from Bernardo Bini was imminent; he received it on 29 November.[36]

There were substantial expenses that had to be met, partly for marble supplies (for the most part paid on delivery) and for the wages of the *scarpellini* at work on the fabric of the monument. But the situation was clearly critical. When Cardinal Leonardo and the Dowager Duchess of Urbino paid their visit to Macel de' Corvi in the following April, they would have encountered the two *Slaves* (pls 29, 30) and the unfinished seated *Moses* (pl. 31). The *Slaves* were probably in the state in which we now see them in the Louvre. They may also have caught sight of the flawed statue of *Christ* undertaken for the chapel of Marta Porcari, and one can only speculate what the cardinal made of this violation of the conditions of the 1513 contract. These four unfinished statues are those referred to in the artist's written instructions to Pietro Urbano of December 1517 about imposing better order on the contents of the Roman property.

The *Rebellious Slave* is, in fact, less worked up than the *Dying Slave*, and it has been widely argued that Michelangelo had abandoned work on it because of the appearance of a prominent crack in the marble running across the face and down into the left shoulder (pl. 30). If this was indeed the case, he was in the disastrous situation of having two impaired statues on his hands by 1516 when the flaw in the head of the Minerva *Christ* must have been apparent. However, when he refers to the unsuitability of the two *Slaves* for the reduced versions of the tomb in letters of 1542, it is on account of their scale; there is no hint of unsuitability because of condition, and it seems more probable, therefore, that the statue incurred the damage on its long journey to France in 1550.[37] In any event, by the summer of 1516 only three statues for the project had been begun and three of the seven years allowed for the completion of the entire programme had already passed.

A partial explanation for this state of affairs may lie in the ill health of the artist, which, as has been seen, is explicitly referred to in the letter recording his encounters with Luca Signorelli in 1513. His condition may have been a consequence of the extreme rigours of the previous years, above all his desperate efforts to complete his work in the Sistine Chapel when he had 'toiled as no man had ever toiled before'. Furthermore, his ill health is actually cited in the Italian text of the imminent new agreement as explanation for the striking concession that he may continue to work on the tomb in places other than Rome.[38] This consideration, taken together with the greatly reduced scale of the new undertaking, leads us back to the artist's words to Buonarroto of thirteen months earlier and his need to complete things soon in order to serve the pope.[39]

At this juncture, the biographer is on uncertain ground, given that the correspondence of this critical period is lost in its totality. If

Michelangelo had wished to cover his tracks, the loss of letters, following the abundant series preserved for the summer of 1515, could have been providential.

Michelangelo would, however, preserve letters injurious to his reputation; one of them, from an enraged Jacopo Sansovino, will engage us shortly. But while he can be exonerated of selective destruction of his correspondence, he cannot be acquitted of wilful misinformation in Condivi's biography. The book's dishonesty concerning events in 1516 and later remained a trap for some of the artist's most accomplished biographers of the nineteenth century.[40] He is presented as the victim of Pope Leo's insistence that he undertake the façade of San Lorenzo, to the profound sorrow of the executors and himself. Furthermore, he was compelled to shoulder the whole project on his own. Although assured by the pope that work on Julius's tomb could continue in Florence, he left Rome a grieving man.[41]

The very marked reduction envisaged for this revised project can, of course, be seen as a painful acceptance of reality by the two cardinals. For the artist, the contract constituted the attainment of something that he had wanted for a decade. Ten years had passed since he had written to Giuliano da Sangallo in May 1506, insisting that he could work to better effect and with greater dedication if based in Florence. Much more recently, he had declared to Lodovico in a letter of January 1514 that he wished to complete the tomb in Florence once he had finished with the marble he had in Rome.[42]

Nevertheless, the timing of the new developments in the summer of 1516 must raise a deep suspicion of opportunism on Michelangelo's part. No one had dissuaded Pope Leo from his objective of expropriating the duchy of Urbino. Just before his death in March 1516, his own brother, Giuliano, had attempted to change the pope's purpose, to no avail. And, as noted above, Elisabetta Gonzaga's plea in April on behalf of Duke Francesco Maria had been rebuffed. The pope, fortified by Alfonsina Orsini de' Medici, Paolo Giovio's 'ambitiosa et importuna femina', had proved inexorable. With the della Rovere in exile in Mantua, the papal troops, under Lorenzo, the pope's own nephew, rapidly crushed resistance in the duchy. The news of the collapse reached Rome in the first week of June, just over a month before the revised contract for Julius's tomb was signed.[43]

That Michelangelo was perceived to have acted badly is clear from comments written hard on the heels of events and the artist's rapid departure for Florence. These reactions are the more telling in that they came from devoted friends. Writing to him on 9 August 1516, Leonardo Sellaio begs him to remain true to the completion of the undertaking so that those who are saying that he has gone and that the work will never be finished will be exposed as liars.[44] Giovanni Gellesi, one of the Tuscan dining group, wrote a day later in even more candid terms. He understands that Michelangelo wishes to regain his honour and is glad to hear that he is now in a positive frame of mind.[45]

The new contract, drawn up in Latin and in a reduced form in Italian, is dated 8 July 1516. Michelangelo's own presence is mentioned in both these texts and in two subsidiary agreements of 10 and 11 July, which concern modes of payment.[46] The important aspects of the contract are twofold: an extension in the time allowed the artist for completion and a reduction in the scale of the project. In the contract of 1513, the artist had been allowed seven years, calculated from 6 May. The period now allowed is nine years from the same date. In other words, he is now granted a deadline of 1522 in place of 1520.

The reduction in the scale of the project was drastic. The number of statues was reduced by nearly half, to twenty-four. But the chance for the artist to reconsider his design led to remarkable results, a far more homogeneous scheme than that of three years earlier and one of great originality.[47]

As already noted, the text of the contract refers at some length to the house at Macel de' Corvi, going so far as to define the boundaries of the property. Michelangelo is allowed to occupy it for nine years without rent, the period to be calculated from May 1513, and this right is to remain even in the event of his working elsewhere than Rome. While these terms are generous, they indicate clearly enough that he was in no way regarded as the owner.[48]

Nevertheless, this new contract was extremely favourable, for the payment that had been agreed for the much more exacting task in 1513 was maintained. A phrase in the text of the contract hints at Michelangelo's gratitude to the executors; he promises to carry out the newly agreed project 'with great beauty and magnificence, according to his conscience'. Later letters suggest that it was Leonardo Grosso della Rovere, rather than Lorenzo Pucci, who was the more involved executor. Increasingly anxious about the delays in implementing this new agreement in the relatively few years of life remaining to him, he could never be accused of ill-will towards the artist.

The actual speed with which Michelangelo abandoned Rome once the contracts had been agreed must have struck many as shocking. Sellaio was left to do what he could to put the house in order; he had been a witness to one of the ancillary contracts. That the artist was impatient to move is clear from a reference to a now lost letter to Buonarroto of as early as 13 June, where he expects to leave Rome within ten days, bringing four assistants with him.[49] In the event, however, no more is heard of Antonio da Pontassieve and his team. Nor is there any further reference to the copper that had been acquired just over a year earlier.

The artist closed his Rome account with the Balducci on 18 July, transferring most of his remaining credit to Florence, but retaining a small sum in cash.[50] He must have left at once, for he was soon in Carrara, where his father addressed a letter to him written on 23 July. He reports that Michelangelo's own copies of the contracts have arrived but, as instructed, he will not forward them. The artist's anxiety to leave Rome in July 1516 recalls his precipitate departure from the city in 1501. His impatience to be gone is confirmed by another letter, which shows that, leaving Carrara after he completed his most immediate business there, he arrived in Florence on 28 July but cannot leave the house as he has no presentable clothes. Soon after, he took steps to acquire a new shirt and, at the same time, a bundle of old clothes arrived from Rome.[51]

The rapid trip to Carrara in July 1516, which had prompted Argentina Malaspini Soderini to write to her brother on 15 July, asking him to extend every kindness to the artist, was only a prelude to a stay of months during the coming autumn, which would begin with Michelangelo's return on 5 September. Two days later, on the seventh, he arranged to rent accommodation in a house owned by Francesco Pelliccia on the Piazza di Sant'Andrea.[52] The Pelliccia were a long-established family of marble suppliers and it would be with Francesco that Michelangelo negotiated the supply of a massive amount of marble on 1 November.[53] But he had already been negotiating for marble as early as mid-September, striking a deal with a supplier in the doorway of the cathedral of Carrara.[54]

At this point, Michelangelo was acting with great energy to see to his needs. Writing to his father at the end of September, he reports that he has arranged to have marble from many different sites at Carrara and, if the weather holds, hopes to have the marble at his disposal at the end of two months. But he has not made up his mind where to work; he mentions Carrara itself, Pisa, or even the option of returning to Rome. His silence about Florence is strange and perhaps studied, a deliberate attempt to avoid the topic of working for the pope.[55] Curiously enough, another marble supplier, offering the master his services on learning of his arrival in Florence, had, in late August, addressed him as 'sculp[t]ore de la Sedia Apostolica', sculptor of the Holy See.[56]

Only a few weeks after his arrival in Carrara in early September, the artist would be back in Florence. From a letter soon to claim attention, we know that the trip was undertaken to meet, along with a designated collaborator, the agent of Pope Leo and Cardinal Giulio to discuss the project of the façade for San Lorenzo.

THE FAÇADE OF SAN LORENZO:
THE COMMISSION

Without the appearance of further evidence, the issue of when Pope Leo decided on the façade project cannot be resolved. Uncertainty also dogs attempts to reconstruct subsequent events. Vasari's statements that record the names of competitive artists and architects who submitted designs are familiar and have been frequently discussed. In the first edition of the *Vite* of 1550 he records five names: Michelangelo, Baccio d'Agnolo, Antonio da Sangallo, Andrea Sansovino and Raphael.[57] In the second, the name of Jacopo Sansovino is added to those that had been enumerated earlier.[58] His information is problematic even if it cannot be discarded. One of the many problems that his passages raise is his complete neglect of the name of Michelangelo's long-standing friend Giuliano da Sangallo. Giuliano had given up his job in the Fabbrica of St Peter's in the summer of 1515 and, in worsening health, returned to Florence. No less than three large and highly finished drawings made by him for the façade of San Lorenzo survive, two of which are prominently dated 1516.[59]

Michelangelo's demonstrable part in the commission emerges only in the late summer of 1516. From that point a wealth of material survives, for the most part provided by a series of letters of Domenico Buoninsegni which present an exceptionally vivid picture of how events progressed – or failed to progress – in the subsequent months. During the autumn and early winter period Michelangelo remained, with scarcely any break, at Carrara. Unfortunately, none of his letters that are referred to in those directed to him has survived prior to March 1517.[60]

Buoninsegni and Michelangelo probably came to know each other soon after the former left Florence for Rome following the election of Cardinal Giovanni as pope in February 1513. He rapidly became one of the most trusted and powerful members of Cardinal Giulio de' Medici's household, in effect his treasurer. As has been seen, to make good Michelangelo's absence from Rome in April 1515, it was

Buoninsegni who was asked to join the Tuscan 'dining club' of which the artist was himself a member. Soon afterwards, friendly relations between the two are indicated by the fact that Michelangelo would arrange to have cloth that he had purchased in Florence for his own use delivered to Buoninsegni in the cardinal's quarters.[61] Buoninsegni would himself refer to Cardinal Giulio as his 'padrone' and would accompany him on his many travels. In a letter of 1517, Niccolò Machiavelli would refer to the multiplicity of his activities, his 'moltitudine delle occupazioni'.[62] Like Michelangelo himself, he had a reputation for *terribilità*.[63] And, as has also been seen, he seems to have been capable of strange behaviour in claiming that the road to Serravezza was close to completion in the summer of 1515.

In a letter of 21 November 1516, Buoninsegni, at that point incensed by the artist's procrastination, had written to Michelangelo recording events that had taken place earlier in the autumn. He recalls that Michelangelo and his collaborator, Baccio d'Agnolo, had met him in Florence to discuss the project of the façade, after which he himself had gone south to join the papal court at Montefiascone. Since a letter of Buoninsegni's to Baccio from Montefiascone, dated 7 October, survives, the encounter must have taken place in the last days of September or early October, and Michelangelo must have come to Florence from Carrara for the meeting. Buoninsegni now recalls that the two had committed themselves to the undertaking, 'vo' due vi movesti e faciesti fantasia di torla sopra di voi'. They had asked Buoninsegni to press ahead and discuss the matter with Cardinal Giulio. Buoninsegni had done so and the cardinal, with Pope Leo's sanction, had agreed and expressed the wish for the two to discuss the matter in person at the court.[64]

Buoninsegni's memory served him well; in the letter of 7 October, preserved because Baccio forwarded it to his collaborator at Carrara, Buoninsegni had urged them both to talk with Pope Leo in person before the court returned to Rome.[65] He adds that a meeting at Montefiascone will have a further advantage: it will allow things to be concluded without the opposition of someone whom he refers to as the 'amicho', the friend, or from allies of his. This 'amicho' evidently enjoyed sufficient power at the Curia to endanger the two men's hold on the commission. We never learn who this man is. But it is plausible to propose that the 'amicho', in reality an enemy, was Bernardo Dovizi, universally referred to after his promotion by Pope Leo in 1513 as Cardinal Bibbiena, one of Raphael's closest backers at the papal court.[66] That the man in question was not with the pope at Montefiascone adds some strength to the argument. For Bibbiena had been made papal legate to Perugia in the consistory of 18 August, the occasion when Pope Leo formally invested his nephew Lorenzo with the duchy of Urbino.[67]

A further episode strengthens the supposition. For, writing a month later to Michelangelo at Carrara, his partner, Baccio d'Agnolo, refers explicitly to a clash that he has had in Florence with Bibbiena and another powerful associate of Raphael, Giovanni Battista Branconio. He feels he can deal with them only with Michelangelo at his side.[68]

Buoninsegni's letters imply that competition for the project still persisted in the autumn of 1516. A further conspiratorial remark in his letter of 7 October to Baccio reveals how tense the situation was at this moment. If he and Michelangelo decide to come to the papal court, they should think up some reason for the journey other than the façade commission so that no one can guess the nature of their business.

His letters also indicate that, from the time when they reveal Michelangelo's explicit involvement in the commission, he had Baccio d'Agnolo as a partner. The patrons must have concluded that he needed an experienced architect in such a demanding undertaking. Baccio was thirteen years older than Michelangelo and had been a prominent figure in Florence for decades by reason of his public appointments as *capomaestro* at the Palazzo della Signoria and, subsequently, as one of the *capomaestri* of the Opera del Duomo, a post he held for much of his life.[69] As head of building activities at the cathedral from 1513, it fell to him to supervise the construction of the still-missing gallery or *ballatoio* around the base of Brunelleschi's cupola. Building work may have begun in 1513 but only one of its eight faces had been completed by 1515.[70] Suspension of the work was ascribed by Vasari in his Life of Baccio to the intervention of Michelangelo, who, on his return to Florence, is credited with dubbing Baccio's work a cricket cage, 'una gabbia da grilli'. If he really played the part referred to by Vasari, this may have come after his break with Baccio in the early months of 1517. Nevertheless, with Giuliano da Sangallo's life at its close – he died on 20 October 1516 – Baccio must have seemed a dependable choice.[71]

In a letter of 3 November, Buoninsegni makes allusion to the respective roles of the two men. On the evidence of a (now lost) letter of Michelangelo to Baccio that has been read in Rome, it seems to him that, at this point, Michelangelo is ready to give Baccio a relatively free hand over the architecture.[72] With respect to the sculpture, the pope has expressed himself happy if Michelangelo carves the most important statues; the rest he can allocate to other sculptors in whom he has confidence with the condition that he is to make the models and keep a firm control of quality.

Turning to the troubled issue of marble supplies, Buoninsegni warns the artist that Pope Leo is insistent on marble from Pietrasanta. For the moment, Michelangelo, with Cardinal Giulio's consent, can divert himself with quarrying marble at Carrara but only until the road is completed. The cathedral *operai* and Pope Leo are each to contribute 1,000 ducats for its construction.

Negotiations made little progress in November. Baccio d'Agnolo was reluctant to go to Rome without Michelangelo. Although the artist's letters of the period are lost, there can be no doubt that at some point in November he had promised to come and had then reneged. His seemingly ceaseless capacity for changing his mind, which would later incite a memorable judgement from the prior of San Lorenzo, provoked an astonishing outburst from Buoninsegni in a letter of 21 November.[73] He has been placed in a false position and has let down both the pope and the cardinal. He writes that he is almost driven mad by Michelangelo's letters.[74] It is at this point that he recalls the meeting the three had had earlier in Florence. He declares that, in the light of Michelangelo's letters, he has had enough. He feels even more betrayed by Baccio. He recalls their complaints when commissions are given to non-Florentines, 'fuori della nazione', and points to their behaviour as the cause.[75] Michelangelo's reaction to this outburst is nowhere recorded, but Baccio d'Agnolo was clearly shaken by this display of Buoninsegni's *terribilità*.[76]

Buoninsegni did not hold to his threat to throw in his hand. He wrote a still longer letter to Michelangelo on 11 December.[77] It is clear that the artist has expressed his suspicion that both Baccio d'Agnolo and a fellow Florentine architect, Baccio Bigio, have been playing him false.[78] Bigio is now in Rome and is evidently keen to have a part in the commission; he has succeeded in meeting both Cardinal Giulio and Pope Leo. Repeating that the cardinal wishes Michelangelo and Baccio d'Agnolo to have the commission, he insists that Michelangelo must make up his mind; the patrons are anxious to see work started; although they know that Michelangelo can serve them best, they may look elsewhere.

Buoninsegni then proceeds to express what he emphasizes is his own opinion. For the artist's personal benefit and honour, to satisfy the pope and other members of his family, and to honour the city, Michelangelo should do all in his power to obtain the commission and come to Rome. In a remarkable premonition of future events, Buoninsegni writes that, although the patrons speak of giving the commission to Baccio d'Agnolo and to him, were Michelangelo to wish to take on everything himself and choose his own collaborator, they will meet his request.[79] In any event, they have rejected a claim of Baccio Bigio that Pope Leo had wanted him and Baccio d'Agnolo to carry out the architecture and Michelangelo to make the statues; this would involve an unacceptable position of inferiority for Michelangelo.[80]

The letter is one of the lengthiest addressed to the artist in the entire *carteggio*. It testifies to Buoninsegni's acute grasp of the situation and to his insight into character. It reveals him as a staunch advocate of the artist, ready to put aside past vexations in order to promote what he sees as the best way forward. From this letter, it is clear that Pope Leo and Cardinal Giulio are determined to get things moving and still hold out the hope that Michelangelo will be involved. The earlier letters in the series do not give the impression that they had set out with a completely inflexible plan. Initial realism on their part is indicated by the expectation that Michelangelo will delegate to others the carving of the subordinate statues, but such caution would not last.

What lay behind his reluctance to leave Carrara in the autumn of 1516 is a matter for conjecture. Distrust of Baccio d'Agnolo and Baccio Bigio may have contributed to his self-imposed aloofness. And it is extremely striking that months later, after his share in the commission had been brutally ended, the former would insist that he had not been involved with Raphael. Running by chance into Buonarroto in April 1517, Baccio d'Agnolo goes to great lengths to claim that he was innocent of planning any role without Michelangelo, and that he had never had any intention of getting mixed up with Raphael. By this date in April of the following year, he wishes to have no further part in the façade project. Buonarroto reports to Michelangelo that he had felt compelled to believe him because of his own good nature and the fact that the encounter had taken place on Easter Saturday.[81]

But there may have been reasons simpler than apprehensions of plotting that led to his refusal to move. He may have been anxious to defer the issue on which he was at odds with his patrons, their requirement to leave Carrara and seek materials at Pietrasanta. And, on a more basic level, he may have been simply too busy with selecting the sites at Carrara for quarrying what he needed for the tomb project to get away. We can recall how much time he had spent eighteen years earlier seeking marble for the cardinal's *Pietà*, a single work. As the letter written to his father in late September had made clear, he had ordered marble from many different sites, 'in molte luog[h]i', and his insistent concern to oversee operations himself must have been a disincentive for leaving. This may explain the fact that when Lodovico was seriously ill in November, Michelangelo, anxious as he was, and even going so far as to recommend to Buonarroto both the spiritual and bodily needs of their father, did not leave Carrara for Florence, notwithstanding his self-protective claim in his letter that everything that he had accomplished had been for Lodovico's sake.[82]

It must have been Buoninsegni's letter of 11 December that finally impelled Michelangelo to act. Writing a summary of events later, he no longer accurately recalled the details, for he would state that he had left Carrara for Rome on 5 December.[83] It was around the fifteenth or sixteenth of the month that he set out. He travelled at great speed and spent a minimum of time at the papal court, for already on 22 December Buoninsegni was writing to him in Florence.[84] Nevertheless, as this later letter shows, this encounter with the patrons was decisive. They had been shown a drawing that had won their unqualified backing and which the artist is to adhere to: 'el Papa era resoluto al disegno che avete fatto e che di quello non si uscissi'.

The character of the drawing that Michelangelo either took with him or actually made on his arrival in Rome has been much discussed. It may have been the very large, carefully drawn but still experimental design preserved in the Casa Buonarroti (pl. 32) or, more probably, a project that closely resembled it.[85] The drawing in the Casa Buonarroti still shows very clearly the influence of the drawings that had been made for the façade by his recently deceased old friend Giuliano da Sangallo.[86]

In his letter of 22 December which followed on Michelangelo's return to Florence, Buoninsegni insists on how crucial for the patrons is the issue of speed. Pope Leo is instructing his brother-in-law, Jacopo Salviati, to pay the artist 1,000 large ducats. The patrons are giving thought to the need for spaces where the work for the façade can be undertaken. The issue of Pietrasanta is not referred to. A model is to be sent to Rome. Baccio d'Agnolo is being kept informed about the outcome of the visit.

Not present at the meeting in Rome, Baccio must have been effectively denied the chance of going by the sheer precipitation of Michelangelo's behaviour. The insistence that the design that the patrons had seen in Rome must be strictly adhered to would not withstand the restless inventiveness and sheer persuasiveness of their chosen artist. In any event, the meeting in December in Rome began what has been appropriately called 'la tragedia della facciata'.[87]

THE BLOCKADE AT CARRARA

The enforced move from Carrara to Pietrasanta would provoke a grave setback that can scarcely have been foreseen by the artist, an embargo on the delivery of the many marble blocks ordered at Carrara after he had taken up residence there in 1516. These blocks, destined for the papal tomb, had been ordered in large quantities. Nevertheless, ever pressed for time, he seems to have failed to keep a precise record of their whereabouts.[88]

Michelangelo, in anticipation of the move that was so unwelcome to him, wrote to a Carrara notary as he recovered from his illness in Florence in the autumn of 1517. The letter has not survived but the notary's reply was preserved by the artist.[89] Dated 30 October, he conveys his relief over the artist's recovery. He states that he cannot adequately convey to Michelangelo the good will that Alberico Malaspina has for him. In response to a lost letter of the artist, the *marchese* has asked the notary, Leonardo Lombardello, to carry out an on-site inventory of the marble already quarried for him. He will go first to the coast to check there the number of blocks prepared for him, marked with the artist's sign. Then he will proceed to the mountains to check the blocks not yet transported to the coast. He reassures him that not a single fragment of marble will escape him.

Lombardello's reference to Michelangelo's *segno*, his sign, is, of course, to his personal symbol of three interlocking circles. When he first employed this sign is not known. In a receipt for marble received, dated February 1517, he himself had referred to the fact that they had been marked with his sign, 'segniati col mio segnio', incised in the stone by the quarrymen.[90] From this period there survives a receipt-book in which Michelangelo made drawings of the blocks of marble

that had been delivered; the drawn blocks are given his symbol and
within one of the circles is inscribed the initial of the quarryman
responsible for the delivery.[91] One such symbol is visible on the top
of the huge block from which he began to carve one of the statues
now in the Accademia in Florence (pl. 33).[92]

Much has been read into the significance of the symbol, and it has
been repeatedly pointed out that, later in the century, Florentines saw
in it a reference to the unity of the professions of sculpture, architecture
and painting. To ascribe to Michelangelo this significance in 1517 seems
fanciful.[93]

It is more in keeping with his character to propose that he used the
three circles as a reference to his name, Buonarroti. It is striking that,
only a few years later, he signed one of his letters with symbols representing his names; for Michelangelo he wrote a capital M flanked by
drawn wings on either side, and for Buonarroti the *segno* of the three
circles.[94]

Lombardello's inventory seems not to have survived. But it was
the assembly of the blocks at the sea that would be the object of
revenge on the part of the quarrymen at Carrara, one exacted for
Michelangelo's abandonment of their quarries in favour of those at
Seravezza. They blocked their removal.

The crisis broke before the end of 1517, as a letter of Pietro Urbano
of 2 January 1518 shows. After reporting on the reception of the
wooden model of the tomb in Rome, he goes on to inform his master
that, in a meeting with Cardinal Leonardo, he has tried to quieten
his anxieties over the tomb project and has described at length
Michelangelo's travails with his former allies at Carrara.[95]

The problem of recovering the marble at Carrara would prove
one of the many time-consuming and frustrating episodes in
Michelangelo's career; its resolution took little short of a year. In a
letter to Buonarroto of 2 April 1518, he asks his brother to ask Jacopo
Salviati to help. He has gone as far as Genoa to seek alternative transport. Four boats had reached the loading point at Avenza. But the men

at Carrara have bribed the owners not to collaborate and he is, in effect, blockaded. He plans to search for alternative help at Pisa.[96]

Writing to his brother a few days later, Buonarroto assures him that Jacopo Salviati is ready to help; he has expressed his devotion to the artist: 'portati grande amore'.[97] Replying in turn, Michelangelo expresses his extraordinary gratitude to Salviati; he writes that all of them will be indebted to him for the rest of their lives.[98] Things remained difficult, however, despite his hope that he had found a boat for a fair price at Pisa. In one of the most desperate letters of his correspondence, of 18 April, he reports to Buonarroto that the boats hired at Pisa have not turned up. The workmen whom he had brought from Florence and Settignano have proved hopeless. It is at the end of this letter, in a brief postscript, that his fury overwhelms him, as it will in another postscript written decades later. Cursed a thousand times be the day and hour when he left Carrara: 'Ò maledecto mille volte el dì e l'ora che io mi parti da Charrara'.[99]

The problem dragged on through the summer months of 1518, despite the good offices of the manager of the Pisa branch of the Salviati bank, Francesco Peri. At this point the artist concludes that everyone in Carrara is against him, expressing his conviction that he cannot get marble from Carrara in twenty years. Nevertheless, in June, the Carrara notary who has already been encountered and whom, it seems clear, Michelangelo trusted, wrote to him at length, explaining that many of the marble workers at Carrara would be delighted to resume work for him. He does, however, add the significant cautionary remark that he has not discussed things with Alberico before writing this letter of reassurance.[100]

How far the *marchese*, whose sister Argentina was, as has been seen, devoted to Michelangelo, was behind the blockade is difficult to judge, but it seems unbelievable that the resistance offered to the artist could have happened without his sanction.[101] Those in Michelangelo's circle do not seem to have entertained any doubts about his complicity. One of the *operai* of the cathedral particularly well disposed to the artist, Berto da Filicaia, had discussed the problem with Jacopo Salviati and had concluded that the issue required intervention in the form of a papal brief.[102] Cardinal Leonardo della Rovere, as a letter of Sebastiano del Piombo of 25 September 1518 shows, was desperate that the pope should act, for it was, after all, marble for the tomb that was in jeopardy.[103]

The brief, delayed by the pope's absence from Rome, was finally delivered to the *marchese* by Donato Benti, a man who enjoyed the artist's trust, on 26 October 1518. Its terms had been described as extraordinary by one of Cardinal Leonardo's closest representatives. It cannot be excluded that the *marchese* may have heard of its imminence, for some marble had begun to be loaded at Avenza a little before it was delivered. Alberico was reported to have been stupefied by the contents of the brief and to have declared that he had never acted against Michelangelo.[104] A month later he himself wrote to both Pope Leo and Cardinal Leonardo, accusing the artist of having created every difficulty. Michelangelo, he is reported to have claimed, always fights with everyone. His indictment of the artist anticipates by two years the celebrated remarks of Pope Leo himself that Michelangelo is impossible to work with.[105]

Buoninsegni saw to it that a résumé of events should reach the artist, including Cardinal Leonardo's desperation regarding the tomb.[106] Writing directly to Michelangelo on 18 December 1518, he does not describe the cardinal's anxieties but does report his recent ill health. He conveys the Medici patron's deep satisfaction that Michelangelo has found good marble at Pietrasanta.[107]

The crisis at Carrara thus came to an end. Shipment of the marble ordered for the papal tomb resumed. In the following months, Michelangelo would be in touch, once again, with the men whom he knew so well at Carrara. His way was eased by the intervention of fate, for the *marchese* Alberico would die in 1519, leaving no male heir.

A SPACE FOR WORKING

As early as December 1516, after Michelangelo's successful journey to the papal court, his patrons had recognized his need for spaces where he could work.[108] For a time, the issue seems to have been put on one side. But in early 1518, following the ratification of the contract for the San Lorenzo façade, the issue re-emerged with real urgency. In April 1518 Jacopo Salviati reported hearing of excellent accommodation close to the church of San Lorenzo where the marble both for the architecture and the statues could be worked, but for unknown reasons the proposal was not pursued.[109] Another site was proposed in May, but was evidently turned down, probably because it was too expensive.[110] The artist did effect a purchase in July 1518 from the canons of the cathedral; the site was close to the city walls and was a substantial piece of land. Writing after the purchase to Cardinal Giulio in Rome, he explains that it is a site to be built on to accommodate his marble. But he complains to his patron that he has been overcharged.[111] The cardinal promptly replied, assuring him that Pope Leo himself would see that the price was reduced.[112] But, for reasons that have remained unknown, Michelangelo never began building work there.[113]

Another promising site for a future working space emerged in the autumn of 1518. Writing to Cardinal Giulio at some point in November, he explains that he has never found a property ample enough to provide for his needs; he mentions work on both marble and bronze statues. Now, he reports, Matteo Bartoli, father of Cosimo Bartoli, the future writer and close friend of Vasari, has found him an excellent site for a workshop on the *piazza* in front of the church of Ognissanti. He specifically states that he could work there on both marble and bronze statues. The prospects for the sale appeared to be good but, for reasons we do not learn about, this project also never went ahead.[114] It is worth noting that Matteo was a well-known bronze caster and that Michelangelo could well have seen in him a future collaborator for the bronze statues for the façade.[115]

A solution was found in late November 1518. The sale of the site was effected on the twenty-fourth of the month. It was on what was called the Via Mozza, now Via San Zanobi. To this site, which cost 113 large gold florins, was added a further adjoining property and yet another one in February 1519.[116] Work began in December and the process of construction is densely documented in the artist's surviving *ricordi*.[117] Michelangelo would frequently, although not invariably, refer to the structure as a *stanza*, and it has been reckoned that the interior constituted an area of about 200 square metres.[118] The cost of the purchase was put to expenses for the project of the San Lorenzo façade, a step permitted him by the terms of the contract. Writing to Leonardo Sellaio in December, the artist explains that roofing his new workshop is being held up; wood for the timbering cannot reach Florence because lack of rain has prevented its arrival by way of the Arno. Nevertheless, he assures Sellaio that, once the *stanza* is completed, he will be able to work on twenty statues at a time.[119]

Although the new accommodation had been acquired for work for the façade, there can be little doubt that it was marble for the papal tomb, liberated at Avenza in the previous autumn, that was the first to arrive. Among these blocks was the one that Michelangelo had selected at Carrara for the new, replacement, statue of *Christ* for Santa Maria sopra Minerva in Rome. Indeed, it was the four *Slaves* now in the Accademia in Florence, and the *Christ* (pl. 28), that were the first carvings undertaken there. Large deliveries of marble were arriving in the Via Mozza in the summer of 1519, as his *ricordi* show. But from the evidence of one dated 17 May, it is clear that, by this date, the artist had already begun to block out marble, aided by his latest assistant, Topolino.[120]

The workshop on the Via Mozza would be the place where the artist would prepare the sculpture for a new project at San Lorenzo, the New Sacristy. But it was also the scene of a strange incident some years later. A *ricordo* preserved in the Casa Buonarroti states that, three months before the siege of Florence began in October 1529, the *stanza* was broken into and around fifty figure drawings, some made for the

Medici tombs, and four models in wax or clay were stolen.[121] Vasari refers to the episode in his Life of Michelangelo of 1568. He states that the theft was the work of Bartolommeo Ammannati and Nanni, son of Baccio Bigio; that the drawings and models were recovered by the Otto di Guardia; and that Michelangelo was persuaded not to pursue the matter further. Ammannati, a future colleague of the artist, would have been just eighteen years old at the time.

After Michelangelo's definitive move to Rome in 1534, the *stanza* lost its function as a working space. It remained a kind of depositary for the monumental carvings that Michelangelo had left there in different stages of completion and a storehouse of pieces of marble that had never been worked at all. Some of these unworked blocks were sold off to Duke Cosimo by 1544.[122] While the statues for the New Sacristy were removed to the chapel during the 1540s, the four huge *Slaves* and the group of *Victory* were still in Via Mozza at Michelangelo's death. They would be surrendered to Duke Cosimo by Michelangelo's nephew and heir, Leonardo.

SETBACKS AND SUSPENSION

At Pietrasanta, on 15 March 1518, Michelangelo contracted with nine quarrymen for marble for the façade of San Lorenzo. No less than eight of them he had summoned from Settignano or its neighbourhood. One of them was the ever faithful Michele di Pippo. The ninth was from close to Pietrasanta; none, therefore, came from Carrara.[123]

The road was an immediate concern. Already as early as January 1517 it had been estimated that the cost of its construction would far exceed what had been provided.[124] By March 1518 Michelangelo was anxious to assume overall control of the enterprise. Some resistance was offered by the Florentine commissioner at Pietrasanta, who felt that the man who had daily charge of the operation, Donato Benti, would feel injured by his replacement by Michelangelo. But the Opera of Florence cathedral insisted that the artist must be given overall control: this was the express wish of the patrons in Rome.[125] Michelangelo had accepted the undertaking by 31 March.[126] In effect, his faith in Donato Benti was shown by subsequent correspondence and by the fact that he appointed him his deputy when he himself was absent. Benti had undertaken work at Pietrasanta for many years, and his devotion to Michelangelo is expressed in a touching letter of the following June.[127]

The artist explained his reasons for wishing to take over control in a letter to Buonarroto of 2 April. Only he knows where the finest marble is located, a statement that, given his acute instinct for the material, must have been true.[128] In a letter of May to Buoninsegni in Rome, he enlarges on the issue of the road. There is excellent marble for building purposes to hand and he expresses optimism about getting it to the sea. But the quality of marble he requires for figure sculpture is situated above and beyond Seravezza. To gain access to it he needs to extend the road a further two miles, one of which must be dug out with pickaxes. He warns Buoninsegni that, if Pope Leo wants marble for his commission, as opposed to that for building at St Peter's, he will have to find the money.[129]

While it is tempting to accuse the artist of dramatizing the problems presented by the building of the roads to the *cave* and to the sea, it may be nearer the truth to suggest that both he himself and the cathedral Opera initially seriously underestimated the problems that Medicean policy provoked. Upkeep of the roads, as well as their construction, posed many difficulties. Convalescing from his second illness in Florence in the autumn of 1518, it was reported to Michelangelo that the road through the marshes to the sea was complete.[130] Yet only a little over a year later, Donato Benti would report that the bridge over the worst of the marshland was in bad condition and required urgent attention. He refers also to the fact that water was threatening the viability of the road to the quarries above Seravezza.[131] In 1521 it was reported that this latter stretch of road was in a state of near ruin.[132]

The months preceding Michelangelo's second bout of illness in the early autumn of 1518, which provoked the impassioned letter of

Buonarroto referred to earlier, were some of the most troubled of the artist's life. Where he chose to live after moving to Pietrasanta seems not to have been recorded. A rare glimpse of his lifestyle is, however, provided by the shopping list he jotted down on the back of a letter addressed to him at Pietrasanta, dated 18 March 1518. Evidently seizing the nearest piece of paper to hand, the artist wrote down what he needed for three meals (frontispiece). Alongside his written instructions he drew little sketches of what he required. It has been rarely noted that these little drawings must have been made because the *garzone* entrusted with the shopping, and perhaps also the victuallers who were to supply the items, could not read. None of the three menus includes meat, and the modesty of Michelangelo's needs that are here recorded confirms the legendary austerity of his way of life.[133]

If, however, the letters of these months are frequently marked by a more than usual nervousness, one issue that fed his anxiety was of his own making. At some point Michelangelo decided to press the Arte della Lana, in charge of the cathedral Opera, for a remarkable concession, their consent to his freedom to take marble from the quarries ceded to the city in 1515 without any payment. The first surviving reference to the issue appears in a letter to his brother Buonarroto of 20 March 1518, and it is clear from this and subsequent correspondence that the artist has asked Jacopo Salviati to act on his behalf, a choice determined by their extraordinary mutual regard and by the fact that Jacopo was one of the *operai*. Jacopo wrote to the artist about his wish on 4 April, reassuring him that he appreciated him more than anyone else in Florence.[134] But the delays that followed, actuated by the need to obtain a joint decision on the part of consuls and *operai*, provoked an astonishing outburst from the artist. Despite a reassuring letter from Buonarroto, Michelangelo wrote to him on 18 April the letter already referred to, one marked by desperation on many counts: the shortcomings of his marble workers, the blockade at Carrara and, not least, the lack of news over the outcome of his demand. He fears that Salviati has failed to arrange the affair and goes as far as to threaten to go to see Cardinal Giulio and Pope Leo, abandon the undertaking at Seravezza and return to Carrara.[135]

On 23 April 1518 Buonarroto wrote to reassure him that all had gone well: his request has been met. The document that prescribes his freedom is dated 22 April. The Arte della Lana, aware of the great efforts that he has expended in opening up the quarries, especially those of Monte Altissimo, has decided to allow him to use whatever marble he may require for whatsoever purpose he chooses, without payment, for the rest of his life.[136] The artist could not have asked for more. Yet despite the almost desperate insistence revealed in his letters, the affair remains one of the many paradoxical episodes in his life. Given his aversion to working at Seravezza, the extraordinary concession would prove of no lasting significance for him. Indeed, by early 1519, actuated by the need for speed in getting the project under way, Pope Leo himself had expressed his willingness for Michelangelo to return to Carrara for marble for two or three of the twelve columns required for the façade.[137]

The concession must have been a response to the setbacks that dogged operations through 1518. In part, the problems that Michelangelo had with the workforce he had assembled in early 1518 owed to their inexperience with marble. But, perhaps in part due to their inexperience, they seem to have been reluctant to work. In August the artist reported to Buonarroto that those he had summoned were useless and concerned only with receiving their wages.[138] One in particular, a member of the extended Fancelli clan and brother of the Topolino who would show loyalty to him on many occasions, had left by the end of August, after spending his time fishing and philandering.[139]

Reporting to Berto di Filicaia of the Opera in mid-September, the artist informs him of the loss of the first column brought down from the quarry. Not properly secured in transit, it had slipped, killing instantly one of the workmen and nearly causing his own death. The scale of the monolithic columns was huge; a contract with the Alessandro Fancelli who would leave in August records their length as 11

Florentine *braccia*, or well over 6 metres.[140] Another column has exposed a flaw that required very extensive reworking.[141]

Nevertheless, Michelangelo once more conveys his confidence in the outcome. In a familiar passage he explains that the place where the quarrying is proceeding is rugged. The men are inexperienced. Great patience is required for some time, until the mountains are tamed and the men instructed. Echoing the claim he made to Buoninsegni many months earlier, he declares that, if God helps him, he will, as promised, create the most beautiful work ever made in Italy.[142]

Jacopo Salviati wrote to Michelangelo on 20 September, reporting that he has heard about the broken column and the artist's deep mortification. He tries to give him encouragement and assure him that the entire city of Florence will be indebted to him and the family for what he is undertaking. Great men, he reminds the artist, grow stronger through adversity.[143] He has heard that the artist does not feel well and urges him to come to rest in the Salviati house in Pisa. The letter is yet one more indication of Jacopo's devotion to the man whom he had recently addressed as 'mio quanto fratello'.

That Michelangelo had been profoundly upset by the loss of the column is confirmed by a letter of the same day from the cathedral Opera addressed to the son of Berto di Filicaia. It refers to his unhappiness over the event but urges Berto's son to console the artist, at the same time expressing wishes for the recovery of his health.[144]

The ordering of marble for the façade continued in the autumn of 1518. On 29 October the artist contracted with Topolino for marble that was to include two columns. His assistant would be paid 40 large gold ducats for each. And another column was ordered in December.[145] Michelangelo left for Pietrasanta a day after Topolino's contract had been drawn up but he did not stay for long. The site he had bought on the Via Mozza required his presence, and he was back in Florence only a few days later, where he would remain until January 1519.

The destruction of the column in September 1518 would not be the last. No less than three further quarried columns were destined to be lost. One had been broken in early April 1519. The setback had reached the ears of the cathedral *operai* by the sixth of the month. They lament the loss and express their concern. They urge that the undertaking must go ahead and express the hope that the Lord will bring it to a happier conclusion. Pietro Urbano, at this point in Florence, has also heard about what he calls 'la disghratia della cholouna' and has been deeply depressed by the news.[146]

Michelangelo would write a long letter to Urbano from the quarries on 20 April, describing a disaster to a column. It has been assumed that he is writing of the same incident. But this seems not to be the case. He is referring to the disaster having occurred on the previous Saturday, 16 April, and is writing of this to his *garzone* as a 'novita'. He explains the circumstances: it had been the faithful Donato Benti who had caused the disaster. One of the rings of the tackle holding the column had broken because the man entrusted by Donato with its making had used poor-quality iron. The column had fallen into the riverbed, shattering in a hundred pieces.[147]

A further column was broken later, in December 1520, months after the project had been suspended.[148] On the occasion of the arrival of the first intact column in Florence in April 1521, the dependable chronicler Giovanni Cambi would report that, in all, six columns had been quarried for the façade, of which four had been broken in transit. His information confirms that two had met with disaster in April 1519.[149]

These were serious blows for the man whose near-veneration for the purity and well-being of his chosen material emerges time and again in his letters. But there was also the issue of the serious financial lessons involved. Looking back later, Michelangelo, in one *ricordo*, reckoned that the first transported column had cost no less than the huge sum of 60 ducats; the second one had cost 30.[150]

The patrons in Rome cannot have been unaware of such setbacks and they would have learnt more at first hand from Jacopo Salviati. He had left Florence for Rome near the end of 1518, a move prompted by his worsening relations with Duke Lorenzo. Rumours were rife in

Florence that, following his return from France in the previous year, Lorenzo planned to establish a personal regime in the city, a despotic Signoria. Salviati had always favoured a restricted form of government but could not accept the plan now nurtured by Lorenzo.[151]

In reality, Lorenzo was already a sick man by the end of 1518. Confined to Palazzo Medici, reliant on only a handful of close advisers, his condition brought Cardinal Giulio to Florence in late January 1519. Writing to the artist on 15 January, Salviati had referred to Pope Leo's intention to come to Florence and wish to see some sign of a start on work for the sculptural decoration of the façade.[152]

Cardinal Giulio would remain in Florence for many months, his main task to attempt to strengthen the Medicean regime after Duke Lorenzo's death in May. It was during his stay, which extended until October, that the decision to suspend the façade project must have been taken; but his presence (and also that of Buoninsegni) in Florence meant that no informative exchange of letters between patron and artist was required. And Michelangelo's own account of events, chiefly concerned to vindicate his financial rectitude, was committed to paper only a year later, in 1520.

That the patrons' aims had, by June 1519, shifted from the façade to two new projects at San Lorenzo, a burial chapel for the family dead and a library in the convent, is evident from a remarkable memorandum written years later by the man who had been made prior by Leo in 1514, Giovan Battista Figiovanni.[153] The text vividly records his conversation with the cardinal in Palazzo Medici in June. Cardinal Giulio tells him of the two new projects that have been decided on and states that they have in mind an expenditure of approximately 50,000 ducats. Asked if he is willing to take on the responsibility, Figiovanni accepts with the condition that he is spared the burden of overseeing the financing. He continues that work began in early November 1519 and that Michelangelo was in charge of the architecture.[154]

There is a striking absence of contemporary reference to the suspension of the project for the façade. Even the ever informative Giovanni

Cambi, while noting the start of work on the New Sacristy at San Lorenzo and recording the delayed arrival of marble destined for the façade, makes no reference to the halt of work on it. Suspension, nevertheless, is probably a more appropriate word than termination. A few shreds of evidence strengthen the supposition that Cardinal Giulio did not put the façade altogether out of his mind and that, after his own election as pope in 1523, he still nursed the idea of the project's resumption. Writing to the artist in April 1524, Michelangelo's mediator at the court, Giovan Francesco Fattucci, conveys the pope's satisfaction that the artist has dropped the idea of situating the library on the *piazza*, out of consideration for the façade.[155] The same concern for the possibility of a future façade reappears in a letter of Figiovanni of the autumn of 1531 when the project of a tribune for the display of the church's relics was under renewed consideration.[156]

We do not gain from Michelangelo himself a clear idea of why work on the façade was halted. His own self-justification is contained in the surviving draft of a letter. It is neither dated nor addressed to the recipient, but in all probability it was written in late February or early March 1520 and sent to Buoninsegni.[157] The artist went to great lengths to prepare the letter, for there survive no less than five *ricordi* in his hand that document his efforts to reconstruct events since the autumn of 1516 and establish the payments he had received and the expenses incurred and time consumed.[158] The reason for this exercise was a demand from Cardinal Giulio for an account of the moneys received and spent.

Increasingly resentful in tone, Michelangelo points out that he has lost three years and, indeed, has incurred ruin over the project.[159] He demands a written guarantee from Pope Leo that he is free of any future financial claims. On what led to the work's suspension he makes only a brief allusion, writing that work had been stopped by the patrons because they wished to release him of the burden of supervising marble supplies. He then refers obliquely to a new contract but he offers no details of what this 'nuova chonventione' is.[160] In one of his preparatory *ricordi* he had been a little more candid. He had written that Pope Leo, perhaps in order to allow a quicker completion than that envisaged in the contract, with his agreement had liberated him from the undertaking.[161]

That it was Michelangelo's refusal to countenance assistants that had led to the breakdown of the undertaking was a view already voiced even before the appearance of Vasari's Life of 1550. An extraordinary letter from Baccio Bandinelli to Duke Cosimo survives that levels this accusation, dated 7 December 1547. In the context of explaining his own need of helpers, he reviews the employment of assistants by great sculptors of the past, citing among others Donatello. He recalls that, the contract for the façade concluded, it was decided that the sculpture should be executed under Michelangelo's guidance by youthful assistants. Duke Cosimo should realize that the reason Michelangelo had never delivered any works was his refusal to be helped by anyone, so as not to create 'maestri', in other words rivals. Bandinelli informs the duke that he was told this by Pope Clement who could never succeed in getting Michelangelo to make large models.[162]

In his *Lives* of Michelangelo of 1550 and 1568, Vasari levelled two accusations at the artist. Writing of the architecture, he explicitly criticizes him for rejecting colleagues who could have helped him, and, on a more general level, he states that it was the delays that led to the money that had been set aside for the project being diverted by Pope Leo x to carry on the war in north Italy.[163]

In his newly prepared Life of Bandinelli for the second edition, Vasari came up with a completely different explanation for the breakdown. He states that Domenico Buoninsegni, in charge of the finances for the façade, wished to involve the artist in a conspiracy to defraud Pope Leo. On Michelangelo's refusal, Vasari alleges that Buoninsegni developed so great a hatred of the artist that he contrived to have the façade project abandoned.[164] There is, however, nothing in the tone or content of two subsequent letters concerning the New Sacristy, which Buoninsegni addressed to the artist in December 1520, to lend any substance to the theory of a break between them. There are, it can be said, scattered in Buoninsegni's lengthy correspondence with

Michelangelo, moments when he gives his own opinion of affairs 'off the record', but nothing to lend substance to the thesis of conspiracy advanced in Vasari's passage.[165] The most satisfactory explanation for the abandonment of the project lies in the increasing concern of the patrons over the lack of tangible progress and the new urgency that had arisen to honour the Medici dead.

VIII

UNDERTAKINGS IN ROME
AND FLORENCE

THE SECOND *CHRIST*

Problems older than those provoked by the quarries above Pietrasanta
would re-emerge in this period of adversity. Michelangelo, before
leaving Rome in the summer of 1516, had probably promised Marta
Porcari's trusted nephews that he would carve a new statue of *Christ*
for Santa Maria sopra Minerva to replace the one irretrievably compromised by the dark vein in the face (pl. 28).

Nothing is heard about the issue for nearly a year, when Michelangelo
evidently asked that the 150 ducats banked in the 'statue' account with
the Balducci should be transferred to Florence. A letter from Rome
of 3 October 1517, confirming the transfer, shows that the request had
come from the artist.[1]

Metello Vari, a nephew of the deceased Marta Porcari, signatory of
the contract of 1514 and the only man who would prove steadfast in
seeing the project through, wrote to Michelangelo on 13 December.
He reminds him that the money has been sent and that more than
three and a half years have passed since the contract had been drawn
up for what he refers to as 'un Cristo nudo'. He has assumed, in the
absence of any word from the artist, that the carving had been carried
out. He impresses on the artist the importance of completion.[2]

This letter of Vari's of December 1517 is the first in a surviving
series of no less than twenty-five that he would write to Michelangelo

between 1517 and 1532 regarding the project. His letters are only a part of a much larger correspondence relating to the marble *Christ* from Michelangelo's Roman circle, which includes letters from Leonardo Sellaio, Sebastiano del Piombo, and Pietro Urbano, who would travel to Rome to put the final touches to the statue after its arrival.[3]

Michelangelo's request for the money that had been put on deposit in the Balducci 'statue' account shows that he had not touched it while working between 1514 and 1516 on the carving that would be abandoned. Back in Tuscany, he needed a new block and, although precise details are lacking, he probably included an order for the needed marble after he had taken up residence at Carrara in the late summer of 1516. It would appear that, while recovering from his serious illness in Florence in the early autumn of 1517, he had decided that he must take steps to provide the replacement.

These steps proceeded with painful slowness, but he was not responsible for this. It is likely that the new marble block for the Minerva statue was among those held up by the blockade at Carrara. Indeed, this seems corroborated by a letter of his of December 1518, to be discussed below.

In the meantime, further letters from Vari reached the artist, one of 26 July 1518, another of 24 November. Preoccupied by many problems, of which the delay to the statue's implementation was only one, Vari goes so far as to press the artist to engage an assistant to carve the figure and to propose that he, Michelangelo, should limit himself to providing the final touches, 'l'ultima mano'.[4] From the second letter, we learn that Cardinal Giulio de' Medici has been pressed to intervene. He had evidently arranged for the issuing of a brief granting an extension of time for the work to be delivered, easing the predicament of the executors. Vari writes that he wants the statue to be in place in Santa Maria sopra Minerva by Easter Sunday of the following year, 'a Pasqua di Risurexo'.[5]

Michelangelo's own letter of late December 1518 was written in reply to one from Leonardo Sellaio in Rome. He explains that the marble block has reached Pisa, which goes far to confirm that it had been held up by the blockade of the Carrarese. But a new obstacle has emerged. The same lack of rain that has prevented the wood arriving to roof his new workshop has meant that much of his marble cannot be transported up the Arno. The block for the commission will be among the first to arrive, but he feels unable to reply to Vari's letters until he can begin work. He writes that he is dying of shame and that he has become a swindler against his will.[6]

Further, increasingly urgent, letters were written by Vari in the spring of 1519. Evidently losing faith in the provision of a new statue, he goes so far as to propose that Michelangelo should at least finish the one that is in Rome.[7] In another letter of April, Vari reminds him that the extension of time achieved through the intervention of Cardinal Giulio expires in May; if the statue is not in a state to be dispatched, he should write to the cardinal for a further prolongation. Writing again a day later, he again proposes that the flawed statue in Rome should be completed.[8]

At some point in the course of 1519 Michelangelo did begin the new statue. There is no written record of when this happened; all we know is that Vari would write in January 1520 to inform the artist that he has heard from Leonardo Sellaio that the figure is close to completion.[9]

The rediscovery of the earlier abandoned statue has demonstrated that, despite the constraints of the new enterprise of the chapel at San Lorenzo and the need to satisfy Cardinal Leonardo della Rovere over the papal tomb, Michelangelo did not choose the easier option of repeating his earlier intervention. He began all over again.[10] The new statue of Christ is conceived in a much more heroic form than its predecessor. The contrast could serve to rebut the accusation levelled against him in Lodovico Dolce's *Dialogo della Pittura*, that to see one figure of Michelangelo's is to see them all.[11] One of the drawings made in preparation for the new conception was drawn over a small ground plan relating to the projected new chapel at San Lorenzo.[12]

Michelangelo must have worked with extraordinary dedication on the new *Christ* during 1519. But further delays would follow and here the artist was himself implicated. The carving was substantially finished by early March 1520. The news was communicated to the parties in Rome by Michelangelo himself in a letter now lost. Vari replied on 24 March, acknowledging the fact of the outstanding 50 ducats. But here a problem arose. Vari's fellow heir of Marta Porcari, Pietro Paolo Castellani, had recently died and his executor refused to pay Castellani's half share of the sum required. Vari informed the artist of his difficulties but begged him to send the statue to Rome, notwithstanding the delay over payment.[13] In a further letter, he writes that he will take upon himself the payment of all 50 ducats outstanding, if Castellani's executor refuses to collaborate. He again urges Michelangelo to dispatch the statue.[14]

The artist did not comply. Sellaio would urge him not to send the sculpture until he had been paid. In the meantime, he cannot have been gratified to hear from Sebastiano that a rumour was circulating in Rome that the statue had been carved not by him but by Pietro Urbano.[15] Finally, from a letter of Vari's of January 1521, we learn that the money was finally on its way; the heirs of Castellani had agreed to contribute their share. He again urges that the statue be sent so that it can be installed at Easter.[16] A *ricordo* of Pietro Urbano shows that he had supervised the loading of the statue at Pisa by 12 March. Entrusted by Michelangelo with the installation of the statue, Pietro set off for Rome, travelling by land.[17]

Michelangelo's stubbornness over the issue of the final payment could be seen as another case of his financial avarice. But this would be manifestly unjust. He had, in reality, bought two marble blocks and carved two statues – or had begun one and completed another – for the price that had been agreed in 1514 for one. Other expenses, which could not have been foreseen, followed from the fact that the second carving had been undertaken in Florence rather than in Rome. The block, undoubtedly excavated at Carrara, had been transported to Florence, only with delays beyond the artist's control. After the statue had been completed, the work had to be returned to Pisa in order to be shipped to Rome.

The contract of 1514 had stipulated that while the socle or base of the statue was the artist's responsibility, the overall setting was to be paid for by the heirs.[18] The latter issue had begun to engage the artist well before the work was dispatched and, characteristically, he chose a Florentine working in Rome to undertake the surround. His choice was a little-known sculptor called Federigo Frizzi, whom Michelangelo seems to have regarded as dependable, for he had recommended him to Piero Soderini in 1518 to help with the project in San Silvestro in Capite.[19]

Frizzi thanked Michelangelo for recommending him in a letter of 10 March; he has heard that the statue is finished. Armed with the work's measurements, he has attended a meeting with those concerned in Santa Maria sopra Minerva to discuss the location of the statue. It seems that Marta Porcari had wished that her altar should be located in the left transept. Frizzi has objected to the poor light there and has proposed a column or pilaster in the nave. He has succeeded in persuading the heirs and adds that he will construct only a shallow niche, to allow the statue greater visibility. In the end, the site chosen for aedicule, statue and altar was against the pier to the left of the entrance to the choir, in an arrangement destroyed in the nineteenth century but recorded in a drawing. The episode is striking for the emphasis given to concerns of visibility even when these may have conflicted with patronal wishes.[20]

If the setback involving the earlier version of the *Christ* might suggest that the enterprise was born under an unlucky star, the history of the artist's replacement would go some way to confirm the suspicion. The statue's arrival in Rome was much delayed by protracted bad weather. After it had arrived at the Ripa, it was subjected to customs duty, a *gabella*, before being allowed to proceed any further, an action that aroused outrage in Michelangelo's circle.[21] Pietro Urbano would himself contribute to the ill fortune of the enterprise. Trusted to put the very final touches to the statue, he succeeded in inflicting substantial damage which the painstaking Frizzi had to do his best to make good.[22] But the young man would give cause also for other concerns. Letters to Michelangelo from his Roman circle would describe how Urbano, unmindful of the artist's instructions on his earlier journey to Rome, had thrown himself into a life of self-indulgence and even crime. Weeks later, he would leave Rome for Naples and would effectively disappear from Michelangelo's life.[23]

Michelangelo's deep mortification over what had happened to the statue led him to remarkable gestures towards Vari. He acceded, it seems without demur, in meeting the patron's request that he be given the first, abandoned, version of the statue, which had remained locked away at Macel de' Corvi since 1516.[24] The work was handed over to him in January 1522, despite the hard-headed Sellaio's resistance to the move. Metello was anxious to have the work on view to quell ugly rumours and to make public the artist's generosity in making a new one.[25] He planned to install it in a renovated courtyard at one of his houses where, as already mentioned, it would be carefully recorded by Aldrovandi soon after 1550. But Michelangelo went even further and offered to make a third statue for his patron. This gesture led to renewed protests from members of his Roman circle and Sellaio went as far as to try to keep such generosity concealed from Vari.[26]

On another issue, Michelangelo would be much less accommodating. Vari would repeatedly ask him for a receipt for the money that had been sent to Florence; he needed this to settle affairs with Castellani's heirs. For years Michelangelo did nothing, and it was not until 1532, more than ten years after the statue had been installed, that the artist finally responded.[27]

In doing so, he evidently asked Vari for a written declaration that he had received the statue and was satisfied with it. Vari's written acknowledgement the artist carefully preserved. Dated 1 June 1532, he refers to the statue as nude and as representing Our Lord's resurrection, 'una figura innuda de relevo tonna, che fa la resiretione de Nostro Signore Iesu Cristo'.[28]

The Minerva *Christ* has been frequently referred to by modern art historians as a Man of Sorrows. Yet a number of the attributes associated with that subject are conspicuously absent. And Vari's own reference points to what should be described in modern terminology as a Risen Christ, a *Cristo Risorto*. To characterize the statue we see in the church, one of almost Apollonian beauty, as a Man of Sorrows is, in effect, to accuse Michelangelo of artistic ineptitude.[29]

The story of the Minerva *Christ* is one of repeated setbacks. And to its troubled history there must be added yet a further misfortune. Only a few years after its installation, the statue was vandalized.[30] Nevertheless, its fame was rapidly established; just over twenty years later, it would be described as a marvel to behold.[31] And Francis I would write to the artist himself, asking, among a number of favours, permission to have a cast made, to be brought to France.[32] The statue prompts a further reflection. It was the first work in marble that Michelangelo had brought to completion since the dispatch of the *Virgin and Child* to the Netherlands more than fifteen years earlier.

TWO DEATHS

Raphael died on Good Friday, 6 April 1520. Writing to Michelangelo six days later, Sebastiano del Piombo reports the news, although he presumes that his friend has already heard it.[33] Although Sebastiano does not refer to the fact, news had reached Rome that, once again, Michelangelo was himself ill in Florence. The reports proved to be untrue.[34]

One of the many consequences of Raphael's unexpected death was to raise Sebastiano's hopes that he might inherit some of the projected undertakings in the Vatican, above all the decoration of the Sala di Costantino. Much of the letter of 12 April is concerned with the issue. He is anxious that Michelangelo intervene on his behalf with Cardinal Giulio, who had returned to Florence in February to take control of the city. He warns Michelangelo that one of Raphael's assistants is on his way to Florence in order to obtain the projected commissions from the cardinal.[35]

This was not the only favour that Sebastiano had sought from his absent friend in recent months. The problem of payment for the *Raising of Lazarus* had arisen in the last days of 1519. Since there had evidently been no formal contract, Cardinal Giulio had suggested that Michelangelo should decide on the remuneration; Sebastiano points out that he had seen the painting at an earlier stage, and reminds him that there are no less than forty figures in the painting, excluding those in the landscape. Baldassare Peruzzi had been called in and had recommended payment of the enormous sum of 850 ducats, but Sebastiano was prepared to accept 800. The problem dragged on for months and it remains unclear whether Michelangelo got involved.[36]

There can be no doubt, however, that he did so over the issue of commissions in the Vatican, although his only known intervention took a singular form. A draft of a letter written on behalf of Sebastiano's claims survives, and the text that went to Rome is referred to in a letter of Sebastiano's own of 3 July. This shows that Michelangelo had written to Cardinal Bibbiena, with whom, as has been seen, his relations were, at best, uneasy.[37]

The text of the draft is very eccentric. In it, Michelangelo refers to himself as a man of no significance. He declares that he is poor and mad, but asks that Sebastiano be awarded a share of the work. He writes that, even if His Lordship thinks the favour would be thrown away, in favouring the mad some pleasure may be found, as when one turns to a diet of onions after a surfeit of capons. He, Bibbiena, is for ever granting favours to men of real account. Michelangelo proposes that he try a change with him, concluding by praising Sebastiano's competence.[38]

In adopting a tone of mock self-abasement, the artist was indulging with great skill in a form of humour of which Bibbiena himself was a highly accomplished exponent. The cardinal would, for example, on occasion sign his letters 'Moccicone', the sniveller; other self-mocking forms of signature are frequent. And it was Bibbiena who was entrusted with the leading role in Book II of Castiglione's *Il Cortegiano*, a long exchange about many kinds of jokes.[39] We know from Sebastiano's letter of 3 July that Michelangelo's had provoked general merriment at the Curia and had been the chief topic of conversation.

Sebastiano continued to agitate at the court for months. His letters demonstrate his hatred of Raphael's pupils, whom he describes as acting like demigods. They also reveal his belief that any chance of his gaining work in the Sala di Costantino would depend on Michelangelo's advocacy; he may even have hoped for drawings. Pope Leo can never have seriously considered Sebastiano for the Sala, but seems to have found the whole situation difficult to cope with.

It is in his letter of 15 October that we find Sebastiano's account of how Leo regarded Michelangelo. All painters have learnt from him, including Raphael. But the artist is 'teribile' and is impossible to work with.[40] In a further letter of two weeks later, Sebastiano again reverts to Leo's attitude to him. He has spoken of him near to tears, describing Michelangelo as a brother and recalling that he and the artist had been brought up together. He is devoted to him, but Michelangelo frightens everyone, even popes.[41]

The pope's words, conveyed to Michelangelo in Sebastiano's letters, are the most candid that have been recorded of any of his papal patrons. *Terribile* has a number of meanings in Italian. But Sebastiano's second letter suggests that Leo's employment of it refers to the artist's sheer intractability.[42] Recent developments, such as the elimination of Baccio d'Agnolo and Jacopo Sansovino, could well have distressed the pope, despite the fact that both he and Cardinal Giulio had extended great latitude to the artist over the façade. However badly Alberico Malaspina had behaved in 1518, his recorded remark, that Michelangelo always wanted to fight with people, may have evoked a sympathetic response in Leo. Increasingly, it would be left to Cardinal Giulio to handle the artist, although the death of Cardinal Leonardo Grosso della Rovere created a crisis that Leo could not ignore.

Cardinal Leonardo died on 27 September 1520. He had recovered from a serious illness in December 1518, and, to judge from contemporary reactions, his death had not been expected. Michelangelo seems first to have heard of the loss in a message of Buoninsegni, written on the day he died.[43]

His death would prove a disaster for the artist. Cousin of the dead Julius, it seems to have been his concern over the tomb project that provided the real hope that something would be accomplished, for, although it had been Cardinal Pucci who had been responsible for the earlier instalments of payment, he makes no appearance in the correspondence. Cardinal Leonardo's mounting anxiety over the delay in implementing the contract of 1516 is evident from his letters to the artist. Nevertheless, the tone is unfailingly warm and his solicitude over Michelangelo's grave illness in the autumn of 1518 was clearly not prompted by simple self-interest. In a letter of 23 October 1518, he alludes to a promise from the artist to undertake two new statues.[44] By the following December he was beset with anxiety about the blockade of the marble at Carrara and it was at this moment that he fell seriously ill.[45]

By early 1519 he had been assured by Jacopo Salviati, now resident in Rome, that during the coming summer Michelangelo would execute four statues.[46] This, together with further promises from the artist's Roman friends, seems to have allayed his anxiety. His closest aide, Francesco Pallavicini, was on his way to Florence in the summer of 1519, but there is no record of what he found in the new workshop on the Via Mozza. It is unlikely that the artist had done much to carry out what Salviati had promised for he was, at this very time, engaged in carving the second statue of *Christ* for an increasingly desperate Metello Vari. Only as late as February 1522, in a letter of Leonardo Sellaio, do we find a reference to the statues that had been promised by Jacopo Salviati; Sellaio, writing from Rome, exhorts Michelangelo to press on with 'those nudes', in his own words 'chotesti ingnudi'.[47] This neglected remark must refer to two or, perhaps, all four *Prigioni* or *Slaves* now in the Accademia in Florence (pls 34, 35). Sellaio had been in Florence in the autumn of 1520, after the Minerva statue had been completed, and his words seem to imply that he had seen the beginning of work on them.[48] The condition of the four incomplete sculptures in the Accademia, destined for the front of the pope's tomb and still in the Via Mozza workshop in 1564, shows the failure of the artist to follow his devoted friend's urging. Work for the Medici would intervene.[49]

Cardinal Leonardo's death left the della Rovere without their most committed advocate in Rome. Contemporary report stated that he had left no directions for future steps regarding the project and, indeed, he seems to have died intestate. Time was now running out; the contract made in 1516 had stipulated completion of the whole monument by 1522. Urged to come to Rome, Michelangelo did not move.

Sebastiano's letter of late October, quoted earlier, not only reported Pope Leo's view of Michelangelo, it also described his dilemma and his incapacity to resolve the issue of competing claims. On the one hand, he was not prepared to countenance delay to the new Medicean projects under way in Florence, while on the other, he was unwilling to abet a formal halt to the tomb project.[50] Accepting commissions he should have refused, the artist was caught up in the conflict between della Rovere and Medici interests, a conflict that would take a new turn, much more threatening to himself, when Leo died in December of the following year.

An immediate issue that arose was the future of the property at Macel de' Corvi. Owned by the della Rovere, the contract of 1516 had permitted Michelangelo to live there until the agreement reached its term in 1522. Following the cardinal's death, it seems that Michelangelo planned to make a formal appeal to Pope Leo but was dissuaded by his Roman friends, who thought it more prudent to remain silent. From the correspondence, it appears that the pope was disposed to make over the property to the artist but did not do so, because the problem re-emerged in 1524.[51] Macel de' Corvi would then become a pawn in the bargaining that would proceed between the della Rovere, the Curia and the embattled artist.

FAMILY DISCORD

Economic adversity is rarely absent from the letters of Lodovico and the artist's brothers in the period following his return to Florence in 1516. But worse was to come. In the agreement that had established the family wool business in early 1514, it had been stipulated that Michelangelo was at liberty to claim the return of the 1,000 florins he had invested, after a lapse of ten years, if he so wished. At some point prior to the deadline in January 1524, he had decided to exercise his right.

His relations with Lodovico had been bad for some time. In February 1521 there had been a furious row between father and son; Lodovico had left Via Ghibellina for the family house at Settignano and had spread word that he had been thrown out by Michelangelo. What is known about the quarrel comes from a letter from the artist subsequently written to his father, shortly before he was due to leave for Carrara to superintend marble supplies for the New Sacristy. He expresses his utter amazement over what Lodovico has been saying, rebuts the charges but, at the same time, asks for his pardon if he feels he has been badly treated.[52] He asks Lodovico to return to Via Ghibellina for a meeting. If an elusive note of Lodovico's is to be believed, he had been met with blows.[53]

Where the truth lay in this extraordinary episode seems impossible to establish. A stray comment of Michelangelo's suggests that Pietro Urbano, soon to leave for his ill-fated work on the Minerva *Christ* in Rome, may have been involved. A year later, however, needing a week in Florence, Lodovico would ask Gismondo to find him accommodation, which suggests an unwillingness to stay in the Via Ghibellina. In this letter, Lodovico paints a rather poignant picture of his condition. He wishes to put all his affairs in order since he feels he has not long to live. He expresses the wish to die in Florence rather than Settignano. The letter is dated 26 November 1522. Lodovico was now seventy-eight years old.[54]

From a few weeks later, there survives another letter of Lodovico's, addressed to Michelangelo.[55] Its contents suggest that, already by this date, the artist had resolved to call in what he felt he was owed. The letter suggests that Lodovico was in an agitated state, fearful of contracting the plague that, at this moment, was endangering the populations of both Rome and Florence. He dwells on his physical frailty, and proceeds to authorize Michelangelo to sell a sufficient number of his Monte shares to pay off what he owes him for help in reaching the settlement with Cassandra Bartoli in 1509. He repeatedly asks his son to forgive any wrongs he has committed. Yet, in the very same letter, he lies about what he had been compelled to spend to reach the 1509 agreement. This had stipulated a payment on Lodovico's part of 196 florins. He now informs Michelangelo that it had cost him 700.

In reaching his decision to demand the return of the substantial sum he had loaned his father and brothers in 1514, Michelangelo may well have been prompted by fears that the family business might collapse and that his investment would be irretrievably lost. In deciding to act, it could be argued that he was confirming a bitter judgement passed on him by Lodovico years earlier, that Michelangelo wanted what he had for himself.[56] Yet it should be recalled that his purchase of the properties in Via Ghibellina as long ago as 1508 had served, almost exclusively, to benefit his father and brothers. Between the date of the purchase and his return to Florence in 1516, his own presence there could, at most, be counted in terms of weeks, on hasty trips from Rome.[57]

Despite the spectacular wealth constituted by the numerous properties that he had acquired in and around Florence, at just this moment Michelangelo may have been anxious about his financial situation on a score that has been overlooked. His security was now threatened by a restored Francesco Maria della Rovere, who was no longer confronted by an implacable enemy in Rome after Pope Leo's death in December 1521. The consequences can be returned to later. At this point, it is enough to note that, by the spring of 1523, Michelangelo would inform one of his most dependable friends that he might be confronted with financial penalties for his failure to honour his obligations to the della Rovere family for Julius's tomb.[58]

The artist's claim for the return of his money precipitated something of a family crisis. His determination to proceed was, no doubt, fortified by the fear that, if Lodovico died intestate, his estate would be divided among the four brothers and Michelangelo could run into serious problems in regaining what he was owed.[59] This amounted to the 1,000 florins he had put into the family business in 1514 and a further 200 florins to reimburse what he had paid out to settle Cassandra Bartoli's claim in 1509. His request for payment revealed that, even acting together, father and three sons could not find the money. Consequently, family arbitrators were agreed on and a contract drawn up on 16 June 1523. It was established that Lodovico's estate, comprising the family home at Settignano, his effects and his Monte holdings, should be valued at 2,200 florins. It was laid down that Michelangelo was to become legal owner of the Settignano house, of its contents, and of Lodovico's Monte credits. It was stipulated, however, that Lodovico could occupy the house for his lifetime and could enjoy the income from the Monte up to his death.[60]

Suffering from acute old age anxiety, Lodovico believed that he had been deprived of his possessions and Monte income. Two letters addressed to him by Michelangelo survive from the days following the agreement; both are harsh, the second one even brutal in explaining the implications of the contract.[61] It would take a series of letters from one of the arbitrators to quieten the old man.[62]

The most immediate consequence of the events of the summer of 1523 would be the dispersion of the family. Lodovico retired to the house at Settignano. Buonarroto also moved out. Perhaps rueful over the break-up, Michelangelo is quoted in August as confessing to a sense of complete isolation; he feels he no longer has a father or brothers or anyone else in the world to count on.[63] A year later, he himself would move to a house close to San Lorenzo; the rent would be met by Pope Clement.[64] How long it took the family wounds to heal is difficult to establish. There are no letters now surviving from Michelangelo to Lodovico or vice versa for some time. Three years later the son would be sending gifts to his father at Settignano, and the death of Buonarroto in October 1528 would prompt Michelangelo once more to act as the family's mainstay.

WORKING FOR CARDINAL GIULIO

The building of the New Sacristy and a library at San Lorenzo had been decided on when Cardinal Giulio had his discreet conversation with Figiovanni in the family palace in June 1519. Giulio had used the plural 'we' when discussing the new undertakings, and it cannot be excluded that the decision had been made in Rome before the death of Duke Lorenzo on 4 May.[65] The event, feared for many months, provoked deep concern about the stability of the Medicean regime, and brought Giulio back to Florence less than two months after he had returned to Rome, in late February.[66] As the cardinal explained to Figiovanni, provision was to be made for the fitting burial of four Medici dead, the two recently deceased dukes and the fathers of Pope Leo and himself.[67] Inevitably, given the circumstances, the burial chapel took precedence.[68]

Figiovanni's own reference to Michelangelo as *capomaestro* of the work is notoriously unflattering, a reflection of the troubles he would endure with the artist; Job, he states, would not have had patience with him for a single day.[69] Yet, despite the setbacks that had dogged the project for the façade, the patrons' faith in Michelangelo had survived. It appears that Cardinal Giulio did not share Pope Leo's misgivings about the artist's personality; on the contrary, he seems to have viewed him with warmth and understanding. As has been seen, he had been ready to intervene in the crisis provoked by the delays in the delivery of the second statue for Santa Maria sopra Minerva. And it seems telling that, while the patrons were prepared to spend around 50,000 ducats, a sum greater than that agreed for the façade, for the sacristy and the library, they do not seem to have felt it necessary to draw up a formal contract for the new undertakings.[70] Nevertheless, Figiovanni's memorandum shows that Cardinal Giulio now insisted on a strict record of expenses; he was no longer willing to tolerate the chaotic financial arrangements that had been employed for the façade. Figiovanni declined to handle the money himself, although he did keep books that were subsequently destroyed.[71] The role of paymaster was initially given to the cardinal's chamberlain, Bernardo Niccolini, who had played a part in the financing of the façade. He was later to be replaced by Giovanni Spina, much to Michelangelo's satisfaction.[72]

Although the new projects had been agreed on by the two cousins, pope and cardinal, circumstances would create a situation where Cardinal Giulio would come to play an almost exclusive role as patron. This was a consequence of his repeated presence in Florence, where he was needed to shore up the fragile Medicean regime.[73] But his leading role as patron of the chapel reflected a more general accession of power that he came to enjoy. His ever greater accumulation of authority was remarked on by observers at the papal court. By 1517 it was recorded that he had effectively supplanted Bibbiena as Leo's closest confidant.[74] In June 1520 one well-informed Venetian envoy would report that, although in no way threatening the pope's authority, everything passed through his hands.[75]

For his part, Michelangelo seems to have developed a confidence in the cardinal that survived the crisis provoked by the suspension of the façade. Already in 1518, beset by problems, he had declared himself to be the cardinal's man.[76] Mutual respect would grow ever stronger in the coming years, and the surviving exchanges between them after Giulio's election as pope is one of the most extraordinary records of partnership of patron and artist to have survived. Adding a personal postscript to a letter addressed to the artist in December 1525, Giulio, now Pope Clement VII, would address Michelangelo not as 'voi' but with the intimate 'tu'.[77]

It is not known when the paths of the artist and Giulio de' Medici first crossed. Giulio was three years younger. He had been born out of wedlock in May 1478, just a month after his father, Giuliano di Piero, had been murdered by the Pazzi conspirators. A persistent but unsubstantiated tradition would claim that the newly born child was entrusted to the care of Antonio da Sangallo the Elder, younger brother of Giuliano da Sangallo.[78] True or not, the mature Giulio would come to display an understanding of architects' and artists' requirements unmatched among patrons of his time.[79] Now that it has been confirmed that the young Michelangelo worked for Piero de' Medici after the death of Lorenzo the Magnificent, an early acquaintance between Giulio and the artist becomes more plausible.

The exceptional authority that Giulio de' Medici enjoyed by the time he became de facto ruler of Florence in 1519 had been favoured by two events years earlier, the Medicean restoration in September 1512 and his cousin's election as pope in March 1513. A further stroke of good fortune had been the death of the incumbent archbishop of Florence, Cosimo Pazzi, in April 1513. One of Leo's first acts was to appoint Giulio as his successor. He was created a cardinal in Leo's first creation in September.

His subsequent accumulation of preferments was exceptional. On the death of Sisto della Rovere in March 1517, he was appointed Vice-Chancellor of the Church. Following the alleged cardinals' plot to murder Pope Leo, the great palace of Raffaello Riario, the artist's first Roman patron, was seized. The seat of the chancery was removed to this palace. In the events that followed, Giulio was given San Lorenzo in Damaso, within the palace complex, as his titular church and the palace itself was henceforth known as the Cancelleria. It would remain Giulio's residence in Rome until his election as pope in November 1523.[80]

Inevitably, many of the judgements passed on Giulio de' Medici were deeply coloured by the disaster that shattered his pontificate in 1527. For Guicciardini, he was a supreme example of the fickleness of fortune. Another Florentine recorded, but found it difficult to explain, the passage from his greatness as a cardinal to his loss of reputation as pope.[81] A third witness, Bartolommeo Cerretani, wrote a perceptive appreciation of his character in the years we are concerned with here, emphasizing his wisdom, patience and pertinacity.[82] Many years later, Michelangelo would pay his own tribute to Giulio de' Medici.[83]

The early building history of the New Sacristy cannot be written; much important evidence is missing. In part, our lack of information owes to Cardinal Giulio's repeated presence in Florence, which has robbed us of the kind of exchange of letters that survives for the façade and, later, for the library. Many of the early decisions were, no doubt, made in discussion between patron and artist. It is not known, for example, when the initial intention to create a replica of the Old Sacristy was dropped. The decision may have been urged on Giulio by the artist, who, in his first written reference to the chapel that survives, refers to his intention to diverge from the form of tomb in the centre of the earlier building.

A feature of the New Sacristy is the notorious discrepancy between interior and exterior, most obtrusively evident at the level of the exterior drum. To explain these anomalies, it has been proposed that, during construction, there was a change in the design of the elevation, a proposal that has been contested.[84]

Nothing more is heard about the chapel project for many months. Cardinal Giulio had left for Rome in October and the artist must have devoted much of his time during the autumn of 1519 to working on the second statue of *Christ*, which was near completion in early 1520. As already noted, he was reported to be ill in April 1520.

It was in the month that the cardinal left for Rome that Michelangelo, assuming a rare public role, became involved in an attempt to have the remains of Dante brought home from Ravenna to Florence. Some attempt to achieve this had been made four years earlier, in 1515, and both the earlier one and the renewed attempt now in 1519 were the initiatives of the Sacred Medicean Academy, a body of Florentines that had been granted a charter and a modest annual subvention by Pope Leo. It was to Leo that both appeals were addressed. Of the twenty

signatories of the petition of 1519, a number were members of a conspicuous group that met regularly in the gardens of the Rucellai,
known as the Orti Oricellari, to discuss philosophical, literary and
political issues. Michelangelo certainly knew some members of the
group, but whether he himself took part in their meetings, as has been
proposed, remains doubtful.[85]

His own submission stands apart from the others. Unlike these,
written in Latin, Michelangelo, with his determination to adhere to
the vernacular, composed his in Italian and, after expressing his wish,
went on to offer his willingness to execute the tomb of the Divine
Poet in an honourable location in the city.[86] His devotion to the poet,
whose work he had studied with Gianfrancesco Aldrovandi in Bologna
a quarter of a century earlier, could scarcely have prompted a more
deeply felt expression of homage. But the request by the Florentines
had no effect in Rome, and Dante's remains would rest in Ravenna,
in the mausoleum commissioned from Pietro Lombardo in 1483.

Cardinal Giulio returned to Florence in February 1520, the month
when the façade project seems to have been formally suspended. As a
consequence, issues concerning the new chapel could be discussed
personally with the artist. But at some point before leaving for Rome
in November, he entrusted a further project to Michelangelo, to
design windows for Palazzo Medici on Via Larga, the celebrated
'kneeling windows' or *finestre inginocchiate*. The project sprang from a
decision on the cardinal's part to close a loggia at the southern corner
of Michelozzo's palace. Two windows were to be substituted for the
fifteenth-century loggia's arched openings and a third added to replace
a doorway on the main façade. These windows would become one
of Michelangelo's most imitated works, their form repeated with vari-
ations everywhere in Florence (pl. 36).[87]

The windows have, for the most part, been dated to 1516 or 1517.
This is, however, a misunderstanding of Vasari's passage about the
project in the second edition of the *Vite* of 1568. He states that
Michelangelo undertook them when he returned to Florence, but the
context shows that he is referring not to the return from Rome in

1516, but to that from Seravezza, where he had laboured to gather marble for the San Lorenzo façade.[88]

This implies a date of 1519 or 1520. The later is the likelier. Vasari states that Michelangelo made a model for the windows, information likely to be correct, for he would himself be employed in this very area of the Palazzo Medici in the first half of the 1530s. It is probable that it is this model that is referred to by Domenico Buoninsegni in two letters addressed to the artist in December 1520. From them, we learn that the model has been undertaken at the cardinal's request. And in the later of the two, dated 28 December, he reports that Giulio is delighted to hear that the model has been finished, although he is not yet certain where it is to go.[89]

That the windows were constructed in the first half of 1521 is a conclusion strengthened by the further fact that plans for decorating the interior space were being made in September. The work would be undertaken by Giovanni da Udine, so esteemed by the cardinal, but, for reasons unknown, he did not complete it. In April 1522 Giovanni da Udine, now in Venice, would write to Michelangelo in the warmest terms, adding his regards to Piloto, a friend of Michelangelo involved in the project. For it was to him that the master entrusted the execution, on his design, of the celebrated metal gratings, now lost, to cover the windows.[90]

The design of the windows is one of great boldness. But an even greater ambition is found in the surviving drawings made at about the same time for the *ballatoio* of Florence cathedral. The move to involve Michelangelo probably came from Cardinal Giulio, and the artist responded, perhaps spurred on by the memory of his invitation to make a drawing for the project as long ago as 1507. Vasari describes Michelangelo's involvement in his Life of Baccio d'Agnolo of 1568. He states that he reached the stage of making a model, which was much discussed in Cardinal Giulio's presence.[91] He gives no date, but the evidence of writing on the two sheets of drawings involved suggests a date of 1519–20.[92] Some of the artist's sketches even go so far as to show him contemplating replacing Brunelleschi's drum altogether with a radically revised design of his own. It could well have been the alarming implications of his thoughts that led to the abandonment of the project. All that we see today is Baccio d'Agnolo's fragment facing the Via del Proconsolo. Nevertheless, Michelangelo did not forget the experience, and some of his thoughts for the project in Florence cathedral would re-emerge decades later when he turned to the challenge of the cupola of St Peter's.[93]

THE MEDICI CHAPEL

In one of the summary ground plans that the artist had drawn at some point in 1519 for the funerary chapel in San Lorenzo, he had briefly indicated wall tombs. They are not, however, the four that Cardinal Giulio had discussed with Figiovanni in May, but five. This suggests that, even at an early stage, the cardinal was not excluding the idea of having his own tomb included, close to that of his murdered father.

The idea re-emerges in the early correspondence about the tombs, exchanges prompted by the return of Giulio to Rome. The cardinal wrote to Michelangelo on 28 November 1520, in reply to a letter of the artist's of which only a fragmentary draft has survived.[94] The artist had evidently proposed relinquishing wall tombs in favour of a new idea, a monumental sepulchre in the centre of the chapel that would house the dead. These followed an interesting exchange of views, in which the patron expressed his concern that such a solution would crowd the chapel space. He himself proposed a central monument based on the antique form of an *arcus quadrifons*, which would include his own tomb in the centre. Throughout, however, he repeatedly expresses his readiness to let the artist decide.[95]

The idea of a centralized tomb would be abandoned. But this did not happen before Michelangelo had made a number of striking designs for such a monument, some of which included figurative sculpture. The series forms just a part of an astonishingly rich surviving group of drawings for tomb designs. Probably made in a relatively brief span of time, the group reveals an almost inexhaustible wealth of ideas that none of his fellow sculptors could have rivalled in a working lifetime.[96]

At some point in the genesis of the tombs, Cardinal Giulio abandoned the idea of his own inclusion in the project, leaving Michelangelo to confront the issue of planning tombs for the two dukes and two *magnifici* on three walls; he chose the solution of a single ducal tomb on each lateral wall and a double tomb for the entrance wall that abutted the church. He opted for this only after having also experimented with a double tomb on each of the side walls. The final decision is likely to have been discussed with his patron in person, for Cardinal Giulio was back in Florence on 2 February 1521.

The design of the tombs, and many of the carved figures envisaged for them, must have been settled before the artist left for Carrara in early April. On 9 April he recorded that he had received 200 ducats from Buoninsegni, who was acting for the cardinal; the purpose of the trip, to commission marble, is expressly stated.[97] Accompanied by a stone cutter from Settignano, he may have left on the same day. He remained there for just under three weeks, making measured drawings of the blocks he needed and contracting with two different companies for their supply.[98]

Michelangelo had not been to Carrara for over three years. No longer do we hear of Medicean insistence on his confining himself to supplies from Pietrasanta, despite all the investment of money and time that had been made in establishing access to the quarries above Serravezza. Repeatedly, Cardinal Giulio insists on speed and there can be no doubt that he had learnt from the setbacks incurred in the supply of stone for the façade that Michelangelo's judgement over the best source for his materials deserved respect.

Recent events could have confirmed this. In the previous December news had reached Rome that Francesco del Lucchesino, widely known as Cecchino, who had been asked to supply the sandstone, *macigno*, for the interior of the chapel in October 1519, had been implicated in the breaking of a column at Seravezza, destined for the façade.[99]

Michelangelo's absence at Pietrasanta must have contributed to the hold-up in the construction of the sacristy. He was back in Florence in January 1521, when the stone that had been contracted for the autumn of 1519 was reordered; this delay had evidently held up progress on the *pietra serena* membering of the lower level of the interior. By April this work was well under way.[100]

Events in Florence after Michelangelo's departure for Carrara once more indicated his reluctance to deputize. A problem arose over how the entrance from the church into the sacristy should be constructed. He had placed overall supervision of the building work in the hands of Stefano di Tommaso Lunetti, a man whose activities ranged from book illumination to building.[101] He wrote to Michelangelo on 20 April, explaining that no one knew how the entrance was to be constructed. The problem had brought Buoninsegni himself to the church and it had become clear that it could not be designed along the lines of the entrance to Brunelleschi's sacristy.[102]

Stefano had been summoned to the cardinal's presence, and the latter insisted that none of the cornices of the lowest order of the chapel be put in place in Michelangelo's absence. A further letter was written by a man who would come to play a crucial role in the artist's life in the next few years, Giovan Francesco Fattucci, one of the chaplains attached to the cathedral and a man who enjoyed the cardinal's closest confidence. He reports that the cardinal has emphasized that not a stone be built without Michelangelo's approbation. Further, no building material is to be used without the artist's personal approval.[103]

Cardinal Giulio's demand for speed would not be met. Despite Michelangelo's restored relations with the marble workers at Carrara, things would move very slowly. Why this happened is never fully spelt out, but the artist's dissatisfaction with the slow progress prompted a second trip to Carrara; it is likely that the *garzone* he had left there to keep an eye on the work had a negative report. The artist was also being kept informed by the ever dependable Donato Benti. In a letter from him of 7 July 1521, we learn that Cardinal Giulio had appointed him to oversee quarrying operations on Michelangelo's recommendation. He is grateful for the honour and expresses his warmest thanks but, at the same time, requests that he be paid.[104]

A *ricordo* of the artist's shows that he made a second visit to the quarries at Carrara in July. He stayed there for nine days but refused to give any further money to the Carraresi because they had not carried out his instructions.[105] This second visit seems to have had some effect, for members of the two companies who had contracted to deliver marble came to Florence in August. They were each handed a further 30 ducats, but we are given no further details.[106]

In the following month, there was better news. Writing to the artist from Carrara on 24 September, the team headed by Jacopo Pollina reports that the figures, 'le figure', have been quarried and they are now engaged in rough hewing them into shape. They assure him that work will continue on obtaining the other pieces that he had ordered in April.[107]

On the other hand, progress made by the other company that had been entrusted with supplies seems to have been poor. They wrote to Michelangelo on 11 November, seemingly stung by an angry letter of remonstrance from him, which had been sent to the Medici agent at Pietrasanta, Galeotto de' Medici, by no less than Silvio Passerini, who had been created cardinal by Pope Leo in 1517 and who would assume control of the city from 1524. They claimed to have six *charrate* of marble to hand but attribute delays to bad weather.[108]

The company complained of lack of payment and this would become a constant note in the correspondence relating to the supply of marble in this period. In a letter sent to Buoninsegni in the late summer of 1521, Michelangelo himself, while stressing his absolute devotion to the cardinal, points to a lack of money for the ongoing expenses. Persistent complaints from the marble workers at Carrara lend credence to what he writes.[109] Problems continued throughout the autumn and, in an attempt to improve matters, the ever faithful Topolino was dispatched to Carrara in November.[110]

Medici funding may have suffered because of the cost of the war against the French in Lombardy, in which Cardinal Giulio was personally involved. A further adverse event was the completely unexpected death of Pope Leo at the age of forty-five in December 1521. His death precipitated a financial crisis in the papal city because of the enormous debts he had accumulated. Guicciardini would write that he would be immortalized by their scale.[111]

Progress on the construction of the sacristy cannot be followed in detail because there is a lack of evidence. The first *ricordi* of the artist relating to the ongoing work date from February 1524, when work began to prepare the interior of the cupola for coffering in stucco.[112] In a letter of 30 January from Fattucci in Rome, he had referred to the patron's wish to see what Michelangelo intended for the coffering, and a drawing of the artist's, almost certainly made with this request in mind, has survived.[113] A little later, Michelangelo would write to his patron. Addressed no longer to Giulio as cardinal but as pope, he informs him that the chapel's lantern has been completed under the supervision of Stefano Lunetti and has been greeted with universal approbation. The ball that would crown the lantern is in the process of being made by Piloto, Michelangelo's friend who had made the grilles for the windows of Palazzo Medici. With an implicit allusion to his patron's wish for 'fantasia', he adds that, to distinguish it from others, it will be faceted.[114]

Work on the tombs seems to have lagged. This may have been a consequence of slowness in the delivery of marble. Surviving references to money for its transportation date only from as late as 1524 and it seems likely that the stone that did arrive was confined to that required for their architecture rather than the sculpture.[115] How far this reflected failures by the suppliers or, on the other hand, must be attributed to a lack of funds, about which earlier correspondence is so vocal, depends in part on how a letter of Michelangelo's to Fattucci of April 1523 is interpreted. He writes that it is now two years since he went to Carrara to order marble for the tombs. Looking back, he states that he had met Cardinal Giulio before he left for the war against the French in Lombardy, implying a date of September 1521.[116] Nothing was agreed about his payment. On the cardinal's return, which implies a date early in 1522, there had been a further meeting, which had arrived at no conclusion. Reporting that nothing came of it, the artist writes that he had said that they should meet again once his marble had arrived.[117]

In this same letter, Michelangelo records that he had promised the cardinal that he would undertake wooden models, to be carried out to scale, for the architecture of the ducal tombs, to expedite the work. Work on this task began in January 1524, although, in the event, it seems that only one was made. This could suggest that marble had already arrived or was expected. Cutting and dressing the marble was under way by the end of March.[118] The detailed work sheets the artist made, which date from April, invariably refer to work proceeding on both tombs, and their evidence therefore excludes any significant lapse of time between the execution of the two *quadri*.[119]

If financial problems had, in reality, held up work within the chapel, Giulio's election as pope in November 1523 would transform the situation. He had been expected to be elected in the conclave that had followed Leo's death in midwinter of 1521–2. And the election of a non-Italian, who took the title of Adrian VI, would cause grave problems for Michelangelo, which will be discussed below. Now, in November 1523, writing to Topolino at Carrara after the news of Giulio's success had reached Florence, Michelangelo refers to universal rejoicing and expresses his belief that the event will bring great benefits for art.[120]

Soon after, he left for Rome, after an absence from the city of three years. As in the past, his decision seems to have been made quite suddenly.[121] From subsequent correspondence, it is clear that a number of issues had been on the agenda. It was at this moment that Pope Clement decided that work begin on the library at San Lorenzo. For, even before the end of December, Fattucci, now entrusted by the pope with much of the correspondence, had received a drawing for the library project sent from Florence, which he had shown to Jacopo

Salviati prior to discussing it with the pope. Another issue that seems to have arisen was the way in which the artist was to be paid. And a third was the problem of the tomb of the dead della Rovere pope, which Pope Adrian's policies had left in a state of crisis. Whether the artist had been subjected to personal confrontation over the issue while in Rome is unknown. But the letters that followed his return to Florence indicate the gravity of his situation.[122]

From March 1524 Michelangelo was occupied with the task of making clay models for the statues of the two ducal tombs. He was still working on them in October.[123] He probably planned a model for each of the ten statues and we learn from a letter of his faithful correspondent, Leonardo Sellaio, of March 1526 that by that date eight had been completed.[124] As the one survivor shows, these models, like those for the tomb architecture, were made to scale; the reclining *River God*, now in the Casa Buonarroti, was originally 4 *braccia* in length, or just over 230 centimetres.[125] A whole series of purchases testify to the complexity of the undertaking; for example, it has been calculated that more than 500 kilograms of clay, of two different kinds, were acquired to make them.[126] In this case, as with the wooden models for the architecture, it is probable that Michelangelo went to such lengths in order to satisfy his exacting patron.[127]

Marble for the statues had not arrived by October 1524, three and a half years after it had been ordered. This is indicated by an event late in the month, when the artist arranged for the transportation of a block of marble from his workshop in Via Mozza to San Lorenzo. His *ricordo* explains that he has done this to allow him to begin work on one of the reclining *Times of Day* projected for the two ducal tombs, sufficient evidence to indicate that marble was still lacking. He records the length, depth and height of the block and adds that it has been slightly used.[128]

It has been proposed that this substituted block was employed to carve the *Day*, but the depth is too shallow to accommodate the figure and there can be little doubt that this Via Mozza block went to create the *Night*. The two statues of *Day* and *Night* on the tomb of Giuliano present an anomaly, in that their bases are straight, unlike those of *Dawn* and *Evening*, whose bases are curved to follow the curve of the sarcophagus lids (pls 37, 38). The block he now decided to employ for the *Night* had not been rough hewn with the Medici chapel tombs in mind, and, inevitably, the *Day* had to conform.[129]

Michelangelo's decision to employ marble that had been quarried eight years earlier for the tomb of Pope Julius indicates the depth of his frustration in the early autumn of 1524. Earlier letters had expressed his growing concern over the delays at Carrara. In one of February that year, he had deplored the situation to Pope Clement himself.[130] In a later one of July, he had informed Fattucci that he was still awaiting delivery and took the opportunity to complain that he faced having to pay what he regarded as arbitrary taxes.[131]

Topolino remained at Carrara and his letters to the artist in Florence express at one moment optimism, at another despair over the behaviour of the quarrymen. In March, in a moment of desperation, he had gone to see the widow of the *marchese* Alberico Malaspina. She had had a letter from the patron himself in the spring of 1522, complaining about the workforce at Carrara and she had promised, in reply, to call them to order.[132]

In August 1524 the two partners, Marcuccio and Francione, wrote to Michelangelo in Florence informing him that they had ready all the marble owed him, which is awaiting transportation at the coast. They add that Topolino has mobilized them for further work on his behalf. If their remarks relate to the original 100 *carrate* ordered from them by Michelangelo in April 1521, it must be concluded that it had required more than three years for the marble to reach Avenza, prior to its subsequent shipment first to Pisa and then to Signa on the Arno.[133]

While the flow of Topolino's letters from Carrara are a valuable source of information, on occasion they require to be read with a certain caution. In a letter of 13 August 1524, he refers to the quarrying of two blocks which he describes as 'Papi', that is, popes.[134] It has been concluded from what he writes that blocks for statues of Pope Leo and Pope Clement were now ready for transportation.[135] That Michelangelo, in addition to his current obligations, should undertake the tombs of the two Medici popes had recently been proposed in Rome. Fattucci, in a letter of 23 May, had reported that Jacopo Salviati, in conversation with Clement, had proposed that the pope should make provision for the tomb of his deceased cousin and also one for himself.[136] Clearly, the blocks of 'Papi' referred to by Topolino cannot have been prepared in response to this new proposal in August. The papal tombs were still under discussion in April 1525.

Topolino seems, therefore, to have been confused about the purpose of these two blocks, which were in all probability destined for the two *capitani*, the dukes Giuliano and Lorenzo. This seems chronologically persuasive, for it is known that Michelangelo had made sufficient progress in carving one of them by mid-June 1526 to contemplate turning his attention to the other.[137]

Despite his periodic dejection – at one moment he begs the artist to release him – the importance of Topolino's presence at Carrara is once more underlined by the fact that he was entrusted with the task of finding the marble for the most remarkable architectural features of the chapel, the eight door-and-tabernacle bays in the corners (pl. 39). Drawings for these had been sent to Rome along with that for the coffering of the cupola, and they were returned to him with an accompanying letter of Fattucci of 9 February 1524. The designs had greatly pleased Clement, and Fattucci urges Michelangelo to get the masons to start work.[138] Constituting a new style, it is a remarkable indication of the pope's responsiveness to architectural innovation that he reacted to them with such enthusiasm, a reaction that preceded by more than two decades Vasari's celebrated passage devoted to them in his Life of 1550, where he saw in them an emancipation from the bonds of the past.[139]

Inevitably, Michelangelo was dependent on many helpers who were closer to hand than Carrara. His wish to carve the principal figures himself is expressed in an important passage in a letter to Fattucci of June 1526. It is his aim to carve the two dukes, the four *Times of Day*, the four *River Gods* and the statue of the Virgin destined for the tomb of the two *magnifici*.[140] For the decorative carving of the tombs and architecture he required highly skilled assistants. This decoration was very different from that which he had planned for the tomb of Julius II and which had got under way with the team headed by Antonio da Pontassieve in 1513. The decoration in the chapel, essentially funerary in character, although highly telling, is sparingly employed. In this, it constitutes a step in the artist's progress towards an ideal that he would express many years later to Vasari: 'Where there are marble figures, there should be no ornament.'[141]

Among those involved in carving the decorative elements such as the pilaster capitals and the friezes, two names stand out. One strikes a familiar note, that of Francesco da Sangallo, son of Michelangelo's old friend Giuliano, who, as a boy, had been carried by his father, in the company of Michelangelo, to inspect the newly discovered *Laocoön* group. Aged about thirty in 1524, he occupies a place in the master's lists of assistants, although his work was not always to Michelangelo's satisfaction.[142] A much more gifted *intagliatore* was Silvio Cosini, whose experience in executing Michelangelo's designs would do much to form his own mature style as a sculptor. His name appears in the artist's *ricordi* between April 1524 and April 1525.[143] Vasari, in his second edition of the *Lives* of 1568, would single out for lavish praise the virtuosity he displayed in carving some of the pilaster capitals and the astonishing friezes of masks, which probably included that extending behind the statues of *Night* and *Day*.[144]

The destructive passage of time conveyed by the imagery of the two tombs of the dukes seems inescapable. It finds striking confirmation in a celebrated inscription of five lines that Michelangelo added to a sheet of studies of architectural profiles that relate to the chapel. It reads:

Day and Night speak and say: We have with our swift course led Duke Giuliano to his death. And it is only just that he has his revenge for this, as he does. And the revenge is this: that we, having brought about his death, he, thus dead, has deprived us of light and, with closed eyes, has sealed our own, which no longer shine upon the earth. What would he have done with us while he lived?.[145]

A further confirmation that all-consuming time was in the artist's mind can be found in what he told Condivi decades later. Alluding to the chapel, which his biographer never saw, he remarks that *Day* and *Night* signify time which destroys everything, 'il tempo che consuma tutto'.[146]

These words, probably inscribed on the drawing in 1524, would not be the last that the artist would assign to *Night*. Almost exactly two decades later, she would voice a very different lament, to which we can return. But before leaving this earlier one, it is worth adding that the artist's explicit association of *Night* and *Day* with Duke Giuliano cannot be reconciled with a proposal advanced in the nineteenth century, that the statue we regard as representing Giuliano is, in fact, of Lorenzo, while it is the abstracted duke, with head bowed, who is Giuliano. As characterized, their appearance undoubtedly conflicts with the realities of the two men's careers and personalities. And that this lack of verisimilitude was already apparent at an early date is confirmed by a passage in an extraordinary letter of a fellow Florentine, Niccolò Martelli, written in July 1544. Michelangelo had not modelled his two statues on their natural appearance. Rather, he had given them a grandeur, a proportion, a decorum, a grace and a splendour that he believed would bring them greater praise, for a thousand years hence, no one would perceive any difference.[147]

THE DELLA ROVERE RESTORED

When Michelangelo made his brief trip to the papal court in December 1523, shortly after Giulio's election as pope, the issue of how he was to be paid for his work at San Lorenzo was one of the matters discussed, as is clear from subsequent letters. What had gone before is impossible to deduce, for the evidence of what he had received is extremely fragmentary. It is at least possible that the remuneration, whatever it had been, had broken down after Leo's death in December 1521 and that the issue was reappraised after Giulio's election in November 1523.[148]

Writing to the artist immediately following his visit, Fattucci raises the subject. He refers to a conversation he has had with Jacopo Salviati. The idea that Pope Clement should grant the artist a pension, based on the income from a benefice, had come up. This would have the advantage of protecting Michelangelo in the event of the pope's death, whereas there could be no such security were he to be paid a salary. Salviati liked the idea, happy that the Church's money be spent in the Church.[149]

Fattucci wrote again on 2 January 1524. The pope has expressed his consent to giving the artist a pension, but this would involve his promise not to marry and to his taking Minor Orders. Otherwise, all at the Roman court are determined on his having a proper salary, a *provisione*.

Throughout 1524, the artist showed no disposition to accept an appropriate salary, despite the pleadings of Fattucci. From one of his letters, it appears that he had asked for the modest sum of 15 ducats a month, one that Fattucci described as shameful. Salviati had given his instructions to Spina of the Pisa bank to pay Michelangelo 50 ducats a month, apart from his expenses.[150] A little later, Fattucci recommends him to rent a house near San Lorenzo, which will be paid for by the Salviati bank. In the summer, it emerged that the artist was not drawing his salary, and only in late August would he write to Spina expressing his decision to take it.[151] But, once more, his reluctance to accept it arose and the situation persisted into 1525. As late as the autumn of 1525, Spina was still remonstrating with him over his failure to draw his salary and refers to the fact that he himself has been sharply rep-rimanded by those in Rome for his own negligence.[152]

Even if the gravest charges of avidity that have been levelled at the artist are resisted, his refusal to draw his salary for his all-consuming

work at San Lorenzo is a remarkable fact. To explain it requires returning to the issue of his failure to take steps to complete the tomb of
Pope Julius; the failure provoked a protracted crisis following Leo x's
death in December 1521.

Leo's own attitude toward Francesco Maria della Rovere, following
the duke's loss of the duchy of Urbino, had remained implacable. After
Lorenzo de' Medici's death in May 1519, the duchy was formally
annexed to the Papal States, with the exception of San Leo and Mon-
tefeltro, which had been given to Florence in recognition of the huge
sums that the city had been compelled to contribute to the costs of
the war. In 1520, because Federico Gonzaga had become Captain of
the Church, Duke Francesco Maria had had to leave Mantua, which
had been his chosen place of exile. The pope's unexpected death
changed everything. Francesco Maria had re-entered his duchy before
the end of December.

Following Leo's death, and before his successor, Adrian vi, had
arrived in Italy, the Curia had come to terms with the duke. The
Sacred College had negotiated a provisional treaty with him in Febru-
ary 1522, and a little later he was formally absolved from all censure.
Francesco Maria's journey to Rome was delayed by illness, but he
arrived there in mid-March 1523. His visit sealed his rehabilitation.
Peace was declared, and he was formally reinstated with his duchy by
Pope Adrian.[153]

His restoration was a threatening event for Michelangelo. And even
before the duke's visit to Rome in 1523, the spring of 1522 had already
marked a moment of danger for him. The terms of the contract drawn
up in the summer of 1516 had laid down that the entire project was
to be completed nine years after the earlier agreement of 1513 had
been drawn up. In other words, the time allowed him expired in May
1522.[154] The deadline can scarcely have escaped him, however engaged
he was with the work going forward at San Lorenzo, work expressly
forbidden by the terms of the contract of 1516, which had allowed
him the freedom to move elsewhere only if this contributed to the
completion of Julius's tomb. And the executor most involved, Cardinal

Leonardo della Rovere, a man who had always believed the best of
the artist, was no longer alive to act as a protective mediator. It may
well have been his growing anxiety to know how things stood with
the Urbino court that prompted an exchange of letters with his young
Florentine friend Gherardo Perini in Pesaro in early 1522. Michelangelo's, undated, was probably prompted by one from Perini in which he
offers his services to the artist in any way he can, dated 31 January
1522. Michelangelo writes that he will await Perini's return to learn
how things have gone; he will then hear all the details, which much
concern him. Further letters of Perini's of July show that he has not
yet returned to Florence, but expects to see him soon.[155]

   This exchange could suggest that the celebrated drawings that
Michelangelo is recorded as having made for Perini, already described
in Vasari's Life of 1550, could have been presents actuated not only
by the artist's attachment but also as an acknowledgement of things
he had attempted to do to help him. Perini had been born in Florence
in June 1503 and was, therefore, twenty-eight years the artist's junior.
His letters show that he was of Michelangelo's circle and a friend of
Piloto. The artist's feelings for him are less circumstantially recorded
than those he would later display for Tommaso de' Cavalieri (pl. 46)
and the drawings given to him less ambitious, but it is the earliest
episode of the kind that has been reported.[156]

   The early stages of the crisis cannot be followed because much of
the artist's correspondence of 1522 is lost. But it seems clear that the
della Rovere had taken steps by November. Writing to Michelangelo
in the middle of the month, Jacopo Salviati reports a meeting that he
had had with Girolamo Staccoli. He was the deputy of the della
Rovere envoy in Rome, Giovan Maria della Porta, and it was he who
would undertake much of the day-to-day negotiations regarding the
tomb. Staccoli demands some resolution of the problem, but talks have
been hampered by his illness. In his letter, Salviati adopts an optimistic
tone, which subsequent events would prove to be misplaced.[157]

   The full danger facing Michelangelo is revealed in a letter of his
own to Fattucci of April 1523. The timing of what he writes is

significant, for, as has been seen, the Duke of Urbino's arrival in Rome was imminent. He spells out the facts, which he presumes Fattucci is already aware of. A *motu proprio* has been drawn up, which awaits Pope Adrian's signature. The sums that he has had from the della Rovere are to be established, and, if the artist is not prepared to complete the work, the money is to be returned to the family with appropriate penalties and interest. If Michelangelo does not wish to carry out the tomb, Adrian is reported to have declared, these events will follow.[158]

Unless freed from his obligations to the della Rovere, he goes on, he cannot continue to work at the New Sacristy. If Cardinal Giulio achieves this, he declares that he will work for him without payment for the rest of his life. If he is not freed by the cardinal, who, nevertheless, wishes his work at San Lorenzo to proceed, he will endeavour to find time to satisfy his wishes while he works on the della Rovere tomb.

It was this crisis of the spring of 1523 that precipitated the artist's decision to call in the money that his family owed him.[159] The letter also explains why Michelangelo so persistently declined to claim his *provisione* for his work at San Lorenzo and why he had actually left the house rented for him just behind the Medici Chapel. Payment, and perhaps even more the provision of a house, could only have added to the sense of outrage nursed by the della Rovere.[160]

The death of Pope Adrian and the election of Cardinal Giulio as his successor in November 1523 eased the immediate crisis. But in the longer term, it could only worsen the problem for, as Giulio declared, he wanted Michelangelo for himself. That the issue of the tomb was discussed on the artist's brief trip to Rome in December is clear from subsequent events. Fattucci wrote to him on 22 December to report that he had met the dead Cardinal Leonardo's closest adviser, Francesco Pallavicino, together with his brother, Bartolommeo della Rovere. To their insistence that the project must be finished, Fattucci had claimed that Michelangelo had not been paid following the death of Cardinal Leonardo but that he had not ceased to work for the project, a statement that Michelangelo's start on the four *Prisoners* in the

Accademia could confirm. He asks the artist to send him the information he needs regarding events from the very beginning of his work
for Pope Julius. He recalls that Michelangelo had told him that there
had been no contract for the project of painting the ceiling of the
Sistine Chapel and that his payment for that work had ended by being
adapted for the tomb project. Michelangelo must send to him his
reckoning over his payments for the latter, together with the text of
the 1516 contract. Spina can see to it that it is safely forwarded to
Rome.[161]

Like so many of the letters addressed to the Curia, Michelangelo's
reply is lost. But two drafts, already frequently referred to earlier,
survive. Both were written to convince Fattucci, and those to whom
it would be shown, of his blameless record. The lengthier of the two
actually opens with an aggressive challenge to what had been proposed
while Pope Adrian still lived: he writes that it is to him, the artist,
that damages and interest should be paid. Michelangelo takes his survey
of the past back as far as 1503, when he gained the commission to
carve the marble apostles for the cathedral of Florence. As earlier
quotations have already shown, no opportunity is neglected to present
himself as a man persistently ill-done by. Even Agostino Chigi's theft
of two pieces of marble ordered for the tomb is brought up.[162]

Fattucci's need of information had not been met by the artist's letter.
Writing on 30 December 1523, he presses Michelangelo to inform him
how much he had earned on account of the tomb from the date of
the contract of July 1516 up to the present time, adding that he needs
to establish the value of what Chigi had stolen. It is not known how
the artist met this request.[163]

In the end, it was the surviving executor, Cardinal Lorenzo Pucci,
who came to his aid. He would argue that Michelangelo had received
8,500 ducats. Since the total payment for the tomb in the contract of
1516 had established a total sum of 16,500 ducats, he still was creditor
to the total of 8,000.[164] For him to complete the project, this outstanding sum was to be handed over by the della Rovere and put on deposit
until completion. If the sum was not put down, the project would

remain unfinished.[165] Pucci went even further and argued that the house at Macel de' Corvi should unconditionally pass to the artist. From having been initially hostile to Michelangelo's claims, Pucci had become his ardent advocate. Behind this volte-face, remarked on by the artist's Roman circle, there lay pressure from Pope Clement.[166] Nevertheless, even such protection could not shield the artist from his critics in Rome. In a letter of 24 March, the ever faithful Leonardo Sellaio reminds him that he does not lack enemies and must act to silence those who are saying that he never accomplishes anything.[167]

By late 1524 Michelangelo's readiness to continue the struggle had deserted him. He repeatedly failed to send the notarized document that was required to allow Fattucci to act for him. He urges him to give up his role as advocate of his cause and return to Florence, where he had left an ageing mother. And in April 1525 he sent the draft of a letter to Giovanni Spina; he asks him to write a more finished text and forward it to Rome. Earlier in the month, he had heard from Leonardo Sellaio that legal proceedings with the della Rovere were imminent. He now writes that he does not wish to become involved in a lawsuit that he will lose. He is ready to acknowledge his responsibility for failing to complete the project. He wants Pope Clement to act as intermediary and declares his readiness to return what is due to the della Rovere. Once restitution has been made, they can choose whom they wish to carry out the commission. Pope Clement can aid him by arranging that he pay the minimum that is due; he can accept his argument about all the time that he had spent working for Pope Julius, specifically citing the period he had spent in Bologna. Once the sum is agreed, he will sell what is necessary and make restitution. Then he will be free to give his mind to the pope's projects. As things are, he cannot live, let alone work.[168]

He refers to the depth of his depression in a letter to Sebastiano del Piombo. Invited out to dinner by friends of the Venetian, he has accepted and gained satisfaction from hearing their praises of his friend as a painter; the occasion has, for a while, allowed him to escape his melancholy.[169] But the magnitude of his anxiety was not understood

by his allies in Rome. The plea to end the crisis, which he had sent
to Spina to be forwarded to Rome, fell on deaf ears. The most powerful of his supporters, Jacopo Salviati, seems also to have been the most
militant; he reportedly urges the artist to leave the settlement to
them.[170] Fattucci remained in Rome and, at some point, the artist was
prevailed upon to have the document authorizing him to act, the
mandata di procura, sent from Florence. It arrived without the notary's
signature, however, and had to be returned.[171]

In August Fattucci, still clinging to the proposition that the della
Rovere should hand over the residue of the money prescribed in the
contract, wrote to tell him that Duke Francesco Maria's instructions
were expected and that neither he nor his representatives were prepared to spend any further money on the tomb, not a 'quatrino' more.
Neglecting the artist's own wishes, he had declared that Michelangelo
had no available money to return and that some other solution would
have to be found. He now asks him for his suggestions, ignoring what
the artist proposed so recently. He should consider all solutions except
that of paying back money to the patrons. Well-intentioned as they
were, Michelangelo's friends were in effect condemning him to
repeated crises in the future.[172]

A further attempt to reach a solution would be made in the late
summer of 1525. The idea was mooted in Rome that the artist should
design a tomb along the lines of those of Pius II and Pius III in St
Peter's. These were shallow wall tombs, without the deep returns on
either side that had characterized the project of 1516. It is not known
whose proposal this was but it attracted the artist, as a letter of his to
Fattucci shows.[173] He once again expressed his approval of the idea in
a letter of 24 October. He could carry out the project little by little,
always with the proviso that he should return no money to the patrons
and that he would be left the house and its contents in Rome. He
would undertake the carving of the statues himself. He expresses his
devotion to Pope Clement; if he receives the salary from him, he will
work for him for the rest of his life. However, he complains that he
is old; in fact, he had reached his fiftieth birthday just eight months

previously. Anticipating a more celebrated pronouncement he would make in the final crisis over the tomb, still seventeen years in the future, he declares that one cannot work on one thing with one's hands and another with one's head, least of all when carving marble.[174]

Fattucci was pleased with his response and asked him to send a drawing that could be forwarded to the della Rovere. The artist should shed his fantasies and concentrate on his work.[175] But a new problem was emerging that will occupy us later. Despite the many different tasks Pope Clement was now giving him at San Lorenzo and despite his repeated references to his incapacity for work, his restless ambition would be aroused by the pope's revival of the project of a marble group to form a pendant to the marble *David*, the commission he himself had been given by Soderini as long ago as 1506.

The new scheme for Julius's tomb, which was initially welcomed by all parties, was subject to repeated delays. Duke Francesco Maria's representative in Rome was frequently ill. Differences would arise over the length of time to be allowed for the completion of this reduced project. Fattucci would write only as late as October 1526, acknowledging that Jacopo Salviati had shown him the drawing that Michelangelo had sent to Rome. It will be forwarded to Urbino when the artist agrees.[176] The hope in Rome had been that, once the new design was approved, the contract of 1516 could be annulled. All these expectations would come to nothing.

The exact details of what happened are not clear. But, writing to Fattucci on 1 November 1526, the artist is found once more plunged in crisis over the tomb. He had insisted that the dependable Giovanni Spina write to Rome regarding the tomb project. He wrote in heated terms, a consequence of his mounting anxiety. Now, given the state of the times they are living in, Michelangelo feels he has made a mistake.[177]

He has had news from Rome that has caused him acute alarm, provoked by the ill will that the relatives of Julius bear him, not without reason. The lawsuit is going ahead and they are demanding damages so great that a hundred of the likes of himself could not meet them. Reflecting on his situation, he writes that if Pope Clement were to fail him, he would not survive in the world. He is not clear about his patron's intentions but does not believe that he would wish to see him ruined. He is aware of the pope's economic problems and asks whether these would give him the opportunity to begin something, in Florence or in Rome, for the dead pope's tomb, for he wants to be rid of his obligation even more than to live. He repeats his wish for Fattucci to clarify the pope's intentions. He hopes his letter is not unintelligible for he is out of his mind.[178]

The letter leaves a great deal undisclosed. But it can be presumed that the news that had come from Rome was of the rejection by the della Rovere of what we can call the 'Pius II solution'. The sculpture of the fifteenth-century tomb had been modest when considered in the light of the expectations Michelangelo had raised; the della Rovere cannot have been unaware of the two *Prisoners* and the *Moses* in the house in Rome and were probably outraged by the inadequacy of what was now being offered. Negotiations were still under way in Rome in December without any hint of an outcome. Five months later, everything would change. Rome would be sacked, with the pope a fugitive in Castel Sant'Angelo, and the Medicean regime in Florence would collapse. Nevertheless, despite his recent declaration of his dependence on Clement conveyed to Fattucci, Michelangelo would survive the eclipse of his greatest patron.

THE SAN LORENZO LIBRARY AND OTHER PROJECTS

The election of Cardinal Giulio as pope in the conclave of November 1523 led to the decision to proceed with the plan of constructing a library at San Lorenzo for the Medicean book collection. As Figio-vanni's later memorandum shows, the intention had been conveyed to Michelangelo in his meeting with the cardinal in June 1519.[179] The lack of any fitting resting place for Lorenzo the Magnificent, Giuliano (Giulio's own father) and the two dukes so recently deceased, had determined the precedence of the project for the sacristy. Cost control may have contributed to the delay. But it is more likely that the library was postponed for fear that the double burden on the artist would have slowed progress on the chapel and its tombs. Even well after the library got under way, it remained a constant apprehension of the pope that this second project would threaten progress with the first.[180]

Like the construction of the chapel, the intention to found a library was an expression of family *pietas*. Medicean associations with libraries went back to the patronage of Cosimo, *Pater Patriae*, of the library at San Marco.[181] His son, Piero, made some additions to the family's own collection, but it was Lorenzo who had bought on a massive scale to augment it. Cosimo's munificence in paying for the construction of the library of Michelozzo at San Marco was a constant reminder of family tradition. As late as 1533, after work on the San Lorenzo library had resumed, following the breakdown of work precipitated by the sack of Rome, Sebastiano del Piombo would write to Michelangelo that Pope Clement had two wishes concerning the reading desks, the 'banchi'. He wants them to be constructed of walnut and that they follow the precedent of Cosimo's; that, in other words, they follow those in the library at San Marco.[182]

Lorenzo's intention to build a library for the family collection seems to have been formed as early as 1472, although it is unlikely that a specific site had been chosen. We are dependably told that, as he lay dying at Careggi in April 1492, some of Lorenzo's very last words concerned his scheme for Greek and Latin libraries.[183] After the fall of Piero in the autumn of 1494, the family library had been taken over by the Signoria and lodged at San Marco.[184] In 1506 Cardinal Giovanni, the future Leo x, now resident in Rome, expressed his wish to gain restitution of the books and, in 1508, succeeded in buying almost all of them from San Marco.[185] Son of Lorenzo, he had even better reason than his cousin to pursue the plan of a permanent home for the family library at San Lorenzo, but his early death in December 1521 prevented his witnessing the beginning of the undertaking.

Like a number of his decisions where travel was concerned, Michelangelo's departure for Rome in December 1523 seems to have been undertaken without long deliberation. One of his motives was to discuss the issue of payment for his ongoing work at San Lorenzo, another to attempt to ward off the consequences of della Rovere displeasure over the papal tomb. But the issue of the library was probably the most immediately important for him, to judge from the fact that a drawing for the project had already reached Rome before the end of the month.[186]

Nevertheless, although the decision to proceed with the second San Lorenzo project had been taken, much seems to have been left unclarified. It may have been the pope's intention that much of the work could be left to Stefano Lunetti, thereby ensuring that work on the chapel would not be held up. An early drawing for the project had left those in Rome uncertain whether it had been made by Stefano or Michelangelo. A letter of the artist's of early January suggests a certain confusion about how things stood. He writes that he does not know where the library is to be situated. He explains that he will do what he can once Lunetti has returned from Carrara, qualifying his remark with a disclaimer of a lack of competence that almost exactly echoes the one he had made years earlier when engaged on the Sistine ceiling.[187]

The remarkable series of letters directed to the artist from Rome, for the most part written by Fattucci, indicate an engagement with the library project on Clement's part even more intensive than that with the sacristy. An increasing concern would be cost, but for the early stages of the enterprise nothing escaped his attention, be it practical or an issue of stylistic choice.[188] A particular preoccupation was the danger of fire. Even before the final site for the library had been agreed, Clement was adamant that, if situated over conventual quarters, the lower rooms should be vaulted. Fattucci, recording one of Clement's not infrequent examples of caustic humour, writes of his patron's fears about a fire hazard from a drunken priest.[189] Another concern, expressed before the site had been selected, was one involving the ceiling of the library. As early as March, Fattucci would pass on his insistence on some new form of ceiling, a 'fantasia nuova', which would diverge from the pattern of heavy coffered wood ceilings prevalent in Rome.[190]

The choice of the present site for the library was made only after lengthy discussion of two other possibilities. One was to situate the library across the smaller of the two cloisters of the *canonica*, involving the destruction of some of the canons' cells, a proposal that alarmed the pope. The other, drawn concurrently on the same sheet by Michelangelo, was to situate the library on the south side of the *piazza* in front of the church, extending to the Borgo San Lorenzo.[191]

The final solution was agreed only at the beginning of April. Clement was now ready to leave the decision to Michelangelo and to accept the site he had proposed, happy that the abandonment of the *piazza* plan would leave future decisions over the façade for the church without any constraint.[192] The library was to form an additional storey along the west side of the canons' complex. To the library was to be added an entrance vestibule to house the staircase, required to allow access to the library itself. The choice of an elevated site was in strict conformity with tradition, for all previous Italian monastic libraries had similarly responded to the two needs to avoid damp and achieve good light.[193] But since the project involved building the library over existing structures, these would require some form of buttressing to meet the problem of weight.

For the task, Michelangelo felt he needed professional assistance and turned to Baccio Bigio, an architect with long-standing Medicean associations. The choice could have been seen as a curious one and, it seems clear, was in no way actuated by the pope, for he is reported to have given way to laughter at the news. Yet Baccio proved his worth, a fact that came to be acknowledged at the papal court.[194]

The library elevation that we see today from the main cloister of San Lorenzo is not what Michelangelo had originally intended. He had initially envisaged a continuous elevation for both reading room and vestibule, with a common roof and with uniform fenestration, with the exception that the vestibule windows were to be blind, to allow for an elaborate interior articulation.[195]

This left outstanding the issue of how the vestibule was to be lit, one that provoked an animated exchange with Rome. The subject emerges in the correspondence in late November, when work on the construction of the library was well advanced and the step of turning to the building of the *ricetto* was occupying both artist and patron. In a letter of 29 November Fattucci responds to a radical idea of Michelangelo's that the vestibule should be lit by overhead skylights. Clement has been much taken by so beautiful a novelty. But he fears that two friars from the Gesuati in Florence would have to be paid to do nothing other than sweep off the dust.[196] In a further letter from Rome of 23 December, the idea of the skylights, the 'occhi di vetro', re-emerges. Once again, Clement has found it a beautiful idea, but has once more expressed concerns about it: he is still worried that the skylights will receive more dust than light. From this letter, it is clear that in the interim the artist has come up with a different idea, to raise the upper part of the vestibule walls to allow for windows.[197]

This provoked concern in Rome, for it emerges that some of the wooden beams of the library roof already extended over the area of the *ricetto*. A further worry was that of the additional weight involved. Nevertheless, at a date not clearly established, it was this option of heightening the upper walls of the vestibule that would be chosen. But the change was one limited to the upper area of the *ricetto* and did not involve the main order.[198]

There is no record of Clement's reaction to the extraordinary novelties of the vestibule comparable to his reported enthusiasm for the corner bays of the neighbouring chapel. Drawings could never have conveyed to the full the effect of many of its most radical features, such as the recession of the Doric columns and the denial of any function to the huge consoles (pl. 40).[199]

The correspondence shows that Clement assumed that, for the reading room, a 'basilica'-type arrangement would be employed, one with two lines of columns, which had been adopted for all recent conventual libraries. And it was one of the artist's most radical decisions to opt for a single central passageway between the desks that would, in turn, abut the library walls, a solution that was decisive in achieving the extraordinary unity that the interior displays.

Yet Clement's intervention over another issue was of great significance. In April 1524 he had accepted the idea of a double staircase of two flights for the *ricetto*, a scheme exemplified in a whole group of the artist's drawings. A year later, he changed his mind. He now proposed that there should be a single monumental staircase from the vestibule to the reading room, one that would effectively fill the *ricetto*, and Michelangelo accepted his proposal.[200] The staircase as built owes much, therefore, to Clement's initiative. Built many years after the artist's move to Rome and his patron's death, the fact reminds us that Clement was destined to see none of the works in progress with which he had been so intensively engaged. His wish to come to Florence to see the ongoing work was reported to Michelangelo in late October 1525, but remained unfulfilled.[201]

The rapid progress with the building of the library, completed by the end of 1525, had been achieved with a substantial number of workers, their pay and identities listed in some of the artist's *ricordi*. There had been a cost in terms of human relations, for the prior of San Lorenzo had bitterly complained to Rome about the chaos that Michelangelo's project had wrought.[202] But the completion prompted the patron to turn his attention to other features of the project. Earlier in the year, he had decided on the addition of a rare book room at the far end of the library, an idea still reflecting a similar small area reserved for Greek books at San Marco. Problems existed, however, springing from restrictions of space caused by adjacent property. Michelangelo, his capacity to find solutions to intractable problems once more coming to his aid, designed a triangular room in order to conserve space. Two drawings for the project survive, the more finished of them one of his most striking unexecuted projects.[203]

By April 1526, as work went forward on the vestibule, Michelangelo had sent to Rome a drawing for the doorway into the library, which provoked extraordinary enthusiasm on the part of his patron (pl. 41). The design, which had to make provision for an inscription, the object of a discussion with Paolo Giovio, had drawn from Clement the statement that he had never seen a more beautiful design, antique or modern.[204] In early June Fattucci returned the drawing to the artist together with what would seem to be a selection of epitaphs that Michelangelo should hand to others to read, a telling reminder, as mentioned in this book's introduction, that he was not up to the task of understanding the Latin.[205]

The same letter reminds us that other projects were occupying the mind of Michelangelo's patron. One was that of tombs for Pope Leo and himself. As noted earlier, the issue had arisen as early as May 1524, seemingly at the instance of Jacopo Salviati, but work on the interior of the sacristy was much too advanced to allow for any additions to the programme, as had been unrealistically proposed. The artist had subsequently proposed as sites the two small areas on each side of the sacristy's choir, referred to in the correspondence as the *lavamani*. A little later, in the summer of 1524, Clement himself had suggested, as a more realistic site, the choir, or some other location, within the church of San Lorenzo.[206]

There followed a lull in the surviving letters until Fattucci's return to the topic in the letter of June 1526 that had concerned the doorway design. He has advised against the *lavamani* in the sacristy because of their inadequate size; he feels that the papal tombs would be eclipsed by those of the two dukes. Fattucci had expressed to Clement his own preference for the church. But he then proceeds to air a bizarre idea, that the fourteenth-century church of San Giovanni, close to the *piazza* of San Lorenzo, could be pulled down and replaced by a centrally planned church that would accommodate the tombs of the two popes. Clement had observed that such a project would cost 50,000 ducats, to which Fattucci had retorted that, to find the money, one would have to pray for longevity.[207]

One month later, a very different message would be received in Florence. While there should be no economies where the sacristy was concerned, expenditure on the library would have to be cut back in a drastic fashion. The monthly outlay had to be reduced to a third of the sum being currently spent.[208]

The request reflects the worsening political and economic situation of the pope. Ever since his election in November 1523, Clement had had to contend with financial adversity. In part, this was the effect of the dire problems left by his cousin Leo; Adrian's pontificate had been too brief to allow for significant improvement. Regarded as parsimonious by many contemporaries, his lack of money was evident by as early as 1524, as a letter of Baldassare Castiglione indicates.[209] The situation in the following years would grow worse, for papal revenues would come to be depleted by the apostasy of the reformist states in Germany.

The most serious financial burden was, undoubtedly, that of military expenditure. For example, Clement would spend significant sums, to no avail, in the attempt to save Hungary from the Turks; its total loss in 1526 depressed him deeply. As some observers recognized, his very rectitude contributed to the financial crisis, for he resolutely refused to engage in the wholescale sale of offices pursued on a massive scale by Leo x.[210]

Nevertheless, despite this prevailing economic adversity, the project for two papal tombs remained alive and fired the artist's imagination, as one of his most monumental designs shows.[211] And another project envisaged for San Lorenzo was pursued with great energy, a ciborium to house the cherished Medicean collection of relics. Unlike the two tombs, which were never realized by Michelangelo, the scheme to house and exhibit the relics would be brought to fruition, but only following the Medicean restoration in 1530.

The project emerges in the surviving correspondence from Rome no later than October 1525. It was one with which Clement was deeply engaged. Several sites within San Lorenzo were contemplated, but, before all correspondence comes to a halt in late 1526, it emerges that he opted in favour of the construction of a ciborium over the high altar.

He reached this decision only with misgivings, and, when finally built, the site, one mooted by Clement, would be above the central door of the interior entrance wall of the church. As Fattucci explains in a letter of 8 February 1526, the pope is anxious that an unimpeded view into the choir behind the altar be preserved, in the light of the possibility that it may some day come to be decorated.[212] In a further letter of 23 February, Fattucci returns to the issue, explicitly referring to a wish of Michelangelo's own to decorate the choir, one evidently expressed in a letter now lost.[213] The interest of this remark is strengthened by the fact that, probably in the previous year, Clement had entrusted the project of painting lateral wall frescos in the choir to an artist who, at this point, had become the object of Michelangelo's most bitter enmity, Baccio Bandinelli, although, in the event, the paintings had not been carried out.[214]

TWO *GIGANTI*

When Jacopo Sansovino wrote to Michelangelo in June 1517, furious over his exclusion from any share in the sculpture programme for the façade of San Lorenzo, he had declared that he had heard from Jacopo Salviati that Bandinelli, 'Bacino di Michelagniolo', was the ablest sculptor to hand. It is implied that this is Michelangelo's judgement and that Bandinelli was being considered as a collaborator.[215]

A role for Bandinelli may well have been urged by Pope Leo and Cardinal Giulio. Their support for the artist, which would become progressively more pronounced, was inspired not only by a genuine respect for his skills but also by earlier ties, for his father Michele di Viviano, an outstanding jeweller and metalworker, had been patronized by Lorenzo the Magnificent and, subsequently, Piero. And his service for the Medici would resume following the family restoration of 1512, and now included work for the two *magnifici*, Giuliano and Lorenzo.[216] Vasari stated that it had been Giuliano who had helped the artist gain the commission for the statue of *St Peter* for the series of apostles for Florence cathedral, a work completed in the period when Sansovino addressed his letter to Michelangelo.[217]

If Bandinelli's involvement in the San Lorenzo façade sculpture did find favour with the patrons, no tangible trace of such support now survives other than Sansovino's letter. In the event, Michelangelo's uncompromising rejection of collaborators would have prevailed, as it had done in the case of Baccio d'Agnolo. And no one would more unerringly point to this as a cause of the failure of the enterprise than Bandinelli himself in his extraordinary letter addressed to Duke Cosimo in December 1547.[218]

Bandinelli's hatred of Michelangelo emerges as one of the recurrent themes of Vasari's *Vita*, although the older artist's attitude to his younger competitor, born in November 1493, is initially less clear. But the favours extended to Bandinelli by Pope Leo and Cardinal Giulio may have provoked uneasiness. And it is telling that, once in Rome after a period spent working at the Santa Casa in Loreto, members of Michelangelo's circle such as Sellaio and Sebastiano would report on Bandinelli's current activities, just as they had done earlier with their reports of Raphael's. Commissions such as the projected copy of the *Laocoön* were reminders to Michelangelo that he was not the Medici's only sculptor. But the most brutal realization of this fact came in the period that is our present concern. Clement would choose Bandinelli to carve the companion statue to the marble *David* before the Palazzo della Signoria.[219]

Bandinelli probably coveted the commission many years earlier. Telling is the familiar fact that, for the celebrations for Pope Leo's visit to Florence in late November 1515, among a number of contributors to the decorations of the *entrata*, he had made a huge statue of *Hercules*, variously reported to have been made in clay or stucco, which he had painted to simulate bronze. It had been situated in the close vicinity of Michelangelo's *David*, in the bay of the Loggia della Signoria closest to the palace. One contemporary informs us that Bandinelli's figure was of the same scale as the *David*. And that it was a conscious challenge to the earlier sculpture, and a claim to carry out the statue that Michelangelo had failed to carve, seems implicit from what we are told in the sources. Contemporary references to this statue of Bandinelli's even adopt the nomenclature that had been adopted for the *David*; it is called the *Gigante* (pl. 43).[220] Another reminder of his ambitions as a sculptor on an heroic scale were the two very large stucco statues subsequently carried out for Cardinal Giulio at Villa Madama in Rome.[221]

The issue of Bandinelli's successful procurement of the commission for the second statue for the Piazza della Signoria erupts in Michelangelo's surviving correspondence only in October 1525. The earlier silence about an issue that would so deeply mortify him is not easy to explain. That Bandinelli's involvement must have been known is suggested by the fact that, as early as late April 1523, present in person at Carrara, he had contracted with three Carrarese quarrymen for the delivery of a block approximately 8 *braccia* high.[222] In the restricted world of Carrara, it seems strange that Michelangelo's own workers could have been unaware of such a striking event, and odd that the news had not reached him.[223] In April 1523, however, it must be recalled that he was plunged in the crisis of Pope Adrian's implacability over the della Rovere tomb.

Perhaps at that point the artist had abandoned proprietorial concerns over the project and it was only when the reality of Bandinelli's success became a highly public one that he was seized by competitive fury. But it remains a possibility that he had never entirely put Soderini's project out of his mind. Two neglected comments in the letters are worth noting. Writing to his master from Carrara in August 1519, Pietro Urbano had referred to a large block, a 'sasso', owned by Alberico Malaspina, and had alluded to the possibility of Michelangelo acquiring it. Urbano seems to have had in mind its usefulness for the façade of San Lorenzo.[224] What could well have been the same *sasso* is referred to by a Carrara marble worker in a letter to Michelangelo of June 1524. He informs him that he is to 'finish' the block that Michelangelo wishes to obtain from the *marchese* and adds that, if the artist is to make 'this work', it would answer his requirement.[225]

Soon after he had received this letter, the task of quarrying the block for Bandinelli was completed.[226] There then followed the problem of its transportation to Florence, a journey marked by the notorious setback of the marble falling into the Arno, an event that gave rise to public ribaldry. For the date of its arrival in Florence we are dependant on the account of Giovanni Cambi, who states that it reached the city on 20 July 1525.[227] Wood required for the salvage operation had been advanced by the *operai* of the Palazzo della Signoria, who would be subsequently reimbursed by the Opera del Duomo, telling evidence that the practicalities of the project were now in the hands of the city's public bodies. The block would arrive at the Opera no later than December.[228]

Michelangelo's letter of protest to the Curia over the preferment of Bandinelli was written on 3 October. Like almost every letter sent to Rome, it is lost, but we have Fattucci's reply of 14 October. It can have done nothing to pacify the artist, for Clement seems to have reacted with ill-judged disingenuousness, disclaiming what must have appeared a fait accompli to any observer, and stating that the project would be awarded to the artist who would present the best model. But Fattucci spells out the overriding concern of the pope: he requires Michelangelo for his own projects.[229] These include not only the ciborium for the display of the Medicean relics but also a very different *Gigante* from that projected for the Piazza della Signoria. Clement wishes the artist to undertake a huge statue, to be situated behind the Palazzo Medici, to overlook the *piazza* before the church of San Lorenzo. He wants it to be not less than 25 *braccia*, or 14.5 metres, in height, and to be carved in pieces.[230] Clement's determination to keep Michelangelo for himself is again made clear in a subsequent letter of Fattucci's of 10 November. He has instructed the latter to warn the artist not to concern himself with public works, a reference to the

carving of the second statue before the Palazzo della Signoria, but only
with his, the pope's. That this was the reason for Michelangelo's exclusion from the project must have been well known to informed Florentines. In a remarkable passage devoted to the project, Giovanni Cambi
states that it was the popular wish that Michelangelo should carve the
companion statue to the *David*, and explains that the work was given
not to the greatest sculptor of his time but to another, in order that
the tombs of the Medici should not remain unfinished.[231]

It fell to Jacopo Salviati to attempt to console the artist and provide
encouragement. In a remarkable letter written on 30 October, he urges
him to rid himself of the fantasies that are troubling him. He expresses
his amazement that Michelangelo could be so affronted by the choice
of Bandinelli and imagine that he could ever be considered his equal.
He urges him to concentrate on the work under way at San Lorenzo
and promises to make sure that he will be properly paid.[232]

In his Life of Bandinelli, Vasari attributed a significant role to
Domenico Buoninsegni in the decision to award the commission to
Bandinelli; he is alleged to have stated that Michelangelo wanted everything for himself.[233] As seen earlier, Vasari's charge that Buoninsegni
had fallen out with Michelangelo when the artist had refused to con-
spire with him to defraud the Curia over the San Lorenzo façade is
unlikely to have been true. However, when Buoninsegni, together
with Bernardo Niccolini, had been put in charge of the supplies of
money for the New Sacristy, relations deteriorated and their replacement by Giovanni Spina of the Salviati bank came as a great relief to
the artist. More significant was Buoninsegni's accusation, a true one,
that Michelangelo's claim that money he had received for work in the
Sistine Chapel had been put towards expenses for the pope's tomb was
false. Fattucci's report of what Buoninsegni had said, of late October
1524, and his own significant reaction have already been noted. The
letters leave no doubt that both he himself and Jacopo Salviati came
to regard Buoninsegni as an enemy.[234] But even if Vasari's report was
true, and Buoninsegni had taken the part of Bandinelli over the second
piazza statue, his role can never have been a determining one. The

letters from Rome abundantly confirm Cambi's recognition that Clement would allow nothing to hinder the ongoing work at San Lorenzo.

Michelangelo's only surviving letter about the *Hercules* project, existing in a preparatory draft, is of early November. Perhaps calmed by Salviati's counsel and by Florentine friends, it is a restrained response to an enquiry of Fattucci's about who in Florence has supported him in his wish to carry out the work. Michelangelo mentions, along with two others, his close friend Piero Gondi; but he also alludes to general public opinion. He is willing to undertake the project as a gift, when the pope permits it; without his consent, he can work on nothing other than his projects. Recently, he has been told that the *operai* would be prepared to wait for two or three years until the papal projects have been completed, provided that he would undertake it. The *operai* he refers to were, in all likelihood, those of the Palazzo della Signoria. His reference to popular support, rumours of which must have reached the Curia, matches what the anti-Medicean Cambi writes and would be confirmed by events that followed the collapse of the Medicean regime in Florence.[235]

Fattucci's successive letters from Rome show that Michelangelo had maintained silence over Clement's project for his own *Gigante*. In the meantime, the pope had changed his mind about the figure and had expressed the wish that it should face Palazzo Medici.[236] He finally broke his silence in an undated letter of December, which has good claim to be the most extraordinary to have survived, adopting a tone of mordant irony about his patron's project that has no parallel elsewhere in his correspondence. He refers to a project of 40 *braccia*, thus almost doubling the scale of what Clement had proposed. The statue should not impede the street, presumably Via de' Ginori, but should be situated on top of a barber's shop, facing the *piazza*, and be a hollow construction, facilitated by its construction in pieces. Since the shop has a chimney, the figure can hold a cornucopia to allow the smoke to escape. As a friend has suggested, the hollow head could serve as a dovecote. But he himself has had a better idea: to carve the figure on a still larger scale in the form of a tower. The head can serve as a much-needed bell-tower for San Lorenzo and the sound of the bells would issue from the giant's mouth, crying mercy, *misericordia*. As for the transportation of the materials, to ensure secrecy they could enter the city by night; problems over access through the city gates could be resolved by employing that on the Via San Gallo.[237]

This astonishing letter could, perhaps, be regarded as confirmation of an observation Michelangelo would make a little later, that the pen is always more expressive than the spoken word.[238] Yet its brutal irony does not seem to have caused excessive disturbance at the Curia. Pier Polo Marzi would reply on behalf of Clement in late December, alluding only briefly to the issue, assuring him that the pope regards the project a serious one, not a joke, and that if time permits, the assignment will go ahead. Marzi's allusion to time seems to have prompted Clement to add the autograph postscript that has been referred to earlier, reminding Michelangelo that popes do not live long.[239]

It has been suggested that the letter discloses the artist's contempt for Medicean projects such as this and reveals, even at this point, a distaste for his patron that would find violent expression later.[240] The letter, however, must be read in the light of Clement's resolve to deprive him of the colossus he so passionately wished to undertake and which would be given to him after the collapse of the Medicean regime in May 1527. That the choice of Bandinelli to carve the *Hercules* had plunged Michelangelo into depression is borne out by a letter of the well-disposed Giovanni Spina of only a few weeks earlier.[241]

IX

A VULNERABLE ARTIST

MONTHS OF OBSCURITY

Information about the artist in this period preceding the collapse of the Medicean regime in Florence is slender, but one episode sheds light on Michelangelo's self-imposed isolation and his apprehensions about the political situation. Writing to his agent in Florence, Giovanni Borromeo, on 22 February 1527, Federico Gonzaga, Marquis of Mantua, presses him to obtain some work from the artist that would contribute to the embellishment of his current enterprise, the Palazzo Te on the outskirts of the city. The *marchese* writes at length, expressing his long-standing admiration of Michelangelo's work. He wants either a sculpture or a painting, leaving the choice to the artist. If current obligations render an immediate response impossible, he will, for the present, settle for a chalk drawing. But he goes so far as to urge Borromeo to seek the help of the leading figures of the Medicean regime and to approach Cardinal Silvio Passerini and Ippolito de' Medici.[1]

Borromeo hastened to reply, writing on 1 March. He has sought out people who could influence the artist, but these are few in number, 'pochissimi'.[2] Writing again on 7 March, he is able to report some progress. He has gained access to Michelangelo through a common friend and has established some degree of familiarity with him. He hopes to obtain a work in marble which depicts nude figures in combat, a reference to the *Battle of the Centaurs and Lapiths* (pl. 2). Borromeo reckons that he has made some progress, in persuading Michelangelo to show him the work, since he never shows anything to anyone. All whom he has consulted have told him that the essential task is to divine the artist's whim. Michelangelo, although friendly, has explained that he is entirely subject to the wishes of the pope and the latter, in turn, is continually being warned that the work that the artist is engaged on will never be finished.[3]

Borromeo would fail to secure the *Battle of the Centaurs and Lapiths* for his master. Writing once more on 3 April, he reports that he has met with Michelangelo several times but has obtained no satisfactory response. He believes, like many others, that the artist is made deeply anxious by the threat of war, for he is rich and he laments that he finds himself in Florence. Borromeo has urged him to come to Mantua, where he has told him he would be warmly received. At some moments, the artist seems to have given the idea serious thought; but he fears to travel and perhaps is unwilling to leave his money. behind He has expressed his willingness to approach Cardinal Passerini and Ippolito de' Medici at an appropriate moment, thereby avoiding conflict with the pope.[4]

Few letters surpass these of Borromeo in evoking the artist's solitary existence and self-protective character. The latest also indicates awareness in Florence of gathering danger, for on 30 March the imperialist army had begun to move south, the troops almost out of control because of lack of pay. The universal fear that they would descend on Florence was lifted by the proximity of the army of the League of Cognac, part of which was commanded by Francesco Maria della Rovere, Duke of Urbino. Instead, Bourbon's army proceeded towards Rome and had reached Viterbo by 2 May. The papal city would be stormed on the sixth.[5]

The artist's growing concern about the deteriorating situation is reflected in what is certainly the last of his letters to have survived before the eclipse of his patron. Unfortunately, it is undated, but may have been written in February 1527, just a few weeks before Borromeo's abortive attempt to secure a work for his master. Addressed to a man whom he could trust, Giovanni Spina, Michelangelo confesses that he has lacked the courage to bring up the issue that concerns him, the future of his salary, given what he laconically refers to as the adversities of the times, which are unfavourable to his art. Even without his salary, he will continue to work for the pope, but will no longer be able to keep what he refers to as 'open house'. He can live elsewhere with much less expense, and this would also relieve Spina of having to pay the rent on the house where he now lives. If his salary is maintained, however, he will stay where he is. The artist's characteristic reference to his financial burden cannot be reconciled with the observation passed by Borromeo on the money he is reluctant to leave, were he to go to Mantua.[6]

The letter is not free of ambiguities. The artist cannot have planned to move back to his own property on the Via Ghibellina. He had rented out the main house on Via Ghibellina after the quarrel with his family; *ricordi* show that he received rent of 22 florins a year, a sum that he would continue to collect until 1537, three years after he had left Florence for ever.[7] His domestic outgoings seem to have been relatively modest. Apart from the invaluable presence of Antonio Mini, whose life with Michelangelo will be returned to, the artist seems to have had two domestic helpers in the house, a boy and a serving woman. It seems clear that all papal subvention for the rent of the house on Via dell'Ariento came to an end with the sack of Rome in May 1527. Nevertheless, the artist remained there for a further two years, moving to rented accommodation in what is now the Via di Mezzo in May 1529.[8]

One *ricordo* of the spring of 1527 is of particular interest. On the evening of 29 April the artist records that, some days earlier, his friend Piero di Filippo Gondi had asked him if he could hide some articles in the New Sacristy at San Lorenzo. And on the same evening, Gondi began to carry into the sacristy certain clothes that belonged to his sisters. Unwilling to intrude, Michelangelo discreetly absented himself, giving Gondi the key to the chapel.[9]

He records that Gondi had made his request because of the dangers facing Florence. However, when the artist refers to the danger 'in which we find ourselves', he does not make clear whether he here refers to all Florentines or to those associated with the deeply unpopular Medicean regime.

Gondi's request must have been prompted by events in the city on Friday, 26 April, when there had been a popular uprising against the regime headed by the widely despised Cardinal Silvio Passerini. It had been prompted by a brief absence of Passerini, two fellow cardinals and Ippolito de' Medici, when they left Florence to meet with the leaders of the army of the league at Cestello, just outside the city. For a few hours, the government had been thrown out and the constitution of 1512 restored. By the evening the government had been re-established.[10]

Its days, however, were numbered. News of the sack of Rome reached Florence on either 10 or 11 May, and the scale of the disaster would inevitably lead to the collapse of Medicean rule in Florence.[11] Cardinal Passerini and Ippolito de' Medici were permitted to leave the city on 17 May. The first Signoria of the new regime was established on 31 May, and Niccolò Capponi, a long-standing opponent of the Medici, was subsequently elected *gonfaloniere* for a one-year term.[12]

How did the artist view such profound changes? There is no evidence to tell us and we have almost no information about his life in 1527, a fact that has scarcely changed since Symonds lamented a dearth of material in 1893.[13] Nevertheless, one piece of evidence survives that demonstrates Clement's faith in his artist while he himself was a prisoner in Castel Sant'Angelo. The beleaguered pope issued a brief on 29 September 1527 appointing Michelangelo superintendent of fortifications of Bologna, one of the few cities not lost to the papacy following the events of May. The nature of the work with which he was entrusted constitutes a remarkable anticipation of the role that he would undertake for the Florentine republic in the months ahead.[14] Clement's commission, which Michelangelo may never have received, also brings to mind what Piero Soderini's wife, Argentina Malaspina, had written to her mother as long ago as 1516, describing the artist's familiarity with military architecture and the capacity to prepare defences.[15]

While Michelangelo did not cease to write *ricordi* throughout 1527, these are almost exclusively concerned with minor outgoings or the details of what he was receiving from his properties. From a letter of August, we learn that he has been elected to a minor office, which he has decided not to take up. A further one counsels Buonarroto not to accept it in his place on account of the plague, which he describes in a characteristic phrase as going from bad to worse. It is not worth risking one's life for an annual salary of 40 ducats.[16]

The counsel was sound but did not save Buonarroto's life. He would die of the wave of plague that swept through Tuscany less than a year later, on 2 July 1528. It was the same onset of plague that would kill Vasari's father in Arezzo in August. It was a particularly cruel fate, for, of the artist's surviving brothers, he alone was a married man with children and the only one who had shown some capacity for business.[17] Already on 30 June Michelangelo had made payment to an apothecary on account of Buonarroto's illness. A series of *ricordi* document the payments relating to his brother's burial in Santa Croce, dated 6 July; they include outgoings for candles and for the transportation of the body from Settignano.[18]

Of the brothers, there can be no doubt that Buonarroto meant the most to him. We can recall his passionate concern when he got the news of Buonarroto's grave illness in 1510 and his readiness to drop everything to come to Florence. And Buonarroto would be associated with Lodovico in the artist's heartfelt verses written following their father's death in March 1531. A further touching allusion to Buonarroto's death appears in a letter from Michelangelo's former assistant and companion of long ago, Piero d'Argenta. From what he writes, it emerges that the artist had informed him of Buonarroto's death. Piero's reply, from Argenta, is dated 31 March 1529, and is one of the most moving of the entire *carteggio*. For he ends his letter with the heartfelt message that he has the artist always in his mind and that there is not a day when he does not think of him. There could be no more striking indication of the feelings that, despite his notoriously rebarbative personality, Michelangelo could inspire in those who had been close to him.[19]

We can follow some of the artist's public activities from the late summer of 1528. But we are very much in the dark as to the events of 1527 until early 1528. In his later Life of the artist of 1568, Vasari would assert that despite the adversities of his Medicean patron, the artist continued to work secretly in the sacristy at San Lorenzo, a statement that has occasioned much discussion. But the increasing anti-Medicean sentiment in the city would surely have rendered so politically charged an act of clandestine loyalty unlikely. By early 1527 the celebrated epitaph in San Lorenzo honouring Cosimo Vecchio de' Medici was under threat. Images of members of the family at Santissima Annunziata were destroyed and the obliteration of Medici arms in churches that had enjoyed their patronage was sanctioned by the Otto di Guardia. This *damnatio memoriae* was particularly bitter for Pope Clement, and scarcely an encouragement for an apprehensive artist to continue with his assignment.[20]

More persuasive is the suggestion that his thoughts turned once more to the project of the dead Julius's tomb. That the two-figure marble group that Vasari would later refer to as the *Victory* is a work begun in this time between 1527 and 1530 has been proposed in the past and the suggestion has much to recommend it (pls. 42 and 44). In 1527 the artist was a relatively free man.[21]

A further neglected fact might be regarded as strengthening the argument. On the evening of Friday, 26 April, when the anti-Medicean uprising was put down, the artist's della Rovere patron, Duke Francesco Maria, in his capacity as one of the generals of the league, would enter Florence. On that same evening, the terms on which the insurgents surrendered were drawn up in Or San Michele. Duke Francesco Maria was one of those present. And on Sunday, 28 April, he would proceed to wring from the Florentine regime the surrender of the fortress of San Leo, which Pope Leo had bestowed on Florence after his expulsion of the della Rovere from their state exactly ten years earlier. We can only speculate as to how Michelangelo may have reacted to the presence in Florence of the fearsome patron whose threats had so recently unnerved him. Francesco Maria left Florence on 2 May, which could have allowed him time to make contact with the artist over his neglected obligations.[22]

It may be no coincidence that the group of *Victory* is one of the least recorded of all his carvings and that the year 1527 is one so sparsely documented. If the date for its inception here suggested is correct, one of the earliest artists to have caught sight of it may have been Bartolommeo Ammannati, when he broke into Michelangelo's workshop just before the siege, in 1529.[23]

SERVING THE REPUBLIC

On 22 August 1528 the republican government, headed by Niccolò Capponi as *gonfaloniere*, commissioned Michelangelo to undertake the carving of the block that had been ordered by Bandinelli at Carrara in April 1523 and transported to Florence in the summer of 1525. They refer to the fact that the marble had been planned for 'la imagine et figura di Cacco', in other words for a Hercules and Cacus. Notwithstanding that the marble had been assigned to others in the past – Bandinelli's name is nowhere mentioned – they now concede the marble to Michelangelo, their cherished citizen. He is to carve a figure together with, or united with, another, according to the artist's judgement. The statue is to be placed where the government will decide. And the artist is to begin work by the Feast of All Saints, 1 November.[24]

Thus, twenty-seven years to the month after he had been commissioned to carve the marble *David*, Michelangelo is now asked to undertake the companion statue, a commission formally denied him by Pope Clement three years earlier in favour of Bandinelli. This document is sparing of details. No time limit is laid down for the completion of the work. Nor is there any reference to payment. In the light of his consuming wish to carve the sculpture, he may well

have offered the Signoria to undertake it for nothing. It may be
recalled that in his letter to Fattucci of early November 1525, desperate
to acquire the commission, he had offered to undertake the work as
a gift.[25]

Although, as has been seen earlier, the artist seems to have worked
on a project for the *piazza* of Hercules fighting Antaeus in 1524, the
government retained the subject of Hercules and Cacus established by
the Medicean regime; in this case, political change did not lead to any
radical refashioning of public imagery.[26] Many questions concerning
this new undertaking arise. It is unknown how far Bandinelli had
proceeded with the project. Vasari, who wrote an extensive biography
of Bandinelli for his second edition of the *Vite* of 1568, did not allow
his deep distaste for the artist to limit his aim to provide a very detailed
account. He wrote that, the final design established, Bandinelli made
a clay model of the scale of the projected marble, but does not give
details as to how far carving had progressed.[27] Vasari states that
Michelangelo, at a point not clearly defined, abandoned the subject of
Hercules and Cacus in favour of Samson fighting with two Philistines.[28] As has been seen, the Signoria had referred to a Hercules and
Cacus and it is probably for this initial subject that the artist made the
clay model now in the Casa Buonarroti, the only surviving example
of a multi-figured model by him to have survived. The project of
Samson, although no autograph model survives, enjoyed a greater fame,
recorded in a striking number of bronze renditions.

Any prospect that Michelangelo would proceed with carving the
sculpture planned for the Piazza della Signoria would be excluded by
very different demands from the Florentine government, demands
provoked by the steadily deteriorating political situation. As Vasari
would write, Michelangelo had other things to think about than pol-
ishing marble. The pope had left Viterbo and returned to a devastated
Rome in early October 1528. Of his many tribulations, one of the
most bitter was the behaviour of the Florentines in proclaiming an
anti-Medicean regime and indulging in ever more violent manifesta-
tions of hostility to the family; even Clement's illegitimacy was brought

up. While Niccolò Capponi remained *gonfaloniere*, all hope of an accommodation with Clement was not lost, but his attempts to mediate through the offices of Jacopo Salviati would steadily weaken his position and lead to his loss of office in the spring of 1529.[29] He had already been anxious to renounce power in February 1529, and he would be driven out in April, to be replaced by Francesco Carducci, a passionate anti-Medicean. Two months later, a treaty was drawn up between Pope Clement and the Emperor Charles v in Barcelona that would spell the future destruction of Florence's last republic.[30]

Michelangelo would become progressively more involved in the urgent requirements to defend the city. In June 1528 the government reconstituted a body that had been a feature of Soderini's regime, the Nove della Milizia, its primary duty to strengthen the physical protectorate of the city.[31] Michelangelo would be appointed a member of the Nove on 10 January 1529. There can be no doubt, however, that he had become involved with the ongoing preparations months earlier. A letter written on 3 October 1528 requests his presence at a meeting at San Miniato, where Capponi himself would be present.[32]

Evidence of his involvement earlier than this is provided by the remarkable group of drawings in the Casa Buonarroti that he made to prepare new defences at different points around the city; some of these sheets are exceptionally large. The precise sites for which the designs were made are not always identifiable. But a number were drawn for the gate leading to Prato, the Porta del Prato, others for the gate of San Piero Gattolini, today Porta Romana, still others for a bastion at the Prato d'Ognissanti. The series of drawings appears to have been made in the summer of 1528.[33] Their range and ambition may strike us as unrealizable in any plausible time scale, but it must be recalled that these were designs for earthworks, not for fortifications of stone.[34]

It has been observed that none of these elaborate drawings relates to the hill of San Miniato, and the need for its fortification would promote a conflict between Michelangelo and Niccolò Capponi, the artist insistent on promoting this and Capponi unwilling to act. The differences between them would be described in letters that the staunch anti-Medicean Giovanbattista Busini would address to Benedetto Varchi in the late 1540s in order to assist him in writing his history of Florence. Busini knew Michelangelo in Rome in this later period and much of his information was gained from the artist himself. He would write that Capponi would always oppose the artist's wishes and that the *gonfaloniere* would send him on missions away from Florence in order to remove him from the scene. These contributions cannot, however, be depended on, since there is little doubt that the ageing artist would alter the record. In fact, Michelangelo's missions, first to Pisa and Leghorn in June 1529, followed by that to Ferrara in late July, took place only after Capponi had been deprived of office in April.[35]

Capponi's attitude may have sprung from a conviction that the city would escape a siege. He had, after all, been driven from office before the alliance between Clement and the emperor had been forged. But he may also have been influenced by a report on the city's defences drawn up only a little earlier. It had been Pope Clement himself who had recently become concerned about their vulnerability because of the growing threat of an imperialist invasion. One issue had been the fortification of the hills beyond the Arno, from San Miniato to Monte-oliveto. As recently as 1526, in response to these anxieties, a report was ordered by the Medicean regime from Niccolò Machiavelli and a professional military engineer, Pietro Navarra. They had conducted their inspection in March; Machiavelli wrote the report and took it to Rome on 6 April. It had concluded that the area was indefensible. But Clement rejected their conclusions.[36]

Michelangelo's own situation would be radically changed in April 1529. On the sixth of the month, just before Capponi would be forced from office, he was formally appointed to a new post, Governor General and procurator of the fortifications and walls of Florence, by the Dieci di Balìa. The text of the appointment is a remarkable one. He is praised for his professional gifts and described as unsurpassed by any master of his time. He is also extolled for his love of his country, which equals that of any of its citizens. The Dieci point out that up to the present time he has worked without pay. He is now to be paid one large gold florin a day for his services. The appointment, to last for the next twelve months, was confirmed by the powerful Council of Eight the same day.[37]

The creation of the post was a recognition of the need for some controlling presence over the urgent task of attempting to defend the city against attack, above all from the threat of artillery. The issue had preoccupied the artist as early as the summer of 1528, when he had made the drawings now in the Casa Buonarroti. We have no informative letters in these summer months, but it seems probable that he was anxious on many counts, not least the fate of his properties situated outside the city's walls. And we can recall his fearful letters to his family of 1512, when Florence had been threatened by an imperial army. The sack of Prato must surely have been in many minds as the situation continued to deteriorate in the late summer.

As already noted, in his later letters to Varchi, Busini would emphasize Michelangelo's insistence on the need to fortify the hill of San Miniato. The same note is struck in Condivi's biography, where it is implied that serious work began there only after the artist's return from his flight to Venice.[38] Defensive work, however, had begun months earlier; contracts with men entrusted to dig protective ditches at San Miniato date from mid-June 1529 and there can be no doubt that many of the steps required to defend the site were under way at an earlier date.[39] The measure adopted to protect the church's *campanile* from hostile artillery fire included a protective covering of wool to deflect the cannon balls. Condivi refers to the use of mattresses as a protection and the Venetian envoy in Florence, reporting back to the senate in late October, when Michelangelo was still absent, would refer to the woollen protection that effected excellent resistance to enemy fire.[40] Michelangelo's work for the defence of Florence did not escape all contemporary criticism.[41] But his contribution to the defences of the city was acknowledged in an eloquent passage written by Donato Giannotti many years later. Giannotti was an important witness, for it had been he who had served as secretary to the Dieci in these last republican years.[42]

MICHELANGELO AND ALFONSO D'ESTE

Michelangelo left Florence for Ferrara in the last days of July 1529. It was his second absence from the city on official business. In early June he had gone to Pisa, accompanied by his long-standing assistant, Stefano Lunetti. His presence had been sought for some time by the Florentine commissioner there, Francesco Tosinghi. Advice was needed on means to prevent the Arno in flood from damaging the citadel. They arrived in Pisa on the evening of 4 June. With characteristic reticence, Michelangelo had declined the commissioner's offer of hospitality and lodged in a Pisan inn. He followed his stay in Pisa with a rapid visit to check the situation in Livorno, before returning to Florence a few days later. By 17 June he had agreed with the Dieci di Balia on the steps required to solve the problems in Pisa.[43]

The mission to Ferrara was of a different nature, taking him outside Florentine territory. Alfonso d'Este was an ally of the republic and a fervent enemy of Pope Clement; he had seized papal Modena just over a month after Rome had been sacked. Florence would proceed to engage his son Ercole as military commander. However, the formal *condotta* to engage him was subject to repeated delays and was formally ratified only as late as December 1528. It would provide no effective assistance to the embattled republic, although Florentine disillusionment still lay in the future.[44]

Letters of credence were addressed to the recently appointed ambassador in Ferrara, Galeotto Giugni, by the Signoria and the Dieci di Balia on 28 July. The former express the hope that Giugni will arrange a meeting between the artist and Duke Alfonso and that he will return to Florence with the knowledge they are seeking. The Dieci's letter is more explicit. They write that Michelangelo is being sent to Ferrara at the wish of the Nove della Milizia to examine Duke Alfonso's fortifications.[45]

Giugni, a member of one of the most distinguished Florentine families serving the republic, would write from Ferrara to the Dieci on 2 July, reporting Michelangelo's arrival. He is keen that the artist should return with all the information that is required.[46] He has, however, been mortified by the artist's behaviour; he has refused to stay with Giugni, recalling his similar recent rejection of Tosinghi's hospitality. He added a postscript on the following day. He has spent the morning with Michelangelo inspecting the city's defences. Subsequently, they have seen Duke Alfonso, who was anxious to meet the artist. He has spent the rest of the day with him, showing him everything.[47]

From what Giugni writes, there can be no doubt that Michelangelo was shown Alfonso's celebrated *camerino* with its mythological paintings by Giovanni Bellini, Dosso and Titian; Condivi, in a brief passage concerning the Ferrara visit, also states that he was shown everything. And it was on this occasion that the duke brought up the topic they had discussed as long ago as 1512 on the scaffolding of the Sistine Chapel, his desire to have a work by the artist. Condivi even adds the anecdote that Alfonso had threatened to keep him a prisoner until he had promised to supply a painting or a sculpture.[48] No evidence survives suggesting that the duke had previously pressed Michelangelo to fulfil the promise of 1512, whereas he had made great efforts to acquire a work from Raphael. These had begun from as early as 1514 and persisted until Raphael's death in April 1520.[49] Had he exhibited the same zeal with Michelangelo, some trace of this would surely have survived in the artist's carefully preserved correspondence.[50]

The assumption is sometimes made that the work that Michelangelo agreed to undertake for Alfonso was destined for the *camerino*.[51] But this is not plausible. The scale of the *Leda* probably exceeded that of the other paintings made for the room.[52] In addition, by the late summer of 1529 it is unlikely that there was still space available to accommodate a further painting in the *camerino*.[53] Most decisive is the rarely noted fact that the *Leda* was painted on panel, an anomaly in a room of canvases that Alfonso would never have countenanced.[54]

The date when Michelangelo was back in Florence is not recorded. The Dieci would write to Giugni on 8 August, expressing through him their warmest thanks for the pains that the duke had taken; at that point, the artist had not yet returned. By 8 September he was urgently awaited in Arezzo to inspect the defences there. Whether he went is unrecorded.[55]

THE FLIGHT TO VENICE

Although one of the most discussed episodes in biographies of the artist, his flight from Florence to Venice only a few weeks after his return from Ferrara still raises problems of interpretation. And Michelangelo's own subsequent comments go little way to clarifying what precipitated the event.

In a letter that bears no date but which was probably written in late September, addressed to a fellow Florentine, Battista della Palla, he states that he had left Florence with the aim of going to France; but the dangers of making the journey through German territory has deterred him. He nevertheless emphasizes, at the letter's close, that he is consumed by the desire to go.[56]

In choosing to write to della Palla, he was seeking help from a man familiar with France and the court of Francis i and who had played a conspicuous role in procuring works of art for the king. One of these was his own early marble statue of *Hercules*, carved thirty-six years earlier. He asks della Palla whether, if he made the journey, he would accompany him.[57]

Michelangelo refers to his leaving the city in an almost surreal passage. While at work on the fortifications, he was approached near the Porta San Niccolò by someone whom he did not know who urged him to flee the city. Having obtained horses, he took the unknown individual's advice.[58]

We may compare this passage, where it would appear that Michelangelo was unprepared to confide fully in della Palla, with what Giambattista Busini would be told by Michelangelo about the episode in
Rome nearly twenty years later. It had been distrust of Baglione
Malatesta, newly appointed head of the city's defences, that compelled
him to flee. Malatesta had, he states, left artillery unguarded outside the
walls. Questioning a fellow member of the Nove, the latter had replied
that Malatesta came from a family of traitors and that he would betray
Florence. Actuated by the fear these words provoked, he sought out
a fellow Florentine, Rinaldo Corsini. The two, accompanied by the
artist's servant, unidentified by Busini but undoubtedly Antonio Mini,
finally succeeded in leaving the city, after a number of failures, by the
Porta al Prato.[59]

The account that Michelangelo gave to Busini has a certain plausibility, for it would be Baglione Malatesta who would arrange the
surrender of Florence to the imperialists in the first week of August
of the following year. Although he had accepted the role of commander
of the Florentine troops in April 1529, however, the dependable Venetian ambassador in Florence, Carlo Capello, would note that Baglione
arrived in the city only around 17 September, a fact that must weaken
the belief that rumours of his treachery were circulating in the city
early enough to precipitate Michelangelo's flight on the twenty-first.[60]
Capello, in a further letter of 24 September, would describe the general
atmosphere of apprehension in the city and state that a substantial
number of Florentines had fled.[61]

No single event may have precipitated the artist's flight. But by
mid-September it had become clear that those whom the Florentines
still looked to for assistance, above all the French, had abandoned any
plan to come to the city's rescue. The imperial army was drawing
steadily closer. Some of the artist's most devoted friends would refer
to the flight in unvarnished terms. Writing to him on 1 January 1530,
Piero d'Argenta would report that he has heard from Cardinal Lorenzo
Pucci that the artist had fled to avoid the ill fortune of the war in
Florence.[62]

When discussing the idea of the artist's leaving Florence for Mantua in 1527, Giovanni Borromeo had referred to his reluctance to leave his money behind. Now, in 1529, he took money with him. He himself would subsequently tell Sebastiano del Piombo that he left with 3,000 ducats.[63] Varchi, on the other hand, would state that he travelled with no less than 12,000 gold florins carefully sewn into his clothes to escape detection.[64] A much more dependable witness, at San Lorenzo throughout the period of the siege, was Giovan Battista Figiovanni. In his *ricordanza*, valuable, as has been seen, for the history of the New Sacristy, he would write that Michelangelo fled, fearful for his money.[65]

Details about Michelangelo's flight to Venice are lacking. It is known that, en route, he lost the company of Rinaldo Corsini, who went to meet Galeotto Giugni in Ferrara and on his advice returned to Florence.[66] In fact, in the text of the *bando*, issued by the Otto di Guardia on 30 September, denouncing thirteen Florentines, Michelangelo among them, Corsini's name is one of a number cancelled, demonstrating that he had returned. Those who failed to return by 6 October would be subjected to extreme penalties.[67] In a further decree of 7 October, however, Michelangelo's name was excluded from the list of those whose property would be seized by the government.[68]

Almost nothing is known about the artist's stay in Venice; no letters written in the city have survived. It is a commonplace that he chose to live on the relatively secluded Giudecca. This may well be true, but the evidence is not conclusive. In his letters to Varchi, Busini limits himself to stating that Michelangelo took a house in which to live, but he does not specify where it was. Varchi would refer to the Giudecca as the place chosen by the artist in his funeral oration of 1564 and would repeat the statement in his *Storia*. That he lived on the Giudecca is also stated by Vasari in the second edition of the Life of 1568.

Two letters from Battista della Palla to Michelangelo, addressed to him in Venice, have survived. One is dated 24 October and the other

19 November and are not, therefore, immediate replies to the artist's own appeal.[69] In the earlier, della Palla encourages him to return to Florence, giving an almost rhapsodic description of life in the heroic city under siege. In the second, he once again presses him to return, and encloses no less than ten similar appeals from other Florentines and a copy of the safe conduct that had been issued by the Florentine government on 20 October. In fact, the artist had already left Venice before the second letter was written, having reached Ferrara on 10 November.

Della Palla addressed him at the house of a fellow Tuscan, Bartolommeo Panciatichi, but this does not necessarily imply that the artist was living with him. He asks Michelangelo to remember him to Antonio Brucioli. He himself was now living in exile in Venice. Distrusted for adopting Lutheran views, he had also deeply antagonized those with Savonarolan sympathies around the *gonfaloniere*, Carducci. Arrested by the Otto di Guardia in June 1529, he had been subsequently exiled for two years.[70]

Although we lack letters written by Michelangelo in Venice, there has survived a sheet of *ricordi* listing a number of expenses. At the top is written the date 10 September and the location, Venice. This inscription led writers in the nineteenth century to suppose that Michelangelo had travelled to Venice not once but twice, the earlier a secret and unrecorded one that had preceded the notorious flight later in the same month. A more convincing interpretation, published but still frequently overlooked, is that he began a letter with the date 10 September, realized that he had written the wrong month, abandoned the letter and used the sheet to list his expenses; the names of Rinaldo Corsini, Antonio Mini and Piloto appear in the list. So does a Venetian, for he records that he has paid 5 ducats for his rent to a 'messer Loredan'. Which member of this extensive Venetian family has not been established, but the very fact of the payment suggests that Michelangelo made his list shortly before leaving Venice to return to Florence.[71] The appearance of Piloto's name in the *ricordi* might appear to confirm Vasari's statement that Piloto had accompanied him on the flight, despite the absence of his name from Busini's account, where, following the old master's information, there were only two, Corsini and his assistant, Mini. Piloto, however, seems to have travelled to Venice quite frequently in the period that concerns us and could well have already been there before Michelangelo's own arrival.[72]

Michelangelo's intention, to go to France, remained an issue very much alive during the Venice stay. This fact is confirmed by a remarkable series of letters written by the French ambassador in Venice, Lazare de Baïf. The earliest surviving one, dated 14 October, was written to Francis I and his grandmother, Anne de Montmorency. He has heard of Michelangelo's presence in Venice. He states that the artist never sees anyone. Reporting that he does not wish to remain in Venice, he firmly believes that he would accept a good offer from the king. If so instructed, he will attempt to meet the artist.[73]

Baïf repeated his information in a letter of 23 October, once again referring to the artist's lack of appearance. He reiterates that, if offered a good arrangement, Michelangelo would leave for France. He needs to know what terms the king is prepared to offer.[74]

Events would overtake the negotiations. On 16 November Baïf announced the artist's departure from Venice. In the same letter, he pronounced a harsh judgement on the artist's cowardice.[75] A further letter followed on 9 December, after the offer from the king had been received. By this date, Baïf had lost all hope that Michelangelo would enter the king's service. He has, nevertheless, written to the French envoy in Florence, Claude Dedieu, that, in the event of the move, Michelangelo could expect an annual salary of 1,200 livres and a house.[76]

Nothing that Baïf writes suggests that Michelangelo sought a public presence while in Venice; rather, his letters fortify the impression that he remained a recluse. Against this view there can be cited the claim that he was asked by the Venetian government to make a design for the bridge over the Grand Canal at the Rialto. Condivi alludes to such a design in vague terms and implies that the drawing was made recently, a suggestion not compatible with a date of 1529.[77] In his Life of 1568, Vasari writes that it is said that the artist designed a bridge for the Rialto while in Venice, a cautious statement. His reference does not inspire quiet confidence, for he states that the invitation came from Doge Andrea Gritti, who died in 1528, months before Michelangelo's residence in the city.[78]

The Florentine Signoria had issued a safe conduct for his return on 20 October 1529, valid for the whole of the coming November.[79] Just a day earlier, his servant Catarina, on what must have been the artist's instructions, had removed objects, including foodstuffs, from the house. Since the *ricordo* was written by Francesco Granacci, it is evident that Michelangelo's devoted friend of many years was acting for him.[80] Another *ricordo*, again written by Granacci, records that a shoemaker, Bastiano di Francesco, had been paid on 22 October to travel to Venice to find the artist. We are told by Varchi that Bastiano was a man held in deep affection by Michelangelo and that he took the safe conduct with him.[81]

Michelangelo must have decided to return to Florence towards the end of the first week of November, for on the ninth Galeotto Giugni, in Ferrara, would report to the Dieci di Balìa that the artist had arrived there. The Dieci had taken the step of informing Giugni of the safe conduct on the day that it had been issued and he would contribute to the easing of the fugitive's return.[82] Alfonso d'Este would also help, providing the artist with a safe conduct for his journey through his territory on 10 November.[83] Michelangelo must have left Ferrara with a sense of gratitude towards the man for whom he would undertake a monumental painting.[84]

The artist appears to have reached Florence before 23 November, on which date he and a fellow fugitive were released from the terms of the *bando* of 30 September. Michelangelo's punishment was a modest one, which was subject to review: exclusion from the Great Council for a period of three years.[85] He would, however, be one of the forty citizens required to pay a forced loan of 1,000 ducats to the embattled government in the coming months.[86]

THE *LEDA*

There can be little doubt that Michelangelo began to prepare for the painting of *Leda* for Alfonso d'Este in early 1530 (pl. 45). One of his earliest sketches for the work was drawn on a sheet of paper containing an autograph *ricordo* of 6 January 1530.[87] Perhaps, at this point, the most intensive work to strengthen the city's defences had been concluded, leaving him sufficient time to implement his promise to Duke Alfonso.[88] His preparation for the work was evidently undertaken with great care. He went to the length of making a full-scale cartoon for the painting, which, as already noted, was carried out on wood. As far as is known, this was the first time he had put brush to panel since the *tondo* painted for Agnolo Doni.

Patron and artist must have discussed the subject of the proposed work before Michelangelo left Ferrara to return to Florence; that this had been already settled on the scaffolding of the Sistine Chapel as long ago as 1512 is unlikely. Alfonso himself probably proposed, and certainly sanctioned, the subject of *Leda and the Swan*, one of Jupiter's sexual conquests briefly referred to by Ovid in his *Metamorphoses* and a frequent subject in antique sculpture. It has been pointed out that the choice could have had particular significance for the duke. The Ferrarese poet Ariosto had specifically associated Alfonso and his brother Ippolito with Castor and Pollux, the male offspring of Jupiter and Leda, in his *Orlando Furioso*; they make an appearance in the most complete surviving records of Michelangelo's painting.[89]

The dramatic changes in Florence following the fall of the city in August 1530 aroused Alfonso's concern about his painting. This is confirmed by a letter he wrote to Michelangelo from Venice on 22 October 1530, two months after the Medici had regained Florence. He has heard from his former envoy in Florence that the artist had mentioned the painting to him; every hour will seem a year until he sees it. He will send his agent, Pisanello, to arrange its delivery. With regard to payment, he leaves the matter to the artist because he has not seen the work.[90]

As all who are familiar with the project will know, Duke Alfonso would never see the painting, for his agent succeeded in totally alienating the artist. We are told by Condivi that Pisanello had called the work he had come to collect a small affair, 'una poca cosa'. Michelangelo, referring to Pisanello's activities as a merchant, had replied that he was doing bad business for his master and threw him out.[91]

In the months that would elapse between the abortive visit of Pisanello and the artist's decision to give the painting to his assistant, Antonio Mini, the *Leda* had come to public notice. This emerges from a remarkable reference to the painting from one of Michelangelo's circle in Rome, Benvenuto della Volpaia, dated 26 November 1531. The stir that the work had provoked in Florence had been reported to the Curia and no less than Pope Clement himself had asked for information about the painting. It seems that Michelangelo had not secreted the work away as might have been expected. It is likely that he had worked on the panel in his studio in the Via Mozza.[92]

Michelangelo's lost painting was an astonishingly literal representation of the sexual encounter of the disguised god and a human. Its impact was achieved by the scale: the naked woman occupies almost the whole space in the painting and the force of the invention is heightened by the way she holds her lover between her legs.[93] The composition is indebted to an antique relief that was on the Quirinal Hill in Rome until late in the sixteenth century and to an onyx cameo that the artist could have seen as a boy in the Medici Palace; but in Michelangelo's hands his sources have gained an astonishing power.[94] Although dependant on a painted copy of the *Leda* sent to Venice, Aretino, some years later, would express his rapt admiration of the work.[95]

Michelangelo would not sell the painting despite the stir it had created in Florence. Instead, he would give it as a present to his long-standing assistant Antonio Mini. Born in July 1506, Mini entered the artist's service in 1523. Michelangelo's previous record over hiring assistants had been one dogged by excessive expectations and poor judgement. His employment of Pietro Urbano had ended particularly badly. Mini would prove to be a dependable aid and also, like other assistants before him, an aspiring draughtsman.[96] His repeated appearances in Michelangelo's *ricordi* indicate to what lengths the master depended on him. As has been seen, he would accompany Michelangelo on the flight to Venice and would take care of many tasks on his behalf. It is in a *ricordo* of his, for example, that we learn of the break-in of Michelangelo's workshop in the summer of 1529.[97] A number of Mini's exercises as a draughtsman survive and constitute a record of his copying of the master's drawings and his attempts to achieve a competence of his own.[98]

He received not only the painting but also the artist's preparatory cartoon and a wealth of other objects, comprising models and drawings. His setbacks in France need not be recounted here; he would die there, his ambition to make his fortune unrealized, in late 1533. Although Francis I would ultimately acquire Michelangelo's painting, Mini had not succeeded in his aim of profiting from the treasures assigned to him.[99]

Michelangelo may have come to regret his generosity as an act of ill judgement, but it nevertheless reveals an altruism often denied him. And the very fact of his carrying the painting to completion points to a fortitude that is in stark contrast to the panic that had led to his flight only a few months earlier. By May 1530, when work on the painting was probably under way, the dead in Florence, a city reduced by hunger and plague, were so numerous that they went unburied.[100]

X

FLORENTINE EPILOGUE

THE RETURN OF THE MEDICI

The formal surrender of the city took place on Friday, 12 August 1530. Weeks earlier, Malatesta Baglione, at odds with the extremist *piagnoni* in the government, had concluded that the republic was no longer capable of prolonged resistance.[1] Fears grew that, if the besiegers succeeded in entering the city, it would be put to the sack. It has been calculated that, by August 1530, as many as 36,000 Florentines had perished from plague or starvation.[2]

The terms of the surrender, agreed at the headquarters of Baccio Valori, Pope Clement's commissioner, were to be ratified by the emperor and the pope within two months. But many of the clauses agreed on 12 August would be ignored, particularly the one that had promised an amnesty for those involved in the service of the republic.[3] Benedetto Varchi would provide a remarkable review of the fate of those who had served the republic, listing those executed or sent into exile.[4] Mention can be made of two cases, since both the men involved played a role in Michelangelo's life. He informs us that Donato Giannotti, who had served as secretary to the republican Dieci, a body abolished by the new regime, was subjected to exile from the city. The case of Battista della Palla was much worse. He was arrested in his own house, tortured and then condemned to life imprisonment in the citadel at Pisa, where he would die in 1532, probably from poison.[5]

Michelangelo's going into hiding at this critical moment is an episode that has attracted less comment than the flight to Venice but is, nevertheless, one that biographers have not neglected. Vasari made no reference to the event in his Life of the artist in the *Vite* of 1550, although he can scarcely have been unaware of it. Condivi made good this failure in his Life of 1553, writing that a search for the artist was instigated by the victors and that his house was subjected to a vigorous but fruitless intrusion. Condivi writes that the artist, fearful of what the authorities might do, had taken refuge in the house of a great friend, where he remained for many days. Revising his Life in 1568, Vasari would treat the episode only in reticent terms.[6]

Who was the artist's great friend who gave him shelter? An old story referred to Michelangelo having been hidden in the *campanile* of San Niccolò sopr'Arno.[7] This in turn led to the suggestion that he had been taken in and protected by members of the Quaratesi family, for one of their palaces was situated close to San Niccolò. It was above all with the youthful Andrea Quaratesi, born in November 1522, that Michelangelo enjoyed close ties. There is evidence that Andrea took informal drawing lessons; a sheet at Oxford contains his attempts, marked by a striking lack of success, to copy drawings by his mentor. A much more striking testimony to the friendship is the artist's black chalk portrait of Andrea, made either before or soon after the siege of Florence.[8]

The belief, however, that it was the Quaratesi who had sheltered the artist has been put in doubt by the relatively recent discovery of Figiovanni's *ricordanza*, which has been quoted earlier when examining the events surrounding the history of the New Sacristy at San Lorenzo. He writes that, following Michelangelo's disappearance in 1530, Bartolommeo Valori wished to have the artist killed by Alessandro Corsini. Figiovanni states that it was he who saved Michelangelo from death and secured his belongings.[9]

That Valori planned to have the artist killed may seem scarcely credible, although it must be recalled that no other Florentine who had so conspicuously served the republic escaped death or exile. The reference to Alessandro Corsini is also noteworthy. He had recently fled Florence to serve the pope. Condemned as a traitor, the republican government had had his effigy painted on one of the walls of the Bargello, a traditional treatment meted out to traitors.[10] Another fact that favours the dependability of Figiovanni's account is the noteworthy improvement of relations between Michelangelo and himself in the post-republican period. And, as will be discussed below, it was for Valori that Michelangelo would undertake both architectural and sculptural assignments.

A further aspect of Michelangelo's evident dread of reprisals after the siege ended is again owed to Varchi. Referring to the fact that, in 1506, the Bolognese had destroyed the palace of the Bentivoglio family after their expulsion from the city, he goes on to state that many credited Michelangelo with the idea of destroying Palazzo Medici and creating in its place a public square that could be called the Piazza de' Muli, a savage reference to Pope Clement's illegitimate birth. Varchi concedes that he never discovered the source of the story but adds that the artist had expressed sympathy with the idea.[11]

He returned to the issue in a subsequent passage of his book when he discusses Michelangelo's going into hiding. He expressly disclaims that the artist had been responsible for the idea, but adds that the remarks had spread and their notoriety had further added to Michelangelo's terror of the pope.[12] The artist may have been innocent of such indiscretions. But there can be no doubt that extreme supporters of the regime had aimed to destroy prominent properties of the Medici and their adherents and in some cases had succeeded.[13]

OLD AND NEW ASSIGNMENTS

Even in the months of his deepest adversity following the sack of May 1527, Pope Clement did not forget his cherished artist. As noted earlier, he had issued a brief, while a prisoner in Castel Sant'Angelo, appointing Michelangelo director of the defences of Bologna, which still remained a papal city. After his flight to Orvieto, despite the intractable political problems that confronted him and the sheer physical privations of his life there, the work at San Lorenzo was not forgotten.[14]

This is shown by a letter from a Florentine who had travelled to Orvieto in the spring of 1528. Writing from the papal court to Michelangelo in the first days of March, he informs him that Clement had asked whether he, the artist, was still at work. He had reported to the pope that Michelangelo was weighed down by his financial outgoings, having lost the rent of his house, and did not know where to turn for money. Lorenzo Niccolini, his correspondent, informs the artist that, if he is ready to resume work, Clement would send him an immediate subvention of 500 ducats, to be followed by *ad diem* payments. Niccolini offers to look after Michelangelo's interests at the court. The offer was exceptionally ill-timed, made just one month before the artist would be appointed head of the city's defences.[15]

The pope would lose no time in providing for the resumption of work in the New Sacristy. On 20 October 1530 his secretary, Pier Polo Marzi, would write to Figiovanni that arrangements have been made with a Florentine bank to pay the artist his monthly stipend.[16] A later letter, as well as an undated *ricordo* of Figiovanni, would confirm that this was a monthly provision of 50 ducats.[17] On 11 November Marzi, acknowledging a letter of Figiovanni, conveys the pope's wish that, above all, Michelangelo should be treated with every indulgence, 'carezato'.[18]

Several other letters from Marzi to Figiovanni would follow, expressing Clement's deep satisfaction over the way that Michelangelo is working. In one of them, Marzi writes of his 'grandissimo piacere'.[19] The care with which he followed events is further indicated by an event in November. Writing to Michelangelo on 17 November, Figiovanni informs him that Cardinal Innocenzo Cibo, passing through Florence on his way to Rome, wishes to speak with him and, if the artist is willing, would like to see the sculpture in the chapel. He adds that Cibo will report to the pope.[20]

The prominence of Figiovanni's role in these events indicates his enhanced authority following the Medici restoration. Once referred to in a moment of exasperation at the Curia as 'una bestia' by the pope, he is now addressed affectionately in the letters from Rome as 'Figi', and his importance would be confirmed by his appointment as prior of San Lorenzo in 1534. His relations with the artist would also assume an unprecedented warmth. In a number of notes written to Michelangelo at this time he would address him as 'Amantissimo'.[21]

In the following year, the artist's life, taxed by the expectations of his patron, would be further troubled by requests that came from others. In the spring of 1531 Federico Gonzaga, frustrated in his attempt to procure a work from him in 1527, returned to the struggle. Giovanni Borromeo, who had tried to lure the artist to Mantua at that time, wrote to Federico in late May, reporting that he had pursued Michelangelo on a number of occasions. The artist had explained that he could serve only the pope on a project begun long before and where he works day and night. He has been asked to provide something for the Marchioness of Pescara, Vittoria Colonna, but permission to undertake anything has been refused in Rome. He lives in fear of the pope, whom he feels he has greatly offended, and speaks of the threat that he will be deprived of everything he has if the work remains unfinished. Borromeo concludes that his undertaking is such that he does not believe that the artist's lifetime will be enough to see its completion.[22]

Borromeo's discouraging letter induced his master to approach the pope directly. Writing to the Mantuan envoy at the Curia, Francesco Gonzaga, on 26 May 1531, he asks Pope Clement to allow the artist to satisfy his wish.[23] Francesco replied on 5 June, reporting that he has spoken with the pope. Clement's response indicates his guile. Not referring to his own exclusive needs, he responded that it would be very difficult for the artist to turn to painting at a time when he is habituated to working on sculpture. The duke must await the completion of the work on which he is engaged.[24]

The request for a work for Vittoria Colonna would have a different outcome. Borromeo had reported that it had been Alfonso d'Avalos, Marquis of Vasto and Pescara, who had asked Michelangelo to carry out a painting for his adoptive mother. The artist had responded that permission to accept the invitation had been forbidden in Rome. In this case, however, a solution would be found: Michelangelo would provide a full-scale cartoon and the painting based upon it would be handed to another artist to carry out.

The compromise was achieved through the good offices of the man who had replaced Valori as de facto ruler of Florence in January 1531 and who would arrive in the city in February. This was Nicolas von Schomberg, Archbishop of Capua, a man implicitly trusted by Clement. But Figiovanni also played an important role in furthering the project. In a letter to the artist of 11 April 1531, he had proposed that he should first make a drawing.[25] For many months, Michelangelo seems to have declined to collaborate. In a subsequent but undated letter, however, Figiovanni refers to a cartoon that Michelangelo has made and extols it as a 'cosa divina'.[26] A third letter, again undated, conveys to Michelangelo Schomberg's satisfaction with the outcome: employing the cartoon, another artist can carry out the painting. He is unidentified by Figiovanni, but it would be Jacopo Pontormo who would execute it.[27]

The subject requested by Vittoria Colonna is briefly referred to by Figiovanni in one of his letters as a 'Magdalena'. It was, in fact, the narrative episode of the Noli Me Tangere, a choice expressive of her deep devotion to the saint who was the first to witness the Resurrection. Painted transcriptions of Michelangelo's lost cartoon by both Pontormo and Bronzino survive.[28]

A more serious diversion from work in the sacristy was provided by a request of Baccio Valori, de facto ruler of Florence until his replacement by Schomberg in early 1531. At some point during his administration of the city, he asked Michelangelo to undertake no less than a carving for him and, alongside this time-consuming undertaking, approached him to design a new palace in the Via Pandolfini to replace the one that had been vandalized by the republican government in December 1529.[29]

Michelangelo was in no position to resist Valori's wishes, and his unfinished statue of *Apollo*, now in the Bargello in Florence, testifies to his need to ingratiate himself with Clement's powerful lieutenant, a fact well known to Vasari when he referred to the carving in both editions of his *Lives*.[30] In a letter to Michelangelo, undated but perhaps written in the spring of 1532, Valori, now appointed governor of the Romagna by the pope, refers to his promised statue. He writes that he feels there is no need to urge the artist to press on with it. There is nothing he desires more than the work.[31]

In writing to Michelangelo, however, Valori's chief concern is the future of his projected palace. The artist had sent his assistant, Francesco del Lucchesino, to Valori armed with a letter.[32] From what Valori writes, Francesco may have been equipped with a ground plan, for Valori's chief concern is with the prospective space for the new building. He regards the projected courtyard as too small without the addition of an adjacent property. No further correspondence survives and we cannot follow the course of the project. Nevertheless, that Michelangelo proceeded with the undertaking is not in doubt. Indeed, the design of the seven window tabernacles of Valori's palace on Via Pandolfini has been ascribed, not without some plausibility, to Michelangelo himself.[33]

Notwithstanding Clement's great enthusiasm over the way that Michelangelo resumed work in the New Sacristy, subsequent letters from Rome would display an increasing concern over the health of the fifty-six-year-old artist. In a letter of 29 April 1531 Sebastiano de Piombo reports that the pope has heard that Michelangelo is working day and night, words recalling those of Federico Gonzaga's agent, and that he is enormously pleased.[34] By June, however, a note of anxiety has crept into the correspondence lest the artist's exertions damage his health. Clement has suggested that he should occasionally go for a walk.[35] Concern over his health again emerges in a letter of his secretary, Pier Polo Marzi, of 20 June, replying to a letter of the artist's that had reported on the state of work in the chapel.[36]

The issue of Michelangelo's physical deterioration would emerge most clearly in a letter that Giovan Battista Mini, Antonio's uncle, would write to Baccio Valori in Rome on 29 September. Mini recounts how Michelangelo is rarely seen for fear of the plague. But he had visited Mini twice, who had his nephew and the artist's *garzone* present, as well as his old friend, the painter Bugiardini.[37] They had proceeded to the New Sacristy to see the two female allegories, 'le dua femine [*sic*]' as Mini calls them. He declares to Valori that they are wonderful. He recalls that Valori himself has seen the *Night*; but the other female statue, unnamed by Mini but, of course, the *Dawn*, in beauty eclipses everything else. He goes on to state that the artist has finished one of the old men, 'uno di que' vechi', and it would be impossible to see anything to surpass it. Mini is here referring to the *Evening*, for the statue of *Day*, 'il Giorno', is, today, less finished, the head only roughly blocked in.[38]

Mini's purpose in writing to Valori is, however, more urgent than extolling the carvings. He expresses deep concern about the artist's health and way of life, which he has discussed with Bugiardini and his nephew. If nothing is done, Michelangelo will not live long. He overworks, eats little and badly and does not sleep. For a month he has suffered from headaches and dizziness. Although his basic health is sound, his head and heart are affected. He urges that the artist should not work in the adverse conditions of winter in the sacristy. He could work elsewhere and finish the group of the *Virgin and Child*, on which Michelangelo had worked in the Via Mozza workshop, or carve the statue of Duke Lorenzo. Mini wishes the pope to intervene through Figiovanni, who frequently sees the artist.

Mini ascribes the heart condition to the artist's anxiety about the della Rovere tomb. He writes that the whole predicament could be resolved by the pope paying out 10,000 ducats and thereby freeing the artist for ever. He points to the problem that would face the pope were Michelangelo to die.

Clement had once declared that he wanted Michelangelo for himself. The increasing alarm over the artist's health and the persistent demands of others like Valori, whom Michelangelo was unable to ignore, drove him to action, for he needed him not only for the completion of the New Sacristy but also for the library and for the reliquary tribune that had been discussed before disaster struck in 1527. A papal brief, dated 21 November 1531, addressing Michelangelo in the familiar second person singular and written in warm terms, expresses concern for his health. He is forbidden, under pain of excommunication, to engage on any work in painting or sculpture except the della Rovere tomb and the work that Clement has commissioned: 'nisi in sepultura et opera nostra quam tibi commisimus'.[39]

A subsequent letter from Rome would shed further light on the circumstances relating to the brief. Bernardo della Volpaia, brother of the now dead Benvenuto whose drawings Michelangelo had copied in 1516, wrote to the artist on 26 November. Close to the pope and about to be lodged in the Vatican, Bernardo explains the reasons behind the issue of the brief: Clement has taken the step to save Michelangelo from the importunities of others and hopes that it will serve to discourage them. Bernardo actually refers to the case of Valori and reports that the pope has said that he will concern himself with the issue. Bernardo goes on to report that Clement has said that the artist must not continue to work in the chapel and has mentioned alternatives. He also turned to the need for assistants to work from Michelangelo's models.[40] In the light of Bernardo della Volpaia's allusion to Valori in this letter, it seems likely that it was at this point, in the autumn of 1531, that Michelangelo ceased work on the marble *Apollo*.[41]

THE DEATH OF LODOVICO

Once believed to have lived until 1534, it is now known that Lodovico died prior to 23 March 1531. He had reached the advanced age of eighty-seven. His last years were difficult ones, for he did not escape the adversities that had afflicted the republic in the last months of its existence.[42]

The straits to which the government was reduced are shown by the demands made upon him. In January 1528 he had been elected to the office of the Cinque del Contado, which he had refused to accept. In the following year, he had again been drawn for office, that of the *podestà* of a small town in the lower Valdarno. This he accepted, probably at the insistence of his sons, who saw in the appointment the chance to escape, with his two grandsons, Leonardo and Simone, children of the dead Buonarroto, from the dangers threatening Florence.

The move had not been accomplished without difficulties. Referring to his father's appointment in a letter of June 1529, Gismondo, the youngest of Lodovico's sons, would point to the need of a dependable assistant. He notes that the salary would be useful.[43] In early July Lodovico was still resisting the idea of taking his two grandsons with him. Complaining as ever, he writes to Giovan Simone that he is utterly ruined in body and soul.[44] He would be prevailed upon to take them with him and, writing a profoundly despondent letter after his arrival, he would describe them as ill behaved.[45] Despite his wish to see his father, Gismondo would explain that he is forbidden to leave Florence. He writes to him that he would die of sorrow, were he to witness the privations in the city.[46] By December Lodovico had deserted his post and had fled to the greater security of Pisa. And it would be during the stay in Pisa that the younger Simone di Buonarroto would fall ill and die, leaving Leonardo, who had been born in 1522 and was not eight years old, the unique male heir of the Buonarroti family.[47]

Lodovico needed financial help during the months he remained in Pisa. And aid in transferring funds, a difficult task at the time, was given by members of the Quaratesi family. A note of the artist shows that Andrea facilitated the transfer of funds to the stricken Lodovico in Pisa, where his brother, Giovanni, had taken refuge.[48] Letters show the continued devotion shown to Michelangelo by Andrea. In one, he insists that, although suffering from an attack of fever, he will come to supper, even if on all-fours.[49]

The custody of Buonarroto's three children had remained with the Buonarroti family; following a common Florentine practice, his widow, Bartolomea della Casa, would go back to her family's house with her dowry returned to her.[50] The eldest, Francesca, born in 1519, would return to the convent of Boldrone, east of Florence, after the siege had ended. Michelangelo paid for her upkeep and would visit her there.[51] She would leave to marry a Guicciardini in 1537 and Michelangelo would pay for her dowry.

The care of Leonardo was a greater problem. Lodovico had briefly looked after him after Buonarroto's death and he had then gone, for a brief period, to Michelangelo. Following Lodovico's death, he would be cared for by the two younger uncles and, in the end, it would be Giovan Simone who would be formally appointed as the boy's guardian in the summer of 1531.[52]

Despite the successive crises that had marked Michelangelo's relations with Lodovico, his attachment was profound, and the feeling was reciprocated. In the last letter of Lodovico's to have survived, written on 15 January 1531, his father thanks him for all the help he has recently received; he and God have saved him from famine. He recommends his son to take care of Leonardo, who is of their flesh. And he ends with more than the traditional wishes that God preserve him, as if he may have had some premonition that he had not long to live.[53]

Michelangelo's sense of the double loss of Buonarroto and Lodovico would find expression in a poem that he never completed.[54] And his devotion to Lodovico's memory emerges in a letter that he would write to Giovan Simone in the summer of 1534, shortly before he made his definitive move to Rome. He insists that his brother, for whom he nursed an undisguised contempt, take good care of the servant who had tended Lodovico at Settignano.[55] As he lay dying, Lodovico had recommended Michelangelo to take care of *monna* Margherita. Despite his leaving Florence, the artist would maintain a close interest in her fortunes as later letters reveal; he would periodically help her finances with gifts. The news of her death in 1540 would deeply grieve him; he felt he had lost more than a sister.[56]

A FURTHER CONTRACT

When Antonio Mini's uncle, Giovan Battista, had written to Baccio Valori in September 1531, he had attributed a part of Michelangelo's ill health to his constant anxiety about the prospect for Pope Julius's tomb. The issue had, however, emerged many months earlier, as we learn from a letter of Sebastiano del Piombo of 29 April 1531.

The artist's Venetian friend, still shattered by the events of the sack, had returned to Rome in the early months of 1531. He describes the adversities he has suffered in a letter of February; he is not the 'Bastiano' he had been before the devastation of May 1527.[57]

In the same letter, he refers to a disaster that has struck the house at Macel de' Corvi. He would enlarge on the problem in a letter of 16 June 1531. Rome had been stricken by a further disaster in early October 1530, when the city was swept by a flood provoked by forty-eight hours of torrential rain. Water from the Tiber had reached a height of up to 3 metres in those areas of the city close to the river. The artist's house had not been spared. Water had poured through the roof, and the marble fabric of the lower storey of the tomb, on which Antonio da Pontassieve and his colleagues had begun work in 1513, had been submerged.[58]

A different form of storm would gather strength during 1531 over the lack of any progress on the project of Julius II's tomb. Sebastiano had passed through Pesaro on his way back to Rome from Venice. He reports that he had found Duke Francesco Maria della Rovere furious over the situation.[59] By midsummer the crisis was recognized at the papal court and Pope Clement had agreed to intervene. As so often, the artist's side of the correspondence is in large part lost. But by July it seems that he had offered to return 2,000 ducats to the della Rovere, surrender the house in Rome, and promise to complete the work within the space of three years, terms that Pope Clement found far too generous.

These events emerge from a letter of Sebastiano's of 22 July 1531.[60] He had assumed the role of negotiator that Fattucci, now back in

Florence, had played in the previous decade. Sebastiano has met with two men. One was the duke's ambassador to the papal court, Giovan Maria della Porta. The other was an agent of the duke's, Girolamo Staccoli. Both had been in Rome for nearly ten years and were only too familiar with the saga of delays that had dogged the enterprise. Staccoli would prove the more intransigent of the two. He had, for example, met the artist's offer to surrender the house with the obser- vation that it was not his to give. It is in this letter that we first find reference to an idea that the duke's representatives would return to transport to Rome the statues that had been undertaken for the tomb in Florence.

Sebastiano was not the most subtle of negotiators, a fact that clearly emerges from this letter. He writes that he has reminded the two della Rovere representatives that the skies did not rain Michelangelos. He had gone further and claimed that two of his statues alone were worth 10,000 ducats, no doubt referring to the two unfinished *Prisoners* in the workshop at Macel de' Corvi. This was the sum of money that Michelangelo had, more than once, himself referred to as the total amount that had been agreed for the entire project in Julius's lifetime. The fact is referred to in the contract to be drawn up in the following April of 1532.

Exceptionally, there survives an autograph copy of a letter that the artist sent to Rome, probably in the previous August. The text shows his deep concern. He feels he is faced with one of two courses. One is to provide the tomb, but this will antagonize the pope, for it will mean an end to his work on Clement's own projects. Were he to adopt the second, he would provide models, add the statues already made and pay back the 2,000 ducats. In some way or other, he would find the money.[61]

Sebastiano would reply that Clement still found the offers excessively generous. The exchanges make melancholy reading, for they recall the abortive negotiations that had gone on before the sack of May 1527.

A resolution, however, would emerge. Staccoli had returned to Urbino to discuss the issues with his master, Duke Francesco Maria.

Again, Sebastiano would recount what had happened.[62] The duke, determined on spending no more money, had agreed to a reduced project and asked for a drawing from the artist. He is happy to annul the contract of 1516. Michelangelo must complete the new project within three years. In a long postscript that Sebastiano added on 21 November, the date of the pope's brief, he states that the statues, now in Florence, undertaken for the project of 1516, must be brought to Rome. As noted earlier, Clement reported that he had seen these statues, the four *Prisoners* now in the Accademia, before he left Florence, never to return, in September 1523.

Michelangelo probably left for Rome on 6 or 7 April. He lodged with Benvenuto della Volpaia in the Vatican. He would leave Rome before the contract, the fourth, was drawn up on 29 April 1532.[63] All previous contracts for the project are annulled. Michelangelo is to provide six statues, which he has already begun in Florence and Rome. Other parts of the monument he is permitted to delegate to others. As had been discussed in the earlier correspondence, he is to pay 2,000 ducats, money that will include the sum that will be paid for the house at Macel de' Corvi. The whole project is to be completed within three years.[64]

Many of this contract's clauses would not be observed. In the exchange of letters between Rome and Florence, it is clear that Michelangelo had never accepted the idea of transporting the Florentine statues to Rome, an extremely laborious and potentially hazardous undertaking. The mishap when Bandinelli's block for the Piazza della Signoria statue had fallen into the Arno was a very recent memory. The clause that demanded the moving of the huge and still only roughly worked blocks, today in the Accademia in Florence, would never be honoured. The real importance of this new contract lay in the fact that what was now prescribed was a true wall tomb, unlike the wildly ambitious designs that had been envisaged in 1513 and 1516.[65]

Clement still wanted Michelangelo for himself. By the terms of this contract, he took the step of allowing Michelangelo to work on the project, but his concession was scarcely a generous one. During the three years allowed for the completion of the work, he grants him leave to come to Rome for two months, more or less, as he pleases. In the event, this clause would also be ignored.

Giovan Maria della Porta would write to his della Rovere master on the following day in celebratory mood. To have secured the promise of six statues carved by the master is worth the whole world; they will be without compare. He turns to the issue of the site of the tomb, something nowhere alluded to in the contract. St Peter's must be excluded because of the rebuilding. He had favoured Santa Maria del Popolo, but Michelangelo had objected because of lack of space and light. He reports that many are in favour of San Pietro in Vincoli, because of its della Rovere associations.[66]

The issue of the site of Julius's tomb was not settled without further debate. In a letter of 19 June to the duke, della Porta would return to the issue. From what he writes, it seems that Duke Francesco Maria had remained in favour of Santa Maria del Popolo, a choice seemingly favoured also by the pope. The issue had been discussed before Michelangelo had left. He had been to Santa Maria del Popolo and remained firm that the church lacked space and light; only San Pietro in Vincoli would be suitable. Clement had apparently given way and agreed to move the altar dedicated to the chains of St Peter to the high altar of that church. The correspondence confirms, therefore, that the artist's choice was respected: the site we see today was the one that Michelangelo himself had pressed for.[67]

Fired by his new project, Michelangelo was anxious to get back to Rome, where he had left instructions that the house at Macel de' Corvi be put in order. But no less than the della Rovere ambassador, Giovan della Porta, would write to discourage him from returning in the heat of August.[68] Uneasiness about his presence in Rome in the hottest season was also expressed by Clement. But he had realized why the artist was eager to face the heat: modelling in clay was much easier in these conditions.[69] His comment indicates that Michelangelo was intent on beginning work on models for the sculpture for the tomb.

But the tasks that remained in Florence were formidable: the completion of the carvings in the New Sacristy, which included the *magnifici* tomb, the supervision of work at the library of San Lorenzo, and the construction of the reliquary tribune within the church. One comfort lay in the pope's recognition that the sculpture in the chapel required assistants.

TOMMASO DE' CAVALIERI

Michelangelo would follow the advice of those who had written to him from Rome, dissuading him from moving in the great heat of August. On 13 August Sebastiano had written to report that the house at Macel de' Corvi had been put in order and cleared for his arrival.[70] When he left Florence is not recorded, although a letter addressed to him on 19 September suggests that he had been in Rome for some time. Before he left, he had had the chance to see Giovanni da Udine's preparations to start work on the decoration of the cupola of the New Sacristy.[71] Another concern was the building of the reliquary tribune for the interior of San Lorenzo, which would provoke a lively correspondence after he had left.[72]

Michelangelo would remain in Rome until the end of June 1533. At some point following his arrival he would fall in love with a youthful Roman, Tommaso de' Cavalieri (pl. 46). This passionate attachment would, in succeeding years, change into a friendship that would last until his death. But the initial period of his love would provoke a poetic outpouring that was unprecedented. It has been calculated that his love for Cavalieri prompted the writing of at least fourteen sonnets and a number of other poems.[73]

Many of the poems express an ineradicable sense of guilt. And one of his long-established Roman friends, Bartolomeo Angiolini, who would write to him repeatedly after the artist had returned to Florence in the summer of 1533, commented that one of the sonnets sent to Rome expressed travail rather than happiness.[74] They are profoundly subjective, one of them expressing the fear that his passion may be construed as carnal rather than spiritual.[75]

How Michelangelo met Cavalieri is not recorded, but this could have happened through the offices of a relatively unknown sculptor, Pier Antonio Cecchini, who belonged to the household of the anti-Medicean cardinal Niccolò Ridolfi. It had been Cecchini who had put the artist's Roman house in order in anticipation of his return to the city.[76] The Cavalieri family lived in the area now formed by the modern Largo Argentina, only a brief walk from the house at Macel de' Corvi. They possessed a number of antique carvings.[77]

The meeting between the fifty-seven-year-old artist and the young Roman, aged a little over twenty, must have taken place in the autumn months of 1532.[78] The first tangible evidence is the draft of a letter of Michelangelo to him, which is undated. It may have been written on the day on which Cavalieri replied, acknowledging the receipt of two drawings that had been brought him by Cecchini; the reply can be plausibly dated 1 January 1533. Michelangelo had addressed his young friend in extravagant terms as unique in the world; Rome produced divine men. Cavalieri should read his heart rather than his letter. Cavalieri replied in more measured terms that he had never felt greater love for a man than his for the artist. Responding to the present of the two drawings, he expresses his intention to study them for two hours every day.[79]

The two drawings delivered as a New Year's present were the *Rape of Ganymede* and the *Punishment of Tityus* (pls 47–8). They formed a kind of mythological diptych, the subjects readily available from Ovid's *Metamorphoses* and perhaps expressing some of the intense feelings of the artist. Vasari, when he came to refer to the drawings made for Cavalieri, listed the pair and added a further two: the *Fall of Phaeton* and the *Children's Bacchanal*.[80] Elsewhere in the *Vite* of 1568 he made mention of another drawing given to Cavalieri, a *Cleopatra* (pl. 50).[81] This sheet would leave Cavalieri's collection, for he was compelled to give it as a gift to Duke Cosimo de' Medici in January 1562. The letter that he wrote to the duke survives. In it he expresses his pain

at parting with it, comparing his loss with that of a child.[82] The rest
of the drawings seem to have remained together. When he died in
1587, they were acquired by Cardinal Alessandro Farnese, who paid
500 *scudi* for them.[83]

What Vasari seems not to have known was the fact that Michelangelo
had drawn no less than three versions of the *Fall of Phaeton*. The earliest, now in the British Museum, he carried out before he left Rome
for Florence in the summer of 1533.[84] In making it, he closely followed
the text of Ovid's *Metamorphoses*. At the same time, he took some of
the narrative elements from a depiction of the scene on a Roman
sarcophagus, at that date situated outside the church of Santa Maria in
Aracoeli, the family church of the Cavalieri family.[85] Along the lower
edge of the sheet he addressed a message to his friend, addressing him
as 'Messer Tomao'. If the sketch does not please him, he is to tell
Urbino, so that he can make another one the following evening. If
he likes it, he is to return it and he will finish it.[86]

Michelangelo did finish the drawing but probably remained dissatisfied with it himself, prompting him to begin again. The result was the
superlatively finished and more expressive drawing of the *Fall of Phaeton*
now at Windsor (pl. 51). It would be sent to Rome in the late
summer. Cavalieri acknowledged it in a well-known letter of 6 September. He recounts how the drawing has created a sensation. Everyone, including Pope Clement himself, has seen it. His nephew, Cardinal
Ippolito de' Medici, had successfully wrested the *Tityus* from him as
a loan, in order to have it copied in crystal, a medium the cardinal
was much attached to. Cavalieri writes that he has succeeded in
holding on to the *Ganymede* only with the greatest difficulty. The
episode indicates the unprecedented significance now attached to
drawings.[87]

As referred to earlier, Michelangelo's moving portrait drawing of
Andrea Quaratesi has survived. That he also undertook one of Cavalieri
is referred to by Vasari in his *Vite* of 1568, who, unaware of the Quaratesi sheet, claimed that the Cavalieri portrait was unique in the artist's
work.[88]

A description of the Cavalieri drawing exists, written in a copy of
Vasari's *Lives* of 1568 preserved in the Corsini library in Rome. The
note was probably written in the early years of the seventeenth century.
The unidentified writer provides a eulogistic description of the portrait. Like the earlier drawing of Quaratesi, it is in black chalk and
highly finished. Cavalieri is described as unbearded and holding a
portrait or medal in his hand.[89] Long deemed lost, there survives in
Bayonne a very damaged drawing that is probably the original.[90]

Michelangelo's love for Cavalieri was widely known. His Roman
correspondents refer to his feelings quite openly, and knowledge of
his passion was not confined to the city. This is shown by the later
taunt of Pietro Aretino. Frustrated in his attempts to acquire a drawing
by the master, he would write that only 'Gherardi e Tomai', a reference to both Perini and Cavalieri, could hope to receive them. But
the widespread knowledge of the relationship may be interpreted as
an indication that, passionate as the artist's feelings were, it remained
chaste. This is unlikely to have been true of another friendship, for
which the evidence is much slighter, dating from his last months spent
in Florence before his move to Rome.

A MARBLE *APOLLO*

In the later months of 1530 Michelangelo's relations with Pope Clement
would be restored and his recent role in the defence of anti-Medicean
Florence exonerated. Letters written by Pier Polo Marzi at the Curia
to Figiovanni at San Lorenzo in Florence reveal the steps taken to
make peace with the artist. He is to be treated with every consideration now that he is resuming work in the New Sacristy. Marzi
expresses anxiety concerning Michelangelo's health, most emphatically
in a letter of June 1531, and his concerns would be shared by Sebastiano
following his return to Rome.[91]

These issues would be most vividly evoked in a letter of Giovan
Battista Mini to Clement's powerful lieutenant, Baccio Valori, in a

long letter of 29 September 1531. He writes of Michelangelo's loss of
weight and indicates that his anxieties are shared by a common friend,
the painter Bugiardini. He believes that if remedial steps are not taken,
Michelangelo will not live long. Mini insists that Pope Clement must
forbid the artist from working in the New Sacristy at San Lorenzo in
the winter. He should seek a place elsewhere to proceed to complete
the statues of the *Virgin and Child* and of *Duke Lorenzo*. He goes on
to explain that troubles that the artist is having with his heart are
provoked by his anxieties over the project of the dead Pope Julius's
tomb and his continued involvement with the issue with the Duke of
Urbino.[92]

Clement would now insist that the artist be provided with every
aid and assistance, 'sopra tutto Michelangelo sia accarizzato'. He would
also act with uncharacteristic firmness in reassigning projects to other
artists. Perhaps the most striking example of this would be the project,
still not carried out after so many years, of the monumental sculpture
to stand before Palazzo Vecchio as a companion to the marble *David*.
The commission would now be assigned to Baccio Bandinelli and
would comprise two figures. It would be completed in 1534.[93]

Michelangelo did not entirely escape other commitments. It was
probably soon after Baccio Valori had been appointed head of the
Florentine administration by Clement that the former commissioned
from the artist a carving that he would carry far towards completion,
the marble statue of *Apollo*, now in the Bargello (pl. 52). Following
his transfer to become president of the Romagna by Clement, Valori
would write to Michelangelo early in 1532, referring to the statue,
something he wished for more than anything else.[94]

Whether Valori took possession of the carving, despite its unfinished
state, is not recorded. Its future history would not exclude the possibility. Following the failed attempt by Valori and his colleagues to
overthrow Cosimo's regime in 1537, which would lead to Valori's
execution, at some point, not yet established, the statue would be
acquired for the Medici collection, listed in an inventory of 1553, where
it would be misidentified as a statue of David. These events do not

strengthen the belief that Michelangelo had held on to the sculpture in the 1530s. It could be concluded that, despite its lack of finish, Valori had taken possession of it when Michelangelo left for Rome and that it passed to Duke Cosimo following Valori's downfall and subsequent execution.[95]

The statue of *Apollo* undertaken for Baccio Valori was not the only contact between the two men. Valori's palace in the Via Pandolfini had been destroyed by the republican government after he had been formally declared a rebel along with other Medicean sympathizers in 1529.[96] Following the fall of the republic, it appears that Valori solicited Michelangelo's advice. A letter of his of early April 1532 could imply that the artist was involved in Valori's plans to replace the building destroyed three years earlier. As remarked above, it has even been suggested that the window tabernacles in the newly reconstructed palace in Via Pandolfini bear indications of Michelangelo's intervention.[97]

Michelangelo's decision to leave the Florence of Alessandro de' Medici, taken in 1534, would prove to be irrevocable. Many close associates he would never see again, including a recent young protégé, Febo di Poggio, who would feel resentment over the way he had been treated.[98] But he would make no secret of his profound dislike for the new ruler of Florence, son-in-law of the Emperor Charles V, whom he would later describe to Condivi as 'feroce e vendicativo'. He could have regarded as a confirmation of his view of Alessandro de' Medici the latter's construction of a menacing new monument in Florence, the Fortezza da Basso, which would follow his departure. Not even much later conciliatory behaviour of Alessandro's successor, Duke Cosimo, would persuade the ageing artist to abandon papal Rome, where he would settle in 1534 and where no less than three decades of active life still awaited him.

NOTES

ABBREVIATION

ASF   Archivio di Stato di Firenze

PREFACE

1 *Il Carteggio di Michelangelo*, ed. G. Poggi, P. Barocchi and R. Ristori, 5 vols, Florence, 1965–83.
2 *Il Carteggio indiretto di Michelangelo*, ed. P. Barocchi, K. L. Bramanti and R. Ristori, 2 vols, Florence, 1988–95.
3 *I Contratti di Michelangelo*, ed. L. Bardeschi Ciulich, Florence, 2005.
4 *I Ricordi di Michelangelo*, ed. L. Bardeschi Ciulich and P. Barocchi, Florence, 1970.
5 It had been Giovanni Poggi's long-standing ambition to edit the publication of material he had collected over many decades, but this was not to be. For his material, see Tampieri 1997.

CHAPTER ONE

1 *Carteggio* II, p. 245, no. CDLXXIII. The count addresses the artist as 'mio molto amato et parente honorando messer Michelle Angelo Bonaroto de Canossa, scultptoro dignissimo in Roma'. He was unaware that Michelangelo was not in Rome; at this point he was in Florence.
2 *Carteggio* IV, p. 288, no. MC. About to send the letter to his nephew, he urges him to take care of it. Frey 1907a, pp. 5ff., dismissed the story of the count's visit to Rome as a fiction. Canossa, situated in mountainous terrain to the west of Modena, had been the scene of a celebrated episode in the late eleventh century when the Emperor Henry IV had submitted to Pope Gregory VII.
3 For the drawing, see Wilde 1953, no. 87, pl. CXLIII. The subject's helmet bears

the crest of a dog with a bone, a playful reference to the name 'Canossa'. For Condivi's account, see his *Vita* (Condivi 1998), pp. 7–8. Referring to the claim in his second edition of 1568, Vasari treated it with great caution; see Vasari 1987, VI, p. 4. It had been referred to in Varchi's funeral oration of 1564. The story's credibility was rejected by Campori 1855, pp. 100ff., and Frey 1907a, pp. 5ff., who also dismissed the count's visit to the artist as a fiction. For the cult of constructing genealogies to stress familial antiquity, see Bizocchi 1995, passim.

4 See Ristori in *Carteggio indiretto* I, pp. X–XIII, and Hatfield 2002, pp. 201ff.

5 Hatfield 2002, p. 202. For a pioneering attempt to list the major offices held by the family, see Frey 1907a, pp. 13–14.

6 Hatfield has shown that more recent members of the family frequently experienced exclusion from offices because they owed taxes to the commune, known as being *a specchio*. He also notes that Michelangelo himself, when resident in Florence, showed little enthusiasm for taking up offices for which he was drawn. For general comments on the adverse situation in which the Buonarroti found themselves after the Medicean restoration of 1434, see Spini 1991, pp. 10–11; he observes that they belonged neither to the Popolo Minuto nor to the ascendant Medici party.

7 *Carteggio* IV, pp. 249–50, no. MLXX. The letter is returned to later in this book. It is in this letter that Michelangelo memorably requests Leonardo to find somewhere in Florence for the last of his brothers Gismondo (Sigismondo) to live, so that he himself can be spared reports that he has a brother who ploughs with the oxen at Settignano.

8 *Carteggio* IV, p. 365, no. MCLXIII. He writes: 'Non mi vo'distender più a narrarti la miseria in che io trovai la casa nostra, quand'io cominciai aiutarla; che non bastarebbe un libro'.

9 For this setback, see Passerini's note on Simone Buonarroti in Gotti 1875, II, p. 17; and for caution over the issue, Ristori in *Carteggio indiretto* I, pp. XII–XIII.

10 For an informed account of Giusto Giusti's life, see R. M. Comanducci in *DBI*, LVII, 182–6. He was born in 1406, and his marriage to Lisa was his third. The author states that the dowry that precipitated the crisis was 300 florins. Lisa bore him nine children and died on 13 April 1473. For an excellent edition of his *ricordi*, see Newbigin 2002. For his *ricordo* of his marriage to Lisa in February 1449 (1448 Florentine style), ibid., p. 125.

11 The financial crisis of 1449 is referred to in Leonardo Buonarroti's tax return for the *catasto* of 1458, a year before he died, in which he refers to the ceding of his property to his son-in-law; see ASF, Catasto 1458, Santa Croce, Lion Nero, 1536–1001, no. verde 807, fols 640ff. A marginal note in a previous return of 1446 seems to imply that his daughters had no protection by a holding of shares in the Monte delle Doti, or Dowry Fund. For a detailed study of the Monte's

foundation, function and its subsequent vicissitudes, see Molho 1994, passim, but especially pp. 27–79. The *catasto* returns of the Buonarroti family were first published in Frey 1885 and Frey 1907a, pp. 14–17; a more critical edition is required. For an outstanding survey of Florentine taxation in the fifteenth century, see Conti 1984, passim.

12   ASF, Catasto 1469–70, Santa Croce, Lion Nero, no. verde 914, fol. 334, published by Frey 1885, pp. 189–92. Their legitimate deductions exceed their capitalized assets.

13   ASF, Catasto 1427, Santa Croce, Lion Nero, Campione no. verde 72, fols 145–6. The property is referred to as 'Uno podere chon chasa da lavoratore e da signiore e maserizie a uso di detta casa ... Un pezzo di terra apartenette a detto luogho chon suoi vochaboli'. In the return of 1469, referred to in the previous note, there is an impressive list of products from the property, which must have helped the family economy. Farm and animals were being cared for in 1469 by a long-standing associate of the family, Piero Basso, who would briefly join Michelange-lo's team in the Sistine Chapel in 1508 to help with practical needs.

14   For the issue of the dowry, which is returned to below (p. 255), see Ristori in *Carteggio indiretto* I, p. XVIII.

15   ASF, Catasto 1480, Santa Croce, Lion Nero, no. verde 1005, fol. 265.

16   The correct identification of the house, a large building of six floors, owes to extensive research by Brenda Preyer, who has traced its history up to the nine-teenth century. For comments on fraternal households, see Kent 1977, pp. 3–15, and for a wide-ranging analysis of families, with an extensive bibliography, Kent 1991. There is a wealth of information, based on the *catasto* returns of 1427, in Herlihy and Klapisch-Zuber 1985, pp. 280ff.

17   For the return of 1498, see ASF, Decima Repubblicana, no. verde 58, fol. 353, published in Frey 1885, pp. 195ff. The drama of the house had ended with Lisa's death and the property's subsequent return to the family. The brothers sold it in 1484. For their present accommodation, they were paying a rent of 12 large florins a year. Their taxable liability had remained negligible.

18   Lodovico's reported remark to Lorenzo, as recorded by Condivi, reads: 'Io non feci mai arte nessuna, ma sempre sono fin qui delle mie deboli entrate vivuto, attendendo a quelle pochi possessioni che da' miei maggiore mi sono state lasci-ate, cercando non solamente di mantenerla, ma accrescerle quanto per me si potesse, colla mia diligenza'. See Condivi 1998, p. 12.

19   There is little information about Lucrezia degli Ubaldini da Gagliano; she brought Lodovico a dowry of 600 florins of *suggello*, a slightly debased form of currency. See Ristori's note in *Carteggio indiretto* I, p. XIX, who reports that she came from an impoverished branch of her family.

20   *Carteggio* I, p. 7, no. V.

21   For the error, see Barolsky and Wallace 1993, subsequently acknowledged by

the former. Lodovico's rejection of the office is correctly referred to in Hatfield 2002, p. 207. I am grateful to Gabriella Battisti for checking the source.

22 See, most recently, Hatfield 2002, p. 205. The text, printed in Frey 1907a, p. 2, permits Lodovico the services of two notaries, three servants and a horse. His salary of 500 lire was to cover all his expenses. The dates of Lodovico's term of office conclusively establish Michelangelo's year of birth as 1475, a point often neglected; see, for example, Lippincott 1989, who, however, provides a rewarding discussion of the artist's horoscope.

23 *Carteggio* IV, pp. 296–7, no. MCVII.

24 The text was already published by Milanesi in the nineteenth century. For a correct text, see *Carteggio* IV, p. 296. It reads: 'Ricordo come ogi, questo dì 6 di marzo 1474, mi nacque uno fanciullo mastio. Posigli nome Michelagnolo; et nacque in lunedì matina, inanzi dì 4/o 5 ore; et nacquemi essendo io potestà di Caprese, et a Caprese nacque ... Batezossi addì 8 detto nella chiesa di Santo Giovanni di Caprese'. There follow the names of the two priests and seven witnesses, one a notary, who were at the baptism.

25 Condivi 1998, pp. 8–9. For a fourteenth-century formulation of the belief, see Paolo da Certaldo's *Libro di buoni costumi*, in Branca 1986, pp. 3–99, the passage on the power of the wet-nurse's milk on p. 88. Warning of the need for care in selecting a wet-nurse, he writes: 'che molto spesso i fanciulli ritraggono e somigliano da la natura del latte che poppano'. The literature is extensive; see the debate in Alberti's *I Libri della famiglia*, ed. R. Romano and A. Tenenti, Turin, 1980, pp. 44ff.; and for a documented review of the issue, Klapisch-Zuber 1985, pp. 132–64. It may be presumed that Michelangelo was sent to Settignano as soon as Lodovico had completed his term of office at the end of March 1475.

26 For a fine discussion of *libri di famiglia*, see Ciapelli and Rubin 2000, pp. 26–38, with an outstanding bibliography. For a pioneering list of Florentine books, see Anselmi, Pezzarossa and Avellini 1980, pp. 93–149, which offers more than three hundred items. The celebrated *ricordo* concerning Michelangelo's apprenticeship, which Lodovico entered in a book of Domenico Ghirlandaio, is discussed below, pp. 9–10.

27 The pages, written and numbered in a later hand, are in Archivio Buonarroti, XXIV, labelled 'Quadernuccio di spese di Lodovico di Lionardo Buonarroti'. Entries run from September 1477 to September 1480. They were known to Poggi; see Tempieri 1997, I, IIIA, 5, pp. 155–82. The payments on behalf of Michelangelo are on fol. 8. A previous entry relates to Lodovico sending his eldest son, Leonardo, to learn to read with Don Mauro, the priest at Santa Maria at Settignano. Another shows that Piero Basso was already employed by the family in 1477, helping Lodovico sell wine.

28 See the Quadernuccio, fol. 19: 'Richordo questo dì 15 d'ottobre mandai a Fiesole a chasa madonna Bonda la Francesca e tutti altri e mia fanciulli e anche

io v'andai in persona per fuggire la moria'. They returned to Florence on 27 December, and Lodovico records that he gave Bonda some money, no doubt to help with expenses incurred. It is clear from the Quadernuccio, however, that Leonardo and Michelangelo had already stayed with her earlier in the year, and visits may have been quite frequent.

29   For this suggestion, see Wallace 1992b, pp. 151–2, and the sceptical response concerning the family tie in Kent 2004, pp. 8–9 and 158.

30   For the villa at Fiesole, see Lillie 1993, pp. 193ff.; Kent 2004, pp. 114ff. The del Sera villa was located close to that of the Medici.

31   Pitti's letter to Vasari, dated 10 October 1563, was published and discussed in Frey and Frey 1930, pp. 9ff. He writes: 'Dice [Michelangelo] che ha ottantotto anni, che per il caso de Pazzi era portato in collo'. As Frey saw, he was referring to the execution of Jacopo Pazzi, to which Lodovico evidently carried him on his shoulders. The episode, for the most part neglected, was noted in Vasari 1962, IV, p. 1832. In his diary, Landucci reports that the executions took place on the evening of 28 April 1478: 'E in questa medesima sera de 28 dì d'aprile, circa a ore 23, fu impiccato alle finestre del Palagio de' Signori, sopra la ringhiera, messer Iacopo de' Pazzi e Renato de' Pazzi e molti altri loro fanti'; see Landucci 1883 / 1969, p. 19.

32   Condivi 1998, p. 9.

33   I owe these suggestions to Robert Black, who has pointed to the education of Niccolò Machiavelli as a parallel.

34   See, for the evidence, Ulivi 2002, pp. 161ff. Leonardo, Michelangelo's elder brother, is recorded as having been abused by his *abaco* teacher in April 1483 and was denounced by Lodovico. I owe the reference to Robert Black.

35   Vecce 1998, p. 236. It is worth noting that Francesco da Urbino had a number of distinguished pupils, including the deceased Filippo Strozzi's sons in 1498. He is recorded as being paid a salary of 60 florins by the Studio Fiorentino from 1497 to 1502 for teaching in the quarter of Santo Spirito; see Verde 1973, pp. 264–5.

36   For the text of the letter and the list of signatories, see Gotti 1876, II, pp. 82–4. The artist's contribution reads: 'Io Michelagniolo Schultore il medesimo a Vostra Santità suplicho, offerendomi al Divin Poeta fare la Sepoltura sua chondecente, e in locho onorevole in questa Cictà.'

37   See *Contratti*, nos. xx and xxi, pp. 45–51. In both these cases, the tomb of Julius II was involved. Their significance was appreciated by Frey 1907a, pp. 16–17, who concluded that Michelangelo had little or no Latin. Striking evidence that eluded Frey can be found in a document published by Frediani; he discovered that a notary at Carrara had recorded Michelangelo's insistence on a vernacular translation of one of his texts. The notary wrote: 'Ho scripto in vulghare questo contracto perchè lo excelente homo maestro Michelangelo no

po soffrire che qui da noi d'Italia s'habia a scrivere non chomo se parla per tractare de chose pubbliche'; see Frediani 1875, p. 20.

38 For details of the Granacci family, see Holst 1974, especially pp. 12ff. The *catasto* return of 1479–80 is published on pp. 209–10.

39 Condivi 1998, p. 9. A candidate for this panel painting is in a British private collection. The style relates to Ghirlandaio, but does not substantiate the claims made for it; the saint in the panel is a reduced version of that in the print, completely at odds with the young artist's monumentalizing of prototypes, so clear in his early drawn copy of Giotto. For the painting, see Weil-Garris Brandt et al. 1999, pp. 326–33.

40 Condivi 1998, p. 10.

41 For the passage, see Vasari 1987, VI, p. 6. It records that Lodovico, on 1 April 1488, has established that Michelangelo should stay with Domenico and Davide Ghirlandaio for the following three years. He is to learn to paint and carry out the two brothers' directions: 'ch'l Michelagnolo debba stare con i sopradetti detto tempo a imparare a dipignere et a fare detto essercizio e ciò i sopradeii gli comanderano'. For the three years, he is to be paid 24 florins of the lower value known as *di sugello*: 6 in the first year, 8 in the second and 10 in the third. A subsequent *ricordo* had confirmed that Lodovico received a payment of 2 florins on 16 April.

42 As Thomas 1995, p. 72, noted, it was not unusual for boys substantially younger than fourteen to be admitted to workshops. And the terms extended to Michelangelo were in no way exceptional, as many examples in the records of Neri di Bicci show; for parallels, see Neri di Bicci 1976, pp. 153, 228–9 and 244–5. It could, however, have been Michelangelo's age that led Lodovico to write the agreement.

43 For this striking evidence of Michelangelo in the workshop, see Cadogan 1993, republished in Cadogan 2000, p. 355. The entry runs: 'Domenico di Tomaso del Grilandaio de'dare a dì 28 di giugno 1487 fiorini tre larghi portò Michelagnolo di Lodovico'.

44 Giuliano da Sangallo's involvement was already known in the nineteenth century; see now Cadogan 2000, p. 350.

45 Cadogan 2000, p. 241, concluded that most of the fresco painting was carried out only in 1489–90.

46 For the influence of Ghirlandaio in the technique of painting that Michelangelo would adopt in one of his earliest works on panel, the *Manchester Madonna*, now in the National Gallery in London, see the analysis by Dunkerton in Hirst and Dunkerton 1994, pp. 88ff. Ghirlandaio's profound influence on the drawing styles of the artist has long been recognized.

47 *Carteggio* I, p. 3, no. 11.

48 *Carteggio* III, p. 240, no. DCCLX, addressed to his dear friend Giovan Francesco Fattucci.

49 Michelangelo twice requests that he should not be designated 'scultore' by his
    correspondents. He had requested his nephew Leonardo to drop the practice in
    a letter of 1543; see *Carteggio* IV, p. 166, no. MIX. In a later one of 2 May 1548,
    he asks Leonardo to request that Fattucci should drop the designation; see *Car-
    teggio* IV, p. 299, no. MCIX. It is in the latter letter that he expressed the familiar
    declaration that he was never a painter or sculptor who kept a workshop: 'se
    un cictadino fiorentino vuol fare dipigniere una tavola da altare, che bisogna
    che e'truovi un dipintore: ché io non fu' mai pictore né scultore come chi ne
    fa boctega'. The statement was, in fact, accurate.

50 See Vasari 1987, VI, pp. 9–10, and Condivi 1998, pp. 10–11. Kent 2004, p. 129,
    does not refer to Vasari's account and points to a lack of evidence of a personal
    relationship between Ghirlandaio and Lorenzo. Nevertheless, it should be
    recalled that the artist painted a striking portrait of Lorenzo in the Sassetti Chapel
    in Santa Trinita and was one of the painters employed at Lorenzo's villa at
    Spedaletto around 1490. For subsequent relations between the Medici and
    Ghirlandaio, see Cadogan 2000, p. 166.

51 Condivi 1998, p. 13: 'Era Michelangelo, quando andò in casa del Magnifico d'età
    d'anni quindici in sedici, e vi stette fin alla morte di lui, che fu nel novantadue,
    intorno a due anni'. For comments regarding the date of Michelangelo's depar-
    ture from the Ghirlandaio shop, see p. 10 above.

52 It has been proposed that Michelangelo received training as a sculptor in the
    workshop of Benedetto da Maiano, based on the suggestion that the right-hand
    marble *putto* on Benedetto's Curiale altarpiece in Sant'Anna dei Lombardi in
    Naples is his earliest work. The proposal was made by Lisner 1958, pp. 141ff. The
    attribution has been accepted by Carl; see now her *Benedetto da Maiano* (Carl
    2006), especially pp. 21 and 104. Lisner conceded that her proposal involved
    accepting the Naples figure as a work prior to the celebrated relief of the
    Madonna of the Stairs now in the Casa Buonarroti, a work technically less assured
    than the figure in Naples and yet one deeply personal, showing no trace of
    Benedetto's influence.

53 Chastel 1959, pp. 19–25, rejected the possibility that there was some form of
    school in the garden. Gombrich 1966, pp. 56–7, even voiced doubts that the
    garden ever existed.

54 The existence of the garden was vindicated, with an impressive body of docu-
    mentation, in Elam 1992c, pp. 41ff. See also the comments of Draper 1992,
    pp. 62–75.

55 For Roman sculpture collections, see the valuable material in Magister 1999,
    pp. 129–204, and Magister 2002. The most spectacular assembly of sculpture
    available to Lorenzo's inspection was that of Prospero Colonna, which included
    the Belvedere Torso. However, it is worth noting the existence of Poggio Brac-
    ciolini's sculpture garden in the upper Arno valley dating from decades earlier,
    which attracted distinguished visitors.

56 The Anonimo Magliabechiano, writing earlier than Vasari, stated that the young Leonardo da Vinci, given a salary by Lorenzo, was employed by him and worked 'sulla piazza di San Marco di Firenze'. Cited by Elam 1992c, p. 66, note 6; see Frey 1892, p. 110. Leonardo left Florence for Milan in 1482.

57 See Draper's comments, Draper 1992, p. 67, for the fact that a number of the alleged students were not in Florence around 1490.

58 The episode of Torrigiano's attack on Michelangelo is recorded in the second edition of Vasari's *Lives* (Vasari 1987), IV, p. 126, and confirmed in a passage of Cellini's autobiography, Book I, XIII. Both sources refer to the fact that the damage inflicted on Michelangelo's appearance would remain for the rest of his life; Cellini's passage cites remarks by Torrigiano himself. The best evidence for Michelangelo's aged appearance, Daniele da Volterra's bronze bust, confirms the two writers' statements.

59 Alamanni's letter of 22 July 1489 has been cited many times since its initial publication in 1897; see Villata 1999, no. 44, pp. 44−5. Lorenzo's reply was first published only in 1992 by Fusco and Corti, pp. 16−17; see Villata 1999, no. 45, p. 45. Lorenzo explains that he can find no master whom he considers fit for the job. He writes: 'in effecto qui non truovo maestro che mi satisfaccia. Non deverra mancharne alla Excellentia Sua, alla quale fate intendere questa charestia et manchamento, che mi duole assai.' Kent 2004, pp. 23−4, has appropriately referred to the letter, which strikes a note that brings to mind Vasari's passage in his Life of Michelangelo where he reports Lorenzo's awareness of a lack of sculptors: 'Dolendosi adunque Lorenzo . . . che ne'suoi tempi non si trovassero scultori celebrati e nobili . . . deliberò . . . di fare una scuola'; see Vasari 1987, VI, p. 9.

60 For a fine discussion of the development of the small bronze in Florence, see Wright 2005, pp. 323ff.

61 For this document, see the important contribution to Bertoldo studies by Böninger and Boschetto 2005. The text is discussed on pp. 238ff. and published on p. 262.

62 See Vasari 1987, VI, p. 9, where his inability to work is ascribed to old age. However, from a document discovered by Elam, referred to in Kent 2004, pp. 58−9, it seems that Bertoldo was still actively working for Lorenzo in the late 1480s.

63 The letter is discussed in Draper 1992, pp. 7ff., and, more recently, by Böninger and Boschetto 2005. Their revised transcription is published as their document 13, pp. 266−7. Lorenzo is addressed as 'domino meo singularissimo'.

64 See Fusco and Corti 2006, p. 309, their document 113. The letter is dated March 1489.

65 For Bertoldo's room, see Spallanzani and Bertelà 1992, p. 22, and for works that can be associated with him, pp. 20, 71, 72 and 81. The identifications of the inventory items are clarified in Draper 1992, p. 278.

66 The precedent was noted by Agosti in Barocchi 1992, p. 174, and more recently referred to by Kent 2004, p. 18. Cosimo's hospitality is referred to in a letter of 1458, re-transcribed in Caglioti 1993, pp. 4–5, who adds information on Andrea dall'Aquila.

67 The influence of Bertoldo's *Battle* is not confined to Michelangelo's marble *Battle of the Centaurs*. The emphasis on struggling male nudes, a number depicted from behind, clearly influenced Michelangelo when he designed the figures in the cartoon for the never executed *Battle of Cascina*. Justi 1900, p. 223, acutely observed that Michelangelo's Victory groups in his drawings for the project of 1513 for Julius II's tomb are derived from Bertoldo's Victories standing on captives in the same relief.

68 Evidence that the *Orpheus* could be a work referred to as early as 1471 has been published by Böninger and Boschetto 2005, pp. 240 and 262–3.

69 His figure of Pegasus in the well-known group now in Vienna (for which see Draper 1992, pp. 176ff.) clearly inspired a figure in Michelangelo's *Battle of the Centaurs*, as has been long recognized, although the original bronze was no longer in Florence at the period that concerns us. More remarkably, on the reverse of his medal of Filippo de' Medici, Bertoldo, in depicting Christ standing and half-naked in his rendering of the Last Judgement, anticipated Michelangelo's Christ in his fresco in the Sistine Chapel. For a clear reproduction of Bertoldo's composition, see Tolnay 1960, fig. 276, and for comments, Draper 1992, pp. 85–6. The connection was proposed more than a hundred years ago by Wilhelm von Bode (Bode 1925, p. 30).

70 Condivi 1998, pp. 12–13.

71 *Carteggio* II, p. 253, no. CDLXXVII. Writing of Leo X, Sebastiano reports to Michelangelo: 'quando parla de vui par rasoni de un suo fratello, quassi con le lacrime algli ochii, perché m'a decto a me vui sette nutriti insiemi, et dimostra conoscervi et amarvi'.

72 *Carteggio indiretto* I, p. 41, no. 24.

73 Since Bertoldo had inherited works left in his master's workshop, for which see Vasari 1987, III, p. 226, it is possible that Michelangelo could have had access to works in perishable materials no longer known. Wind 2000, p. 177, saw in the melancholy of the Virgin a reference to her foreknowledge of her Son's death. He pointed out that the five steps, which have given the relief its name, could relate to the symbolic numerology in Domenico Benivieni's *Scale della Vita Spirituale sopra el nome di Maria*, which would be printed in Florence in 1495.

74 Michelangelo's remark that the work was unfinished was made years later in surviving comments made in a copy of Condivi's book once owned by Ugo Procacci. For a review of these latter-day reflections and the identification of the hand as Tiberio Calcagni's, see Elam in Condivi 1998, pp. XXI–XLVI. In his funeral oration Benedetto Varchi stated that the relief had been found in the artist's workshop.

75 For Ovid's lengthy account of the event, see *Metamorphoses*, XII, 210–535. The motif of the figure dragged by the hair, given prominence in the relief, is explicitly referred to in ibid., 220ff. The debate over the sources employed has been extensive; see Vasari 1962, II, pp. 100–01, to which should be added the discussion in Lisner 1980. The subject was not confined to sculpture; for a mural image, see Chambers 1992, p. 87, recording a representation ordered by Cardinal Francesco Gonzaga.

76 Many observations on Poliziano's role relating to the visual arts can be found in Agosti's contributions in Barocchi 1992, pp. 104ff. Worth noting here is his sustained polemic against the ideal of imitation; see, for example, Jüren 1975. It should be added that Poliziano's homosexuality was notorious.

77 It is useful to compare Alberti's dictum in *De Statua*, 2, with two of the artist's sonnets, 'Si come per lever, donna, si pone in pietra alpestra' and 'Non ha l'ottimo artista alcun concetto', the latter the subject of a later celebrated lecture of Benedetto Varchi. For the two texts, see Girardi 1960, nos. 151 and 152, and Saslow 1991, with the same numeration. For comments, see Vasari 1962, II, pp. 229ff. The idea can already be encountered in Plotinus.

78 Parenti 1994, pp. 21ff.

79 Poliziano's long and moving letter was already published in Roscoe before 1800; see Roscoe-Bossi 1816–17, II, pp. 84–90. For rewarding comments, see Godman 1998, pp. 1ff.

80 Masi 1906, pp. 17–18. He writes that Lorenzo was regarded as one of the wisest men in all Italy. He had, however, critical comments for his sons.

81 For his remarkable encomium, see Landucci 1883 / 1969, p. 65. Lorenzo had ennobled his own family and also the entire city.

82 Condivi 1998, p. 14.

83 The episode of the snowman may have been introduced to emphasize Piero's basic frivolity. However, there were exceptionally heavy snowfalls in Florence in January 1494 (1493 Florentine style). See Hirst and Dunkerton 1994, p. 17, citing Tibaldo d'Amerigo de' Rossi.

84 The document relating to the *Hercules* was first published in Merisalo 1999, p. 60; for an improved transcription, see Caglioti 2000a, I, p. 263. That the *Hercules* was made for Piero was proposed in Hirst 1985, p. 155; the same view had been reached by Elam 1992c, p. 60. In deciding on commissioning an image of Hercules, Piero was, of course, following a long-standing Florentine tradition. For the significance of Hercules for the city, see Ettlinger 1972 and Wright 1994, pp. 323–39. Hercules was already a highly conspicuous presence in Palazzo Medici, exemplified in the monumental canvases painted by Antonio del Pollaiuolo, most informatively discussed in Wright 2005, pp. 75ff.

85 Condivi 1998, p. 15. For a very similar indictment of Piero, see Guicciardini 1931, p. 84, who wrote of Piero: 'la sua natura era tirannesca ed altiera'.

86 See the comments of Hirst in *Carteggio indiretto* II, Appendix 2, pp. 323–4.

Writing to the artist's brother from Venice, Lorenzo Strozzi, in a letter of June 1506, refers to the fact that he has heard that the 'figura' is now housed in Palazzo Strozzi, where the two brothers, Lorenzo and Filippo, together with their father's second wife, Selvaggia, already lived in the part completed. The identification is the more probable in that Buonarroto was, at this point, associated with the two Strozzi brothers in their wool business in the Via Porta Rossa. Michelangelo's own letters of this period show his wish to gratify them. The later fate of the *Hercules* is commented on below.

87 For the problem of the appearance of the lost work, see Cox-Rearick 1995, pp. 302–13.

88 For the passage, see Condivi 1998, pp. 14–15. He records that the work was made to gratify the prior of Santo Spirito, that it was made of wood and that it was, when he wrote, still to be seen above the high altar of the church. There follows a description of the close relations between Michelangelo and the prior, identified by Frey (1907a, pp. 107ff.) as Fra Niccolò di Giovanni di Lapo Bichiellini, and a remarkable reference to the dissections he allowed the artist.

89 For Piero's election, see Botto 1932, p. 36, note 1.

90 See Frey 1907a, pp. 107ff. The presence of the sick is recorded in Frey's documents. His material seems to have been neglected by students of hospitals of the period.

91 See Frey 1892, p. 115, where we read that, among other corpses, Michelangelo dissected one from the Corsini family, which provoked a scandal. Summoned to appear before Piero Soderini, the latter laughed and exonerated him, since he had done it for his art.

92 The wooden crucifix was discovered by Lisner in 1963 and discussed by her in Lisner 1966, pp. 295–316, and on later occasions. The attribution has not gone unchallenged, but the singularity of the piece confirms its accuracy. We may note that Bertoldo had also worked in wood; see Draper 1992, pp. 275–6.

93 The sequence of events is well described by Nardi 1838–41, I, pp. 35ff.

94 Nardi 1838–41, I, pp. 47ff.

95 Frey 1907a, p. 76.

96 For the identification, see Cummings 1992, pp. 37–8.

97 For the episode, see Condivi 1998, pp. 15–16, and for Bibbiena, see Moncallero 1953; he exercised great influence over Piero. The ever closer ties between them provoked the bitter criticisms of Poliziano and others; see Picotti 1955, p. 124, and Godman 1998, p. 125.

98 The letter was first published by Poggi 1906 and by Frey 1907a, pp. 119–20. Poggi's text reads: 'Sapi che Michelagnolo ischultore dal g[i]ardino se n'è ito a Venegia sanza dire nulla a Piero, tornando lui in chasa: mi pare che Piero l'abia auto molto a male'. That the letter confirms the reality of the garden was noted in Hirst 1969, p. 763; see also Elam's comments, Elam 1992c, p. 58. Frey believed that Michelangelo probably left on 10 or 11 October.

99   Parenti 1994, pp. 102–3.

100 Condivi 1998, p. 16. The practice was a long-standing one; see Simeoni 1934–5, pp. 73ff.

101 Giovan Francesco Aldrovandi has not received a monographic study and he does not appear in the *Dizionario biografico italiano*. There is an account of his career in Ciammitti 1999, with an informed bibliography. He would later serve Pope Julius II and lived until 1512. He is repeatedly referred to in Ghiradacci's *Historia di Bologna*.

102 For Baccio da Montelupo's sculptural group for San Domenco, see Gatteschi 1993, pp. 34ff; documents for his work in Bologna, first published by Supino, survive. The group is now only a fragment. Baccio, born in 1469, was Michelangelo's senior by six years. He would flee from Florence a second time in 1498 on account of his Savonarolan sympathies.

103 Niccolò's contract to decorate the Arca with statues was drawn up in July 1469. The document was already published by Gualandi in the nineteenth century and has been reprinted in Dodsworth 1995, Document XLIII, pp. 166ff. Niccolò seems to have abandoned work on the project many years before he died.

104 Condivi 1998, p. 17.

105 The *ricordi* of Fra Lodovico da Prelormo, for many years the archivist of San Domenico, provide the following passage: 'Sciendum tamen est quod Imago Sancti Petronii quasi totta, et totta Imago Sancti proculi, et totta Imago illius Angeli qui genua flectit, et e posto sopra il parapeto che fece Alphonso scultore, qual è verso le finestre, queste tre Imagine ha fatto quidam Juvenis florentinus nomine Michael angelus imediate post mortem dicti M.ri (magistri) Nicolai'. The passage can be found in Fra Lodovico da Prelormo, 'Memorie manoscritte', in the Archive of the Convent of San Domenico, fol. 24. It was published by Bonora 1875, p. 17, and republished in Dodsworth 1995, Document LIV, pp. 179 80. Leandro Alberti, associated with San Domenico since 1495, attributed all these statues to Michelangelo in a book published in Bologna in 1535; see his 'De Divi Dominici Calaguritani obitu et sepultura', fol. 9.

106 The literature devoted to the Arca is too extensive to be reviewed here. However, it must be noted that Frey's contention, Frey 1907b, p. 133, that the *St Proculus* is not by Michelangelo conflicts with the sources cited here.

107 For the culture of the two brothers and their role as patrons, see Cecchi 2005, pp. 148ff. For the presence of Botticelli's *Primavera* in their house on the Via Larga, see Shearman 1975a, p. 25, no. 38. And for Lorenzo di Pierfrancesco's contacts with Rome, which would play a role in Michelangelo's subsequent career, see Baldini in Weil-Garris Brandt et al. 1999, pp. 152ff. The two brothers came to be known as the *popolani*, indicating their hostility to Piero de' Medici; at one point prior to his fall from power they had been compelled to leave the city.

108 Shearman 1975a, p. 25, no. 33; the work is referred to as 'Uno San Joanbaptista

di marmo di rilievo'. It is striking that Michelangelo's carving, long lost sight of, was given the same valuation as Botticelli's painting.

109   Landucci 1883 / 1969, p. 108. Landucci wrote: 'Era il Frate in quell tempo in una tanta stima e divozione in Firenze, che ci era molti uomini e donne, che se gli avesse detto loro entrate nel fuoco, l'arebbono subito di fatto. Stimavasi per molti che fussi profeta, e lui lo diceva.' For a more measured view, see Parenti 1994, p. 310: 'E in effetto divisa era la città: una parte totalmente a frate Ieronimo credeano; l'altra, la quale minore era di numero di homini, ma più potente di danari e di credito, contrarii li erano.'

110   In a sermon of 29 May 1496 he had accused the papacy of selling Christ's blood: 'vendono insino al sangue di Cristo'. Lanckoronska saw in Savonarola's words an influence on Michelangelo's celebrated sonnet 'Qua si fa elmi di calici e spade', which will be returned to later; see Lanckoronska 1932–3, pp. 122ff.

111   Condivi 1998, p. 62.

112   The letter was published by Poggi, who correctly identified the writer; see *Carteggio indiretto* II, Appendix I, pp. 321–2. Piero refers ironically to Savonarola as 'vostro sarafico', and mockingly suggests that he would be canonized if he were to come to preach in Rome.

113   *Carteggio* I, p. 85, no. LX. Of 'Iachopo di Sandro' he refers to his good appearance but reminds his son of how often he has warned him about the Frate's followers: 'ma già più volte ti dissi che tutti questi piangnioni erano chattivi huomini'.

114   For Michelangelo's comments, see *Carteggio* III, p. 28, no. DCVIII. Frey 1907b, pp. 111–18, in a searching examination of the topic, rejected the conclusion that Michelangelo had ever been a *piagnone* sympathizer, but he failed to appreciate the artist's remark in full for he was unaware that Lunetti had been a long-term supporter of Savonarola. He had even taken part in the defence of San Marco when it had been under attack in April 1498. For these events, see Villari 1898, II, p. CLXXXIV.

CHAPTER TWO

1   *Carteggio* I, pp. 1–2, no. 1. Although the letter is addressed to 'Lorenzo di Pier Francesco de' Medici', it is directed, as often noted, to Sandro Botticelli. What seems not to have been noticed is that, in referring to his safe arrival, Michelangelo uses the plural 'we', implying that he did not travel alone. That his companion was Jacopo Gallo cannot be excluded.

2   Condivi 1998, pp. 17–18. For Baldassare del Milanese, see Baldini in Weil-Garris Brandt et al. 1999, pp. 149ff. It should be recalled that the episode of the deception over the *Cupid* was familiar decades before Vasari and Condivi described it.

Writing in the 1520s, Paolo Giovio refers to the burial of the *Cupid* in order to age it and to the great price for which it was sold; see Barocchi 1971, p. 11. Condivi's account, dependent on the artist, confirms that Riario paid 200 ducats for the sculpture, and Vasari explicitly names Baldassare del Milanese; see Vasari 1987, VI, pp. 12 and 14.

3   See Hirst and Dunkerton 1994, p. 72, note 25: 'Lo Reverendissimo Cardinale di San Giorgio de'avere a di 5 di magio ducati 200 di charlini 10 per ducato'.

4   Isabella's correspondent writes: 'Chi lo tene antique e chi moderno. Qualunque se sia, è tenuto et è perfectissimo'.

5   Vasari 1962, II, p. 152: 'Quel Cupido è moderno. E lo maestro che lo ha facto è qui venuto; Tamen è tanto perfecto, che da ognuno era tenuto antiquo. E da poi che è chiarito moderno, credo che lo daria per manco prezio'.

6   Vasari 1962, II, p. 153.

7   For a brief survey of Riario's eventful career, see Schiavo 1964, pp. 414–29, and for both patron and palace, the valuable contribution in Frommel 1989. It should be noted that Frommel 1992 (pp. 450ff.) proposed that Riario had invited the artist to Rome, but the evidence he cites seems insufficient to confirm the suggestion.

8   This and other aspects of Riario's interests are discussed in Daly Davis 1989, pp. 442ff. It was generally believed that the new palace was built on the site of the Theatre of Pompey.

9   Bober and Rubinstein 1986, fig. 396. For the discovery of a remarkable antique bronze relief in 1490 on the site of the Cancelleria, acquired by Riario and now lost, see Carl 1999.

10 The Gallo family property lay to the north of the Cancelleria; see Schiavo 1964, p. 92, and his figs 6 11, and Lodico 1999, pp. 155–8.

11 See the informative discussion in Frommel 1992.

12 For the remarkable archival resource of the Carte di Lemmo Balducci, records of the activities of the bank run in Rome by Jacopo Gallo and the Florentines Baldassare and Giovanni Balducci, now in the Archivio di Stato, Florence, see, most recently, Hatfield 2002, pp. 2ff. Known to Giovanni Poggi, they were first brought to public notice by Mancusi-Ungaro 1971. Michelangelo appears to have opened a credit and debit account there not later than March 1497.

13 The payment was recorded on 19 September 1496; see Hirst and Dunkerton 1994, p. 74, note 15. Already in August Michelangelo is recorded as resident in Gallo's house; see Frommel 1992, p. 454, note 31. A year later, when Buonarroto visited him in Rome, Michelangelo explained to Lodovico that he could not put him up because he was living in the quarters of others; see *Carteggio* I, p. 5, no. III; the remark suggests a lengthy period as Gallo's guest.

14 For the texts of these payments, initially referred to in Hirst 1981a, pp. 590–93, see also Hirst 1991 and Hirst and Dunkerton 1994, p. 74, notes 8–11.

15 *Carteggio* I, p. 3, no. II. Michelangelo seems to intimate that he is encountering

problems over payment by his patron: 'e partir no' mi voglio se prima io non
sono sodisfatto e rremunerato della fatica mia'.

16   No sixteenth-century source appears to refer to Riario's commissioning of the
Bacchus; in both editions, Vasari (1987, VI, p. 15) implies that it was made for
Gallo. Condivi's passage is more aggressive, citing Michelangelo's statements that
Riario understood little about sculpture – scarcely borne out by the cardinal's
antiquities – and that throughout the year he passed with him he received no
request to make anything for him; see Condivi 1998, p. 19. It was Wilde 1932,
pp. 53–4, who first proposed that Riario had commissioned it.

17   See Aldrovandi 1556, pp. 172ff. The issues surrounding Michelangelo's lost
Cupid for Gallo have been clouded by the promotion of a fragmentary statue
now in New York as an early work of the artist. For the proposal, see Weil-
Garris Brandt 1996, and contributions in Weil-Garris Brandt et al. 1999, passim.
The attribution is not convincing, and a possible connection with the work
referred to in the sources is, therefore, not relevant. It is worth notice that
Condivi appears to list the early works in the order in which they were made.

18   For the drawing of the *Bacchus*, see Tolnay 1943, pl. 69. The right wrist and
hand are shown as broken off, perhaps a consequence of vandalism during the
sack of the city in 1527. The *Bacchus* is referred to in a book published as early
as 1506, confirming its ownership by the Gallo family: 'Item quamquam profa-
num, attamen operosum Bacchi signum in atrio domus Jacobi Galli civis'; see
Maffei 1506, Cap. XXI, p. 495. It would pass by inheritance to Jacopo's sons,
Giuliano and Paolo, with whom, Condivi states, Michelangelo had always
maintained a close friendship. Jacopo's father, Giuliano Gallo, had enjoyed a
reputation as an expert on antique objects and had been consulted on the celebrated Phaethon gem acquired by Lorenzo de' Medici in 1487 just prior to his
death in 1488; see Fusco and Corti 2006, Document 73, p. 298.

19   *Carteggio* I, p. 4, no. III.

20   See, for example, the document of May 1496, published in Fusco and Corti
2006, Document 215, pp. 340–41. Michelangelo's involvement with Piero is
confirmed by the fact that he would repay him the sum of 30 ducats as late as
March 1498; see Hatfield 2002, p. 351, no. R12.

21   *Carteggio* I, p. 3, no. II.

22   Michelangelo sent 9 large ducats to his father in Florence on 23 March
1497; see Hatfield 2002, p. 349, no. R2. See also Poggi's note in *Carteggio* I,
p. 359.

23   De Bilhères' remarkable career in Rome as a representative of the French crown
is described in a useful monograph by Samaran 1921, passim. For more recent
assessments, see Weil-Garris Brandt 1987, especially pp. 8ff., and the detailed
account in Voci 2001, pp. 27–42. De Bilhères was an avid pluralist. He is inaccurately referred to in contemporary references, including the payments to
Michelangelo for the *Pietà*, as the Cardinal of Saint-Denis.

24   For a detailed discussion of the mausoleum, see Weil-Garris Brandt 1987, pp. 77ff. For ground plans that indicate its location on the left of old St Peter's, see her reproduction after Tiberio Alfarano, ibid., p. 108, and Voci 2001, fig. 1. These plans indicate that the mausoleum contained six bays that could have housed altars.

25   For this proposal, see Biering and von Hesberg 1987, p. 181, note 139. A location on a side wall, specifically that on the left of the chapel dedicated to St Petronilla herself, has been suggested by Voci 2001, pp. 83ff. Such a position would have rendered the gesture of the Virgin's left hand, one of the most evocative in Renaissance art, completely invisible to the viewer.

26   See Piras in Weil-Garris Brandt et al. 1999, p. 160.

27   For the letter, see Milanesi 1875, p. 613, and Gotti 1875, II, pp. 33–4. Milanesi's text is the less dependable, printing 'pietra di marmo' instead of Gotti's correct 'pietà di marmo', an error followed in Weil-Garris Brandt 1987, p. 105. The cardinal refers to the projected sculpture as 'una Pietà, cioè una Vergine Maria vestita, con Cristo morto nudo in braccio'. He refers to the artist as 'statuario fiorentino'.

28   See Hirst 1985, p. 156, and Hatfield 2002, pp. 6 and 350.

29   Hirst 1985, p. 156, and Hatfield 2002, p. 351.

30   Carteggio indiretto I, p. 1, no. 1.

31   See Frey 1907a, p. 140.

32   For the letter written by Topolino, one of the artist's most dependable assistants in the 1520s, see Carteggio III, p. 98, no. DCLVIII. It is briefly noted in Wallace 1994, p. 110. From the letter, it is clear that the marble for the Pietà had been quarried at a place called Polvaccio, located above and behind Carrara and a far from accessible site. For a map of the quarries, see Klapisch-Zuber 1969, p. 131. She noted that Michelangelo's choice of Polvaccio enhanced its subsequent importance.

33   The payment, of 9 February 1498, was published in Hirst 1985, p. 196. The four-wheeled carts traditionally employed for transporting the marble to the sea came to be called carretti, and from this sprang the term carrata, adopted to refer to the weight of the blocks; see Klapisch-Zuber 1969, pp. 71ff. The carrata has been reliably estimated to weigh 1,000 kilograms.

34   For this letter, see Milanesi 1875, p. 613, note 1. It is dated 7 April 1498.

35   Frey 1907a, p. 140, wrongly presumed that the man held up at Carrara was Michelangelo himself, an error followed by Tolnay 1943, pp. 146–7.

36   Carteggio indiretto II, pp. 321–2. He describes Savonarola as 'vostro sarafico', and reports on Mariano da Genazzano's attacks on him. Pope Alexander VI would excommunicate Savonarola in May.

37   For a pioneering study of Michelangelo's visits to Carrara, see Frediani 1875, passim. Early references to sculptors' visits are rare, but the undistinguished sculptor who had served the Opera of Florentine Cathedral, Bernardo Ciuffagni,

seems to have gone there several times; see, for example, Poggi 1909/1988, I, nos. 271 and 275.

38 For the outgoings for marble, see Hatfield 2002, pp. 351ff., and his remarks on the implications, pp. 7ff.

39 The artist paid six months' rent on 21 August; see Hatfield 2002, p. 352. There are no details about the nature of the property.

40 For the contractual agreement, which it has been suggested is a copy written for Michelangelo by Gallo, see *Contratti*, pp. 5–6.

41 In favour of a date in the summer of 1500 is the large sum that Michelangelo received from the Ghinucci bank of no less than 232 florins in July 1500. This bank had been used by the executors of the deceased cardinal to pay for his funeral expenses; see Hirst and Dunkerton 1994, p. 78, note 34, citing Burchard 1907–42, II, p. 157.

42 See Hirst 2000b, pp. 487.

43 For a discussion of the employment of the imperfect, see Jüren 1974, pp. 27ff., who refers to its usage by Michelangelo's early mentor, Angelo Poliziano. The form of the imperfect would be adopted by Andrea Sansovino only a few years later. See also Jüren 1975, pp. 131ff.

44 See Hirst and Dunkerton 1994, p. 75, note 1, and Hatfield 2002, pp. 5 and 350. The entry reads: 'A Michelagnolo carlini 3 per 1° chuadro di legno per dipignerlo'.

45 See Hirst and Dunkerton 1994, p. 37.

46 The suggestion has been made by Weil-Garris Brandt; see Hatfield 2002, p. 5, note 21.

47 Vasari 1987, VI, p. 15. Vasari had evidently seen it for he refers to its small scale, describing it as a 'tavoletta'. An earlier source, the Anonimo Magliabechiano, had already referred to the work, writing that the painting had been designed by Michelangelo and perhaps painted by him: 'di mano di Michele Agnolo disegnato et forse colorito'. The writer lavished praise on the figure of the saint. See Frey 1892, p. 129.

48 For an assessment of Céspedes as a source, see Agosti and Hirst 1996. For the text, see their p. 683. He refers to 'un San Francisco que está en San Pedro de Montoro en Roma, aunque algunos dizen que es de mano de un cierto Pedro de Argento, discipulo o practicante suyo'. The passage was already published by Ceán Bermúdez in 1800.

49 For the drawing, its appearance, provenance and authorship, see Agosti and Hirst 1996; it is reproduced on their p. 684.

50 The two letters are published in *Carteggio indiretto* I, p. 1; and II, p. 321. That of March contains the ironical reference to Savonarola cited earlier.

51 For examples from the group, see Hirst and Dunkerton 1994, pls 24–6, and for comments on their style, ibid., pp. 38–40. Since Piero is still described as 'garzone' in 1508, Hatfield 2002, p. 10, note 40, has contested the association.

Michelangelo himself, however, would refer to painters older than himself, called in to help in the Sistine Chapel in 1508, as 'garzoni'; see *Ricordi* 1970, p. 1, no. 1. As late as 1512 he would allude to Alonso Berruegete, born about 1488, as a 'garzone'; see *Carteggio* I, p. 125, no. XCII. Piero could have come from a family of painters: a Jacopo Filippo d'Argenta was a noted miniaturist in Ferrara who died around 1501; see Cittadella 1868, pp. 176–7.

52 To limit discussion to two cases: Hirst, in Hirst and Dunkerton 1994, pp. 42ff., proposed 1497; Penny and Weil-Garris Brandt, in Weil-Garris Brandt et al. 1999, pp. 354–40, argued for an earlier date, close to the artist's stay in Bologna.

53 For these circumstances, see Hirst 1981a, pp. 582ff.

54 See Hirst 1981a, p. 581, and Hatfield 2002, pp. 11 and 360.

55 Hirst 1981a, p. 590, Appendix B. It records that De Dossis and Jacopo Gallo had paid out 60 cameral ducats for the altarpiece of the deceased bishop's chapel, 'per la depintura dell'ancona per la soprascripta cappella'.

56 See Lodovico's letter to Michelangelo of 19 December 1500; *Carteggio* I, p. 9, no. VI. He writes: 'Bonarroto mi dice chome tu vivi chostì chon grande masserizia o vero miseria.'

57 For this information, see now Jestaz 1994, p. 115, no. 2883. The entry reads: 'Uno in tavola grande, cornice di noce, dipinto un Christo condotto al sepolcro dalle Marie, S. Giovanni e Cireneo, mano di Michel Angelo Buonarota'.

58 For these repayments by Michelangelo, see Hirst 1981a, Appendix A, p. 590, and Hatfield 2002, pp. 362–3. Gamba 1948, p. XIV, proposed that the work was abandoned in 1501.

59 'Maestro Andrea' appears to have become a relatively familiar figure in later years. He seems to have been active as a furniture painter in the pontificate of Julius II; see Hirst in Hirst and Dunkerton 1994, p. 79, note 17. His career is described in Marucci et al. 1983, II, p. 1011. It has been stated that he died in the sack of Rome; but see Gnoli 1923–4, p. 215.

CHAPTER THREE

1 *Carteggio* I, p. 10, no. VI.

2 For the loan of money from Gallo, see Hirst and Dunkerton 1994, p. 81, note 57, and Hatfield 2002, pp. 14 and 361, no. R73.

3 For this letter of Fra Pietro da Novellara, head of the Carmelites in Florence, which includes a remarkable description of Leonardo's cartoon, see Villata 1999, no. 150, pp. 134–5. For Vasari's passage, see Vasari 1987, VI, pp. 18–19, which is compatible with the letter of Lodovico to his son.

4 For an account of the role of the Wool Guild in the administration of the cathedral, see, most recently, Haines 1996.

5   For the documentation of the earlier project, see Frey 1909, pp. 104ff., and Poggi 1909/1988, I, nos. 441ff.

6   Poggi 1909/1988, I, nos. 446–7. The document describes the block as 'al presente allato a' fondamenti', and states that the statue is destined 'per uno de' pinacholi della chupola'; an earlier reference alludes to the site as one of the 'sproni' of the building, that is, one of the buttresses.

7   Vasari 1987, VI, p. 18. He is guilty of anachronism in referring to Soderini as already *gonfaloniere* for life in 1501; the office was created and Soderini elected to it only in November 1502. Soderini's great importance for the artist in the following years is referred to below. Condivi 1998, p. 21, contains a polemical passage that Andrea Sansovino had sought to acquire the block. He was probably not in Florence at this time. The charge indicates Michelangelo's persistent contempt for his fellow sculptor.

8   For this *deliberazione*, see Frey 1909, p. 106, no. 8, and Poggi 1909/1988, I, no. 448. It refers to the block as 'vocato Davit, male abbozatum et supinum [Poggi wrongly gives *scultum*], existentum in curte dicte Opere, et desiderantes tam dicti consules quam operaii dictum talem gigantem erigi et elevari in altum per magistros dicte Opere et in pedes stare, ad hoc ut videatur per magistros in hoc expertos posit absolvi et finiri'.

9   *Contratti*, no. IV, p. 12. An annotation on the left margin of this version in the Archivo dell'Opera di Santa Maria del Fiore states that Michelangelo began work on the block on 13 September after he had removed a knot (*nodum*) on the breast of the figure. This knot has provoked much discussion. Lavin 1993, p. 98, proposed that it could have been a measuring point left by Agostino di Duccio. In his second edition of Condivi's *Vita*, A. F. Gori noted a different and now lost version of the contract that identified the subject as David and added details absent from the generally noted text; see Condivi-Gori 1746, pp. 106–7.

10 For the two documents recording the raising of the artist's payment, see *Contratti*, nos. V, p. 13, and VI, p. 14.

11 This provision for the public showing of the *David* was first published in Hirst 2000b, pp. 487ff. Soderini's role is returned to below. The creation of his brother, Francesco, as a cardinal in the summer of 1503 was a significant and much-celebrated event.

12 A critical edition of the record of the meeting of January 1504 is still required. Partially published in Gaye 1840, pp. 455ff., a more complete text is provided in Milanesi 1875, pp. 620–22. A more recent transcription in Baldini and Giulietti 1999, pp. 65–6, contains new errors of transcription. The correct citation for the text is Archivo dell'Opera di Santa Maria del Fiore, Deliberazioni (1496–1507), fols 71 recto to 72 verso.

13 For a detailed study of Filarete, see Trexler 1978, passim, but especially pp. 47ff. He had taken part in a meeting concerning the future of the cathedral as long ago as 1491 and was present at a disputatious gathering concerning the church

of Santo Spirito in 1495. His astrological interests are discussed in Trexler. His dire views about the problems provoked by the displacement of the *Judith and Holofernes* had already been anticipated by others; see the fine analysis in Caglioti 2000a, I, pp. 302ff. He has shown that the 'other' *David* he refers to is not Donatello's but that of Andrea Verrocchio.

14   The passage, for which see Florence, Biblioteca Nazionale, MS II. II. 134, fols 9 verso to 10 recto, reads: 'Finalmente, in diversi pareri, per consiglio del maestro si condusse in Piazza de' Signori per opera di Simone del Pollaiuolo architecto ... Non fu però tale statua interamente approvata dal iuditio delli intendenti, ma scusàvasene il maestro per havere havuto el pezzo del marmo, secondo dicea, male qualificato'.

15   Landucci 1883 / 1969, p. 268. For the episode of the stoning and the identities of those involved, see Hirst 2000b, p. 490.

16   This is noted by Brockhaus 1909, p. 16, note 1. Savonarola, in one of his Sermons on Exodus, referred to David as 'forte di mano et bello di aspetto'; see Savonarola 1956, II, p. 57.

17   For recent comment, see Lavin 1993, pp. 29ff. Frey 1897, pp. 301ff., who first extensively analysed the sheet, cautiously suggested that 'Rotta è l'alta colonna' could refer to the damaged block, but his point has gone unnoticed. *Rotto* can signify ill-used as well as broken.

18   For a recent discussion of these events, see Caglioti 2000a, I, pp. 334ff; the documents are published on p. 336. However, that the 'Raffaello di Giovanni dipintore' who was involved was no less than Raphael himself is a proposal open to serious doubt. See also Ristori 1986, pp. 77ff., for possible Savonarolan implications.

19   For Argentina Soderini's move into Palazzo Vecchio in early 1503, see Rubinstein 1995, p. 43, who points out that the step was widely resented.

20   Nardi 1838–41, I, pp. 456–7.

21   See the letter of Fabrizio Pellegrini published in Ferrai 1891, p. 44.

22   See Gatti 1994, pp. 437–8, quoting the letter of 10 November 1499 from the Signoria to the Florentine envoys in Milan. He republished much of the extensive diplomatic correspondence concerning the bronze *David*; ibid., pp. 433–72.

23   For a review of the employment of artists and their works in a diplomatic context, see Elam 1988.

24   See Gatti 1994, pp. 439–40. The two Florentine envoys expressly refer to de Gié's affection for the city, formed on his stay there in 1494–5, when he had the opportunity to familiarize himself with its collections of sculpture.

25   Gatti 1994, p. 441. The Dieci write: 'Noi habbiamo cercato chi ci possa gittare una figura di Davit come voi ricerchate per il Maricial de Giés et ci è hoggi charestia di simili buoni maestri.'

26   Gatti 1994, p. 441.

27   For the document concerning the Parte Guelfa and this disposable bronze, see
     Caglioti 2000a, I, p. 314. It is now required for the making of a *David* similar
     to that already in the palace. As Caglioti has shown, Donatello's bronze *David*,
     initially placed in the courtyard of the Palazzo Vecchio, had been removed
     indoors and replaced by Verrocchio's; see his p. 311, based on a brief remark
     in Parenti's *Storia Fiorentina*. The substitution, possibly inspired by Savonarolan
     scruples over the nakedness of Donatello's figure, took place at the end of
     December 1495; see Caglioti 2000a, I, p. 311.

28   *Contratti*, Document VII, pp. 16–17. The reference to the bronze to be provided
     must relate to that referred to in the previous note. The scale of Michelangelo's
     projected statue is stipulated as a little over 135 centimetres. The scale of Ver-
     rocchio's *David* is approximately 126 centimetres, that of Donatello about 158
     centimetres.

29   For this point, see Gatti 1994, p. 460, citing two notes of Piero Soderini,
     one of which states that the statue weighs between 700 and 800 pounds; see
     Gaye 1840, pp. 102–3. What seems certain, to judge from a brilliant preparatory
     sketch, is that, like Donatello's *David*, Michelangelo's was totally nude; for his
     drawing, see Tolnay 1975–80, I, no. 19 recto, and Hirst 1988a, p. 23. Some record
     of the statue must have remained in Florence, since it was adapted by Rosso
     Fiorentino for the naked St Sebastian in his altarpiece now in Palazzo Pitti.

30   Gatti 1994, pp. 441–2.

31   Gatti 1994, pp. 442–3.

32   For the financing of the project, see the exhaustive study in Caglioti 1996,
     passim. He rightly points out, p. 101, that 70 florins was a relatively modest
     overall remuneration for the statue.

33   Gatti 1994, p. 445.

34   For Leonardo's painting, see Kemp 1992, passim. Pietro da Noveralla, who had
     described Leonardo's earlier exhibition at Santissima Annunziata, would refer to
     the *Madonna of the Yarnwinder* in a letter of April 1501; see Villata 1999, p. 136.
     He describes Leonardo's patron as 'uno Roberteto favorite del Re de
     Francia'.

35   Gatti 1994, p. 445.

36   The fiscal implications of the artist's failure to deliver his work have been ana-
     lysed in detail by Caglioti 1996, especially his pp. 104ff. This information of
     Buonarroto, known to Poggi, can be found in Archivio Buonarroti, XXVII, fol.
     48 verso. Buonarroto records that his brother's debt to the commune of the 70
     florins established as the payment for the statue was formally annulled as late as
     17 November 1519. The artist had been declared 'a spechio per fiorini 70 d'oro
     ebe più tempo fa in su uno Davit di bronzo che feciono per donare a 1° francese,
     di che n'avevono fatto debitore detto Michelangelo di detti fiorini 70 e non
     l'avevono fato creditore de la sua faticha e di detto Davite'.

37 Gatti 1994, p. 448: 'Il Davit del quale scrivete per le vostre si trova imperfecto per essere stato levato di qui Michelagnolo scultore per uno breve del Sommo Pontefice per fare certa sua opera a Roma. Nè anchora lo possiamo ritrarre di là per non essergli permesso. Et così nel modo si trova dicto Davit non è per satisfare a persona. Resta rozzo et vi è anchora per fare su qualche tempo.'

38 For the letter asking Michelangelo to choose a sculptor to complete the work, see *Carteggio* I, p. 83, no. LIX. For Michelangelo's payments to Benedetto, see Caglioti 1996, pp. 125ff. His findings indicate that Michelangelo paid Benedetto 10 large florins for undertaking the chasing of the statue.

39 *Contratti*, no. II, p. 7.

40 *Contratti*, no. III, pp. 8–11.

41 For Cardinal Piccolomini's involvement, see Burchard 1907–42, II, p. 157, note 2, and Hirst and Dunkerton 1994, pp. 70–71.

42 For the document of May 1481, see Caglioti 2005, p. 472; and for a fine assessment of Bregno's Roman career, ibid., pp. 401ff. Piccolomini's choice of Bregno reflects the sculptor's standing in Rome and the cardinal's discerning judgement. Both patron and artist could have been brought together by their shared enthusiasm for antique sculpture. The cardinal had acquired the celebrated *Three Graces*, which, later in life, he transferred to Siena. Bregno, well known for his antiquarian pursuits, owned the *Belvedere Torso*; see Agosti and Isella 2004, pp. 47–9.

43 For the densely detailed text, see *Contratti*, no. III, pp. 8–11. The *St Francis* is finished, but it is difficult to identify exactly where Michelangelo intervened.

44 For the will in the Biblioteca Comunale in Siena, see Caglioti 2005, pp. 473–4. There is a further fragmentary text in the Archivio Buonarroti; see *Contratti*, no. X, p. 24. Both are dated 30 April 1503 and convey the deep concern of the cardinal that his project be completed.

45 Caglioti 2005, p. 388, has shown that their correct identifications are Sts Peter, Paul, Pius and Gregory. Frequently impugned as weak creations, they afford a fascinating contrast with the carvings carried out in Bologna nearly a decade earlier. Michelangelo probably carved them in pairs.

46 *Contratti*, no. XIV, p. 33.

47 For Lodovico's letter, see *Carteggio* I, p. 105, no. LXXIII, and for Michelangelo's letter of 1511, ibid., p. 118, no. LXXXVI. In the latter, the artist writes: 'E' cento [ducati] che io ò mandate costà [Florence], mi voglio ingegniare di salvargli per rendergli a quegli del chardinale di Siena, come sapete, che gli ànno avere.'

48 See *Contratti*, no. XCII, pp. 220–23. Michelangelo is referred to as 'in scutis centum remansit debitor': p. 220. For Panciatichi's letter, see *Carteggio* IV, p. 89, no. CMLVI: 'Bene vi priego vi piaccia far quelli disegni che sopra a tal cappella vanno'.

49 *Carteggio* V, pp. 253–4, no. MCCCLIII.

50 *Carteggio* V, p. 268, no. MCCLXIII. He concedes that the work had never been done 'per certo diferenze', leaving any detailed explanation aside.

51 *Carteggio* V, p. 268, no. MCCLXIII. It had been Lorenzo Violi who had drawn up the contract relating to the project of October 1504; *Contratti*, no. XIV, p. 34.

52 See Rota 1937, pp. 47ff., and the lucid explanatory note of Ristori in *Carteggio* V, p. 253, note 2, who states that the sum so deposited remained there untouched until 1601.

53 In his diary of Florentine events, Agostino Lapini, commenting on the display on 8 September, would write: 'Et a' dí 8 di settembre 1504 fu finito di fabbricare in tutto e per tutto il gigante Davit in piazza, e tutto si scoperse. Fabricollo e condussello come si vede Michelagnolo Buonarroti, uomo si può dire unico in tal professione.' See Lapini 1900, p. 63.

54 The literature concerned with the new Sala is abundant. Of especial value are the contributions of Wilde 1944, passim, and Rubinstein 1995, pp. 70ff, who, however, differ on important aspects of the issues involved. For the lack of furnishing of the Sala in February 1496, see Landucci 1883/1969, p. 126. He writes: 'E a di febraio 1495 [1496], si trasse la Signoria nella sala nuova, la quale era fornita di coprire, e non e ancora amattonata, nè fatto panche.'

55 For the ideological implications of the statue, see Wilde 1944, pp. 77ff., and Rubinstein 1995, p. 71.

56 Leonardo was employed in the plan to divert the Arno in the summer of 1503, in the attempt to regain Pisa; see Villata 1999, p. 161, no. 181.

57 For Vasari's brief but significant comment, see Vasari 1987, IV, p. 242. He states explicitly that, to improve lighting in the room, two windows were inserted in the east wall and four in the west wall. Rubinstein's rejection of this information (Rubinstein 1995, p. 114) seriously impairs his discussion of the issue, as Cecchi 1996b rightly points out.

58 There are important comments on the fall of light within the compositions in Wilde 1944, p. 81. His reconstruction remains the most acceptable.

59 For the issue of the keys, see, most recently, Villata 1999, p. 162, no. 183. There is a wealth of documentation on the preparations of Leonardo in Frey 1909, pp. 128ff.

60 For this long and important text, see Frey 1909, no. 175, pp. 130–31. The offer of the Signoria reads: 'Et potrebbe essere, che a detto Lionardo venissi bene cominciare a dipignere et colorire nel muro della sala detta quella parte che lui havessi disegnata et fornita in detto cartone, pero sono contenti, quando questo achaggia'.

61 See the passage of Bartolommeo Cerretani indicated and quoted in Rubinstein 1995, p. 73, and the documents in Frey 1909, no. 210, p. 133.

62 Vasari 1987, VI, p. 23.

63 For this documentary evidence, see Morozzi 1988–9. The permission would extend until December, when the term of office of the current captains would end: 'Item addi 22 di settembre fu concessa per corpo d'arte a' capitani di concedere all Signoria o a Michelagnolo Buonarroti dipintore la sala grande dello spedale durante el tempo de dicti capitani'.

64 See Cecchi 1996a, pp. 102ff.

65 Cecchi 1996a, pp. 106ff. Drawings have survived for episodes in the projected mural other than the *Bathers*, best recorded in the well-known grisaille copy at Holkham Hall. For these drawings, indicating that the composition was planned to be extensive, see Hirst 1986a, pp. 43ff.

66 Frey 1909, no. 193, p. 133.

67 Frey 1909, no. 208, p. 133.

68 *Carteggio* I, p. 15, no. IX. He writes: 'Intesi la vostra giunta a salvamento....Veglio chome di già avete chominciato a lavorare, ch'è segno che avete in animo di tornare presto, finito che di chostà avete quanto avete dato principio'.

69 Albertini 1510, unpaginated. He refers to both Leonardo's and Michelangelo's works in the Sala del Gran Consiglio: 'Nella sala grande nuova del consiglio maiore ... e una tavola di Fra Filippo, li cavalla di Leonar[do] Vinci, e li disegni di Michelangelo'.

70 *Carteggio* I, p. 70, no. XLIX, and pp. 75ff, no. LIII. The 'Sala' must be that in the palace, although the identification has been confused in the literature. The further history of the cartoon, probably cut up in 1516, cannot be discussed here. Condivi would later write that various pieces were scrupulously preserved, 'serbarto con grandissima diligenza e come cosa sacra'; Condivi 1998, p. 28. No one would praise it more unreservedly than Benvenuto Cellini.

71 See Gotti 1875, I, p. 48, and Frey 1892, p. 115.

CHAPTER FOUR

1 Cerretani 1993, p. 115, states that Julius summoned Andrea Sansovino to Rome in October 1505. His safe conduct for Andrea's journey to Carrara is dated the sixteenth of that month; see Baldini and Giulietti 1999, no. 61, p. 71. His employment by the pope thus followed that of Michelangelo by some eight months.

2 For the payment, see Hirst 1991, pp. 762ff., reprinted in Hatfield 2002, pp. 17ff.

3 For this remarkable letter of Alidosi, preserved in the Archivio Salviati in Pisa, see Hirst 1991, p. 763. Of Michelangelo he writes: 'lui essere homo che se li possa credere magiur summa'.

4 In a letter of 23 November 1503 from Rome, addressed to the Dieci in Florence, he writes: 'questa mattina ne andai alla camera di messer Francesco di

Castel del Rio, ch'è il primo che sia appresso ad questo Pontefice'. See Machiavelli 1964, II, p. 672.

5   See the important passage in Vasari's *Vite* (Vasari 1987, IV, p. 144): 'Nel ritorno
    di Giuliano in Roma si praticava se 'l divino Michele Agnolo Buonarroti dovesse
    fare la sepoltura di Giulio . . . aggiugnendo che gli pareva che per quello edifizio
    si dovesse fabricare una cappella aposta senza porre quella nel vecchio San
    Piero'.

6   For a dependable transcription of the letter, see Settis 1999, pp. 110–11.

7   See Hirst 1991, pp. 764ff.

8   For this purchase, Michelangelo's first property, see Hatfield 2002, pp. 61ff.

9   *Contratti*, no. XV, pp. 35–6.

10 *Contratti*, no. XVI, pp. 37–8.

11 For this extraordinary remark reported of the artist, see Condivi 1998, pp. 22–3,
    and Elam's comments, ibid., p. XLI.

12 For documents about the project and the house, see Gaye 1840, pp. 473–8, and
    further comments below.

13 *Carteggio* I, pp. 11–12, no. VII.

14 Condivi 1998, p. 23. For the location of the workshop and further details con-
    cerning it, still occupied by the artist in 1510 when engaged on the Sistine
    Chapel ceiling, see Hirst 1991, p. 766, Appendix B.

15 See Settis 1999, pp. 110ff., for Francesco da Sangallo's letter concerning his father
    Giuliano of February 1567, where he records the episode.

16 *Carteggio* I, pp. 13–14, no. VIII.

17 *Carteggio* III, pp. 7–9, no. DXCIV, and for a briefer version, no. DXCV,
    pp. 10–11.

18 The latest recorded payment from Pope Julius is dated 24 January 1506; see
    Hatfield 2002, p. 410, no. R92. For important comments on this shortfall, see
    Frommel 1977, pp. 26ff.

19 Condivi 1998, pp. 26ff.

20 See *Carteggio* I, p. 15, no. IX.

21 *Carteggio* I, p. 16, no. X.

22 The best transcription of the text is Pogatscher's in Steinmann 1905, pp. 695ff.,
    which is reprinted in Vasari 1962, II, pp. 380–81.

23 Florence, Archivio di Stato, Signori, Carteggi, Minutari 19, c.61 recto. It is
    published in Vasari 1962, II, p. 382. In a successive letter, Soderini refers to only
    one papal brief; Michelangelo probably dramatized the issues.

24 Vasari 1962, II, pp. 382–3.

25 For the artist's remarks, see Condivi 1998, pp. 27–8, and comments by
    Elam, pp. XLII–XLIV. For a fine discussion of the issue, see Sarre 1909,
    pp. 61ff.

26 Vasari 1962, II, p. 383.

27 Vasari 1962, II, p. 385.

28 The passage occurs in Erasmus's *Opus Epistolarum*, where he writes: 'Summus Pontifex Iulius belligeratur, vincit, triumphat, planeque Iulium agit.' See Erasmus 1906, p. 435.

29 Vasari 1962, II, p. 385.

30 *Carteggio* III, p. 8, no. DXCIV. 'Dipoi, la prima volta che papa Iulio andò a Bolognia, mi fu forza andare là cholla choreggia al chollo a chiedergli perdonanza'.

31 *Carteggio* I, p. 15, no. IX. Balducci, one of the artist's closest Roman friends following Gallo's death in 1505, writes that Pope Julius wishes him to return to complete his work.

32 For the drawing, one of extraordinary boldness, see Tolnay 1975–80, I, no. 103 recto, and Hirst 1988b, no. 8. For Vasari, see Vasari 1962, I, p. 25.

33 Tolnay 1975–80, I, no. 102 recto and verso.

34 For Frey, see his *Dichtungen* (Frey 1897, pp. 303–6), unfortunately the only edition commonly employed. Steinmann 1905, II, p. 147, note 6, rejected Frey's date, proposing 1506, accepted by Thode. It had been first advanced by Guasti in 1864.

35 *Contratti*, no. VIII, pp. 18–21, and no. IX, pp. 22–3.

36 Much documentation concerning the house was published by Gaye 1840, pp. 477ff., and Frey 1909, pp. 110ff. For its many vicissitudes, see Vasari 1962, II, pp. 227ff.

37 For discussion of the blocks ordered for the apostles, see Amy 2000, pp. 495ff.

38 For the two editions, see Vasari 1987, VI, p. 22.

39 For the drawings for the apostles, see Tolnay 1975–80, I, nos. 36 recto and 37 recto.

40 Condivi 1998, pp. 27–8, and Elam's comments, pp. XLII–XLIV.

41 For the Mouscheron, see Mancusi-Ungaro 1971, passim. He published extensive documentation of their activities now in the Archivio di Stato, Florence. However, his thesis that the Bruges *Virgin and Child* was originally planned for the Piccolomini Altar in Siena is untenable; see the objections in Hirst 1973, and Caglioti 2005, p. 469.

42 See Mancusi-Ungaro 1971, pp. 160–61.

43 See Mancusi-Ungaro 1971, pp. 168–9.

44 See Mancusi-Ungaro 1971, pp. 170–71.

45 See Giovanni Balducci's letter from Rome to Michelangelo, dated 14 August 1506; *Carteggio* I, p. 17, no. XI.

46 Condivi 1998, p. 22.

47 Four small studies for the Bruges group survive; see Tolnay 1975–80, I, no. 37 recto.

48 Taddeo Taddei was born in January 1470 (1469 in Florentine style). See Florence, Archivio di Stato, Tratte, Libri dell'Età 81, fol. 256. For the earlier history of the

family, see Lightbown 1969, pp. 22ff. For his subsequent importance for Raphael's career, see Cecchi 1984, pp. 39ff. He would die of the plague in 1528.

49   For the poor quality of the marble employed for Taddei's tondo, see Hirst 2005, pp. 548–9.

50   See Florence, Archivio di Stato, Catasto 998, fols 309–10.

51   The bibliography on Agnolo Doni is extensive although he is not included in the *Dizionario biografico degli italiani*. For a relatively recent contribution on him as a patron, see the valuable material in Cecchi 1987, with its references to available source material. See also Hayum 1981–2, pp. 209–33.

52   For the attribution, see Schottmüller 1928, pp. 219ff., and more recently Hayum 1981–2, pp. 209ff. Prominent in its decoration are the lion heads of the Doni and the crescent moons of the Strozzi.

53   Gaye 1840, p. 97.

54   Gaye 1840, p. 107. Soderini writes that Michelangelo's own involvement is essential: 'Et non essendo homo in Italia apto ad expedire una opera di cotesta qualità, è necessario che lui solo, et non altri, là vengha ad vedere et dirizzarla, perchè ogni altro non sapendo la fantasia sua lo potrebbe guastare'.

55   For the letter, see Marchini 1977. It exists in the Archivio dell'Opera di Santa Maria Fiore.

56   For Alidosi's letter, see Gaye 1840, p. 91. He requests that Michelangelo is needed by the pope 'per volere fare alcune opera qui in Bologna'. He asks Soderini to dispatch Michelangelo as soon as possible.

57   Soderini's reply, for which see Gaye 1840, p. 91, is one of the most extraordinary tributes to Michelangelo to have survived. He writes: 'Noi certifichiamo la Signoria Vostra lui essere bravo giovane, et nel mestieri suo l'unico in Italia, forse etiam in universo.' He goes on: 'lui è di modo che colle buone parole et colla carezza, se li fanno, farà ogni cosa'.

58   Condivi 1998, pp. 28–9. One can only speculate whether Bramante, who had accompanied Julius to Bologna, witnessed the scene of reconciliation.

59   For a rewarding account of the stucco statue and the bronze that followed it, see Butzek 1978, pp. 77ff. The projects were first examined in a pioneering article of Podestà as early as 1868.

60   Julius would refer to his payment in a remarkable interview with Bolognese envoys in Rome in 1512, when the statue had already been destroyed; see Butzek 1978, Document XI, pp. 351–4.

61   *Carteggio* III, p. 8, no. DXCIV. In this letter, written many years later, the artist stated that the statue was 7 *braccia* high, although the pope was depicted seated.

62   *Carteggio* I, pp. 18–19, no. XII.

63   *Carteggio* I, pp. 20–21, no. XIII.

64   *Carteggio* I, p. 22, no. XIV. The artist writes to his brother Buonarroto: 'Sappi come venerdi sera a ventuna ora papa Iulio venne a chasa mia dov'io lavoro e

stecte circha a una meza ora a vedere, parte che io lavoravo; poi mi decte la beneditione e andossene; e à dimostrato chontentarsi di quello che io fo.'

65 See Florence, Archivio di Stato, Dieci di Balìa, Responsive 85, fols 10 recto–10 verso: 'e così ne fermano il parlare con andare Sua Santità et 3 cardinali et io fuori ad pie in uno luogo dove fa fare a Michelagnolo la sua statua et li stie un pezo et poi se ne tornò in palazzo'.

66 *Carteggio* I, p. 40, no. XXVI.

67 Valeriano must have seen the statue in 1509 on his way from north Italy to Rome. His lines were first associated with the statue in R. Duppa's pioneering biography of Michelangelo of 1807; the text is discussed in Vasari 1962, II, p. 401. The text was first published in 1550 and runs:

> Quo que tam trepidus fugis Viator
> Ac si te Furiaeve, Gorgonesve,
> Aut acer Basiliscus insequantur?
> Non hic Iulius, at figura Iulii est.

68 See *Carteggio* I, p. 57, no. XLI, and p. 61, no. XLIV. Giuliano da Sangallo seems to have been an intermediary.

69 Gaye 1840, no. XLVI, p. 101.

70 See the information of Giovanni Sabadino in a letter to Isabella d'Este of 24 February 1508, quoted in Tolnay 1943, p. 221.

71 See Gaye 1840, pp. 477ff., and Vasari 1962, II, pp. 227–8. He would be deprived of the house following his move to Rome not many weeks later.

72 For the property of the Via Ghibellina, see Hatfield 2002, pp. 65ff., and for the purchase, Procacci 1965, Appendix I, pp. 215ff. It would cease to be Buonarroti property only in the nineteenth century. Michelangelo rarely lived there.

73 The document was first published in Gotti 1875, I, p. 70, note 1, and is dated 13 March 1507 Florentine style (i.e., March 1508).

74 For general observations on the issue of emancipation, see Kuehn 1982, passim.

CHAPTER FIVE

1 For the payment, see Hatfield 2002, pp. 22 and 373.

2 Hatfield 2002, pp. 23–4 and 373.

3 *Ricordi* 1970, p. 1, no. 1.

4 *Ricordi* 1970, pp. 1–2, no. 2.

5 Requiring precise details of his birth, Michelangelo wrote to his nephew Leonardo in April 1548, asking for them to be extracted from the dead Lodovico's *ricordanze* and sent to him. The text he required, taken from Lodovico's lost book, is printed in *Carteggio* IV, pp. 296–7, no. MCVII.

6 See above, pp. 9–10.

7   Few of Leonardo's *ricordi* survive, but in some of those that do we find an engaging range of comment absent from Michelangelo's utilitarian texts. He recorded, for example, how, on the day he put brush to the wall in Palazzo Vecchio, a huge storm burst over Florence and the rain damaged his cartoon; see Villata 1999, pp. 185–6, no. 219.

8   For Alidosi's movements, see G. de Caro in *DBI*, II, pp. 373ff. The most memorable judgement of Alidosi is that of Bartolomeo Cerretani. He wrote of the cardinal at his death: 'era de' signori da Chastello del Rio, d'età d'anni 42, astutissimo, sanza lettere, righagnato, doppio, sanghuinolentte, chrudele, sodomito, in ogni genere et in ogni modo strupatore di vergini, vituperatore di gentili donne, avaro e chattivo quanto può essere uno huomo'; see Cerretani 1993, p. 244. For Alidosi's correct birth date, see Beck 1990, pp. 63ff. His contention that Alidosi could have contributed to the planning of the chapel ceiling's iconography is not plausible.

9   *Carteggio* I, p. 104, no. LXII.

10 Alidosi's choice of subject could have been influenced by the example of Mantegna's small frescoed *Baptism of Christ* in the Belvedere in the Vatican. The choice of fresco was especially unrealistic, for it would have called for the artist's presence at La Magliana.

11 At the time when Condivi was preparing his biography, Michelangelo's relations with the son and heir of Francesco Maria, Guidobaldo della Rovere, were still deeply troubled.

12 For the payments to Rosselli, see *Ricordi* 1970, pp. 2–3, no. III. The total payment amounted to 85 ducats, a substantial sum. It was to be paid out of the money Michelangelo had received from Alidosi. Rosselli, a fellow Florentine and related by marriage to Cronaca, must have been well known to the artist. His task in the chapel included removing the pre-existing decoration and making good the cracks that had developed in 1504. He did not attempt to correct all the vault's irregularities and created an *arriccio*, the rough ground for the plaster, no more than 1.5 centimetres thick; see Mancinelli 1994c, p. 10.

13 Condivi 1998, p. 34.

14 For an earlier realization of where work was interrupted in 1510 and resumed in 1511, see Wilde 1978, p. 66.

15 For the text, see Steinmann 1905, no. 16, p. 699. De Grassis writes: 'In altis cornicibus capellae fabricabatur cum maximis pulveribus, et operavii ita iussi non cessabant.' He himself had remonstrated with workmen in vain and work stopped only after the pope had twice sent orders for them to cease.

16 For a contrary view, that the programme was unlikely to have been established prior to the construction of the scaffolding, see Mancinelli 1992, p. 43. It should be noted, however, that the decision to include the frescoing of the chapel's sixteen lunettes must have been taken by the time the scaffolding was put in place.

17 For these extensively discussed pen drawings in London and Detroit, see Tolnay 1975–80, I, nos. 119 recto and 120 recto. For Roman ceiling decoration in the period, see Schulz 1962, pp. 35–55, and Weil-Garris Brandt 1992.

18 The familiar statements of the artist where he dismisses the initial scheme planned for the ceiling decoration as a 'cosa povera' are to be found in two texts, *Carteggio* III, pp. 7–9, no. DXCIV, and pp. 10–11, no. DXCV. The former text, the draft of a letter to Giovan Francesco Fattucci, has been traditionally, and correctly, dated to late December 1523. The second, with no address, is much shorter. The two texts have always been assumed to date from the same time. But it has recently been proposed that the briefer one, with no indication of its purpose, was written immediately following the death of Pope Julius in early 1513. See the re-dating by Ciulich in *Contratti*, no. XVIII, pp. 41–2.

19 See Hatfield 2002, pp. 123–4.

20 Shearman 2003, I, p. 181. Evidence such as this is relevant for assessing the scale of Michelangelo's remuneration; what had been paid to Domenico Ghirlandaio in Florence in 1490 is irrelevant.

21 Condivi 1998, p. 58.

22 For the artist's later comments on Condivi's text, see Elam in Condivi 1998, pp. XXXVIII–XXXIX. Some of his criticisms of Bramante are now disclaimed, but this extraordinary passage is not one of them.

23 Ackerman 1974, p. 344, did not fully take the measure of Michelangelo's long-standing hatred of Bramante. As will be noted later, his praise of his great rival was confined to a letter. Vasari 1962, II, pp. 409–10, pointed to the lack of any substantial evidence for the episode. Doubted by Frey, Justi 1900, p. 11, dismissed it as a fable.

24 For an excellent illustration of one of these holes, or *fori*, see Mancinelli 1986, p. 5.

25 For a detailed discussion of the scaffolding, see Mancinelli 1986, pp. 220–34. Already in the nineteenth century, Wilson (1876, p. 119) had realized that the scaffolding must have provided a deck on which movement was possible.

26 For a drawing that shows this form of construction, of this period and formerly attributed to Giuliano da Sangallo, see Mancinelli 1994a, fig. 7 (p. 338).

27 For this acute and convincing interpretation of this much-discussed sketch, reproduced in Tolnay 1975–80, I, no. 133 recto, see Mancinelli 1994a, p. 44.

28 A statement in Paolo Giovio's brief Life of Michelangelo, for which see Barocchi 1971, p. 10, has often been interpreted as implying that the biographer described the artist as lying down while at work. The word Giovio employs, *resupinus*, does not necessarily mean flat or supine; it can also signify bent backwards, and it was in this almost tortured pose that the artist describes his situation in his celebrated sonnet and its accompanying sketch. For an informed comment on what Giovio wrote, see Mancinelli 1986, p. 232. For a further description of

the artist at work, see also an epigram dedicated to him by Lascaris, published in Lascaris-Meschini 1976, pp. 78–9.

29   For the fact that Michelangelo had written an important letter to Alidosi in December 1507, as already noted earlier; see *Carteggio* I, p. 57, no. XLI.

30   The history of the commission is set out in Cadogan 2000, pp. 238–43. The frescos were completed in December 1490.

31   For the probable number of Ghirlandaio's assistants, see Cadogan 2000, pp. 169ff. For a very informative discussion of the artist's teamwork, see Danti 1996, pp. 141ff.

32   *Ricordi* 1970, p. 1, no. 1.

33   For Granacci's letter, see *Carteggio* I, pp. 64–5, no. XLVI. Poggi's decisive arguments for dating the letter in April are published in *Carteggio* I, pp. 375–6.

34   For Vasari's enumeration of the assistants, see Vasari 1987, VI, pp. 34–5. The most helpful account of the issue of the assistants is provided in Mancinelli 1994b, pp. 107–14. A pioneering article by Wallace (1987) is not altogether helpful, since a number of individuals are included who were not 'assistants' at all. His statement that Pietro Urbano was an assistant in the chapel is based on a confusion between Urbano and Piero d'Argenta that is not confined to this article. Piero d'Argenta was about to leave Florence to give help to Michelangelo, of what kind is not known but probably domestic, in early October; see Lodovico Buonarroti's letter, dated 7 October, in *Carteggio* I, p. 86, no. LX.

35   *Carteggio* I, pp. 66–7, no. XLVII. The request for 'azzuri begli' must have been for ultramarine if the order was connected with prospective work in fresco. For the Gesuati as suppliers to artists, among them Michelangelo's own master, Ghirlandaio, see Bensi 1980, pp. 33ff.

36   For the text, see *Contratti*, no. XVII, p. 40.

37   For these payments, see Hatfield 2002, p. 412.

38   *Carteggio* I, p. 73, no. LI.

39   For the artist's letter, see *Carteggio* I, p. 70, no. XLIX. However, relations between the two would undergo a major crisis in the following year, discussed below. For Lodovico's letter of 21 July, see *Carteggio* I, pp. 71–2, no. L.

40   Lodovico writes: 'A·mme pare che · ttu facci troppo, e sammi molto male che · ttu stia chostì male e male chontento, e pagherei assai che · ttu te ne potessi sghabellare di choteste imprese, perché, stando male e malvolentieri, chon dificchultà si può fare bene.'

41   *Carteggio* I, p. 75, no. LIII. For useful details about Piero Basso, father of the Bernardino Basso who would appear repeatedly in subsequent periods of the artist's life, see Wallace 1989, pp. 237–8. He had worked for the Buonarroti family as general handyman since at least 1470, before the artist's birth. He himself had been born as early as 1441.

42   *Carteggio* I, p. 73, no. LI. See the useful comments on what Michi writes in Gnoli 1923–4, pp. 394–7. He correctly excluded the possibility that Michi was

here referring to Pier d'Amelia's work in the Sistine Chapel and concluded that Raffaellino's association with the latter was one of a later date, involving work for either Innocent VIII or Alexander VI. Michelangelo can scarcely have wanted to hire Raffaellino, whose modest capacities were, by this time, in steady decline.

43   For this episode, which convulsed the Buonarroti family, see below, pp. 131–2.

44   For the letter sent to the artist concerning the bronze *David*, see *Carteggio* I, p. 83, no. LIX. Soderini's letter, omitted in Vasari, *La Vita* (Vasari 1962), was published in Gaye 1840, no. LI, p. 107. Soderini writes: 'E non si è mandato ad fare bozzare il marmo, perchè la Santità di Nostro Signore non ha mai permesso a maestro Michelagnolo, nostro cittadino, che si transferischa per insino qui solamente per 25 giorni.'

45   *Carteggio* I, pp. 85–6, no. LX. Lodovico, expressing a profound antipathy for the followers of the Frate, writes: 'già più volte ti dissi che tutti questi piangnioni erano chattivi huomini'.

46   *Carteggio* I, p. 87, no. XLI. His father characteristically laments his tribulations of many past years, no doubt prompted by the current crisis with Cassandra Bartoli.

47   *Carteggio* I, pp. 88–9, no. LXII. He writes: 'Io ancora sono in una fantasia grande, perché è già uno anno chi io no ò avuto un grosso da qesto Papa, e no' ne chiego, perché el lavoro mio non va inanzi in modo che a me ne paia meritare. E questa è la difichultà del lavoro, e anchora el non esser mia professione. E pur perdo il tempo mio sanza fructo.' For an earlier usage of *professione*, where he disclaims his capacity, see his letter from Bologna of 19 December 1506; *Carteggio* I, p. 18, no. XII.

48   For comments on the issue, see Borsook 1980, p. XXVIII.

49   Condivi 1998, pp. 33 4.

50   Analysis of the plaster employed for the ceiling, undertaken during the cleaning that tok place between 1984 and 1989, revealed that it is a mixture of lime (*calce*) and a sandy substance of volcanic origin (*pozzolana nera*), an *intonaco* unknown in Florence. It was a plaster that was exceptionally robust, but was clearly ill prepared, by assistants unaware of its properties.

51   *Carteggio* I, p. 91, no. LXIV.

52   *Carteggio* I, p. 101, no. LXX. He writes: 'Io sto qua in grande afanno e chon grandissima faticha di chorpo, e non ò amici di nessuna sorte, e no' ne voglio; e non ò tanto tempo che io possa mangiare el bisonio mio.' The passage implies that he was now working alone, and that Piero d'Argenta, whose arrival in Rome had been referred to in Lodovico's letter of 7 October 1508, may not have come on a permanent basis.

53   See Girardi 1960, no. 5, pp. 4–5, for the Italian text and his note on p. 158. For an excellent reproduction, see Tolnay 1975–80, I, no. 174. For a more

recent English translation, see Saslow 1991, pp. 70–72. The identity of the
Giovanni whom Michelangelo here invokes remains a problem, despite his
further note on the verso, where he writes: 'A Giovanni, a quell proprio da
Pistoia'. This Giovanni has frequently been identified as the Giovanni da Pistoia
who, decades later, would address his own poems to Michelangelo; for these,
see Frey 1897, pp. 260–62. He became an official in Duke Cosimo's administration and chancellor of the Florentine Academy in 1540. Frey was doubtful about
this identification (ibid., p. 308), but it has been generally accepted. It cannot
be correct, however, for the Giovanni in question was born as late as 1509,
about the time when the poem was written; see C. Reggioli in *DBI*, LVI,
pp. 180ff. It is worth recalling here that Condivi would relate how the artist,
at the completion of the ceiling, had problems in reading letters; for a time he
had to hold them above his head. See Condivi 1998, p. 35.

54   Mancinelli 1994c, p. 21.

55   The point is not a new one; see Klaczko 1902, p. 336.

56   For the dedication ceremony on 15 August 1483, see Shearman 1972, p. 3.

57   A connection between the choice of the Ancestors for the programme and the
reading for 8 September has not gone completely unperceived; see the observation of F. Schneider recorded in Steinmann 1905, p. 425, note 3, who too
hastily dismissed the connection. Steinmann did not appreciate the great importance of the Feast of the Nativity of the Virgin for Pope Julius. For his wish to
dedicate his future burial chapel to this Nativity, see the document published
by Frommel 1976, no. 382(B), p. 126. The Bull refers to its dedication as 'sub
invocatione Nativitatis Beatae Mariae, quae Julia nuncupatur, et in qua corpus
nostrum, nobis vita functis sepeliri volumus'. Also telling is the importance he
attached to the feast when travelling. On his first journey to Bologna in 1506,
he celebrated it at Orvieto, at the same time venerating the relic of the Holy
Blood. On his second journey in 1510 he arranged to celebrate it at Loreto, site
of the Santa Casa. For these occasions, see Grassi 1886, pp. 34ff. and p. 90. It
should also be noted that the reading for 8 September from the Old Testament
is Proverbs 8, 22–35, where the Virgin's existence prior to the episodes of
Creation is invoked.

58   For Julius's passionate hatred of Alfonso, chiefly provoked by his ties with the
French, see, most recently, Shaw 1993, pp. 260–61. Regaining Ferrara for the
papacy was, however, only a part of his plan, as is well brought out by a letter
of Stazio Gadio to the Mantuan court of 29 August, just before Julius's departure. He writes of him: 'vol andar ad far carnevale a Ferrara e la quadragesima
a Comachio et anchor vole Parma e Piasenza, dicendo che le sono de la Chiesa'.
For the passage, see Luzio 1912, pp. 245ff.

59   The vicissitudes of the pope's health can be followed in the reports of the
Venetian envoys at the court; it is reported that death is imminent on 20
October: 'dubita il papa non vadi, e presto; si'l muor, è mala nova'. For this

comment, see Sanudo 1879–1903, XI, col. 549, and for the pope's powers of recovery, ibid., col. 634, where it is reported that his resistance is extraordinary: 'Sono miracoli la sua natura.'

60   The reports of the Venetian envoy who accompanied the pope to Mirandola are extraordinarily vivid. The decision to leave for the front line was taken in December and he left on 2 January 1511 in a great snowstorm. He is described as caring nothing for the adverse weather: 'Et con tal tempo ha voluto venir el pontefice, natura sopra tutte le altre fortissima, et par che niente patisce'; see Sanudo 1879–1903, XI, col. 725. Mirandola would fall, in the face of massive artillery attacks, on 20 January.

61   *Carteggio* I, p. 106, no. LXXIV. He writes: 'Io mi sto qua all'usato, e arò finita la mia pictura per tucta quest'altra sectimana, cioè la parte che io chominciai'.

62   Hatfield 2002, p. 27. His suggestion that this probably marked the end of the first campaign is contradicted by the artist's own letter quoted in the previous note.

63   *Carteggio* I, p. 107, no. LXXV.

64   He writes: 'Non vi date passione, perché Dio non ci à creati per abandonarci.'

65   *Carteggio* I, p. 108, no. LXXVI. Of his dilemma he writes: 'se partissi senza licenza, dubito el Papa no si cruciassi e che io non perdessi quello che ò avere'.

66   This fear of the pope recalls to mind Machiavelli's acute judgement of Julius expressed just a year after his death. He wrote to his friend Francesco Vettori in December 1514: 'Papa Iulio non si curò mai d'essere odiato, purchè fussi temuto e reverito; e con quello suo timore mette sotto sopra el mondo'. See Machiavelli 1984, p. 476.

67   The problems raised by this poem require more comment than is appropriate here, indeed a separate study. Insufficiently emphasized in the bibliography is the extreme eccentricity of the handwriting, matched nowhere else in the artist's manuscripts. Its claim to be autograph is highly doubtful; even the artist's own name is misspelt as 'Miccelangniolo', a usage unparalleled elsewhere. It is more likely to be a copy of a lost text; it is noteworthy, although never remarked on, that line eleven, where reference to the Medusa is made, lacks a needed verb. The date of the text is also controversial. Girardi 1960, p. 164, followed Karl Frey in dating it to April 1512. But the admission that he has no work is utterly incompatible with such a date, a moment when the artist was desperately stretched in completing the chapel ceiling. More recently, it has been proposed that the poem belongs to the period of Michelangelo's first stay in Rome and, with its Savonarolan echoes, should be dated around 1497; see Bardeschi Ciulich and Raggionieri 2001, p. 26. But the emphasis on the pope cannot be reconciled with such a date; Michelangelo had no significant dealings with Pope Alexander VI that would explain its extraordinary allusion. Steinmann 1905, p. 175, note 2, in an observation overlooked, saw that the tenor of the second part of the

text agrees with what Michelangelo wrote in his letters of 1510, above all his dread of the pope. He emphasized its Dantean allusions, especially to Inferno II, 27, and Purgatorio XIX, 104. It is worth notice that Michelangelo's reference to Julius as Medusa is not unique; indeed, it is anticipated in an extraordinary epigram of Piero Valeriano dedicated to the subject of the bronze statue of Julius in Bologna: 'Quoque tam trepidus fugis viator, Ac si te Furiaeve Gorgonesve, Aut acer Basiliscus insequantur? Non hic Julius, at figura Julii est'. For this remarkable text, first noted by Duppa as long ago as 1807, see Vasari 1962, II, p. 401. For an English translation of Michelangelo's poem, see Saslow 1991, p. 10, who dated it to the period following the completion of the ceiling.

68   Hatfield 2002, p. 29.

69   Florence, Casa Buonarroti, Archivio Buonarroti, XXVI–XXVII, Quadernuccio di Buonarroto, 1509–14, fol. 61 verso. Four such books survive but have not been published. For their dates, see Tampieri 1997, p. 33.

70   *Carteggio* I, p. III, no. LXXIX.

71   Lodovico would purchase a large farm on Michelangelo's behalf from the hospital of Santa Maria Nuova on 28 May 1512; see Hatfield 2002, pp. 71–2.

72   *Carteggio* I, p. 118, no. LXXXVI.

73   *Carteggio* I, p. 112, no. LXXX. Manfidi writes: 'Confortovi non essere pigro a ricschuotere quando viene el tempo assegnatovi, ma esser sollecito.' Manfidi reports on Soderini's faith in the artist, a remarkable tribute to his good will towards the man whose defection had caused him so many difficulties.

74   *Carteggio* I, p. 113, no. LXXXI.

75   *Carteggio* I, p. 116, no. LXXXIV. Michelangelo at no point refers to his patron's formidable financial problems created by war. In mid-October a sum of 160,000 ducats had to be sent from Rome; see Sanudo 1879–1903, XI, col. 523. A further 50,000 ducats, kept in Castel Sant'Angelo, were called upon in December; Sanudo 1879–1903, XI, col. 634. When already unwell in September, Julius is reported to have declared that he would spend everything he had to take Ferrara: 'Voglio spender tutti li miei danari per l'impresa: non vojo altro che Ferrara'; see the Venetian ambassador's report in Sanudo 1879–1903, XI, col. 467. But the financial expenses for the work in the chapel were extremely modest when compared with the huge outgoing expenditure on the construction of the new St Peter's.

76   *Carteggio* I, p. 118, no. LXXXVI. For the sums that he did receive, see Hatfield 2002, pp. 44ff. His statement, however, that Michelangelo had not previously received advances of money for work not yet undertaken is belied by the initial payment for the project of 10 May 1508. Michelangelo, in his draft letter to Fattucci of late December 1523, would state that the money agreed on for the project was 3,000 ducats; see *Carteggio* III, p. 8, no. DXCIV. Hatfield concludes that the sum is substantially correct, although possibly a further 200 ducats should be added.

77 That new plans for work on the papal tomb were under way in the autumn of 1511; see Shearman 1995, p. 224.

78 *Carteggio* III, pp. 7–9. He writes: 'In questo tempo, quasi finita la volta el papa ritornò a Bolognia, ond' io v'andai dua volte per denari che io avevo avere, e non feci miente, e perde' tucto questo tempo finché ritornò a·rRoma. Ritornato a·rRoma mi missi a far chartoni per decta opera'. 'Ritornato a Roma' has been assumed, even by translators of the text, to relate to his own movements. But since the words follow his statement that he lost all this time until the pope returned, the word 'Ritornato' must refer not to himself but to the pope. Only after Julius's return did he recommence work.

79 For the general rejoicing, see Paris de Grassis (Grassi 1886), p. 279. He wrote: 'Hoc satis sit, quod nemo doluit de huius morte, omnes toti et universi arriserunt et praelaetitia exultarunt, gratias Deo agents, qui est benedictus. Amen.'

80 Paris de Grassis (Grassi 1886), p. 293. He concluded: 'Et sic finis nostrae peregrinationis fastidiosae et inanis.'

81 *Carteggio* I, p. 118, no. LXXXVI. He writes: 'Però pregate Idio per lui, pel suo bene e pel nostro.'

82 For the text, see Steinmann 1905, no. 72, p. 722: 'Pontifex in vigilia et die gloriosissimae virginis assumptae voluit interesse vesperis et missae in capella maiori palatina per sacristam celebratis festiviter, nam ea capella assumptioni praedictae dicata est, et ad eam pontifex venit vel ut pictures novas ibidem noviter detectas videret, vel quia ex devotione ductus fuit.'

83 The course of the pope's ill health can be closely followed in reports of the Venetian envoys at the court. Already on 18 August he had been unable to hold a public consistory. Two days later, his life was despaired of, and by 23 August an election to choose his successor was openly talked of. Only in the second week of September was he formally declared to be out of danger. For the course of his illness, see Sanudo 1879–1903, XII, cols 434, 440, 442, 449 and 482–4.

84 For the letter, see *Carteggio* I, p. 121, no. LXXXIX. He writes: 'Padre Karissimo, io andai martedì a parlare al Papa; il perché v'aviserò più per agio. Basta che mercholedì mactina io vi ritornai, e·llui mi fece pagare quatro cento duchati d'oro di Chamera'. He ends: 'Pregate Idio che io abi onore qua e che io chontenti el Papa, perché spero, se· llo chontento, aveno qualche bene da·llui. E anchora pregate Dio per lui.'

85 See Hirst 1986b, pp. 208–17.

86 See Colalucci 1994, pp. 80–82. For an examination of the whole subject of cartoons and their usage, see Bambach 1999, especially pp. 249–96.

87 *Carteggio* I, p. 133, no. C.

88 The visit was briefly described in a letter of the Ferrarese envoy in Rome, Ludovico Fabriano, to Cardinal Ippolito d'Este, where there is a reference to the date of 11 July; see Sauer 1912, p. 147. There is a more circumstantial

account by the Mantuan envoy, Stazio Gadio, in an undated letter to Isabella d'Este, which reads: 'Sua Excellentia desiderava assai di veder la volta di la capella grande che depinge Michel Angello et il Signor Federico per il mezzo del Mondovì lo fece che lo mandò a dimandar per parte del Papa, et il Signor Ducha andò in su la volta con più persone, tandem ogni uno a pocho a pocho se ne vene giù de la volta et il Signor Ducha restò su con Michel Angello et non si poteva satiar di guardare quelle figure, et assai careze li fece di sorte che Sua Excellentia desiderava chel gia facesse uno quadro et li fece parlare e pro-ferire dinarij et li ha impromesso de fargiello.' For the text, see Luzio 1886, pp. 540–41, and Shearman 1987, p. 213. It could well have been the case that, already at this date, Alfonso was planning his *studiolo* with works by a number of leading artists. For the subject of his *studiolo*, see Shearman 1987, passim.

89   The destruction of Michelangelo's statue achieved widespread notoriety. For the evidence, see, in particular, Podestà 1868; for a more recent comprehensive review of the episode, see Butzek 1978, pp. 92ff. The bronze produced by the destruction was transported to Ferrara on no less than three wagons. But the event would prove a serious embarrassment to Alfonso d'Este, and Isabella d'Este would attempt to mediate with the pope.

90   Bologna was returned to the Church on 10 June, the Feast of Corpus Christi, and on the following day Francesco Maria della Rovere entered the city. For the reception by Julius of the three Bolognese emissaries, see Butzek 1978, especially pp. 340ff; the audience took place in San Pietro in Vincoli. The fury of the pope is recorded in the envoys' letter to Bologna; see Butzek 1978, pp. 351–4. He was especially incensed because he himself, contrary to tradition, had paid for the statue.

91   *Carteggio* III, p. 184, no. DCCXXVII. Clement wishes for a sparing use of bronze for the reliquary tribune: 'a ciò che in qualche tempo non si avessi a fare, per dispetto, come si fece di papa Iulio – cioè non vorebe se ne facessi altiglierie'.

92   For a discussion of Florentine policy at this point, see Butters 1985, pp. 157ff.

93   For the episode of the Interdict, which, with periodic suspensions, lasted from September to early April, see the excellent account in Trexler 1974, pp. 178–86; contemporaries, such as Bartolommeo Masi, recorded the sufferings incurred, including the breakdown of burial of the dead. Michelangelo's reaction to the lifting of the Interdict would strike a slightly ironical note: 'intendo per l'ultima vostra chome siate ribenedecti, che n'ò avuto piacere assai'. See *Carteggio* I, p. 125, no. XCII.

94   For contemporary evidence describing the sack, see Guasti 1880, especially pp. 135ff. Bombardment began on 29 August, with Cardinal Giovanni de' Medici a personal witness, and the Spanish troops sacked the city on the following day. The death toll, mostly of citizens, was estimated to have been four thousand.

95   For these events, see Butters 1985, pp. 164ff.

96   *Carteggio* I, p. 135, no. CII. He writes: 'ora intendendo di qua chome costà passon

le cose, mi pare di scrivervi l'animo mio . . . che voi tucti veggiate di ritrarvi in qualche parte che voi siate sicuri, e abandonare la roba e oggni cosa, perché molto più vale la vita che la roba'. He goes on: 'E de' casi della terra non vi impacciate di niente, né in facti né in parole, e fate chome si fa alla moria: siate e' pr[i]mi a fugire.'

97 *Carteggio* I, p. 136, no. CIII. Of the return of the Medici he writes: 'Ora s'è decto di nuovo che la casa de' Medici è 'ntrata in Firenze e che ogni cosa è achoncia . . . Però statevi in pace, e non vi fate amici né familiari di nessuno, se non di Dio, e non parlate di nessuno né ben né male, perché non si sa el fine delle cose'. He was probably speaking for a number of fellow Florentines at this point.

98 *Carteggio* I, p. 139, no. CVI: 'Del chaso de' Medici, io non ò mai parlato contra di loro chosa nessuna, se non in quel modo che s'é parlato generalmente per ogn'uomo, come fu del caso di Prato; che se·lle pietre avessin saputo parlare, n'arebbono parlato.'

99 Riario's alleged role in the conspiracy that had cost Giuliano de' Medici's life in 1478 was still in people's minds when the crisis of the cardinals' plot against Leo's life broke in 1517. Here, Riario's involvement was well attested.

100 *Carteggio* I, pp. 140–41, no. CVII.

101 There is a first-hand account of the levy in the *ricordanze* of Bartolommeo Masi (Masi 1906, pp. 109ff). He states that the maximum sum was set at 120 florins, the minimum at 6 florins. It appears, therefore, that Lodovico's assessment was the maximum, to be paid in two successive instalments, one in October and the other in November.

102 The artist writes: 'Bisogna avere patientia e rachomandarsi a Dio, e ravedersi degli errori; ché queste aversità non vengono per altro, e massimamente per la superbia e ingratitudine: che mai pratichai giente più ingrate né più superbe che e' Fiorentini.' Compare Inferno xv, 67–9, where Brunetto Latini speaks of the Florentines as 'quello ingrato popolo maligno', and xv, 61, where he complains of them in similar terms: 'Vecchia fama nel mondo li chiama orbi; gent'è avara, invidioso e superba'. Turning on his family, he writes in tones recalling his earlier onslaught on Giovan Simone: 'E già sono stato cosi circha di quindici anni, che mai ebbe un'ora di bene, e·ctuto ò facto per aiutarvi, né mai l'avete chonosciuto né credito.'

103 *Carteggio indiretto* I, p. 41, no. 24.

104 *Carteggio* I, p. 137, no. CIV. The artist laconically states: 'Io ò finita la chappella che io dipignievo: el Papa resto assai ben sodisfato, e·ll'altre cose non mi riescono a me chome stimavo; incholpone e' tempi, che sono molto chontrari all'arte nostra.' The statement that he had finished his work in the chapel excludes the dependability of Vasari's statement, first advanced in the edition of 1550 and elaborated in that of 1568, that Julius had planned the destruction of the chapel decoration undertaken by his uncle, Sixtus IV. For these passages, see Vasari

1987, VI, p. 34; for an explanation as to why he adopted the proposal, see Hirst 1997, pp. 81ff. The redecoration of the ceiling had been a necessity. But that Julius proposed the destruction of the wall frescos is exceedingly improbable, although re-proposed with intricate arguments by Shearman 1994. Julius revered his uncle; many of the inscriptions of his pontificate refer to himself as *nepos*, his nephew, and that he would indulge in so flagrant an act of disrespect is not credible. It would be a Medici, not a della Rovere pope, who would radically change the Quattrocento appearance of the chapel.

105   For the whole passage, see Steinmann 1905, no. 108, p. 736. Referring to the ceiling, Paris de Grassis writes: 'Hodie primum capella nostra, pingi finita, aperta est; nam per tres aut quatuor annos tectum sive fornix eius tecta semper fuit ex solari ipsum totum cooperiente.' The meaning of the term *solaio* has been much debated; see the comments of Mancinelli 1994a, p. 46.

106   For another example of this attention to detail, one can point to the representation of snakebites on the extended arm of the woman on the left of the *Brazen Serpent*, a scene where the emphasis on violent foreshortening could be read as a retort to Bramante's remark that the artist could not meet such a challenge.

107   *Carteggio* I, p. 134, no. CI. In his letters of the spring and summer, the artist had repeatedly underestimated the time required to complete his colossal task. In this letter of August, for example, he assures Buonarroto that he will be back by All Saints, unless he dies in the meantime.

CHAPTER SIX

1   Julius's decline can be followed in successive entries in the diary of Paris de Grassis, master of ceremonies of both Julius and his successor, Leo X; see P. Grassis, Diarum, British Library, Add. MSS 8442, c.273 verso, 280 recto and 281 verso. For other eye-witness accounts, see the summaries in Shaw 1993, pp. 311ff.

2   British Library, Add. MSS 8442, c.281 verso: 'Addiditque velle, quod in manibus suis duos anulos preciosos ponerem, quos mihi se datur, promisit et in Cappella Sixtina collocarem sic ibi permanendum donec sepulcrum suum, quod iam inchoari mandaverat, perficeretur'.

3   For this payment and Michelangelo's subsequent transferral of credit to Florence, see Hatfield 2002, pp. 30, 48 and document R159 on p. 387. There had been a branch of the Fugger bank in Rome since 1495. Papal revenues from the German States, increasingly swollen by the sales of Indulgences, were channelled through it. For Julius's use of the bank, see, for example, Frommel 1976, nos. 358B, 375B and 376B. The best account of the role of the Fugger remains that of Schulte 1904, I, ch. 3.

4   The Bini bank would assume great importance under Julius's successor; for

Bernardo's career, see the account by M. Luzzati in *DBI*, x, pp. 503–6. Bini, however, may have already served as treasurer to Julius prior to his position as 'depositarius pecuniarum datariatus' under Leo. On Leo's death in 1521, the Bini bank came under serious pressure, owing to extensive unsecured loans. For a fine account of the Florentine bankers in Rome, see Bullard 1980, passim.

5   *Carteggio* iii, p. 9, no. DXCIV. Bibbiena had left Rome at some point prior to Julius's death so that his appeal, if really made, must have taken place in late 1512. The 'Actalante' to whom Michelangelo refers as his other intermediary was identified by Milanesi as Atalanta Migliorotti, illegitimate son of one of the overseers at the Fabbrica of St Peter's from 1513; see Milanesi 1875, p. 428, note 1. He would become one of the founding members of the Accademia Medicea founded by Leo x a few months before his visit to Florence in November 1515; Ciseri 1990, pp. 35–6, note 76.

6   *Carteggio* iii, p. 9, no. DXCIV. Writing of the 2,000 ducats, he informs Fattucci 'che son quegli, chon que' primi mille de' marmi, che è mi mectono a chonto della sepultura'. Hatfield 2002, p. 30, has reached a similar conclusion.

7   British Library, Add. MSS 8442, c.142 recto. For his preferments, see Eubel 1923, p. 12, no. 18. At his death, his annual income was estimated at 20,000 ducats.

8   For Pucci, see Eubel 1923, p. 14. Pucci's long and extremely influential career is described in detail in Hirst 2000c.

9   For the contract, see *Contratti*, no. xx, pp. 45–8. For the sums set aside for the arrangements following Alexander vi's death in 1503, see Burchard 1907–42, iii, pp. 360–61.

10 In one of the drafts to Fattucci of 1523, *Carteggio* iii, p. 9, no. DXCIV, and the draft to the unidentified cleric of 1542, *Carteggio* iv, p. 152, no. MI, the artist states that, in 1513, Cardinal Leonardo Grosso della Rovere wanted the project enlarged. Condivi's Life, however, records that, after Julius's death, the project of 1505 seemed to the executors to be too big: 'parendo loro il primo impresa troppo grande'. For the passage, see Condivi 1998, p. 36.

11 This duty may have been one of his administrative tasks, but it is worth noting that he was particularly close to Pucci; see Luzzati in *DBI*, x, p. 504.

12 *Contratti*, nos. xx and xxi, pp. 45–51.

13 Since one Roman *palmo* measures 22 centimetres, the total breadth of the lower-storey *quadro* as prescribed in this July sub-contract is 660 centimetres. This is not much less than the length of the shorter sides of the monument of 1505 as described by Condivi, 12 Florentine *braccia*. For further comments on its appearance, see below. The text of this revised agreement was published most recently in *Ricordi* 1970, p. 5, no. VI.

14 It has frequently been argued that work on the marble *quadro* began in 1505, prior to the crisis of April. The case seems to have been inspired by Michelangelo's own claims in a letter to Fattucci of 1523 that he had at that time brought assistants from Florence and that work began not only on the tomb's

fabric but also on the statues. He had, it is true, written to Lodovico on 31 January 1506, asking for Michele di Pippo to come to Rome as soon as circumstances allowed, but this could have been prompted by the need for help with the marble expected to arrive from Carrara. And there is no reference to his asking for anyone else. Michelangelo's statements, written at a moment of crisis that will be discussed later, are likely to have been face-saving falsehoods. It has also been proposed that the artist worked on the tomb in 1512. But Thode's argument for this was based on a misdating of one of Michelangelo's letters, *Carteggio* I, pp. 154–5, no. CXVII, by no less than three years; see Thode 1902–12, I, p. 355. For different arguments for this conclusion, see Shearman 1995, p. 240, note 33. But the letters and drawings afford little support.

15   Silvio Falcone, a lad who wished to learn how to draw, was one of the very few *garzoni* of the artist who was not a Florentine. For the troublesome Bernardino Basso, who had left his work in the Sistine Chapel because of bad health, see Wallace 1989 and Wallace 1994, pp. 174ff. Antonio da Pontassieve had been in Rome since 1508 and perhaps before – in that year he was working for Bramante at St Peter's; see Frommel 1976, p. 64, and, for his later activities, Frommel 1996, pp. 309ff.

16   The text of the Bull is, in part, printed in Ducrot 1963, pp. 534–6, and in Frommel 1976, pp. 126–7, no. 382 (B). The materials of the projected chapel are of exceptional richness; its dedication is to the Nativity of the Virgin, 'sub invocatione Nativitatis Beatae Mariae, quae Julia nuncupatur'. See also the comments in Frommel 1977, especially pp. 33ff.

17   Frommel, in Millon and Magnago Lampugnani 1994, p. 416, has suggested that the tomb could have been projected for one of the piers of the transept of the new basilica, but there is no word in any of the sources about its future location. Indeed, an explicit reference to a site for the tomb in the surviving contracts is found only in the agreement of 1542, just under thirty years later.

18   Plate 27 reproduces a weak but faithful copy of a much-damaged original drawing recording a design of May or July 1513. Both copy and original are in the Berlin Kupferstichkabinett; for the original, see Tolnay 1975–80, I, no. 55 recto. Whether this elevation relates to the design of May or the revised scheme of July has been repeatedly debated; see Echinger-Maurach 2009, pp. 26–43. Progress can be made by analysing another drawing, Uffizi 608E recto, the lower half of a truncated sheet. For its autograph status, see the discussion in Hirst 1988a, pp. 82ff, anf pls 172 and 175, and Hirst 1988b, pp. 52–4, no. 20. A more recent assessment by Frommel in Millon and Magnago Lampugnani 1994, no. 304, pp. 612–13, is confused. That this design represents the enlarged scheme of July 1513 can be simply demonstrated. If we apply the scale of the *Dying Slave* in the Louvre of 230 centimetres to the slaves drawn here, we find that the architecture is about 662 centimetres in length (excluding the profiles of the side

elevations), hence almost exactly the 660 centimetres of the July sub-contract. Furthermore, the scale of the *quadro* in this Uffizi sheet exactly matches that in the damaged Berlin sheet; the comparison is facilitated by the juxtaposition offered in Tolnay's *Corpus* (Tolnay 1975–80).

19 For this arrangement, see Hatfield 2002, p. 35, and documents RXI to RX–II.

20 Marta Porcari and her will are extensively discussed in Panofsky 1991, especially pp. 130ff.

21 Marta Porcari entrusted the setting up of her 'cappella' to three men: Bernardo Cencio, a canon of St Peter's and her formal executor, and two nephews, Metello Vari and Pietro Paolo Castellani, described as her universal heirs. Their backgrounds are described by Panofsky 1991.

22 *Contratti*, no. XXIII, p. 54. The wording of the contract prescribes 'una figura di marmo d'un Cristo grande quanto el naturale, ignudo, ritto, con una croce in braccia, in quell'attitudine che parrà al detto Michelagniolo'. For the fact that sculpture had been envisaged by Vari and Castellani already in their meeting of November 1512, see Panofsky 1991, pp. 131ff. Hatfield, ever ready to assail the artist, has pointed out that the payment of 200 ducats agreed in the contract equalled all the funds left by Marta Porcari for her 'cappella'. But the sum stipulated can in no way be regarded as greed on Michelangelo's part. Only two years later, his rival Jacopo Sansovino would be paid 300 ducats for his *Virgin and Child* in Sant'Agostino in Rome, although this much larger sum did include costs for transporting the marble; for this evidence, see Boucher 1991, II, p. 320. If the heirs had opted for a painting, the costs would have been less than half. It may have been Vari who pressed for sculpture; for his collection of antique sculpture, evidently mostly inherited, see Aldrovandi 1556, pp. 245–51.

23 Vari refers to the flaw, a dark vein, in two letters of late 1521. See *Carteggio* II, p. 328, no. DXL, and, for his description, 'reuscendo nel viso uno pelo nero hover linea', ibid., p. 334, no. DXLIV.

24 Aldrovandi 1556, p. 247: 'In una corticella overo orticello, vedesi un Christo ignudo con la Croce al lato destro non fornito per rispetto d'una vena che si scoperse nel marmo della faccia, opera di Michiel Angelo e lo donò a M. Metello'.

25 For this remarkable identification, see Baldriga 2000, and for further background, Danesi Squarzina 2000, pp. 746–51. The church is S. Vincenzo Martire, Bassano Romano. For evidence that, prior to its reworking, the abandoned statue was in much the same state of incompletion as the four *Slaves* and the *St Matthew*, see Baldriga 2000, p. 742.

26 *Carteggio* IV, p. 152, no. MI. He writes: 'Poi, dopo detta morte di Iulio, Aginensis voles seguitare detta sepultura, ma magior cosa, ond' io condussi e' marmi al Maciello de' Corvi, et fece lavorare quella parte che è murata a Santo Pietro in Vincola et feci le fighure che ò in casa.'

27   *Carteggio* III, p. 8, no. DXCI: 'e e'decti marmi, che io avevo chondocti, stectono insino alla creatione di papa Leone in sulla piazza di Santo Pietro'.

28   *Carteggio* III, p. 317, no. DCCCXX.

29   *Contratti*, XXVIII, pp. 75ff. The text refers to 'Unam domum cum palchis, salis, cameras, puteo, horto et aliis suis habituris, posita Roma in Regione Trevi', and proceeds to define the property's boundaries, confirming that the artist had worked there 'per multos menses pro perfectione dicte sepulture'. In a much later letter to Michelangelo from his biographer Condivi, the latter sends it to the house that is defined as 'vicino la piazza di S. Apostolo canto la chiesa di Loreto'; see *Carteggio* V, p. 61, no. MCCXXIV. The best account of the house – or houses – at Macel de' Corvi is that of Apollonj Ghetti 1968, passim. This dispels many earlier mistakes, but was evidently unknown to Hatfield when he wrote his own account of the property; see Hatfield 2002, pp. 98–103.

30   *Carteggio* I, p. 153, no. CXV, and p. 153, no. CXVI.

31   *Carteggio* I, p. 310, no. CCXLIX. Leonardo Sellaio, who is discussed below, writes: 'E di nuovo, presente messer Francesco [Pallavicini], mi promesse, finita l'opera, sopra el paghamento donarvi la chasa e uno ufizio.'

32   For this episode, see the documentation in Lanciani 1902, II, p. 125.

33   *Carteggio* IV, p. 185, no. MXXIII.

34   A room that faced onto the courtyard was very large, its height recorded as 6 *braccia* and its width 11 *braccia*; see *Ricordi* 1970, p. 59, no. CCLV. It may have been in this area that work on the *quadro*, or front face of the tomb, was going on; its scale would have accommodated the team.

35   *Carteggio* III, p. 310, no. DCCCXV. See also the comments in Hatfield 2002, pp. 99ff. The plan of the property, for which see Apollonj Ghetti 1968, his plate following p. 24, shows how extensive the whole complex was.

36   Signorelli had completed his frescos in the Cappella Brizio in the cathedral at Orvieto ten years earlier, in 1503.

37   *Carteggio* II, pp. 7–8, no. CCLXXXV. The *capitano* of Cortona, serving from March to September 1518, was Zanobi di Lucantonio Albizzi (information furnished by T. Henry).

38   *Ricordi* 1970, p. 35, no. XXX, which shows that partial repayment had been made in March 1519. At that date, Albizzi's term of service at Cortona had expired. The 80 giuli that Michelangelo had lent to Signorelli was approximately a sum of 8 cameral ducats. For earlier attempts to regain his money, see *Carteggio* I, p. 322, no. CCLVIII; pp. 326–7, no. CCLXI; and p. 350, no. CCLXXVIII.

39   *Carteggio* II, pp. 7–8. Michelangelo writes: 'Ma send' io allora mal sano, inanzi che decto maestro lucha si partissi di chasa mi dolfo seco del non potere lavorare, e •llui mi disse: "Non dubitare che e' verrano gli Angeli da •cielo [a pi]gliarti le braccia e t'aiuteranno" '.

40   Luschino 2002, pp. 271–5.

41   *Carteggio* I, p. 186, no. CXLV.

42 For the elucidation of the sketch, see Wilde 1953, pp. 44–5.

43 Pope Leo's rather brutal behaviour towards her is recorded in a contemporary letter; see Luzio and Renier 1893, pp. 228–9.

44 *Carteggio* I, p. 101, no. LXX.

45 *Carteggio* I, p. 162, no. CXXIV. In a letter of 10 August, after the artist's definitive leave-taking, Gellesi sends him 'mille saluti' from the Roman circle; ibid., p. 191, no. CXLIX.

46 For these two letters, *Carteggio* I, pp. 188–9, no. CXLVII, and for Argentina's remarkable commendation, see also *Carteggio indiretto* I, p. 51, no. 33. Of the artist she writes: 'è persona tanto da bene, costumato et gentile et tale che non crediamo che sia hogi in Europa homo simile a lui'.

47 For the Roman branch of the bank, see Schulte 1904, I, p. 22, note 1. For some details about the Borgherini, with references to further bibliography, see Hirst 1981b, p. 50, note 4.

48 *Carteggio* I, p. 182, no. CXLII. Hatfield's suggestion that Michelangelo had fallen in love with Borgherini seems extravagant when reading the text of the letter in which he writes: 'non voglio niente da ·llui e vo' lo servire per amore e non per obrigo'.

49 *Carteggio* I, pp. 190, no. CXL.

50 *Contratti*, no. XXVIII, pp. 70–78.

51 We are still in a period where the artist's correspondents did not take the trouble to preserve them.

52 *Carteggio* I, p. 190, no. CXLVIII.

53 *Carteggio* II, pp. 174–5, no. CDXXIII, and *Ricordi* 1970, no. XXII, p. 23. Now fragmentary, Michelangelo's note refers to the statues as 'le fugure bozate, che son quatro'. Every drawing, however small, is to be put in a chest.

54 *Carteggio* I, p. 318, no. CCLV: 'E' dichono avere arssii tutti que' chartone, ma non chredo di tutti. Doghomi, ma la volontà vostra s'à a cseguire, e io per piacervi meterei del mio sangue.'

55 *Carteggio* I, p. 194, no. CLII.

56 *Carteggio* I, p. 309, no. CCXLVVIII.

57 Marble left at the Ripa, the landing place on the Tiber, seems to have been vulnerable to theft. In a later letter of March 1520, Michelangelo is told that, of his blocks there, one has gone missing. It is referred to as the 'màndrola' and would seem to be the piece for the mandorla of the Virgin and Christ Child planned for the *cappelleta* of the tomb. See *Carteggio* II, p. 233, no. CDLIX.

58 *Carteggio* III, p. 8, no. DXCIV.

59 For a fine discussion of Chigi's stay in Venice, see Gilbert 1980, passim. In 1511 the capital of the Chigi bank was estimated at a 100,000 ducats. For the Villa Farnesina, see Frommel 1960, passim.

60 In a letter of 1525, written to Sebastiano in Rome, he explains that an invitation to dinner by one of the Venetian's friends had done something to relieve his

melancholy: 'usci' um pocho del mio malinchonica, o vero del mio pazzo'; see *Carteggio* III, p. 156, no. DCCIV.

61 See Vasari 1987, III, p. 630. He writes that Michelangelo 'lo teneva quasi sempre a mangier seco'; after a violent rupture, relations were restored and the friendship renewed.

62 For Sebastiano's Venetian works and his earliest paintings in Rome, see Hirst 1981b, pp. 1–31 and 32–40 respectively.

63 See Vasari 1987, V, pp. 88–91.

64 Hirst 1981b, pp. 41–8.

65 *Carteggio* I, p. 192, no. CL. Borgherini's chapel is discussed at length in Hirst 1981b, pp. 49–65.

66 *Carteggio* I, p. 243, no. CXCIII.

67 For this suggestion, see Hirst 1981b, pp. 66–7.

68 *Carteggio* I, p. 243, no. CXCIII.

69 *Carteggio* I, p. 301, no. CCXL. As late as July 1518, it seems that Raphael had not begun his own painting for Narbonne: *Carteggio* II, p. 32, no. CCCIV.

70 *Carteggio* II, p. 32, no. CCCIV.

71 For this, see *Carteggio* I, p. 222, no. CLXXV. He writes, in the same letter, that Antonio da Sangallo the Younger has been asked by Raphael to join him in the control of the Fabbrica of St Peter's.

72 In a later letter over the issue of payment for the *Raising of Lazarus*, Sebastiano reminds him that he has seen the painting while it was under way; see *Carteggio* II, pp. 206–7, no. CDXLVIII.

73 For Pope Leo's pardon of the Soderini family, see Cambi, *Istorie*, in *Delizie*, XXII, p. 8, and Butters 1985, pp. 217–18. And for further details of Piero Soderini's residence in Rome, see Lowe 1993, pp. 73ff. In the San Silvestro correspondence, Soderini asks that the enterprise should not be publicly talked about. This has led Wallace 1999, p. 422, unaccountably to assert that he was still a clandestine exile with whom it was dangerous to have dealings. His wish for reticence can be explained by the fact of the disgrace of his brother, Cardinal Francesco, who, just one year earlier, had been accused of complicity in the cardinals' plot against the pope. The episode is discussed in Lowe 1993, pp. 104ff.

74 Rosselli's initial letter is in *Carteggio* II, p. 2, no. CCLXXX. For the ensuing correspondence from Rome, see *Carteggio* II, pp. 15ff., no. CCXC; p. 17, no. CCXCI; p. 20, no. CCXCIV; pp. 29ff., no. CCCII; p. 31, no. CCCIII; p. 39, no. CCCX; p. 102, no. CCCLX; pp. 104ff., no. CCCLXII; and pp. 113ff., no. CCCLXIX.

75 Soderini, in a letter of 7 June, explains his aims; *Carteggio* II, p. 20, no. CCXCIV. He is prepared to spend 500 ducats. With regard to any sculptural decoration, he wishes to have reliefs rather than statues, for, he goes on, today in Rome one sees how the latter are removed from their sites. He was probably here referring to Michelangelo's own marble *Pietà* and its removal from its original

location in Santa Petronilla. For this, see Hirst 2000a, pp. 735–6; Karl Frey had already perceived a reference to events in St Peter's; see Frey 1899, p. 101.

76 Wallace 1999, passim, has proposed that the present altar, excluding its later Baroque accretions, is of Michelangelo's design. For further discussion of the issue, see Popp 1927, p. 464. Wilde 1953, p. 40, note 2, saw that the present structure can scarcely be connected with his designs; his conclusion is unrecorded in Wallace's text.

77 *Carteggio* II, p. 39, no. CCCX.

78 *Carteggio* I, pp. 7–8, no. V. In his letter to Michelangelo in Rome he writes: 'ho cinque figl[i]uoli homini e truovomi d'età d'anni 56, et gratia di· dDio non ò nessuno che mi possa dare sossidio d'uno bicchiere d'acqua'. He further adds that it is his impression that Michelangelo regards him as a hapless case.

79 See a letter in the Archivio Buonarroti, XXIII, 102, noted in Tempieri 1997, series I, IIIA, 5.

80 See Condivi 1998, p. 12: ' "Io non feci mai arte nessuna, ma sempre soni fin qui delle mie deboli entrate vivuto, attendendo a quelle poche possessioni che da' miei maggiori mi sono state lasciate, cercando non solamente di mantenerle, ma accrescerle quanto per me si potesse, colla mia diligenza." ' Even if not entirely dependable, the passage eloquently records the pessimistic tenor of Lodovico's pronouncements, one evident in so many of his letters. After a quarrel with Michelangelo, referred to in the text below, Lodovico writes to Buonarroto in 1510: 'Bisongnia fare pensiero di vivere chon quello pocho che noi abbiàno, e non bisongnia per questo né andarsi chon Dio né darsi maninchonia, perché spero Iddio ci darà grazia.' See *Carteggio indiretto* I, p. 25. Nevertheless, as noted earlier, Poggi found some evidence that Lodovico had dabbled in a modest wine business three years after Michelangelo's birth.

81 *Carteggio* I, p. 3, no. II.

82 *Carteggio* I, pp. 4–5, no. III.

83 *Carteggio* I, pp. 9–10, no. VI.

84 Tempieri 1997, series I, IIIA, 4–5. Poggi's work on Buonarroto was above all based on the latter's surviving Quadernucci, which are four in number and preserved in the Archivio Buonarroti, as yet unpublished. Of Selvaggia's two sons, Lorenzo, the elder, was born in 1482, and Filippo in 1488. She took care that both should enjoy a humanistic education and Lorenzo grew up to be himself a writer of poetry; both were among the Florentine elite and, following the Medicean restoration in 1512, enjoyed the favour of the new regime. For further information, see Goldthwaite 1968, pp. 77ff., and Bullard 1980, passim.

85 Tempieri 1997, series I, IIIA, 4–5, and Ristori in *Carteggio indiretto* I, p. XXXIII.

86 Tempieri 1997, citing Buonarroto's first Quadernuccio. Michelangelo's gift was dated 7 May 1505.

87   These points have been discussed above, p. 20.

88   Tempieri 1997, series I, IIIA, 5.

89   For this new company, see Ristori in *Carteggio indiretto* I, pp. XXXIII–XXXIV.

90   Ristori, in *Carteggio indiretto* I, pp. XXXIII–XXXIV.

91   *Carteggio* I, pp. 93–4, no. LXVI. Later, in 1513, Michelangelo would refer to a gift he had made earlier of 400 ducats to Buonarroto, 'che voi avete di mio'; see *Carteggio* I, p. 143, no. CVIII.

92   *Carteggio* I, pp. 95–6, no. LXVII. The artist writes: 'Io non posso fare che io non ti schriva ancora dua versi: e questo è che io son ito da dodici anni in qua tapinando per tucta Italia, sopportato ogni vergognia, patito ogni stento, lacerato il corpo mio in ogni fatiche, messa la vita propria a mille pericoli solo per aiutar la chasa mia; e ora che io ò cominciato a·rrilevarla un poco, tu solo voglia esser quello che schompigli e·rrovini in una ora quell che i'ò facto in tanti anni e chon tanta faticha'.

93   For references to the crisis with Cassandra, see Ristori's comments in *Carteggio indiretto*, I, p. XX, and the circumstantial account in Hatfield 2002, pp. 42ff. and 88–9. He points out that the experience with Cassandra induced Michelangelo to take careful precautions against any future widow's claims to properties he would be involved with.

94   Hatfield 2002, pp. 42ff. and p. 88. Michelangelo had evidently sent 350 florins to Lodovico by 15 September 1509; in his letter he ill advisedly assured his father that he could draw on money if he needed to. In the event, Lodovico did not need to do so to effect the settlement but, as Hatfield 2002, p. 88, has shown, he deposited only 130 florins in Michelangelo's account. There was no direct confrontation between father and son in September 1510, for Lodovico was serving as *podestà* of San Casciano from 22 September, and the first evidence of Michelangelo's presence in Florence dates from 26 September. For Lodovico's lame letter to Michelangelo, dated that day, see *Carteggio* I, p. 109, no. LXXVII, and for two discomposed ones to Buonarroto, *Carteggio indiretto* I, pp. 25–6, no. 13, and p. 27, no. 14. The artist was finally reimbursed, but the bad impression left by the episode clearly lingered. He would express further complaints in a letter to Buonarroto of 1513; see *Carteggio* I, p. 142, no. CVIII.

95   *Carteggio* I, p. 123, no. XCI.

96   *Carteggio* I, p. 143, no. CVIII.

97   Hatfield 2002, pp. 89–90.

98   *Carteggio* I, p. 153, no. CXVI.

99   *Carteggio* I, pp. 146–7, no. CXI.

100 *Carteggio* I, p. 176, no. CXXXVII.

101 For this fact, referred to by Ristori in *Carteggio indiretto* I, p. XXXV, note 114, see *Carteggio* I, p. 214, no. CLXIX.

102 For the character of this 'accatto' and its arbitrary incidence, see Butters 1985, p. 297. Lodovico had serious problems in raising the required 50 florins and at

one point contemplated selling a family mule. For his predicament, see *Carteggio indiretto* I, pp. 101–2, no. 58; pp. 107–8, no. 61; pp. 117–18, no. 65; pp. 128–9, no. 70.

103 Looking back, Michelangelo commented to his nephew Leonardo, son of Buonarroto, in a letter of 4 December 1546: 'Mi son sempre ingegniato di risuscitar la casa notra, ma non ò avuto frategli da·cciò.' See *Carteggio* IV, p. 249, no. MLXX.

CHAPTER SEVEN

1 From the moment that Francis I had succeeded Louis XII, who had died without male heirs in January 1515, he had determined to reverse the expulsion of the French from Italy in 1513. His campaign in the summer of 1515 profited from brilliant military planning and the disorganization of the Swiss army that confronted him. Milan capitulated on 16 September, leaving Pope Leo and his allies dangerously vulnerable.

2 *Carteggio* I, p. 181, no. CXLI.

3 There is an excellent assessment of the situation in Florence at this moment in Butters 1985, especially pp. 204ff.

4 For Leo's triumphant entry and the wealth of contemporary evidence it provoked, see the pioneering article of Shearman 1975b, and the monograph by Ciseri of 1990. Since Ciseri's publication appeared, a further fact has been revealed, that Michelangelo's unfinished *St Matthew* was removed from the Opera of the cathedral for the occasion and taken to Santa Maria Novella, where, in fact, Pope Leo had actually spent his first night in the city. A document published by Settesoldi 1994, p. 133, no. XXX, records payment for the transportation of the statue back from the convent to the Opera on 5 December 1515. The statue is referred to as 'una bozza di marmo grande che era abozzata di mano di Michelagnolo Buonarroti ischultore più fa'.

5 See the material in Ciseri 1990, p. 233.

6 Moreni 1816, p. 184. For the statement that Pope Leo shed tears before his father's grave, see Roscoe-Bossi 1816–17, V, p. 141.

7 Ciseri 1990, pp. 137–9.

8 For a cautionary comment, see Moreni 1816, p. 181: 'Questo ornamento, e tali sentimenti piacquero assai al Papa, ma egli non avea però certamente bisogno di questo impulso per operare cosa grande'.

9 Moreni 1816, p. 175, and p. 183, note 2, and Leo's subsequent ratification of earlier concessions on 14 February, pp. 184–5.

10 The Bolsena façade was opportunely cited by Shearman 1995, p. 231. For the rehabilitation of Santa Maria in Domnica by Leo, see Frey 1910, pp. 38–43; Frommel 1996, pp. 309–28.

11   For a notarial act of July 1515 that refers to possible future demolition of property
     to reorder the *piazza*, see Elam 1990, p. 51.

12   *Carteggio* I, p. 166, no. CXXVIII: 'Io vorrei che tu trovassi lo spedalingo di Santa
     Maria Nuova e che tu mi facessi pagar qua mille quatro cento ducati di quegli
     che gli à di mio, perché qua mi bisognia fare sforzo grande, questa state, di
     finire presto questo lavoro, perché stimo poi avere a essere a' servit[i] del Papa.
     E per questo ò chomperato forse venti migliaia di rame per gictar cierte
     figure.'

13   This purchase of copper may help to explain a later remark in a letter of August
     where he states that he is making models; see note 18 below.

14   Milanesi 1875, pp. 115, note 2. He wrote: 'Da ciò si rileva che papa Leone
     aveva gia cominciato a ragionare del lavoro della facciata di San Lorenzo.' Thode
     was inclined to accept that the façade plan was already under discussion; see
     Thode 1908–13, II, pp. 85ff. While Ackerman passed no comment on the letter,
     it has been briefly referred to in later accounts of the façade project; see Barbieri
     and Puppi 1964, pp. 834 and 839; Millon and Smyth 1988, p. 4; and, with
     pertinent reference to the early date, Argan and Contardi 1990, p. 162. There
     are further references in Vasari 1962, II, pp. 642, 645 and 650.

15   The expression 'in the service of the pope' points to an extended employment
     by Leo X. It cannot be satisfactorily explained by the existence of a small archi-
     tectural project Michelangelo undertook for him in Castel Sant'Angelo in this
     period, discussed in Argan and Contardi 1990, pp. 64ff. Justi (1900, pp. 259ff.)
     believed that it had been the elderly Giuliano da Sangallo who had encouraged
     the idea of the façade project in his last years in Rome, and it is worth noting
     that this letter of Michelangelo of 16 June was written before the end of
     Giuliano's service for the pope and his return to Florence; his place in the Fab-
     brica of St Peter's appears to have ended on 1 July 1515.

16   For evidence of his involvement at this later date, see the discussion in the
     text.

17   For the early plan for a library complex, see below, p. 211.

18   *Carteggio* I, pp. 172–3, no. CXXIV: 'Io, poi che tornai di chostà, non ò mai
     lavorato; solo ò acteso a far modegli e a mectere a ordine e' lavoro, i' modo
     che possa fare uno sforzo grande e finirlo in dua o tre anni per forza d'uomini.'
     As Justi 1900, p. 253, noted, the 'modegli' the artist here refers to could have
     been executed for reliefs for which the purchase of copper had been made. If
     models were made by the artist in his workshop at this moment, as he states,
     they would have been of fragile material and, therefore, probably perished in
     the flooding of the house at Macel de' Corvi in 1529, an event that will be
     turned to later.

19   *Carteggio* I, p. 176, no. CXXXVII. Whether the artist is here providing a genuine
     explanation or was, in effect, stone-walling, is impossible to determine, despite
     his remark that he could have done with him. Benedetto's recent marble *St*

John the Evangelist for the apostles series for the cathedral, which Michelangelo had not produced, is an undistinguished addition to the series. As has been seen, Soderini had employed Benedetto to effect the chasing of the bronze *David* before its dispatch to France, but Michelangelo never had the chance to inspect the quality of his performance.

20 For the episode, see the comments in Wallace 1994, pp. 15−19.

21 For a remarkable letter just preceding the contract of the gift, see Settesoldi 1994, p. 133, no. XXVIII. In it the officials of the Opera of Florence Cathedral write at length to the Florentine captain at Pietrasanta, explaining that the gift is being made to the Florentine government for the benefit of the Opera, 'per conto della decta fabrica di S. Maria del Fiore'. They emphasize the urgent need for a formal contractual ratification of the gift, since they are under daily pressure to conclude the agreement from Pope Leo and Lorenzo de' Medici, 'in però che siamo ogni giorno sollecitati dalla Santità di Nostro Signore, ma etiam dalla Magnificentia del Magnifico Lorenzo de' Medici'. A further letter was written concerning ratification on 23 May; Settesoldi 1994, p. 133, no. XXIX.

22 Frey 1910, p. 27; the payment is 'per conto della strada per e' marmi'.

23 *Carteggio* I, p. 168, no. CXXX. The artist writes: 'qua m' à decto Domenico Buoninsegni che intende che la strada è presso e facta'.

24 *Carteggio* I, p. 168, no. CXXX; p. 170, no. CXXXII; and p. 171, no. CXXXIII. Despite highly disparaging remarks about Michele in these letters, Michelangelo had always trusted him in the past; it was, after all, Michele whom he had requested to hide his marble *Virgin and Child* in 1506. For a biographical sketch of Michele, see Wallace 1994, pp. 19−20.

25 *Carteggio* I, p. 176, no. CXXXVII, and p. 178, no. CXXXVIII.

26 *Carteggio* I, p. 180, no. CXL. For a note on Domenico Fancelli, see Wallace 1994, p. 34.

27 *Carteggio* I, p. 172, no. CXXXIV. He writes to Buonarroto in the letter quoted in note 18 above, that nothing seems to have been done: 'Intendo chome costà non si fa niente.'

28 This striking letter is in Florence, Archivio di Stato, Archivio Mediceo avanti il Principato, filza 117, document 180, c.179 verso. Although referred to by Luzzati in *DBI*, XV, p. 252, it has not attracted attention. Buoninsegni writes: 'Parlando con Monsignore nostro Reverendissimo circa la strada di Pietrasanta per conto de' marmi mi ha ordinato ne debba scrivere costì alli operai, il che per ancora non ho fatto, et che io dovessi fare loro intendere che se di costà per la parte loro cominciono ad fare la spesa della ditta strada, che subito Nostro Signore darà costí ordine di concorre alla metà di quello che la costassi, ma che si debba cominciarla di verso la marina, a causa che venendo le piove non si potrebbe lavorare in la palude. Et qua è stato referito che di detta strada per ancora non si è cominciato cosa alcuna, che come s' intende sia cominciata,

subito si fará la provisione. Emi parso scrivere a Vostra Signoria come quella sa Monsignore Nostro Reverendissimo m' ordinó ne parlassi con Vostra Signoria e se ci ho ad fare più opera alchuna o in sollicitare la provisione de' danari o altro, Vostra Signoria si degnerà significarlo.'

29 Condivi 1998, p. 37, writing at the artist's direction, refers to the road, which had to be built with pickaxes in the mountains and on piles through the marshes, 'per le montagne per forza di picconi e per il piano con palafitte, come quello che era paludoso'.

30 For Buonarroto as a prior, see Hatfield 2002, pp. 209–10, who gives an excellent account of the offices that he did and did not hold. For the list of all the priors for November and December, see Cambi, *Istorie*, in *Delizie*, XXII, p. 97.

31 *Carteggio* I, pp. 184–5, no. CXLIV.

32 There is what purports to be a late and undependable copy of the text in the Archivio Buonarroti, XXVI, c.134. The whole episode was already described by Gotti 1876, I, p. 205.

33 Landucci 1883/1969, pp. 361–2.

34 The fragility of the Medicean succession was vividly demonstrated as early as 1514, when Lorenzo's mother, Alfonsina, intervened to urge her son not to take part in the jousting planned to celebrate the Feast of St John the Baptist in June. Writing on her behalf to Lorenzo on 10 June, Baldassare Turini da Pescia recounts her anxieties: 'hora, che Vostra Signoria è giovine, et in casa non ci essendo altro che quella et lo Magnifico Iuliano, et tutti dui senza donna et figlioli, et atteso la cattiva complexione del prefato Magnifico Juliano, quella non può fare maggiore errore, che tenere simil vie', a reference to Medicean jousting in the past. He continues: 'Et dice che V.S. la faccia fare ad altri, et lei stia a vedere, et che la pensi ad vivere, et mantenere la casa.' For the text, see Roscoe-Bossi 1816–17, VI, pp. 226–7. The increased precariousness of the situation after Giuliano's death is demonstrated by reactions to the news that Lorenzo had been seriously wounded in the renewed campaign over Urbino in the early months of 1517. Lodovico Buonarroti was expressing a general sense of crisis in Florence when he wrote to Michelangelo on 19 May: 'Qua si dubita che 'l singniore Lorenzo de' Medici non sia morto, di modo che qui la terra sta in grande fantasia e pare che sia sozzopra tutto il mondo.' See *Carteggio* I, p. 284, no. CCXXV. Apart from the deep sense of loss at Giuliano's death, the event involved a heavy financial blow for Pope Leo, who was compelled to return the dowry of no fewer than 100,000 ducats to the widowed Philiberte; for documentation, see Hurtubise 1985, p. 142, note 20.

35 For this extraordinary confession, see *Carteggio* I, p. 183, no. CXLIII.

36 The artist's own notes of payments for the tomb project from 1513 to February 1517 can be found in *Ricordi* 1970, pp. 3–4, no. V. There is a detailed assessment of his financial situation in this period in Hatfield 2002, pp. 30–34. This constant income for the project does, of course, explain the relative ease with which

Michelangelo could fund his acquisitions of property in this period, such as the purchase of the farm at Scopeto in May 1518 and his subsequent acquisition of that called Il Fattoio at Rovezzano in October 1519. For these purchases, see Hatfield 2002, pp. 74ff. and 85ff.

37 See his references to the two statues of July 1542 in *Carteggio* IV, pp. 135–40, no. CMXCII.

38 *Contratti*, nos XX, XXI, pp. 45–53. On permission to work elsewhere than Rome, the Italian text reads: 'Ancora perché detto Michelagniolo è stato e di presente non si sente troppo bene, si convennone che detto Michelagniolo possi a suo piacere lavorare per finire detta opera a Firenze, a Pisa, a Carrara e dove parrà a lui, pure che il lavoro che farà servi a detta sepoltura.' Once again, he is enjoined to take on no other work that will interfere with progress on the tomb.

39 A further indication that Michelangelo's mind was occupied with architecture at this time is the existence of a number of copies he made of another draughtsman's studies of antique Roman architecture. For bibliography, see Hirst 1988a, p. 93, note 2. The draughtsman whom he copied has been convincingly identified as Bernardo della Volpaia. For an excellent brief biography, see N. Pagliara in *DBI*, XXXVI, 792–5. The circumstances surrounding his prototypes point to the near certainty that Michelangelo made his copies in Rome, prior to his departure for Florence in July 1516.

40 This seems particularly true of the pioneering biographers in English. Symonds, in his poetic account of the artist's life, accepted without question Condivi's account; see Symonds 1899, I, pp. 211–14. It was Justi in his remarkable study of 1900 (pp. 259ff) who effectively demolished the myth of the reluctant Michelangelo.

41 Condivi dwells at length on Michelangelo's resistance to taking on the façade commission: 'fece tutta quella resistenza che potette, allegando d'esser ubligato al cardinal Santi quatro e ad Aginense, né poter loro mancare'. The pope is described as forcing executors and artist to comply. He concludes: 'In questo modo Michelagnolo, piagendo, lasciò la sepoltura e se n'andò a Firenze'. For this extraordinary passage, where the biographer was entirely at the mercy of the artist, see Condivi 1998, pp. 36–7, and the comments in Hirst 1997, pp. 74ff.

42 *Carteggio* I, p. 148, no. CXII.

43 The most lucid account of the papal seizure of Urbino and the five attempts of the anti-papal coalition to regain it is Guicciardini's; see Guicciardini 1971, II, pp. 1340ff. For the part played by Alfonsina Orsini de' Medici, see especially Nitti 1892, pp. 70ff. News of the conquest reached Florence on 5 June and a celebratory Mass was held in the cathedral. Such elation would not last, for, as noted below, it was Florence that would bear much of the huge financial burden of what followed.

44 *Carteggio* I, p. 190, no. CXLVIII. Sellaio writes: 'E vi priegho istiate nella buona

fantasia che voi sete di finire questa opera per fare bugiardi quegli che dicono
che voi ve ne siate andato e che non si finirà.'

45   Gellesi's letter seems to have been ignored. He writes (*Carteggio* I, p. 191, no.
CXLIX): 'Intendo che voi volete recuperare il vostro honore e che state ben
disposto poi che partisti di qua'.

46   *Contratti*, no. XXIV, pp. 56ff.

47   For the surviving drawings, see Tolnay 1975–80, IV, nos. 499–506. The wooden
model in the Casa Buonarroti is fundamental in documenting the artist's
intentions.

48   The contract refers to the house in the 'Regione di Trevi'. Many writers have
mistakenly assumed this to be a different house from that at Macel de' Corvi,
but the two are identical, as Ramsden 1963, I, p. 251, rightly perceived.

49   For this little-known reference, see *Carteggio indiretto* I, pp. 49–50, no. 32:
'Stamani ... venne Buonarroto et disse come haveva ricevuta una lettera di
Michelagnolo facta de' xiij di del p[rese]nte, et per quella gli faceva intendere
che infra x dì si partiva da Roma alla volta di Firenze con quatro garzone, per
istanza (et) per lavorare a Firenze, et non voleva star più a Roma, et che facesi
in modo che lui potessi stare in casa.'

50   Hatfield 2002, p. 33.

51   *Carteggio indiretto* I, p. 52, no. 34. A letter addressed to Giansimone in Settignano
dated 29 July explains that Michelangelo has not left the house: 'per anchora
non è uscito di casa per non havere panni'. Details recorded in Buonarroto's
Quaderruccio of 1514–16, now in the Casa Buonarroti, show that clothes were
being ordered and that a bundle of 'panni vecchi' arrived in Florence on 4
August: see the reference in Tempieri 1997, series I, busta IIIA.

52   *Ricordi* 1970, p. 12, no. XI.

53   For Francesco di Giovanni Pelliccia, see Klapisch-Zuber 1969, *ad indicem*. For
the contract of marble on I November, see *Contratti*. Despite his long-standing
experience and authority, it is worth noting that Francesco was unable to write
his own name; see *Ricordi* 1970, p. 19, no. XIX.

54   *Ricordi* 1970, pp. 12–13, no. XI.

55   *Carteggio* I, p. 201, no. CLIX. His estimate of receiving his marble two months
after ordering it exactly matches a later one conveyed to Duke Cosimo by
Vincenzo Danti in 1568, quoted in Klapisch-Zuber 1969, p. 62, note 7: 'A
Carrara cavano ale volte dua mesi prima che possano avere un pezzo di marmo
statuale.'

56   *Carteggio* I, p. 195, no. CLIII. The writer, from a long-standing family of marble
workers, was generally referred to as 'Il Caldana'. The family's activities are
discussed by Klapisch-Zuber 1969, pp. 129ff.

57   They are enumerated in the Michelangelo *Vita* of 1550 and the same list appears
in his *Vita* of 1568; see Vasari 1962, IV, p. 53. A summary of the issues that
Vasari's statement raises can be found in Millon and Smyth 1988, pp. 5–8.

58   The addition of Jacopo Sansovino appears in the Jacopo *Vita*; Vasari states that
      he made his design at Pope Leo's request and that it was carried out as a wooden
      model by Baccio d'Agnolo; see Vasari 1987, VI, pp. 182–3. His design survives
      in the form of an engraving (reproduced in Millon and Smyth 1988, fig. 3,
      p. 76).

59   All three are reproduced in Borsi 1985, pp. 481–9. Two of the three are illus-
      trated on a larger scale in Millon and Smyth 1988, figs 10 and 11. It has been
      suggested that Vasari confused Antonio da Sangallo the Elder with Giuliano.

60   None of the original letters Michelangelo addressed to Buoninsegni in this
      period has survived. The few texts we do have, such as the extraordinary one
      of 2 May 1517 (*Carteggio* I, pp. 277–9, no. CCXXI) and a later one following the
      suspension of the façade project (*Carteggio* II, pp. 218–21, no. CDLVIII), have
      come down to us only because preserved in draft form or copy by the artist.

61   *Carteggio* I, p. 163, no. CXXV.

62   Niccolò Machiavelli to Lodovico Alamanni, 17 December 1517; see Machiavelli
      1984, pp. 497–8. It was from 1517 that Buoninsegni's work multiplied when
      Cardinal Giulio succeeded Sisto della Rovere as Vice-Chancellor of the Church;
      see his complaint, one among many, of May 1517, in *Carteggio* I, p. 281, no.
      CCXXIII.

63   In a letter to Michelangelo of September 1518, Sebastiano del Piombo refers to
      the intractability of Buoninsegni: 'De la terribilità de messer Domenico Buon-
      insegni non ve ne scrivo niente: è corozato con tutti, et parmi sia divenuto oltro
      modo teribile senza uno proposito al mondo.' See *Carteggio* II, p. 86, no.
      CCCXLVI.

64   *Carteggio* I, pp. 219–21, no. CLXXIII.

65   *Carteggio* I, pp. 204–5, no. CLXII, and *Carteggio indiretto* I, pp. 54–5, no. 35.

66   It will be recalled that it had been Bibbiena, on the road from Poggio a Caiano
      with Piero de' Medici in 1494, who had so contemptuously rejected Cardiere's
      premonitions of disaster. And it had been to him that Michelangelo had appealed
      for money in 1513. His friendship with Raphael is attested in every account of
      the latter's life, and that he would have supported him over the façade project
      is not open to doubt. That this 'amicho' could have been Bibbiena has been
      proposed also by Contardi, in Argan and Contardi 1990, pp. 162–3. One of
      Leo's closest confidants in the early years of the pontificate, he would gradually
      lose influence to Cardinal Giulio de' Medici. For an excellent biography, see
      Moncallero 1953, passim, and the profile by Patrizi in *DBI*, XLI, pp. 593–604.

67   P. de Grassis, Diarium, British Library, Add. MSS 8443, fols 381–2. Those letters
      of Bibbiena's that survive do not enable us to establish his movements at this
      date.

68   *Carteggio* I, p. 225, no. CLXXVII.

69   Vasari dedicated a Life to Baccio d'Agnolo in both editions; see Vasari 1987,
      IV, pp. 609–17. He enumerates many of his Florentine projects, which included

the palace undertaken for Taddeo Taddei. He had been involved in the projects undertaken for Pope Leo's *entrata* in 1515. Milanesi, in his edition of the *Le Vite* (Vasari-Milanesi 1878–85, V, pp. 363–5), provided a summary chronology of his activities, first as a wood-worker and then as an architect, which is still useful; but much work has been done in more recent years on his career and architectural *œuvre*.

70   For 1513 as the date of beginning of the work, see Cambi, *Istorie*, in *Delizie*, XXII, pp. 63ff. Marble for the construction was being ordered in May 1513; see Settesoldi 1994, no. XIX, pp. 131–2.

71   Cambi, *Istorie* in *Delizie*, XXII, p. 70, had reported that the section of the gallery completed had aroused much criticism but pointed out that Baccio had been following an earlier model. Michelangelo's celebrated phrase occurs only in the second edition of the Vasari *Lives*; see Vasari 1987, IV, p. 613. It is, of course, possible that Michelangelo expressed disapprobation when he himself became involved with designs of the *ballatoio*, referred to below, p. 188.

72   *Carteggio* I, pp. 207–8, no. CLXIV: 'mi pare che quasi li diate la chomissione libera, che della facciata ne faccia quel tanto che a lui par bene'.

73   *Carteggio* I, pp. 219–21, no. CLXXIII.

74   He writes, *Carteggio* I, p. 219: 'Dipoi, per questa vostra ultima, vedo che avete mutato fantasia, diciendo non volere più venire. E considerato el contenuto di tutte le vostre, le vedo tanto varie che se io non inpazzo non mi parrà far pocho.'

75   *Carteggio* I, p. 220: 'E dichovi anchora che, quando intenda che ciascuno di voi si lamenti che le opere d'onore e d'utile sieno alloghate a giente extra[nee] e fuori della nazione, sempre dirò che voi altri ve ne siete chausa, con le false e abstratte inmaginazione che vi fate.' As observed by Elam 1992a, p. 100, this sounds like a reference to Raphael, the only non-Florentine competitor for the commission referred to by Vasari, and the artist who, by this date, enjoyed supremacy at the papal court.

76   *Carteggio* I, p. 225, no. CLXXVII.

77   *Carteggio* I, pp. 230–32, no. CLXXII.

78   *Carteggio* I, p. 230. Referring to Michelangelo's suspicions, he writes: 'mi dicievi che dubitavi che Baccio d'Agnolo e Baccio Bigio non vi inghannassino'. Baccio Bigio did a good deal of work for members of the Medici family, especially Alfonsina. He would become involved in the building of the library at San Lorenzo in 1524.

79   *Carteggio* I, p. 231: 'E benché chostoro dichino volerva dare a voi e a Baccio d'Agnolo, penso che quando voi volessi el tutto sopra di voi, e pigl[i]are per chompagno chi voi volessi, che la vi sarebbe data. Nondimeno, questo dicho pure di mia fantasia.'

80   *Carteggio* I, p. 232.

81   *Carteggio* I, pp. 274–5, no. CCXIX. Reporting Baccio d'Agnolo's remarks,

Buonarroto notes: 'E più mi dise che mai pensò d'inpaciarsi con Raffaello da Urbino e che gli era suo nemicho chapitale'. The passage seems to provide strong corroborative confirmation of Raphael's involvement in the façade commission.

82 *Carteggio* I, p. 233, no. CLXXV.

83 *Ricordi* 1970, p. 102, no. XCIX.

84 *Carteggio* I, p. 235–6, no. CLXXXV.

85 For the large Casa Buonarroti design, see, for recent bibliography, Millon and Smyth 1988, pp. 27–31, no. 3, and Hirst 1988a, pp. 79ff.

86 There are a number of indications that Michelangelo may have seen Giuliano's drawings; indeed, it has been argued that his final design was, in part, influenced by an elevation of Giuliano's, Uffizi 279A, which appears to date from the pontificate of Julius II; see Millon and Smyth 1988, p. 42 and their fig. 9.

87 For the epithet, see Papini 1949, p. 208.

88 See his remarks in his celebrated letter of 2 May 1517 to Buoninsegni that he has ordered marble here and there at Carrara: 'Io . . . ò allogato molti marmi e dati danari qui e qua, e messo a chavare in vari luog[h]i'; *Carteggio* I, p. 277, no. CCXXI.

89 *Carteggio* I, p. 308, no. CCXLVII.

90 *Contratti*, no. XXXIV, p. 91.

91 The book survives in the Archivio Buonarroti, no. LXXXII. Seventeen of its pages contain drawings of blocks by the artist; the first is inscribed by a Carrarese notary; for excellent reproductions, see Tolnay 1975–80, III, nos. 467–76, and for the notary's text, which has lost its date, ibid., p. 101. Ever since Tolnay first discussed them in 1928, these drawings have been related to marble for the New Sacristy at San Lorenzo; a whole study of them by Wallace 1992b is devoted to this argument, which is repeated in his book of 1994. Bardeschi Ciulich, however, has conclusively shown that one of the identified quarrymen, il Mancino, had died by October 1518, long before marble deliveries for the chapel were contemplated. The blocks must, therefore, have been ordered for the tomb of Julius II; see Bardeschi Ciulich 1994, pp. 100–03. For interesting recent suggestions that two of the blocks represented in the book relate to two of the *Slaves* now in the Accademia, see Rapetti 2001, pp. 49–51.

92 This is noted by both Wallace and Rapetti.

93 Its anachronism is evident when we recall that Michelangelo could not be described as an established practising architect in 1517. The clearest exposition of the three circles as relating to the three arts appears in a much later book, devoted to Michelangelo's funeral in Florence in 1564: the 'Esequie del Divino Michelangelo Buonarroti', published anonymously but perhaps written by Vincenzo Borghini. For a modern edition, see Borghini 1964; the passage is on p. 120. For elaborate comments on the *segno*, see Collareta 1978.

94 This signature seems to have been completely overlooked by commentators on

the *segno*. We find a comparable substitution of images for words, a rebus, elsewhere in Michelangelo's correspondence. Inscribing his address in a letter to Fattucci of *circa* 1522–3, in writing of Via Mozza, he adds 'Canto alla [Macina]', with a millstone substituted for the word 'macina'; see *Carteggio* II, p. 344, no. DLII, and Bardeschi Ciulich 1989, no. 12. Much later, he would draw a crow (*corvo*) when writing his address at Macel de' Corvi; Bardeschi Ciulich 1989, no. 27. For a rather comparable example of adopting an object in place of a word, one can cite Dosso Dossi's only signed painting (*Saint Jerome*, Kunsthistorisches Museum, Vienna), where he employs a rebus for the signature, a capital D with a large bone, thus constituting Dosso.

95 *Carteggio* I, p. 317, no. CCLIV.

96 *Carteggio* I, p. 335, no. CCLXVIII.

97 *Carteggio* I, p. 339, no. CCLXXI. Exchanges between the Buonarroti and Salviati were facilitated by the fact that they were close neighbours in the quarter of Santa Croce. In this letter, Buonarroto explains how he and Lodovico had run into Jacopo in Santa Croce on the previous day, Sunday, 4 April. They had talked of Michelangelo's demand to have his own right to marble at Pietrasanta, discussed below, for a whole hour.

98 *Carteggio* I, p. 342, no. CCLXXIII. He writes: 'tucti noi gli dobieno essere obrighati insino della vita'.

99 *Carteggio* I, p. 346–7, no. CCLXXVI, for further comments on the contents of this letter.

100 For this letter of Lombardello, see *Carteggio* II, p. 24–5, no. CXXCVIII.

101 At least two references to Malaspina's obstructiveness exist in the correspondence of this moment. See *Carteggio* II, p. 75, no. CCCXXXVIII, where he is reported to have imprisoned a man dispatched to expedite the loading. See also *Carteggio* II, p. 72, no. CCCXXXVI, for another allusion to him. In neither letter is the reference to Malaspina identified in the book's index.

102 *Carteggio* II, p. 75, no. CCCXXXVIII. Berto da Filicaia was of great service to Michelangelo in these years. For a note about him, see Wallace 1994, p. 24.

103 *Carteggio* II, p. 86, no. CCCXLVI. Sebastiano was giving the cardinal wildly optimistic news about the artist's progress with the tomb at this time.

104 *Carteggio* II, p. 101, no. CCCLIX.

105 *Carteggio* II, p. 106, no. CCCLXIII. Malaspina is reported to have written of the artist 'che sempre avevi voluto chonbatere cho gl'uomini e fare straneze'.

106 A résumé of what Buoninsegni had written was sent to the artist; in it Cardinal Leonardo's desperation over delays is emphasized: 'si cruccia per conto della sepoltura': *Carteggio* II, pp. 125–6, no. CCCLXXIX.

107 *Carteggio* II, p. 125. Despite the problems that Michelangelo had suffered from those at Carrara, it is worth noting an aspect of his goodwill and generosity. At just this troubled moment, he found the time to respond to the needs of Malaspina's own brother-in-law, Piero Soderini, and Argentina, the *marchese's*

sister, over the work they wished to initiate in San Silvestro in Capite in Rome. The artist did not always fight with everyone.

108 *Carteggio* I, p. 235, no. CLXXXV.

109 *Carteggio* I, p. 338, no. CCLXX.

110 *Carteggio* II, p. 14, no. CCLXXXIX.

111 *Carteggio* II, p. 36, no. CCCVII.

112 *Carteggio* II, p. 37, no. CCCVIII.

113 For an account of the property, its location and its subsequent history, see Hatfield 2002, pp. 75–8.

114 *Carteggio* II, pp. 109–10. The letter has been mistakenly associated with a workplace for the New Sacristy at San Lorenzo, and consequently wrongly dated; for this error, see Ramsden 1963, I, pp. 278–9.

115 Hirst 1997, p. 67, note 9.

116 Hatfield 2002, pp. 79ff.

117 See, for example, *Ricordi* 1970, pp. 45ff., no. XLII; pp. 55–6, no. XLVI; and pp. 69–70, nos. LXII and LXIII. Hatfield has pointed out that this care in keeping details was probably prompted by the fact that the costs were to be charged to expenses.

118 Hatfield 2002, p. 80.

119 *Carteggio* II, p. 129, no. CCLXXXII. He writes: 'Ò a ordine qua una bella stanza, dov'io potrò rizare venti figure per volta'.

120 For the deliveries in the summer of 1519, see especially *Ricordi* 1970, p. 85, no. LXXIX. One very large block there listed as arriving in June required no less than five pairs of oxen for its transportation. For the blocking out of marble by May, see *Ricordi* 1970, p. 86, no. LXXX: 'Martedì a dì diciassette di maggio cominciò Topolino aiutarmi bozare certe figure nella stanza d[i] via Mozza'. Topolino, literally little mouse, was Domenico di Giovanni Fancelli from Settignano, who would provide the artist with a great deal of help, especially in the imminent work for the New Sacristy at San Lorenzo. For a brief outline of his career, see Wallace 1994, pp. 69–70. Ten years older than Michelangelo, he aspired to be a marble sculptor, provoking a scathing assessment of his capacities by Vasari: see Vasari 1987, VI, p. 121.

121 For the *ricordo*, see *Ricordi* 1970, pp. 371–2, no. CCCXIV. It has been proposed that it was written by Michelangelo's assistant Antonio Mini, for whom see below, pp. 243–4. For more about the episode, see Vasari 1962, IV, pp. 1565–6.

122 *Carteggio* IV, p. 179, no. MXX. For the date of the marble, see Hatfield 2002, p. 81, note 129.

123 *Contratti*, no. LI, pp. 133ff.

124 Settesoldi 1994, p. 134, no. XXXVIII.

125 Settesoldi 1994, p. 135, no. XLIII: 'Per il che si risponde a Vostra Signoria che questo è intectione et volontà venuta da Roma'.

126   Settesoldi 1994, p. 135, no. XLIV.

127   For a brief biography of Donato Benti, see *DBI*, VIII, *ad vocem*. In late April Michelangelo appointed Benti his procurator; the contract allows him full authority to supervise things in the artist's absence in Florence. In his letter of 13 June, Benti writes: 'Michelagnolo, io v'ò promesa la mia fè; se la ingnoranza no mi ochupa lo intteletto, di chuore non mancherò mai di fede, e cho' fatti lo vedrette.' See *Carteggio* II, p. 27, no. CCC.

128   He explains that he has not asked to be put in charge of the road for financial reasons: 'se io ò chiesto al Papa o al Chardinale che mi dieno alturità sopra questa strada, l'ò facto solo per potere chomandare e farla dirizare in que' luog[h] i dove sono e' marmi migliori, che non gli chonoscie ognune'. See *Carteggio* I, pp. 334–5, no. CCLXVIII.

129   *Carteggio* II, pp. 9–10, no. CCLXXXVI. For the marble for statues 'bisognia allargare la strada facta, dalla Corvara insino sopra Seraveza, circha dua miglia, e circha u' miglio o mancho ne bisognia far di nuovo tucta, cioè tagliarla nel monte cho' pichoni iusino dove si possono charicare e' marmi decti'. This letter is telling for the emphasis Michelangelo places on the role of Cardinal Giulio in Rome. He goes so far as to call himself the cardinal's man: 'Io sono qua chome suo omo'.

130   *Carteggio* II, p. 95, no. CCCLIII.

131   Settesoldi 1994, p. 136, no. LIII; a letter from the Opera recounts what Donato Benti has personally reported. If the water that has encroached on the road is not dealt with, it will provoke 'danno grandissimo'. The road over the marshes is suffering because it has not been paved.

132   Settesoldi 1994, p. 138, no. LXIV. The letter from the Opera reports that 'la strada fatta per conto de' marmi in qualche parte ruina e, se non si riparassi ne' principii, sarebbe in maggiore detrimento'.

133   For bibliography relating to the sketches, see Tolnay 1975–80, I, pp. 96–7, no. 117 verso. It was he who first proposed that the sketches were probably added to help an 'analfabeta'; his perception has not always been subsequently noted. Both the artist's later biographers describe his frugality. Condivi would write: 'È sempre stato nel suo vivere molto parco, usando il cibo più per necessità che per dilettazione, e massimente quando è stato in opera'; see Condivi 1998, pp. 62–3.

134   For Buonarroto's letter, see *Carteggio* I, p. 330, no. CCLXIV, and for Salviati's, *Carteggio* I, p. 337, no. CCLXX. Salviati explicitly refers to Michelangelo's wish to be granted a free supply of marble: 'il partito del potere cavare marmi senza costo'.

135   *Carteggio* I, p. 346, no. CCLXXVI. If Salviati's efforts fail, he writes that he will immediately ride to Rome: 'monterò subito a chavallo e anderò a trovare el chardinale de' Medici e el Papa, e dirò loro el facto mio, e qui lascierò la impresa e ritorneromi a Charrara: che ne sono pregato chome si prega Cristo'.

136 A version of the document exists in the Archivio Buonarroti; see *Contratti*, no. LIV, pp. 143–5. Another exists in Florence, Archivio di Stato, Arte della Lana 62, c.131 verso. The artist is described in the document as 'oggi scultore excellentissimo et . . . di riputatione e fama sopra ogni altro'. During his life, he is permitted to quarry marble for whatever purpose 'sanza che habbi a decta opera o ad altri pagare premio o cosa alcuna per decti marmi et cavatura et tractura di quegli'.

137 The pope's concession is conveyed to Michelangelo by Jacopo Salviati in a letter from Rome of 15 January 1519; see *Carteggio* II, pp. 143–4, no. CCCXCIV. Salviati writes: 'Quando tu ti contenti di volere pigl[i]are dua o tre colonne per la facciata di quelle di Carrara, come accenni per la tua, la Santità di Nostro Signore et il reverendissimo de' Medici ne saranno contentissimi.' He adds that Pope Leo nevertheless wishes work at Pietrasanta to go forward. For Salviati's move to Rome, see below.

138 See, for example, Buonarroto's letter of 30 July 1518; *Carteggio* II, pp. 42–3, no. CCCXII, and Michelangelo's of mid-August 1518, *Carteggio* II, p. 59, no. CCCXXVI, and of the end of August, pp. 70–71, no. CCCXXXV.

139 *Carteggio* II, p. 70, no. CCCXXXV.

140 *Contratti*, no. XXXVIII, pp. 98ff.

141 *Carteggio* II, pp. 82–3, no. CCCXLIII.

142 *Carteggio* II, pp. 82–3, no. CCCXLIII. He writes: 'El luogo da chavare è qua molto aspro, e gl'uomini molto ignoranti in simile exercitio; però bisognia una gran patientia qualche mese, tanto che e' si sieno domestichati e' monti e ammaestrati gli uomi[n]i . . . Basta che, quello che io ò promesso, lo farò a ogni modo, e farò la più bella opera che si sia mai facta in Italia, se Dio me n'aiuta.'

143 *Carteggio* II, p. 84, no. CCCXLIV. Salviati writes: 'Gli uomini grandi e di franco animo nelle adversità pigliono più quore e sono più gagliardi'.

144 Settesoldi 1994, p. 135, no. XLVII.

145 *Contratti*, no. LIX, pp. 153ff.

146 For the *operai*'s letter, see *Carteggio* II, p. 182, no. CDXXVIII, and for Urbano's, *Carteggio* II, p. 183, no. CDXXIX.

147 *Carteggio* II, pp. 185–6, no. CDXXXI.

148 *Carteggio* II, p. 264, no. CDLXXXVI.

149 See Cambi, *Istorie* in *Delizie*, XXII, p. 177. He writes: 'Del mese d'Aprile 1521, venne in Firenze la prima colonna di marmo per la facciata della Chiesa di S. Lorenzo, ch'era braccia 12, e cavossi della Cava fatta di nuovo a Pietra Santa, donata dal Comune all'Opera di S. Maria del Fiore; e perchè il Papa volle e' marmi si cavassino di quivi, donò all' opera Fiorini 1000 di Camera per fare la strada, e molti più ne spese la detta Opera; e per ancora si cava questi pezzi grandi con difficolta, che si trasse 6. colonne, e roppesene 4. nel mandarle, fatte l'avevano, rotolandole al piano'. Klapisch-Zuber 1969, p. 67, note 26. Cambi's statement that, in all, six columns had been quarried is confirmed by a *ricordo* of the artist where he writes of events in early 1518 and refers to 'sei cholonne

d'undici braccia e mezzo l'una'; see *Ricordi* 1970, p. 101, no. XCVII. In the light of Cambi's figures, it is difficult to accept the conclusion of Wallace 1994, p. 48, when he writes: 'The columns are testimony of the innumerable difficulties encountered, but they are also a measure of Michelangelo's success at Seravezza.'

150 See *Ricordi* 1970, pp. 97–8, no. XCV. For a further reference to these figures, see ibid., p. 99, no. XCVI.

151 Their falling out is referred to by Cambi, *Istorie*, in *Delizie*, XXII, p. 151. On Salviati's political attitude, see Busini 1860, p. 89: 'Jacopo Salviati fu sempre onoratissimo e religioso, ed amava meglio la libertà che la Tiranide per sua natura, ma più lo stato ristretto e di pochi, che la libertà: e questo fu sempre l'animo suo'. Pope Leo did not favour his nephew's plan, which was reported to have reminded him of the follies in 1494 of Lorenzo's father, Piero de' Medici; see the passage of Cerretani quoted in Devonshire Jones 1972, p. 139, note 200.

152 *Carteggio* II, pp. 143–4, no. CCCXCIV. In his letter, Jacopo informs Michelangelo that the pope wishes to see 'qualche modello o principio di figure'. In the event, Pope Leo did not come; for further references to his unrealized intention, see Shearman 1995, pp. 234–5. He is recorded as wishing to return once more to Poggio a Caiano, where, in fact, his sister-in-law Alfonsina was living in worsening health; see Cambi, *Istorie*, in *Delizie*, XXII, pp. 145–6.

153 Giovan Battista Figiovanni, who would enjoy a stormy relationship with Michelangelo in the years to come, was born in 1466 and already enjoyed close relations with the Medici family in the future Leo X's youth. He became one of two Medicean canons at San Lorenzo in 1507 and, as a consequence of Leo's election in 1513, became prior of San Lorenzo in the following year. He was also close to Cardinal Giulio, made archbishop of Florence, it should be recalled, in 1513. See, for his career, V. Arrighi in *DBI*, XLVII, pp. 557–8.

154 In disclaiming financial duties, Figiovanni was declining to handle money; he did not escape a huge burden of bookkeeping. For his extraordinary account of events that, with lessening lucidity, he traces up to the date of Clement VII's death in 1534, see Corti 1964, pp. 24–31. He describes how Cardinal Giulio, for greater privacy, led him into a room and locked the door. He then proceeds to explain that he and Pope Leo planned the two new undertakings: 'Noi siamo d'animo fare una spesa di circa ducati 50 mila app[resso] a San Lorenzo, la libreria et la sacrestia in compagnia di quella gia [fatta] et nome hara di cappella, dove molti sepolcri da sepellirvi li ante nati mancati di vita che sono in deposito: Lorenzo et Iuliano nostri padri et Iulian[o et] Lorenzo frategli et nipoti.' The deceased enumerated by the cardinal are Lorenzo the Magnificent, father of Pope Leo, his brother Giuliano, father of the cardinal, Giuliano the brother of Leo, dead, as has been seen, in 1516, and Lorenzo, Leo's nephew, who had died only weeks earlier.

155   See *Carteggio* III, p. 57, no. DCXXVIII. But, in an earlier letter of April 1523 to
      Fattucci, Michelangelo informs him that Cardinal Giulio had himself declared
      that, if he lived, he would proceed with the façade project. See *Carteggio* II,
      p. 366, no. DLXXI: 'Mi disse ... che, se e' vivea, che farebbe anchora la facciata,
      e che lasciava a Domenico Boninsegni la chomessione di tucti e' danari che
      bisogniavano.' If the account is true, the assurance must have been made in
      September 1521, just prior to Cardinal Giulio's departure for Lombardy.

156   *Carteggio* III, p. 339, no. DCCCXXII. Figiovanni explains that the exterior of the
      tribune must be of marble: 'et così el di fuora di marmo per unirlo con la fac-
      ciata, quando mai l'uno e l'altro s'avessi a fare'. In the event, the tribune was
      confined to the interior of the church. There are also one or two allusions to
      the possible resumption of the project in Vasari's *Vite*. Perhaps the most telling
      is the passage in the Life of Tribolo, where he writes that Pope Clement was
      anxious for the sculptor to go to Florence to finish, under Michelangelo's direc-
      tion, the sculpture in the New Sacristy and then 'tutti potessero, mediante
      l'acquisito fatto sotto la disciplina di tant'uomo, finir similmente la facciata di
      San Lorenzo'. The relevance of the passage was pointed out by Barocchi in Vasari
      1962, III, p. 757. For the text, see now Vasari 1987, V, p. 204.

157   *Carteggio* II, pp. 218–21, no. CDLVIII.

158   *Ricordi* 1970, pp. 97–102, nos. XCV to XCVIII.

159   *Carteggio* II, p. 220. Referring to Cardinal Giulio, he writes: 'non gli mecto a[n]
      chora a chonto el tempo di tre anni che io ò perduti in questo; non gli mecto
      a chonto che io sono rovinato per decta opera di San Lorenzo; non gli mecto
      a chonto el vitupero grandissimo dell'avermi chondocto qua per far decta opera
      e poi tormela, e non so perché anchora'. For an assessment of the profit or loss
      Michelangelo incurred over the façade project, see Hatfield 2002, pp. 138–41.
      Such an assessment cannot, of course, calculate what in effect is incalculable,
      the value of the time lost by the artist over two and a half years. Michelangelo
      adds bitterly that marble he had quarried for the façade was taken by Cardinal
      Giulio and the cathedral Opera for repairing the cathedral, work that began in
      October 1520; Cambi, *Istorie*, in *Delizie*, XXII, p. 173. The complaint may not
      be simply a paranoid outburst by the wounded artist. The Opera addressed a
      letter to Lorenzo Strozzi in early February 1520, just a few weeks prior to
      Michelangelo's own, stating that they have heard that quarrymen recently sent
      to Pietrasanta have availed themselves of marble previously quarried by Michele
      di Pippo and Michelangelo, which is contrary to their wishes: 'secondo inten-
      diamo, gli scarpellini nuovamente mandati costì si vagliono de'marmi chavati
      non solo di Michele ma etiam di Michelagnolo, la qual cosa è contro alla nostra
      intentione e volontà, che non par giusto si vaglino di quell d'altri'. See Settesoldi
      1994, p. 136, no. LV.

160   The sentence reads: 'Dipoi, in questo tempo medesimo, el Cardinale per chom-
      messione del Papa mi fermò che io non seguissi più l'opera sopra dicta, perché

dicevono volermi torre questa noia del chondure e' marmi, e che me gli volevano dare in Firenze loro e far nuova chonventione.' What does this last reference mean? Wilde 1955, p. 66, believed that it referred to a new agreement relating to the façade. But it is difficult to reconcile this interpretation with what the artist put down in the *ricordi* preceding the composition of this letter; see the following note. An alternative interpretation could be that this is Michelangelo's reference to the project for the chapel.

161   *Ricordi* 1970, p. 102. The text reads: 'Ora papa Leone, forse per fare più presto la sopra decta facciata di San Lorenzo che l'allogazione che gli avea facta a·mme, e chosì parendo ancora a·mme, d'achordo mi libera.'

162   For the letter, first published by Giovanni Bottari in the eighteenth century and subsequently lost sight of, see now Waldman 2004, Document 587. The passage most relevant for the present concerns reads: 'E mi ricordo quando stavo con Papa Leone, Sua Santità in Firenze mandò per Rafaello da Urbino e per Bun Aroto [*sic*], e choncluse la faciata di San Lorenzo, e si terminò che facessi e modelli delle istatue e delle istorie grande come li marmi, e sotto la sua guida si facessino lavorare a più giovani. E sappi, Vostra Excellentia, che la causa che lui nonn·à mai fornita nisuna opera di marmo è solo stato perché nonn·à mai voluto aiuto di persona, per non fare de' maestri, perché la S.ta Casa non abia queste memorie, e così mi di disse la felice memoria di Papa Clemente, che non lo potette mai dispore a·ffare questi modelli grandi.'

163   After referring to the different artists involved, Vasari writes: 'Laonde Michele Agnolo si risolse di fare un modello e non volere altro che lui, in tal cosa, superiore o guida dell' architettura. Ma questo non volere aiuto fu Cagione che né egli né altri operasse, e che quei maestri, disperati, ai loro soliti esercizii si ritornassero.' See Vasari 1987, VI, p. 51. Vasari's remarks about the war in Lombardy as a cause of the shortfall of finance for the façade are chronologically confused. The discrepancy between the explanation offered in the Michelangelo *Vita* and that quoted here suggests that different authors were involved and that, for this reason, the conflicting accounts were never reconciled in the published text.

164   Vasari 1987, V, pp. 247–8. He writes of the financing of projects of the façade and New Sacristy: 'Delle spese di queste opere teneva i conti e ne era capo Domenico Boninsegni. Costui tentò Michelagnolo a far compagnia seco segretamente sopra del lavoro di quadro della facciata di San Lorenzo; ma ricusando Michelagnolo e non piacendogli che la virtù sua s'adoperasse in defraudando il Papa, Domenico gli pose tanto odio, che sempre andava opponendosi alle cose sue per abbassarlo e noiarlo: ma ciò copertamente faceva.'

165   Vasari's remarkable charge was accepted by Ramsden 1963, I, Appendix 14, but has been treated with justified caution elsewhere; see Luzzati in *DBI*, XV, pp. 252–3, and Elam 1992a, p. 114, note 62. It is also totally at odds with Michelangelo's own remarks of 1523, cited above in note 155. Nothing in the subsequent correspondence lends credence to the charge. For example, in late 1519

Sebastiano was hopeful that Buoninsegni would be a godparent for his newly born son; see *Carteggio* II, p. 206, no. CDXLVIII. For the relations between Buoninsegni and Michelangelo, see the former's request to the artist for a frank appraisal of his prospective bride. Following the artist's lost response, he announces his imminent arrival in Florence 'per vedere se quella roba è sì buona quanto voi dite'. See *Carteggio* I, p. 325, no. CCLX.

CHAPTER EIGHT

1   The artist's *ricordo* of the receipt of the money survives; see *Ricordi* 1970, p. 22, no. XXI. For the letter sent from Rome confirming the transfer, see *Carteggio* I, p. 304, no. CCXLIII. Bonifazio Fazi, who had seen to the transfer, impresses on the artist how important the matter is: 'voi sapete quanto importa la chosa'.

2   *Carteggio* I, p. 313, no. CCLI. He urgently presses Michelangelo for news, since he has heard nothing.

3   In her monograph on the project (Panofsky 1991), Panofsky lists no fewer than sixty-six letters concerning it. Those most relevant are discussed below.

4   *Carteggio* II, pp. 40–41, no. CCCXI. Vari maintains tones of warm friendship, signing himself 'suo quanto fratello carissimo'. And throughout the correspondence, his evident attachment to Michelangelo survives. On the issue of the assistant, he writes: 'Sapessete farla sgrossare ad un altro de' vostri discipuli che possa continuare lo lavoro, et voi metterence l'ultima mano ad perfectione de quella, secundo se rechiede a vostre perfecte opere.'

5   *Carteggio* II, p. 112. The intervention of Cardinal Giulio seems to have been a consequence of discussions when the artist was briefly in Rome to sign the contract for the San Lorenzo façade in January 1518. We have to recall that the executors were now in breach of their obligations and that, in her will of 1512, Marta Porcari had set a deadline for the implementation of her wishes. In the event of failure to meet her terms, the money bequeathed for the altar was to go to two confraternities instead. For the issue, see Panofsky 1991, p. 43.

6   *Carteggio* II, pp. 129–30, no. CCCLXXXII. He writes: 'io muoio di dolore, e parmi essere diventato uno ciurmadore chontro a mia voglia'.

7   Vari asks for news so that he may sleep more easily and adds: 'Et se la figura lì non la havete fatta, almanco farete finire questa de Roma'.

8   For these two letters, see *Carteggio* II, p. 179, no. CDXXVI, and p. 184, no. CDXXX.

9   *Carteggio* II, p. 208, no. CDXLIX.

10 A number of those writing about the commission divined this without the evidence provided by the rediscovered first statue. See, for example, Hartt 1971, p. 215.

11 Dolce 1557, p. 254. The words are given to Pietro Aretino: 'chi vede una sola figura di Michelangelo, le vede tutte'.

12 Tolnay 1975–80, II, no. 179 recto. There are two rapid sketches for the statue on the sheet; in each the artist was concerned with the profile of the 'open' side of the statue.

13 *Carteggio* II, p. 229, no. CDLXIV.

14 *Carteggio* II, p. 230, no. CDLXV.

15 For these developments, see *Carteggio* II, p. 266, no. CDLXXXVII, for Sellaio's advice, and *Carteggio* II, p. 256, no. CDLXXIX, for the information of Sebastiano. Perhaps this rumour was, once more, the work of the unforgiving Jacopo Sansovino. Pietro Urbano, on his arrival in Rome, would report adversely on Sansovino's recently completed marble *Virgin and Child* in Sant'Agostino: see *Carteggio* II, p. 282, no. DI.

16 *Carteggio* II, p. 271, no. CDXCI.

17 *Ricordi* 1970, p. 105, no. CII. The cost of the shipment was $3^{1}/_{2}$ large florins.

18 *Contratti*, no. XXIII, p. 54.

19 *Carteggio* II, p. 102, no. CCCLX.

20 *Carteggio* II, pp. 222–3, no. CDLIX. Frizzi remained dissatisfied with the lighting. Writing to Michelangelo on 19 October, he expresses his view that it would have enjoyed better visibility in the place he had initially proposed, against one of the piers of the nave. He informs him that the chosen location is near the choir or 'cappella grande'; he explains that this is situated between Michelangelo's statue and the Chapel of the Sacrament on the farther side. If the executors were anxious to establish a link between the statue and this chapel, this would explain the fact, for which see Hirst 1988a, p. 68, that the sculpture is set up incorrectly, not conforming with the artist's own intentions. That this may have happened early is suggested by a similar placement of Taddeo Landini's copy in Santo Spirito in Florence. For Frizzi's letter, see *Carteggio* II, pp. 324–5, no. DXXXVII.

21 Pietro Urbano would write: 'volevano che Christo paghasse ghabella a entrare in Roma'; see *Carteggio* II, p. 305, no. DXXI. Those involved hoped that Cardinal Giulio would effect reimbursement.

22 The damage provoked by Urbano's maladroit intervention is described in Sebastiano's letter of 6 September 1521; he emphasizes damage to the right foot and the beard and nose; see *Carteggio* II, pp. 313–15, no. DXXVIII. Frizzi himself described the problems and asked for Michelangelo's permission to deal with them in a letter of the following day; *Carteggio* II, p. 317, no. DXXX.

23 *Carteggio* II, pp. 331, no. DXLII.

24 Vari first expressed his wish to have the abandoned figure in a letter of 14 November; *Carteggio* II, pp. 328–9, no. DXL.

25 See particularly his letter of 12 December; *Carteggio* II, pp. 334–5, no. DXLIV. He explains that many do not believe that Michelangelo has gone to the lengths of making a new statue.

26 See his letters of 4 and 12 January 1522: *Carteggio* II, pp. 339, no. DXLVII, and

p. 340, no. DXLVIII. Sellaio had reported the public unveiling of the *Christ* at Christmas 1521 in a letter of 27 December. *Carteggio* II, p. 338, no. DXLVI.

27 Vari wrote to Michelangelo with his request in no fewer than five surviving letters between March 1523 and 1526.

28 *Ricordi* 1970, p. 275, no. CCXLIX. The text was published by Gotti in 1875 and has been frequently cited subsequently, but seems not to have received the attention it deserves.

29 The statue has been designated a Man of Sorrows in much of the art historical bibliography. But one of the most important attributes of that subject, the crown of thorns, is absent. Still more damaging to this view is the observation of Lotz 1965, p. 148, that the mechanically executed wounds in the hands and feet are clearly not original and that the wound in the side is conspicuously missing. He concluded that Michelangelo's *Christ* 'ist nicht schmerzensmann, sondern Resurrectus', citing Vari's own words of 1532. We can also recall Vari's wish that the statue be unveiled at Easter. Writing to the artist in November 1518, he asks him to have the work ready for Easter of the following year, 'cioè a Pasqua di Risurexio'. In a further letter, he again emphasizes the need for speed to allow its installation at Easter, 'a ciò che a Pasqua sia messa in opera'. For these letters, see *Carteggio* II, p. 112, no. CCCLXVIII, and p. 271, no. CDXCI. For the usage of 'Pasqua di Risurexio', see Battaglia 1961–2002, XV, p. 916. Panofsky's further refinement that the work represents Christ as the New Adam does not seem necessary.

30 The source for this information is Pirro Ligorio. Lamenting the Dominican friar's wanton destruction of antiquities in both church and convent, he continues: 'non altrimenti che fecono al tempo del pontificato di Clemente VII al più bella statua del nostro Salvatore ala quale tagliarono il membro virile, et poi l'han coperto, non portando rispetto né al testamento di coloro che la feci on fare né a Cristo'. For this statement, contained in MS Canon. Ital. 138 of the Bodleian Library, Oxford, see Schreurs 2000, p. 393. If dependable, the passage explains the much-discussed covering up of Christ's genitals, and dates this to before the death of Pope Clement in September 1534. For the damage, see Tolnay 1948, pl. 69.

31 See Frey 1892, p. 129: 'è una cosa tanto ben fatta, che è maraviglia a vedere'. A statement to the effect that the statue is nowhere mentioned by Condivi, widespread in the bibliography, is incorrect; see Condivi 1998, p. 52.

32 For the French king's letter to Michelangelo, see *Carteggio* IV, p. 229, no. MLIV. Delivered by Francesco Primaticcio, Francis asks the artist to consign any works that are available to him, promising payment. He goes on to ask his permission to have casts made of both the *Pietà* and the Minerva *Christ*, 'affin che j'en puisse aorner l'une de mes chappelles, comme de chose que l'on m'a asseuré estre des plus exquises et excellentes en vostre art'. The artist replied on 26 April 1546; a draft, mostly in Donato Giannoti's hand, survives;

see *Carteggio* IV, p. 237, no. MLXI. It seems that, in the event, a cast was made only of the *Pietà*. For a review of the evidence, see Cox-Rearick 1995, pp. 313–14.

33 *Carteggio* II, p. 227, no. CDLXII.

34 The alleged illness of Michelangelo is referred to in a letter of 7 April from Pandolfo Pico da Mirandola to Isabella d'Este and in one of Marcantonio Michiel of 11 April; see respectively Shearman 2003, I, pp. 575 and 582. However, that the rumour was untrue is confirmed in a letter of Giovanni Gelessi to the artist of 22 April; he reports that news had circulated that 'voi eri malato grave'. See *Carteggio* II, p. 228, no. CDLXIII. He has heard from Sellaio that Michelangelo is well. One is reminded not only of how important news of Michelangelo was held to be, but also of the rumour that had circulated in 1509, that the artist had died.

35 *Carteggio* II, p. 227, no. CVLXII.

36 For the correspondence over the issue, see *Carteggio* II, pp. 206–7, no. CDXLVIII; pp. 212–13, no. CDLIII; p. 214, no. CDLIV; p. 215, no. CDLV; and p. 226, no. CDLXI. There survives among Michelangelo's papers an undated note of Sebastiano's, recording his outgoings and the payments relating to the project already made to him; see *Ricordi* 1970, p. 94, no. XCI.

37 Michelangelo's autograph draft is not dated, but the letter must have reached Rome by the end of June, given Sebastiano's reference to it on 3 July. For its text, see *Carteggio* II, p. 232, no. CDLXVI. For Sebastiano's letter, see *Carteggio* II, pp. 233–5, no. CDLXVII, which shows that, in midsummer of 1520, the issue of payment for his altarpiece had still not been settled.

38 In the draft, Michelangelo refers to himself as 'omo vile, povero e macto'. The most extravagant sentence reads: 'E quando paia a Vostra S[igniori]a inn·un mio pari gictar via el servitio, penso che, ancora nel servire e' macti, che rare volte si potrebbe trovare qualche dolceza, chome nelle cipolle, per mutar cibo, fa cholui che è infastidito da' chaponi.'

39 For one example of the burlesque nature of some of Bibbiena's letters, see Dovizi 1955–65, I, pp. 511–12, addressed to none other than Cardinal Giulio. Self-disparaging signatures are common, particularly in the long series of letters to Isabella d'Este; see, for example, Dovizi 1955–65, I, p. 242. The experienced Florentine Francesco Vettori described Bibbiena as 'uomo astutissimo e faceto', supremely acute and facetious. In fact, Bibbiena would not live to see the end of the year; he died on 9 November, an event accompanied by rumours that Pope Leo had had him poisoned.

40 The celebrated passage had been prompted by Sebastiano's claim that, with Michelangelo's help, he could perform miracles. Leo had replied: ' "Non dubito di questo, perché tutti vui havete imparato da lui." Et, per la fede è tra nui, Sua Santità me disse più: "Guarda l'opere de Rafaelo, che come vide le hopere de Michelagniolo, subito lasso la maniera del Perosino et quanto più poteva si

acostava a quella de Michelagnolo. Ma è teribile, come tu vedi; non si pol pratichar con lui." Et io resposi a Sua Santità che la teribelità vostra non noceva a persona, et che vui parete terribile per amor de l'importantia de l'opere grande havete'. See *Carteggio* II, p. 247, no. CDLXXIV.

41 *Carteggio* II, p. 253, no. CDLXXVII. Sebastiano informs Michelangelo of how esteemed he is by the pope and of his affection for him: 'io so in che conto vi tien el Papa, et quando parla de vui par rasoni de un suo fratello, quassi con le lacrime algli ochii; perché m'à decto a me vui sette nutriti insiemi, et dimostra conoscervi et amarvi, ma facte paura a ognuno, insino a' papi'.

42 Vasari, for example, would describe Bramante's architectural genius as 'terribile', meaning that it was awesome. But that cannot be Leo's meaning here. 'Terribile' was an epithet denoting intransigence employed for Pope Julius II. See, for example, the report of the Mantuan ambassador in Rome of 28 November 1505, where he refers to the pope's refusal to change his mind, 'maxime havendo sempre fatto professione de terribile'. For the passage, see Luzio 1909, p. 848.

43 *Carteggio* II, p. 244, no. CDLXXII. Buoninsegni's note comprises a single line hastily written in red chalk: 'Michelagnolo, noi abbiam nuove che Aginensis è morto.'

44 *Carteggio* II, p. 99, no. CCCLVII. He addresses the artist in the warmest tones.

45 See *Carteggio* II, pp. 125–6, no. CCCLXXIX.

46 See Sellaio's letter of 13 February 1519: *Carteggio* II, p. 160, no. CDIX. He reports that the cardinal has told him of Salviati's assurance: 'e dicemi Iachopo Salviati gl'à detto voi questa state farete per ogni modo 4 fighure'.

47 *Carteggio* II, p. 345, no. DLIII.

48 For Sellaio's presence in Florence, see *Carteggio* II, p. 251, no. CDLXXVI; p. 353, no. CDLXXVII; p. 254, no. CDLXXVIII; and p. 255, no. CDLXXIX.

49 The issue of when Michelangelo carved the four unfinished Accademia figures has been discussed extensively. Tolnay 1954, p. 114, even proposed for them a date after 1530. It has been plausibly suggested that work on the *Youthful Prisoner* and the *Bearded Prisoner* preceded that on the other two; see Echinger-Maurach 2009, among others. In other words, the artist worked on a pair at a time, as he had done with the *Prisoners* now in the Louvre. Wilde observed that, in conversation with Sebastiano del Piombo in 1531, Giulio de' Medici, now Pope Clement VII, revealed a familiarity with the figures and could even remember their attitudes; see *Carteggio* III, p. 345, no. DCCCXXXIII. But Giulio left Florence in April 1523, never to return. For this and other acute comments, see Wilde 1954, p. 12.

50 The situation following the death of the cardinal is described by Sebastiano in a letter of 27 October 1520; see *Carteggio* II, p. 252, no. CDLXXVII. Pope Leo had publicly stated that he did not wish to disturb the work going forward in Florence: 'Sua Santità dice non vi vol turbar de l'opere vostre da Firenze'. On the other hand, as Sebastiano explains, 'non voleva esser origine lui de pervertive

di questa opera', i.e., the tomb. His reluctance to get involved had been strengthened by rumours in Rome that Cardinal Leonardo had been poisoned.

51 See *Carteggio* II, p. 280, no. CDXCIX, and p. 284, no. DIII.

52 *Carteggio* II, pp. 274–5, no. CDXCIV. The letter bears no date, but the editors,
following indications of Poggi, propose the second half of February or early
March 1521. Deeply concerned about the pejorative comments Lodovico has
made, he reminds his father, when recently ill, that he has promised him every
support. His request for his father's forgiveness is not couched in very genial
terms and, once more, he recounts that he has been tried by father and the
other sons for thirty years: 'Voi m'avete pure sperimentato già trenta anni, voi
e' vostri figl[i]uoli, et sapete che io ò·ssempre pensato e factovi, quand'io ò
potucto, del bene. Chome andate voi dicendo che io v'ò chacciato via?'

53 *Carteggio* II, p. 275, note 3. Lodovico's note, written at the foot of Michelangelo's
letter, says that when his son made him go to Florence, 'mi chacciò e dettemi
delle busse'. If this is true, Michelangelo was behaving in the very manner he
had violently admonished in Giovan Simone as long ago as 1509.

54 *Carteggio indiretto* I, p. 194, no. 112. It has been noted that Lodovico was once
more living in Via Ghibellina, for an unspecified period, in 1523; see Hatfield
2002, p. 93, note 199.

55 *Carteggio* II, p. 360, no. DLXV.

56 During the row over Lodovico's covert holding on to Michelangelo's money
in 1510, his father had written: 'Io ò sempre pensato che Michelangniolo voglia
il suo per sé.' See *Carteggio indiretto* I, p. 25, no. 13.

57 Michelangelo had also spent money on improvements to the property in 1514;
see *Ricordi* 1970, pp. 7–11, nos. VII–VIII, and Hatfield 2002, p. 67.

58 *Carteggio* II, especially p. 367, no. DLXXI.

59 The point is raised by Ristori, who, in his introduction to the *Carteggio indiretto*,
carefully examined the events surrounding the arbitration of June 1523.

60 See Ristori in *Carteggio indiretto* I, pp. XXIff., and, in greater detail, Hatfield 2002,
pp. 90–93; the text of the notarial agreement is printed on pp. 473–7.

61 See *Carteggio* II, p. 371, no. DLXXV, and pp. 373–4, no. DLXXVII. The impression
left by the second letter is that the artist had lost all patience with Lodovico; it
ends on an exceptionally savage note, reminding him that one only dies once
and that one does not return to put things right: 'Abbiatevi cura, e guardatevi
da chi voi v'avete a guardare, ché e' non si muore più d'una volta, e non ci si
ritorna a rachonciar le chose male facte.' Michelangelo, however, did offer to
have the whole agreement rescinded if his father wished it. He had also
renounced any claim to the 400 florins he had given the family earlier.

62 For this series of letters to Lodovico from one of the two arbiters, Raffaello
Ubaldini, see *Carteggio Indiretto*, I, pp. 195–8 and 200–03, nos. 113–15 and 117–19.
It emerges that Lodovico had even thought of suing Michelangelo; Ubaldini
draws attention to the cost.

63 As quoted by Ubaldini, the artist has said: 'Io fo conto di nonn avere né padre né
   frategli né persona sia al mondo per me'; *Carteggio indiretto* I, p. 200, no. 117.

64 For this house situated on the Via dell'Ariento, just behind the New Sacristy,
   see Wallace 1994, pp. 104–5.

65 Wilde's conclusion (Wilde 1955, pp. 54ff.), that the sacristy was begun *ex novo*
   by Pope Leo and Cardinal Giulio, was confirmed by the appearance of Figiovanni's *ricordanza*, published in 1964 and discussed above. The argument was
   endorsed by Elam 1979, pp. 155ff. Its rejection by Saalman 1985 fails to meet the
   written evidence, to which can be added the statement by Cambi, *Istorie*, in
   Delizie, XXII, pp. 161ff., that the sacristy was begun by Pope Leo. For further
   evidence that the sacristy did not exist at an earlier date, see Burns 1979,
   pp. 145–54, and Reiss 1993.

66 For deep concerns in Rome about events that might follow Duke Lorenzo's
   death, see Sanudo 1879–1903, XXVI, cols 395 and 419.

67 Figiovanni's memorandum quotes Cardinal Giulio as saying: 'Noi siamo d'animo
   fare una spesa di circa ducati 50 mila app[resso] a San Lorenzo, la libreria et la
   sacrestìa in compagnia di quella già [fatta] et nome harà di cappella, dove molti
   sepolcri da sepellirvi li antenati mancati di vita che sono in deposito: Lorenzo
   et Iuliano nostri padri et Iulian[o et] Lorenzo frategli et nipoti'; see Corti 1964,
   p. 27.

68 A further insight of Wilde's confirmed that the initial plan was to build a replica
   of Brunelleschi's Old Sacristy. He realized that a list of calculations by an unidentified stonemason on a sheet in the Archivio Buonarroti was drawn up to
   cost a 'repeat' of the *pietra serena* membering of Brunelleschi's sacristy; Wilde
   1955, pp. 65–6; for a more recent transcription of the text, see *Ricordi* 1970,
   p. 96. The list is reproduced in Tolnay 1975–80, II, no. 179 verso. In the light of
   Figiovanni's *ricordanza*, the calculations and the accompanying ground plans of
   the chapel can now be dated in 1519 rather than 1520, as Wilde had suggested.
   The earlier date is confirmed by a document published in Elam 1979, p. 178.
   It can be added that studies for the second version of the Minerva *Christ* on a
   part of the same (now folded) sheet confirm the date of 1519; see Tolnay
   1975–80, II, no. 179 recto.

69 See Corti 1964, p. 28: 'Capomaestro della architettura l'unico Michelagnolo
   Simoni, el quale Iob pazienza havuto non harebbe con quello un giorno.'

70 No reference to a contract for the project has appeared; had one been made,
   the artist would probably have preserved a copy.

71 Corti 1964, p. 29. Figiovanni states that he was later ordered to destroy them
   by Pope Clement.

72 As had occurred with the financing of the façade, the money required for the
   chapel and the library was handled by the Pisa branch of the Salviati bank. For
   the role of the bank, see Wallace 1992b, pp. 3ff., and for a detailed publication
   of the material, Bardeschi Ciulich 1993, passim.

73   The periods spent by Giulio in Florence can be followed in Cambi, *Istorie*, in *Delizie*, XXII, pp. 144ff., 159ff., 176ff. and 183ff. He was there from May to October 1519, from February to early November 1520, and again from February to late September 1521, when he left to lead the war against the French in Lombardy. He was in Milan when Leo unexpectedly died in Rome in December 1521. He returned to Florence after the conclave that elected Adrian VI in January 1522, but left in July as legate to the Romagna. Subsequently back in Florence, he was ordered to come to Rome by Pope Adrian in April 1523 and never again returned to the city.

74   Sanudo 1879–1903, XXIV, col. 90.

75   Sanudo 1879–1903, XXVIII, col. 576: 'Il cardinale di Medici, suo nepote, qual non è legitimo, à gran poder col papa, è huomo di gran maneggio, ha grandissima autorità; tamen sa viver col Papa di cosse da conto; hora si ritrova a Fiorenza a governar quella città. Il cardinal Bibbiena è apresso assai dil Papa, ma questo Medici fa el tutto'. A full assessment of Cardinal Giulio's career cannot be attempted here. There is a list of his preferments in Salvini 1782; he enjoyed the income of no less than ten bishoprics, as well as that from the archbishopric of Florence.

76   Writing to Buoninsegni, he had declared: 'Io sono qua chome suo omo'. See *Carteggio* II, p. 10, no. CCLXXXVI.

77   *Carteggio* III, pp. 194–5, no. DCCXXII. Clement signed the letter with the single initial 'I', referring to his baptismal name. Contemporaries referred to the fact that he had originally wished to be called Julius III on his election.

78   For a review of the evidence, see Reiss 1992, pp. 105–13.

79   His grasp of architectural details revealed in the correspondence concerning the chapel and the library is familiar. But the same understanding could extend also to sculpture. In July 1532 he instantly understood what had actuated the artist's decision to come to Rome in August despite the threatening heat; the heat facilitated modelling in clay. As reported by Sebastiano, he had remarked: 'che molto meglio et più presto si conduce l'opere di terra di cimatura per il caldo che per il fredo'. See *Carteggio* III, p. 420, no. DCCCLXXXI.

80   For a fine account of his career, see A. Prosperi in *DBI*, XXVI, pp. 237–59.

81   See Vettori 1972, pp. 187, 207 and 245.

82   Cerretani described Giulio as 'savio, di soma gravistà et patienza, di poche et rare parole, di ingeno grande, giuditio buono, et universale, sollecito, patiente d'ogni disagio, cauto et costumato, di buona giustitia et religione il che aiutava assai il mancar di Giuliano'. The passage, in his Sommario delle cose di Firenze, Biblioteca Nazionale, Florence, II.IV.19, fol. 18 verso, is quoted by Moncallero 1953, p. 331, and Reiss 1992, p. 134.

83   See above, p. 324, n. 129.

84   For the bizarre appearance of the exterior of the drum, see Tolnay 1948, pl. 1.

Wilde 1955, p. 60, proposed that there had been a major change in planning the chapel's elevation, a suggestion contested by Elam 1979, pp. 165–7, on the basis of documents concerning the ordering and reordering of the stone for the architectural membering. For a different proposal, retaining the idea of a change of plan, see Joannides in Androsov and Baldini 2000, p. 122. It is difficult to accept that the anomalies of the exterior of the drum were intended from the start. To do so would be to indict the artist of professional ineptitude.

85   The text, surviving in the Archivio di Stato in Florence, was first published by A. F. Gori in his notes in the edition of Condivi's *Vita* published in 1746, pp. 111–15, and reprinted in Gotti 1876, II, pp. 82–4. For the episode, see especially Kristellar 1956, pp. 287–336. It may have been Bartolommeo Cerretani, one of the signatories, who approached the artist. In his *Ricordi* (Cerretani 1993, p. 212), he claims that he often talked with Michelangelo and actually watched him at work.

86   'Io Michelagnolo Schultore il medesimo a Vostra Santità suplicho, offerendomi al DIVIN POETA fare la Sepultura sua chondecente, e in loco onorevole in questa Cictà.'

87   There has been some confusion over the number of windows made for Palazzo Medici by Michelangelo. That they were three is correctly affirmed by Bulst 1990, p. 105, and his note 88.

88   For this misunderstood passage, see Vasari 1987, VI, p. 52. And for a fuller discussion of the confusion, see Hirst 2004b.

89   For the two letters, see *Carteggio* II, pp. 267 and 268, nos. CDLXXXVIII and CDLXXXIX. In the latter, Buoninsegni writes: 'Anchora, Sua Signoria reverendissima à inteso chome el modello è finito e ne à avuto piaciere assai, e non m'à ache detto dove lui vogl[i]a che si metta. Farò d'intenderlo e ve ne darò aviso, benché penso che di chorto saremo chostà.'

90   A letter to Michelangelo from a friend in Rome shows that the bearer was a close collaborator of Giovanni da Udine, Domenico da Forlì, who is described as on his way to Florence to work for Cardinal Giulio. It is dated 22 September 1521; see *Carteggio* II, p. 319, no. DXXXII. Giovanni's own arrival in Florence is not dated.

91   The issue is discussed by Vasari only in his Life of Baccio d'Agnolo of 1568; see Vasari 1987, IV, p. 613.

92   For a recent account of Michelangelo's involvement, see Nova in Millon and Magnago Lampugnani 1994, pp. 596–7.

93   For this perception, see Saalman 1975, pp. 374–80.

94   For the fragment, first published in 1967, see *Carteggio* II, p. 259, no. CDLXXXII.

95   For the correspondence concerning the project for a centralized monument, see three letters of Buoninsegni to the artist, of 14, 17 and 28 December 1520; *Carteggio* II, pp. 264–5, no. CDLXXXVI; p. 267, no. DLXXXVIII; and pp. 268–9,

no. CDLXXXIX. The cardinal's idea for a square monument, pierced by passages with his own tomb at ground level in the centre, was inspired by antique monuments; for a conspicuous surviving example in the Forum Boarium in Rome, see Nash 1968, I, pp. 504–5. Two arches of this kind had been erected for Pope Leo's entry into Florence in 1515, one of them attributed to Antonio da Sangallo the Elder, the putative protector of the young Giulio de' Medici. For the arches, see Ciseri 1990, pp. 91ff. and 106ff.; and Reiss 1992, pp. 134–5.

96   The abandonment of the centralized tomb allowed for the far more ambitious composition of the chapel that will be discussed at a later point; see p. 189. For analyses of the drawings for the centralized monument, see Wilde 1955, pp. 59ff., and for a recent reassessment, Joannides 2000, pp. 105–31. They are well reproduced in Tolnay 1975–80, II.

97   *Ricordi* 1970, p. 105, no. CIII, and p. 106, no. CIV. In the latter he writes: 'Andai a Charrara e là stecti circha venti dì, e• llà feci tucte le misure di decte sepulture di terra e disegniate in carta'. In other words, Michelangelo left not only drawings but also clay models for the figure sculpture.

98   The earlier of the two contracts is dated 22 April 1521. Michelangelo ordered approximately 200 *carrate* of marble from four suppliers whom he had already employed for marble for the San Lorenzo façade in 1517. There was to be sufficient marble to allow the carving of at least three statues as well as marble for the fabric of the tombs. The suppliers received a down payment of 100 large gold ducats and promised to have the material ready for the artist within the next eighteen months, a time span that implies delivery in Florence. See *Contratti*, no. LXVIII, pp. 170–75. The second agreement was drawn up on the following day, 23 April, with two marble workers who were paid 50 ducats and were to supply approximately 100 *carrate* within a year. A block for Michelangelo's projected statue of the Virgin, 'una figura di Nostra Donna a sedere', is explicitly prescribed in the text. In the case of both contracts, Michelangelo is obliged to accept the marble quarried even in the event that the project is suspended or cancelled by Cardinal Giulio, a clause reflecting the recent troubled history of the façade.

99   *Carteggio* II, p. 264, no. CDLXXXVI.

100 *Carteggio* II, p. 292, no. DX.

101 For Stefano, see especially Colnaghi 1928, pp. 164–5, who notes his previous experience as an architect, and Wallace 1994, p. 83. A few years later Michelangelo was having problems with him, as we learn from a letter to Piero Gondi. If he sacks him without apparent justification, he will be denounced by the *piagnoni* as a traitor, an ironical usage of the term adopted for Savonarola's followers. See *Carteggio* III, pp. 27–8, no. DCVIII. However, he would entrust to Stefano the actual construction of the chapel lantern.

102 For an engaging account of the event, see Elam 1979, p. 166.

103   *Carteggio* II, p. 292, no. DX. This is the earliest letter of Fattucci to survive and shows that he has been on friendly terms with the artist for some time. Fattucci would become the chief spokesman of Giulio de' Medici as cardinal and subsequently as pope, but his concerns for the artist's well-being were extensive; in this letter he expresses his anxiety over the delay in the arrival of the Minerva *Christ* in Rome. Biographical details concerning Fattucci are hard to find, but it can be stated that he was seventeen years younger than the artist. For his birth date of 21 August 1492, see Archivio dell'Opera di Santa Maria Fiore, Battesimi Maschi, 1482—92, fol. 73 recto. Fattucci died in July 1559; see Florence, Biblioteca Nazionale Centrale, Poligrafo Gargani 785, scheda 266. He had made his will in May.

104   For Benti's letters, see *Carteggio* II, p. 296, no. DXII, and p. 298, no. DXV.

105   *Ricordi* 1970, p. 106, no. CIV. The journey must have been slow, for his youthful companion travelled on foot.

106   *Ricordi* 1970, p. 106, no. CIV.

107   *Carteggio* II, p. 320, no. DXXXIII.

108   *Carteggio* II, p. 327, no. DXXXIX.

109   *Carteggio* II, p. 322, no. DXXXV. The text is a fragment of a draft for a letter now lost. It contains a remarkable expression of devotion to Cardinal Giulio, where he declares that he is ready to sacrifice all for him when required: 'Domenicho, io sono parato ogniora a• mmectere la persone e la vita, quando [bisogna]ssi, per el chardinale de Medici'. But he adds that he is completely out of funds.

110   *Carteggio* II, p. 332, no. DXLIII. Topolino's stay at Carrara would be protected and his presence there became of critical importance.

111   For a lucid account of Leo's financial problems and the desperate expedients he resorted to in attempting to resolve them, see Bullard 1980, pp. 199—28. The crisis provoked by Leo's death was particularly grave for the Florentine bankers in Rome. Bernardo Bini, for example, familiar from his role as paymaster for the della Rovere tomb, was gravely jeopardized by numerous unsecured loans. Adverse criticism of Leo was widespread; for Guicciardini's indictment, see his *Storia d'Italia* (Guicciardini 1971, IV, pp. 1545—5).

112   *Ricordi* 1970, pp. 114ff., no. CXVI.

113   *Carteggio* III, p. 31, no. DCX. The artist declined to allow Lunetti to make the drawing and his own was sent to Rome and subsequently returned to Florence. For the sheet, see Hirst 1988b, pp. 74—5, no. 30. The tiny addition of figures in one of the rectangles represents the scene of the *Sacrifice of Abraham*, and it is perhaps not coincidental that a large drawing of this subject survives in the Casa Buonarroti, 70F recto. See Tolnay 1975—80, II, no. 183.

114   *Carteggio* III, p. 131—2, nos. DCLXXXVII and DCLXXXVIII. The date of early 1525 ascribed to the two drafts in the *Carteggio* is in conflict with the traditional dating of 1524, which is supported by payments of early 1524 to Piloto for his work

on the 'palla', published by Gronau 1911, p. 66, evidence that eluded the editors of the Carteggio. It was republished in Vasari 1962, III, p. 793. It may be useful to note that Gronau's contribution was omitted in Steinmann and Wittkower 1927.

115   Gronau 1911, pp. 66ff.; Elam 1979, pp. 179–80, Document 9; and Wallace 1992a, p. 8 note 6.

116   For Giulio's movements in this period, see A. Prosperi in *DBI*, XXVI, pp. 244ff.

117   *Carteggio* II, p. 366–7, no. DLXXI. Michelangelo's dependability in this letter to Fattucci is open to question, but it may have been the case that serious financial constraints followed Leo's death in late 1521. Evidence for renewed substantial funding for the chapel appears to date from only after Giulio had succeeded Adrian VI as pope in November 1523. From April to October 1524, however, expenditure was impressive; see Gronau 1911, p. 66, and Wallace 1992a, pp. 6ff.

118   *Ricordi* 1970, p. 123, no. CXVIII.

119   It has frequently been proposed that the architecture of Duke Lorenzo's tomb preceded that of Giuliano's on the grounds that it displays more decorative detail; see, for example, Tolnay 1948, p. 55. But *ricordi* of the artist first published by Bardeschi Ciulich in 1970 show that work went on on both at the same time; see *Ricordi* 1970, p. 134, no. CXXIV; p. 139, no. CXXX; and pp. 142–3, no. CXXXII. One tomb was evidently in place by June 1526, if we can trust Fattucci, and the construction of the other is imminent; see *Carteggio* III, p. 227, no. DCCLII. That one was still awaiting assembling in late November 1526 is evident from the correspondence; see *Carteggio* III, p. 245, no. DCCLXIV.

120   *Carteggio* III, p. 1, no. DLXXXIX. He writes: 'Arete inteso chome Medici è facto papa, di che mi pare si sia rallegrato tucto el mondo; ond'io stimo che qua, cirche l'arte, si farà molte chose.' The rejoicing in Florence, however, was not universal; see the remarks of Cambi, *Istorie*, in *Delizie*, XXII, p. 246.

121   Piloto had not been told of Michelangelo's intentions: *Carteggio* III, p. 3, no. DXCI.

122   *Carteggio* III, p. 12, no. DXCVI.

123   For an initial reference to the purchasing of materials for models, dated 8 March 1524, see *Ricordi* 1970, p. 122, no. CXVII. For the protraction of the work, see *Ricordi* 1970, p. 158, no. CXLIX.

124   *Carteggio* III, p. 214, no. DCCXLIII.

125   For its original scale, see Bartolommeo Ammannati's letter of 1583, quoted in Tolnay 1948, p. 147.

126   For the fact, and a fine assessment of the models' making, see O'Grody 2001, especially pp. 36ff.

127   See O'Grody 2001, p. 37.

128   *Ricordi* 1970, p. 124, no. CXVIII. Just prior to 27 October he had the block moved to San Lorenzo from the workshop on the Via Mozza, 'che mi serve per una figura di quelle che vanno in su' chassoni delle sepulture decte che io

fo'. He gives the measurements as 4 *braccia*, or 232 centimetres in length, $1\frac{1}{8}$ *braccia*, or 65.5 centimetres, in depth, and $1\frac{2}{3}$ *braccia*, or just over 96 centimetres, in height. He adds that it has been slightly worked. This very same block is drawn on one of the sheets of the *quaderno* discussed above, recording delivery of marble for the tomb of Julius II; the measurements of the drawing agree exactly with those given in his *ricordo*; the sheet in question is Archivio Buonarroti, I, 82, fol. 230, reproduced in Tolnay 1975—80, III, no. 474 recto.

129   That this Via Mozza block was employed to carve the *Day* was proposed by Wilde 1954, pp. 15—16, note 3, and was accepted in Hirst 1988a, p. 62. The identification, however, was questioned by Lavin 1965, pp. 380—81.

130   *Carteggio* III, pp. 131—2, nos. DLXXXVII and DCLXXXVIII, unconvincingly dated to 1525 by the editors, following Poggi. Mad and bad as he is, if his plans for the marble had been followed, he would have had it by now.

131   *Carteggio* III, p. 89—90, no. DCL. He expresses his belief that the marble will never arrive: 'non credo che é veng[n]ino mai'. In a letter of August, however, Topolino will report that the marble for the four *Times of Day* will soon be to hand: 'io spero che noi aveno in pochi dì marmi per le figure nude.' *Carteggio* III, p. 102, no. DCLXI.

132   The cardinal's letter has not been found. For Lucrezia d'Este Malaspina's reply, see *Carteggio indiretto* I, p. 189, no. 107, evidently forwarded from Rome to the artist and now in the Archivio Buonarroti.

133   *Carteggio* III, p. 97, no. DCLVII. Both they and Topolino, in a subsequent letter, ibid., pp. 98—9, no. DCLVIII, refer to the fact that the marble quarried at Polvaccio has come from the very location where the artist had found his marble for the *Pietà* of 1497—8. For the fame of Polvaccio marble, which had been employed for Trajan's Column, see Klapisch-Zuber 1969, p. 74, note 59. Bandinelli, no friend of Michelangelo, is reported to have declared that, of all the marble ever delivered from Carrara, the most beautiful was that employed in the New Sacristy: 'Io credo che i più bei Marmi che fuesser mai cavati da Carrara sien quegli che Michel Agnolo mirabilissimo ha lavorati nella sagrestia di San Lorenzo: e principalmente, que due capitani sopra le sepulture.' See Doni 1552—3, Seconda Parte, pp. 46—7; reprinted in Vasari 1962, III, p. 994.

134   *Carteggio* III, p. 98, no. DCLVIII.

135   See, for example, Tolnay 1948, pp. 172ff.

136   *Carteggio* III, p. 76, no. DCXL.

137   *Carteggio* III, pp. 227—8, no. DCCLII: 'Io lavoro el più che io posso, e infra quindici dì faro chominciare l'altro chapitano'.

138   *Carteggio* III, p. 35, no. DCXIV. It was in this letter that Fattucci refers to a formula for the making of stucco gleaned by Giovanni da Udine from Vitruvius, which he has sent in a different letter.

139   For Vasari's celebrated encomium, where Michelangelo is extolled for having broken the prescriptive rules of the past, see Vasari 1987, VI, pp. 54—5. For an

assessment of the corner tabernacles, see Ackerman 1961, I, p. 31, who rightly stresses the stylistic change from the architectural language of the tombs, and for a fine analysis, Portoghesi 1966, p. 213, who provides an appreciation of the dialectic between architecture and sculpture. Even the tabernacles were subject to delays, in part owing to Michelangelo's 'memoriale', his instructions having gone astray. See Fattucci's letter in *Carteggio* III, p. 133, no. DCLXXXIX.

140   Michelangelo writes: 'Le quatro figure in su' chassoni, le quatro figure in terra che sono e' fiumi, e' dua chapitani e la Nostra Donna che va nella sepoltura di testa sono le figure che io vorrei fare di mia mano: e di queste n'è chominciate sei'. He adds that the other figures are less important and can be carved by others. Thus, some delegation of execution was already envisaged at this point, well before the issue of collaboration re-emerged after 1530. For the text, see *Carteggio* III, pp. 227–8, no. DCCLII.

141   Vasari would record the old artist's maxim in the context of the Del Monte family chapel in San Pietro in Montorio. He quotes him as saying: 'dove vanno figure di marmo, non ci vuole essere altra cosa'. See Vasari 1987, VI, p. 82, and for fine comments on his progressive abandonment of decoration, Schottmüller 1928, especially pp. 229ff.

142   Michelangelo did not always find Francesco's work up to standard; for his complaint, see *Ricordi* 1970, p. 150, no. CXLI, and pp. 155–6, no. CXLVII.

143   See *Ricordi* 1970, *ad indicem*, under the name of Silvio detto il Pisano.

144   Vasari 1987, IV, p. 259. Two unfinished marble trophies for one of the tombs were also begun by Cosini. For discussion of all these aspects of the chapel's decoration, see Prater 1979, especially pp. 107–9, 113–17 and 129–32.

145   The text, with capitals and punctuation added, reads: 'e Dì e la Nocte parlano e dichono: Noi abiamo chol nostro veloce chorso chondocta alla morte el ducha Giuliano; e ben giusto che e' ne facci vendecta chome fa. E la vendecta e questa: che avendo noi morto lui, lui chosì morto a tolta la luce a noi e chogli ochi chiusi a serrato e' nostri, che non risplendor più sopra la terra. Che arrebbe di noi dunche facto, mentre vivea?' For the text, written on Casa Buonarroti 10A recto, see Tolnay 1975–80, II, no. 201 recto, and Girardi 1960, pp 8 and 166–7, and Hughes 1981, pp. 202ff. Following Frey 1897, pp. 13 and 313, Hughes has argued that the lines were written with the composition of a poem in mind. Giuliano de' Medici had himself written a poem on the destructive power of time; see Battisti 1966, pp. 517ff. Metaphors of light extinguished had been repeatedly employed in praise of the Medici family; for the text of Marcello Virgilio Adriani's funeral oration for the dead Giuliano, see McManamon 1991, particularly pp. 15–20, where he refers to its anticipation of imagery in the chapel. For the image of closed eyes in Michelangelo's text, see also the fact observed in Gilbert 1971, p. 404, that the eyes of the dukes lack pupils.

146   Condivi 1998, p. 41. To strengthen the allusion to devouring time, the artist had planned to carve a mouse that ceaselessly consumes, like time itself, although

whether intended for the *Day* or the *Night* is not made clear. For an engaging discussion, see Panofsky 1964, pp. 242–51.

147   Since the passage is more frequently cited than quoted in Italian, it is worth adding here. Martelli writes that the artist 'non tolse dal Duca Lorenzo, ne dal Signor Giuliano il modello apunto come la natura gli avea effigiati e composti, ma diede loro una grandezza una proportione un decoro una gratia uno splendore quell gli parea che più lodi loro arrecassero, dicendo che di qui à mille anni nessuno non ne potea dar cognitione che fossero altrimenti, di modo che le genti in loro stessi mirandoli ne rimarrebbero stupefatti.' See Niccolò Martelli, 'Il primo libro delle lettere', Florence, 1546, p. 49 recto; Steinmann and Wittkower 1927, pp. 240–41; and Vasari 1962, III, p. 993. The letter was written in July 1544 and shows that the anomalies in the characterization of the two dukes were noted relatively early and does not strengthen the argument proposed by Grimm in the nineteenth century that the identities of the *capitani* were confused, a thesis revived in Trexler and Lewis 1981, pp. 93–160. Their proposal that Benedetto Varchi gave authority to the mis-identification in 1547 is not credible. If the passage reflects remarks of the artist himself, which is plausible, Martelli's informant is likely to have been Niccolò Tribolo, involved in the chapel before Michelangelo's final departure for Rome in 1534 and the artist chosen by the master to make statues of *Heaven* and *Earth* for Giuliano's tomb, work never completed. Two years after Martelli's letter, he arranged the placement of the *Times of Day* on the tombs; see Aschoff 1967, p. 136. Tribolo was a close friend and neighbour of Martelli; see Doni 1552–3, Ragionamento Secondo, p. 26.

148   For this issue, see Hatfield 2002, pp. 153–4, who points out that the artist did not receive his salary on a regular basis in the period between the death of Pope Leo and the election of Giulio as Pope Clement VII.

149   *Carteggio* III, p. 12, no. DXCVI.

150   *Carteggio* III, p. 22, no. DCIV. Fattucci had declared early in 1524 that the artist's decision to ask for just 15 ducats a month for his salary was shameful, 'una vergognia'.

151   After reflection, the artist wrote to Spina on 29 August. He has decided to take up his salary with the arrears he is owed and expresses his willingness to return to the house at San Lorenzo, already put at his disposal. See *Carteggio* III, p. 103, no. DCLXII.

152   *Carteggio* III, p. 181, no. DCCXXIV.

153   Duke Francesco Maria had an audience with Pope Adrian on 20 March. For the new pope's sense of justice, devoutness and austere lifestyle, see the still unsurpassed account in Pastor-Mercati 1944–63, IV, pp. 31ff., and for the duke's stay in Rome, where he was lodged in the Cancelleria, see Sanudo 1879–1903, XXXIV, cols 54ff., perhaps an uncomfortable choice given his hatred of the Medici. Nevertheless, at this moment in May 1523, an observer would emphasize

Cardinal Giulio's standing in the Curia. Notwithstanding Leo's death, Giulio 'è il primo cardinale e personagio di quella corte'. The number of those seeking his patronage is emphasized, and it is stated that four or five cardinals wait upon him every day: 'Ogni dì vi va 4 et 5 cardinali, si indica poi questo sarà il papa.' See Sanudo 1879–1903, XXXIV, col. 221.

154   For comments relating to this highly significant deadline, see pp. 143–4 above.

155   For Perini's letter, see *Carteggio* II, p. 342, no. DL, and for Michelangelo's, ibid., p. 343, no. DLI. Perini wrote again in July; see *Carteggio* II, p. 352, no. DLIX, and p. 353, no. DLX. Michelangelo had written that he wanted to be informed of everything because it was important to him, 'è cosa che m'importa'. As noted elsewhere, the artist's signature to his letter to Perini takes the form of rebus, a large M with two wings of angels, followed by the familiar symbol of three interlocking circles.

156   The birth date of Gherardo di Domenico Perini, 21 June 1503, can be found in Florence, Archivio di Stato, Tratte, Libri di Età, Leon d'Oro, c.428. Papini 1949, p. 243, wrongly claimed that he was only five years younger than the artist, actuated by a wish to exclude any sexual feelings on Michelangelo's part, and hence rebut insinuations in a letter of Pietro Aretino of 1545, to which we shall return. In his first edition of 1550, Vasari referred to Perini as Michelangelo's 'amicissimo', a description dropped in the Life of 1568. The bibliography on the three drawings Michelangelo made for him, now in the Uffizi, is extensive; for a brief discussion, see Hirst 1988a, p. 107. The note of intimacy on the artist's part is confirmed by a message he wrote on one of the drawings; see Tolnay 1975–80, II, no. 308 recto. The drawings were probably made a little earlier than the generally proposed date of 1525.

157   For Salviati's letter, see *Carteggio* II, pp. 355–6, no. DLXII. For della Porta and Staccoli, see Gronau 1906, pp. 1ff., and Vasari-Milanesi 1878–85, VII, p. 379. Almost no correspondence from the two survives from this period; Gronau found only one letter bearing on the issue of the tomb, from della Porta to Duke Francesco Maria, dated 6 September 1523; see his p. 4. He discusses the means to put pressure on the artist, to whom he refers with biting sarcasm as Santangelo.

158   *Carteggio* II, p. 367, no. DLXXI. He writes of Adrian's pronouncement: 'Che questo si facci, se Michelagniolo non vuole fare la sepultura.'

159   The coincidence of dates, overlooked in the literature, substantiates this conclusion. The legal settlement that Lodovico and the brothers were compelled to accept was arranged in June, just two months after he had written this deeply alarmed letter. The threat of having to return to the della Rovere everything that he had received would have jeopardized the carefully conducted property investments he had undertaken over many years. Nevertheless, at a later moment, he would be driven to contemplating such a move, as will be seen. The artist may also have nursed an especial dread of Francesco Maria della Rovere ever since the assassination of his own earlier protector, Alidosi.

160 The reason that provoked this strange behaviour eluded Hatfield 2002, pp. 154—5, but was noted by Wilde 1953, pp. 68—9. The issue of the Rome house was one irritant among many for the della Rovere.

161 *Carteggio* III, pp. 4—5, no. DXCII.

162 Michelangelo's draft letter to Fattucci of late December 1523, Carteggio II, pp. 7—9. In the text, he asserts that the money paid to him by the Fugger bank just prior to Julius II's death had been payment for the Sistine Chapel ceiling and not for the tomb, a claim that one man, at least, knew to be untrue, Domenico Buoninsegni. The point was made by Hatfield in his valuable survey of the financing of the tomb (Hatfield 2002, pp. 126—38). Buoninsegni's disbelief would subsequently provoke an indignant response from Fattucci: *Carteggio* III, p. 114, no. DCLXXII.

163 *Carteggio* III, pp. 12—13, no. DXCVI.

164 For a detailed discussion of these negotiations, see Hatfield 2002, pp. 126—38. He argued that a truer figure for Michelangelo's earnings from the unfinished project would have been close to 11,000 ducats.

165 The strategy to keep the della Rovere at bay can be followed in a whole sequence of letters from Fattucci of March 1523; see *Carteggio* III, p. 43, no. DCXIX; pp. 46—7, no. DCXXI; and pp. 50—51, no. DCXXIV. In the latest, Fattucci refers to handing the project to others, mentioning Jacopo Sansovino, with Michelangelo himself carving the group of the *Virgin and Child*. He argues that the figures already carved, and the marble assembled, could be valued at the huge sum of 9,500 ducats.

166 For Fattucci's reference to Pucci's assuming this protective role, see *Carteggio* III, p. 50, no. DCXXIV, and p. 52, no. DCXXV. One of the staunchest of Mediceans and a man of huge authority, there is a brief summary of his career in Hirst 2000c. He would subsequently press the artist for the design of his projected palace in Rome, seemingly in vain. Pucci was the only figure now left who had been involved with Julius's tomb from the time of the pope's death – other than Michelangelo himself.

167 *Carteggio* III, pp. 52—3, no. DCXXV. The artist's Roman friends repeatedly refer to the jeopardy of his reputation in the city.

168 *Carteggio* III, pp. 144—5, no. DCXCVII. The artist's wish to bring the problem to a close in this letter seems to have been inadequately weighed. Its text conveys a sense of suffering rarely matched in his correspondence. The verb *piatire* appears no fewer than four times.

169 *Carteggio* III, p. 156, no. DCCIV. The artist refers to his condition as 'mio malinchonico, o vero del mio pazzo'. One of his fellow diners was a soldier, a friend of Sebastiano called Chuio Dini, destined to die in the sack of Rome.

170 *Carteggio* III, p. 158, no. DCCVI, and p. 162, no. DCCX.

171 *Carteggio* III, p. 160, no. DCCVIII.

172 *Carteggio* III, pp. 164–5, no. DCCXII. Fattucci ends his letter: 'Et pensata a ogni altra chosa, acietto che pagare danari'.

173 *Carteggio* III, p. 166, no. DCCXIII. In this letter, Michelangelo alludes only to the tomb of Pius II, but a later letter of Fattucci refers to drawings of the tombs of both Paul II and Pius on their way from Rome; *Carteggio* III, pp. 186–7, no. DCCXXVIII, persuasively identified with drawings that still survive in Florence and Dresden; see Caglioti 2000b. For Pius II's tomb, see Poeschke 1990, p. 160, fig. 67, and for Paul II's, ibid., pp. 156–8, figs 60–62.

174 *Carteggio* III, pp. 173–4, no. DCCXIX. He writes: 'no si può lavorare cho le mani una chosa e chor ciereverllo una altro, e masimo di marmo'. Some of the incoherence of this extraordinary letter may, perhaps, be explained by its being not an original but a copy made by Michelangelo's devoted assistant, Antonio Mini.

175 *Carteggio* III, pp. 176–7, no. DCCXXI. Further correspondence touches on the artist sending a drawing for this new project from Florence.

176 *Carteggio* III, p. 238, no. DCCLIX.

177 *Carteggio* III, pp. 239–40. He writes: 'Se [Spina] à facto errore rispecto a' tempi in che noi si àno, l'ò facto io … che l'ò pregato importunamente che schriva.' This is one of the very few comments on current events we can find in this period of his life. The artist in fact is alluding to the notorious sack of the Borgo in Rome by the Colonna in September, a premonition of the much worse disaster that awaited the city in May 1527. The destruction had been extensive and Jacopo Salviati himself had been offered as a hostage.

178 *Carteggio* III, pp. 239–40. From the letter, it would appear that the Urbino court, or Girolamo Staccoli acting on the duke's behalf, had reacted in the worst possible fashion: 'Io ò avuto uno … ragnaglio a questi dì della chosa mia [i.e., the tomb] decta di chostà che m'à messo gran paura; e questo è la mala dispositione che ànno e' parenti di Iulio verso di me, e non senza ragione'. The shock he has undergone has led him to realize how utterly dependent he is on the pope: 'Questo m'à messo in gran travaglio e fammi pensare dov' io mi torverrei se'l Papa mi manchassi, che no potrai stare in questo mondo'.

179 This remarkable encounter has been referred to above, p. 183.

180 See, for example, Fattucci's letter of 17 September 1524, *Carteggio* III, p. 106, no. DCLXIV. He describes the pope's satisfaction that Michelangelo's enlistment of Baccio Bigio as his assistant will leave him more time to proceed with the chapel sculpture: 'voi potresti con più agio atendere alle fighure'. In a later one of 23 February 1526 (*Carteggio* III, p. 210, no. DCCXLI), he cites his patron's words of satisfaction that work on the library vestibule is now going forward: ' "Ringratiato sia Dio che la cosa debe essere in modo aviata che Michelagnolo non v'arà più a perdere tempo" Sì che, per queste parole et alter che e' disse, comprendo che Sua Santità non desidera altro che la fine di queste sepulture'. The pope had once more added his observation on the brevity of life.

181 For a lucid account of Cosimo's patronage of the library at San Marco, see

Ullman and Stadter 1972, pp. 3–32, and for an assessment of Michelangelo's
library, O'Gorman 1972, pp. 56ff.

182 See *Carteggio* IV, p. 17, no. CMX. Sebastiano writes: 'Circha a li banchi, Nostro
Signore vuole che siano tutti di noce sc[h]ietto [et] non si cura de spender tre
fiorini più, . . . pu[re] che siano a la cosimesca, cioé che se asimigliano a le opere
del magnifico Cosimo.' Clement, as early as August 1524, had expressed the
wish that the space between the desks should be the same as that in the San
Marco library, 'colla distantia l'uno dallo altro come quelli di Santo Marcho a
punto'. See *Carteggio* III, p. 95, no. DCLV.

183 See Parenti 1994, p. 21. He writes of Lorenzo: 'Avanti al suo morire affermò
colli amici restarli di 3 cose desiderio: d'avere visto sano el figlinolo suo cardinale,
finite le logge allo edificio suo del Poggio, e fatta la libreria, quale greca e latina
mirabile parava.' The passage was already cited by Frey 1907a, p. 54, note 1. For
sources for Lorenzo's ambition to create a library for the family books, see now
Kent 2004, pp. 8ff. That, in old age, Michelangelo had referred to Lorenzo's plans
to build a library is borne out in Condivi's text; see Condivi 1998, p. 11, and
Kent's comments, ibid., p. 8, and note 27, p. 14.

184 For the fortunes of the Medicean books following the fall of the regime of Piero
in 1494, see the richly documented account in Piccolomini 1874–5, passim.

185 For Cardinal Giovanni's letter to the prior of San Marco, see Piccolomini 1874–5,
XIX, pp. 275–6, and for the documents recording the sale, ibid., pp. 277–8.

186 *Carteggio* III, p. 12, no. DXCVI.

187 *Carteggio* III, p. 20, no. DCII. He writes: 'farò ciò che io sa prò, benché non sia
mia professione'. How far it had been the intention in Rome to give much of
the responsibility to Lunetti, as has been suggested, is difficult to judge. But it
must be recalled that, at this very time, Michelangelo was anxious to get rid of
Lunetti altogether; see n. 101 above.

188 In January 1524 Clement is reported to be ready to spend at least 3,000 ducats
a year in order to quicken the work: *Carteggio* III, p. 30, no. DCX.

189 See the letters of 10 March and 3 April 1524: *Carteggio* III, p. 41, no. DCXVIII,
and p. 57, no. DCXXVIII.

190 *Carteggio* III, p. 41, no. DCXVIII. Clement wants the decoration to be in low
relief, of a depth of not more than two or three fingers. The request shows that
he was not inflexibly bent on having the library itself vaulted, although mention
of this appears in the correspondence, and would have added a further fireproof
aspect to the building, comparable to the vaulting of the library at San
Marco.

191 A brief site plan by Michelangelo, no doubt made in preparation for a more
careful delineation that was sent to Rome, survives on two divided sheets in
the Casa Buonarroti, 9A verso and 10A verso. They are most easily legible in
Hirst 1988a, pls 190 and 191. For a comprehensive discussion of the genesis
of the plans for the library, see Salmon 1990, especially pp. 419ff. The

earlier schemes are abundantly discussed in the letters from Fattucci in Rome: *Carteggio* III, pp. 30ff. It has been persuasively proposed that another Casa Buonarroti drawing, 42A recto (Tolnay 1975–80, IV, no. 541 recto), represents an idea of the artist for the façade elevation of the *piazza* project; see Salmon 1990, p. 425.

192   *Carteggio* III, p. 57, no. DCXXVIII. Fattucci writes: 'vi dico come Nostro Signore dice che faciete la libreria dove voi volete, cioè supra le camere di verso la sacrestia vechia; et piacegli assai la vostra consideratione rispetto alla faccia di Santo Lorenzo'.

193   The need was particularly important in Florence, a city subject to periodic flooding.

194   As noted earlier, Baccio Bigio had meddled in the project for the façade of San Lorenzo and had been suspected of causing mischief in Rome. Fattucci reported the pope's hilarity in a letter of 29 April 1524, quoting him as saying that Baccio had played a ruinous role in building work at Poggio a Caiano. For Baccio's work for Alfonsina, widow of Piero de' Medici, see Reiss in Reiss and Wilkins 2001, especially pp. 129ff.

195   This important fact was first pointed out by Wittkower 1934, pp. 123–8.

196   *Carteggio* III, p. 186, no. DCCXXVIII. Clement's quip gains added point when it is recalled that the Gesuati, the foremost suppliers of pigments in Florence, were also manufacturers of stained glass; see Reiss 1992, p. 91, note 319.

197   *Carteggio* III, p. 194, no. DCCXXXII.

198   Wittkower 1934, pp. 135ff., contended that there was a change to the columnar articulation of the vestibule as late as February 1526. The proposal was rejected by Wilde 1953, p. 72, and Wilde 1978, p. 139. *Ricordi* of the artist relating to the delivery of stone for the vestibule interior and to the start of work, published in *Ricordi* 1970, no. CXCII, pp. 202–11, exclude Wittkower's hypothesis. Wilde argued that the heightening of the upper storey took place in 1533–4, but his reasons for proposing so late a date have remained elusive.

199   The 'sunken' columns of the vestibule have been among the most discussed of the artist's architectural innovations. The idea was not simply a reaction to the *ricetto*'s restricted space, for he had already considered recessed columns on two recent occasions: for the never executed double tomb for the two *magnifici* facing the altar in the sacristy, and for the library's exterior façade for the *piazza* project; see the drawings referred to in note 96 above.

200   For Fattucci's conveyal of Clement's proposal, see *Carteggio* III, p. 141, no. DCXCV: 'Circa al ricetto, quelle scale, se a v[o]I paresis vorrebe che di dua se ne facessi una che tenessi et pigliassi tutto il ricetto'.

201   *Carteggio* III, p. 177, no. DCCXXI: He had told Fattucci that 'solo per vedere le cose vostre aveva desiderio di venire a Firenze, fra uno anno o diciotto messi'.

202   He famously complained to the papal court that the library resembled a dovecote, in Fattucci's words to the artist, 'che voi fate la libreria in colonbaia'. See *Carteggio*

III, p. 108, no. DCLXVI. The remark is frequently ascribed to Figiovanni, but this cannot be correct, for he was elected prior of San Lorenzo only in the summer of 1534; see Moreni 1816, pp. 291–2. Figiovanni himself aroused deep antagonism at the papal court; at one point the pope would refer to him as 'una bestia'. His relations with Michelangelo steadily deteriorated, and in 1526 he resigned his post as *provveditore*, as he states in his *ricordanza*; see Corti 1964, p. 29. Their relations were restored in the changed circumstances after the Medicean restoration of 1530.

203   The two drawings for the rare book room are Casa Buonarroti 79A recto and 80A; Tolnay 1975–80, IV, nos. 559 recto and 560. Fattucci acknowledged the receipt of the two drawings for the *pichola libreria* in a letter dated 10 November 1525: *Carteggio* III, p. 184, no. DCCXXVII. There is a fine analysis of the more finished of the designs that now survive, Casa Buonarroti 80A, in Wittkower 1934, pp. 182–5.

204   For this, one of Fattucci's most remarkable letters, see *Carteggio* III, pp. 220–21, no. DCCXLVII. A carefully drawn autograph *modello* for this door survives, Casa Buonarroti 98A, Tolnay 1975–80, IV, no. 550. Whether this was the drawing sent to Rome and subsequently returned is an attractive hypothesis, but is probably not correct.

205   *Carteggio* III, pp. 224–5, no. DCCL.

206   *Carteggio* III, p. 94, no. DCLIV.

207   *Carteggio* III, pp. 224–5, no. DCCL. The church of San Giovanni degli Scopoli, at the corner of Via Martelli and Via de' Gori, subsequently rebuilt by Bartolommeo Ammannati, would, if so transformed, have emphasized the Medicean take-over of the area.

208   For this letter of 17 July, see *Carteggio* III, p. 232, no. DCCLVI. Fattucci has been told by Jacopo Salviati that what is now spent in one month must extend to three. On the other hand, the artist is given a free hand for work on the interior of the chapel; the patron 'arà sommo piacere che si spenda assai'. In his desperate letter of the following November, for which see p. 207 above, Michelangelo did, for the first time, perhaps impressed by the devastation of Rome wrought by the Colonna, show some understanding of the pope's predicament. In it he acknowledges the expenses at San Lorenzo, which include the rental of his house and his salary, 'che non son pichole spese'. *Carteggio* III, pp. 239–40, no. DCCLX.

209   In a letter of 24 May 1524 to Federico Gonzaga, he writes: 'veggo il Papa povero, e in estrema strettezza di denari'; see Castiglione-Serassi 1769–71, I, p. 112.

210   Clement's financial rectitude was recognized by contemporaries. See, for example, the report of the Venetian Marco Foscari, of 1526, in Sanudo 1879–1903, XLI, col. 282: 'Questo pontafice non beneficii, né li dà per simonia'. But Guicciardini, even before the sack of Rome took place, foresaw that Clement's reluctance to employ these traditional means to raise money was leading to disaster. He would

write to a colleague on 22 October 1526: 'io veggo Nostro Signore, et per natura sua et per le difficultà in che si trova, di animo tanto prostrato et sì male risoluto a fare provisione di danari per quelle vie potrebbe (faccendosi più conscientia o havendo più rispecto a vendere quactro cappelli che a ruinare el papato et tucto el mondo) che io dubito assai che ... gili paia, *etiam* con li augumenti offerti, impossibile a sostenere tanto peso'. See Guicciardini 1962, p. 148.

211 See Tolnay 1975–80, II, no. 279 recto, and the analysis in Hirst 1988a, pp. 82–4.

212 *Carteggio* III, p. 207, no. DCCXXIX.

213 *Carteggio* III, p. 210, no. DCCXLI. Explaining that Clement would like the ciborium over the altar, he refers to his hesitation: 'ma quello che lo faceva pensare altrove, era per non quastare la vostra fantasia, cioè se voi volessi uno dì dipingere la cappella'.

214 The artist's project is referred to in Vasari's detailed Life of Bandinelli. He states that Clement commissioned Bandinelli to paint frescos of the *Martyrdom of St Cosmas and St Damian* and the *Martyrdom of St Lawrence* in the choir. Bandinelli's design for the latter so gratified the pope that he arranged for Marcantonio Raimondi to engrave it. Vasari does not explain why the project fell through. He states that Clement, it would seem to make up for the failure to proceed, made Bandinelli a knight of St Peter. For his account, see Vasari 1987, V, pp. 246–7. The context suggests a date of 1525. A document published in Waldman 2004, no. 159, p. 86, shows that Bandinelli was arranging for the collection of his income in July 1526.

215 For Sansovino's letter, discussed earlier, see p. 216.

216 For Michele di Vivano and the Medici family, see Waldman 2004, pp. 5ff.

217 See Vasari 1987, V, p. 243. For the initial commission, see Waldman 2004, p. 32, no. 76.

218 For this long-lost letter, see now Waldman 2004, pp. 348–9, no. 587.

219 For the contract for the copy of the *Laocoön* group, drawn up in September 1520, see Waldman 2004, p. 56, no. 113. Michelangelo's Roman friends allude to the project. At the same time, Sellaio reports on a staggeringly ambitious project for the tomb of Henry VIII of England and estimates its cost at no less than 40,000 ducats; see *Carteggio* II, p. 336, no. DXLV, and for further information, Waldman 2004, pp. 61ff., no. 118. Almost certainly relating to this project is an extraordinarily bizarre episode recounted by Nardi 1838–42, II, p. 67, that an unidentified 'maestro' showed a wooden model for the project to the dying Pope Leo X, an event regarded as an evil premonition of his imminent death in the first days of December 1521. The depth of feeling hostile to Bandinelli is indicated by the request of Michelangelo's Roman circle that Michelangelo endorse the previously maligned Jacopo Sansovino's claim to a major project in order to exclude Bandinelli; see *Carteggio* III, p. 127, no. DCLXXXIII.

220 The statue is referred to as the 'gigante della Loggia' in the payments for

Bandinelli's contributions to the *entrata* made by the Otto di Practica; see the document first published by Ciseri 1990, Document XXXVII, p. 272, and subsequently by Waldman 2004, p. 40. The well-informed Bartolommeo Masi, in his account of the entry of Pope Leo, writes: 'Et in sulla loggia de' Signori si v'era uno giugante fatto di terra, colorito a modo che se fussi di bronzo, ed era della grandezza che è quello di marmo che è in sulla ringhiera del palazzo di detti Signori.' See Masi 1906, p. 167, reprinted in Ciseri 1990, p. 202. Another witness, Luca Landucci, refers to the work as 'un gigante nella loggia de' Signori, che pareva di colore di bronzo e posato in su le spalliere della Loggia sotto el primo arco verso el Palegio: non fu molto stimato'. See Landucci 1883, pp. 358–9. His critical evaluation of the work would be echoed by Vasari in his Life of Bandinelli. For a review of the evidence concerning the statue, see Ciseri 1990, pp. 86ff., and her pl. VII for Vasari's own later presentation of the work in his fresco in Palazzo Vecchio, depicting Pope Leo in the Piazza della Signoria.

221 They were carried out in stucco and still survive in ruinous condition. For their general appearance, see Ciseri 1990, pl. VIIIa.

222 The contract, alluded to in the nineteenth century, has been published only recently; see Waldman 2004, no. 128, pp. 66–8. The block now ordered was to measure approximately 8 *braccia* in height, $2\frac{3}{4}$ *braccia* wide, and $2\frac{1}{3}$ *braccia* deep. These measurements do not differ very much from the scale of the block given by Giovanni Cambi in his account of its arrival in Florence in 1525, alluded to below; he there refers to the block as $8\frac{1}{2}$ *braccia* long. The contract thus excludes the hypothesis, sometimes proposed, that Bandinelli availed himself of the block that had been ordered for Michelangelo by Soderini. Its total cost is recorded as 100 ducats.

223 Bandinelli actually employed the notary Galvano Parlanciotto, who had been adopted earlier by Michelangelo; see, for example, *Contratti*, pp. 81ff. and 95ff. And it had been Parlanciotto who had checked the delivery of marble blocks for the tomb of Julius II, summarily sketched in the notebook now in the Archivio Buonarroti.

224 *Carteggio* II, p. 198, no. CDXLI. Urbano's letter is scarcely literate, but the meaning emerges that the purchase is being discussed.

225 *Carteggio* III, p. 83, no. DCXLV. The artist's correspondent writes: 'Credo voi sapete che io sono per dovere finire lo sasso che voi voleste pig[l]iare dal Sig[n] ore nostro, e non so dove finire; e se voi avesse a fare questo lavoro, sarebe per lo preposito vostro.' The 'Signore' he refers to must be Scipione d'Este, the first husband of the deceased Alberico Malaspina's daughter, Ricciarda. It cannot be excluded that the *sasso* is the one ordered so many years earlier by Soderini, quarried, but never rough hewn by Michelangelo, as seen earlier in this book. The date of this letter assumes added significance from the fact that drawings by Michelangelo for a sculptural group of Hercules and Antaeus can be assigned

to this same time; for their date, see Wilde 1953, pp. 67–8, and, as is clear from information of 'Cambi' quoted in note 231 below, the artist initially contemplated this subject for the *piazza* group. For the drawings, see Tolnay 1975–80, II, nos. 236 recto and 237 recto.

226 Cambi's *Istorie*, in *Delizie*, XXII, pp. 274–5. For an improved transcription of this remarkable passage, adopted in note 231 below, see now Caglioti 2000a, p. 221, note 291. Vasari states that it was Piero Rosselli, who had prepared the vault of the Sistine Chapel as long ago as 1508, who was in charge of the rescue operation; Vasari 1987, V, p. 249.

227 Waldman 2004, no. 147, p. 78.

228 *Carteggio* III, pp. 170–71, no. DCCXVII.

229 *Carteggio* III, pp. 170–71, no. DCCXVII. At this stage, Clement wishes the statue to be located with its back to Palazzo Medici, at the corner of the *piazza*. Michelangelo is to mention the undertaking to no one.

230 *Carteggio* III, pp. 184–5, no. DCCXXVII. Of Clement's injunction, Fattucci writes: 'Digli che io lo voglio tutto per me, et non voglio che e' pensi alle cose del pubrico né d'altri ma alla mia'. The pressure exerted on the artist by others' demands can scarcely have remained unknown. Several years earlier, he had been approached by Cardinal Niccolò Fieschi for a life-size group of the *Virgin and Child* for the high altar of Santa Maria del Popolo; see *Carteggio* II, p. 306, no. DXXII; p. 309, no. DXXV; and p. 350, no. DLVII. The artist was saved by the cardinal's death in 1524. Similarly, he had been under pressure to produce a small work for the study of the greatly respected Cardinal Domenico Grimani; see *Carteggio* II, p. 376, no. DLXXIX; p. 381, no. DLXXXIV; and p. 383, no. DLXXXV. Michelangelo may have given thought to this request; see Wilde 1953, pp. 64–5, and Hirst 1988b, p. 62, no. 24. Once again, the death of the patron intervened.

231 Cambi, *Istorie*, in *Delizie*, XXII, pp. 274–5, and Caglioti 2000a, I, p. 221, note 291: 'E avàmo allora in Firenze un Michelangelo schultore e dipintore, ciptadino fiorentino, el migliore maestro che · ssi trovassi ne' tempi sua di che se n'avessi notizia, di che il popolo desiderava lo lavorassi lui, perché aveva fatto il G[i]ughante, el quale marmo no era grande a suo modo ... Ora, questo Michelagnolo Simoni lo tolse a chavarnelo lui, essendo givoane di circha an[n]i XXI, e però dexideravano lo faciessi lui [the newly arrived block], perché speravano faciessi qualche coax degnia d'un Erchole che scopiassi Anteo giughante. E perché e' lavorava le sepulture de' Medici facieva fare papa Chlemente 7mo, disegniava detto papa lo faciessi un' altro schultore fiorentino, acciò e' sua sepolcri non rimanessino imperfetti.'

232 *Carteggio* III, pp. 178–9, no. DCCXXII. In what is clearly a response to Michelangelo's lost expression of indignation over Bandinelli's preferment, Salviati writes: 'non conosco ho vegho che in conto alcuno Baccio si possa equiperare ad te, o

fare minimo paragone alle cose tua, et mi maraviglio assai che tu li voglia dare questa riputatione'.

233 Vasari 1987, v, pp. 247–8.

234 See, for example, *Carteggio* III, p. 114, no. DCLXXII.

235 *Carteggio* III, p. 183, no. DCCXXVI. He writes that he has been approached by Florentines who are engaged with the issue, 'di quegli a chi s'apartiene'.

236 *Carteggio* III, p. 185, no. DCCXXVII.

237 *Carteggio* III, pp. 190–91, no. DCCXXX. Extensively discussed, the passage concerning the project is also printed in Vasari 1962, pp. 1149–50.

238 *Carteggio* III, p. 250, no. DCCLXIX, where he writes to Spina that 'la penna è sempre più animosa che la lingua'.

239 *Carteggio* III, pp. 194–5, no. DCCXXXII: 'Tu sai che li pontefici non vivon molto; et noi non potremo, più che facciamo, desiderare vedere, o almeno intendere, essere finita la cappella con le sepulture delli nostri et anche la libreria.'

240 Elam 1990, p. 53.

241 *Carteggio* III, p. 181, no. DCCXXIV.

CHAPTER NINE

1 The text of this long letter was published by Luzio 1913, pp. 246–7. Difficult to consult, it was not included in Vasari, *La Vita* (Vasari 1962), where other fragments of the correspondence are quoted. Federico writes: 'Sono molt'anni che siamo amatore dello excellentissimo messer Michele Angelo per la fama della virtù sua, non meno celebrato et rara nell'arte della sculptura, che unica et illustre nel mestiero della pittura, come anche per la experientia che havemo visto in qualche lochi delle non mai abastanza laudate opera sue?' He expresses his 'ardentissimo desiderio' to have a work of his to embellish Palazzo Te. The provision of a drawing will, only for the moment, assuage his 'honestissima voglia et intentissimo desiderio'.

2 Luzio 1913, p. 247.

3 Luzio 1913, p. 248. The letter warrants lengthy quotation. Borromeo writes to his master: 'Io ho facto per mezzo d'uno amico mio amicitia com Michelagnolo schultore et sono in qualche praticha com lui. Et spero havere certo quadro di figure nude che combatteno, di marmore, quale havea principiato ad instantia d'un gran signore ma non è finito. È braccia uno e mezo a ogni mane, et così a vedere è cosa bellissima, e vi sono più di 25 teste e 20 corpi varij et varie actitudine fanno. Mi è parso sino qui havere facto un bel passo che habbi voluto mostrarmelo, che non mostra cosa alchuna ad alchuno, et anche mi pare haverlo aceso talmente dello amore e benivolentia sua verso V. III.ms S. che non sia

meno el desiderio suo di servirla che V. Ex. di havere qualche cosa del suo. E ciaschuno con chi mi sono consigliato m'à dicto che el tucto sta a indovinare la sua fantasia e che comincia a volermi per amico; pure si schusa assai essendo obbligato a N.S. quale non resta farli grandissima instantia dolendosi che non lavora como se vuole e che ha alchuni che continuamente dicono a S. B.as che non fornira mai questa opera, e che ogne minima cosa che si vedesse di sua mano andare fuora gli saria di gran carichio appresso S. S.th et che vuole pensare a qualche modo per il quale possa servirla e fuggire le imputatione gli potessino essere date. Io gl'ho offerto farnelo pregare al R.mo et al S.re Ippolito et che se serà bisogno V. Ex. Ne scriverà alla S.tà di N.S. suplicando la licentia; me ha dicto non parli com persona alchuna et che me dirà presto quello sarà da fare et non mancherò sollicitare in quello destro modo che io pensi potere condurre la cosa.'

4   Luzio 1913, p. 248. Borromeo writes: 'Io sono stato più volta con Michelangelo scultore et non posso anchor vitrar sustantia quando voglia fare, et credo lui come gl'altri stia sospeso di queste cose della guerra, perchè è richo et nel suo parlare si dole esser qui'.

5   A review of the events leading to the sack of Rome cannot be undertaken here. For a detailed and balanced view of Clement's failings, see Pastor-Mercati 1944–63, IV, 2, pp. 233ff. Guicciardini, himself in the service of the pope, believed that the disaster had been precipitated by the dilatory tactics of Francesco Maria della Rovere, whose hatred of Clement is assessed in Clough 2005, pp. 101ff. For Guicciardini's assessment, see his letter to Roberto Acciaiuoli of 28 May 1527, where he writes: 'Di tucto è stato causa el Duca di Urbino, quale, o per havere piacere che Nostro Signore si perda, o perchè giudicassi troppo pericoloso lo accostarsi, ha temporeggiato el cammino studiosamente'; Guicciardini 1857–67, IX, p. 26.

6   Carteggio III, p. 250, no. DCCLXIX. Poggi proposed, with a query, February 1527, as its date; Ramsden 1963, I, p. 170, favoured December 1526.

7   For details concerning the rentals of the main and ancillary properties on Via Ghibellina, see Hatfield 2002, pp. 68–9.

8   Ricordi of the period of 1525–6 afford a clear picture of Michelangelo's domestic arrangements. For the move to new accommodation in 1529, see Hatfield 2002, pp. 68ff.

9   Ricordi 1970, p. 228, no. CCII: 'Ricordo chome più dì sono che Piero di Filippo Gondi mi richiese della sagrestia nuova di San Lorenzo per naschondervi certe loro robe per rispetto del pericolo in che noi ci troviàno. E stasera, a dì ventinove d'aprile 1527, v'à cominciato a offar portare certi fasci: dice che sono panni lini delle sorelle; e io, per non vedere e'fatti sua, né dove e'si nasconde dette robe, gli ò dato la chiave di detta sagrestia detta sera'.

10   There is an accessible description of the events of this remarkable day in Roth 1925, pp. 23ff. For the sources, see Varchi 1843, I, pp. 102ff., and Nardi 1838–41,

II, pp. 132ff., himself a protagonist and whose defence of Palazzo Medici would lead to the inadvertent shattering of the left arm of Michelangelo's *David*, specifically referred to by Varchi. In his Life of Francesco Salviati of 1568, Vasari would claim that he and his friend, after a lull of three days, crossed the picket lines outside the palace to gather up the pieces, which were handed to Salviati's father for safe-keeping. The later restoration of the arm has been referred to above, p. 48. There is an excellent account of the Passerini regime in Stephens 1983, pp. 164–82. The exactly contemporary letters of Francesco Guicciardini afford a damning indictment of the cardinal's ineptitude.

11 Cambi, *Istorie*, in *Delizie*, XXII, p. 313, states that Florentines first heard the news of the sack on 11 May.

12 Capponi's situation and political sympathies are extensively discussed in Varchi 1843, I, pp. 172ff. His differences with Michelangelo are alluded to below.

13 Symonds 1899, I, p. 4.

14 For the text of the brief, first published in 1912, see now *Contratti*, p. 184.

15 See *Carteggio* I, pp. 188ff., no. CXLVII, and *Carteggio indiretto* I, p. 51, no. 33. She had written of the artist: 'è persona che intende di architectura et di artigl[i] arie et di saper monire una terra'.

16 For the two letters, see *Carteggio* III, p. 251, no. DCCLXX, and p. 252, no. DCCLXXI.

17 For a valuable survey of Buonarroto's life, see Ristori in *Carteggio indiretto* I, pp. XXIX–XXXVIII.

18 In the immediate aftermath of Buonarroto's death, Michelangelo took on a number of the duties caused by the event. There survives, for example, a list of expenses incurred to provide his niece Francesca with clothes, and in mid-September he took her to live in a convent of sisters at Boldrone, outside Florence. He had, a little earlier, arranged the repayment of the dowry of Buonarroto's widow, Bartolomea della Casa. For a time, his nephew Leonardo came to live with him. For details about the dispositions made following Buonarroto's death, see *Carteggio indiretto* I, p. 345, note 4.

19 See *Carteggio* III, p. 269, no. DCCLXXXVIII.

20 A letter addressed to Michelangelo from the court in exile at Orvieto of 2 March 1528 asks for news of whether he is still at work. Niccolini, newly arrived at the court, had told Clement of Michelangelo's expenses and the pope has responded by offering to pay him 500 ducats at once and then his daily stipend. From a later letter written by the pope's secretary after the return of the court to Rome, dated 25 November 1530, it appears that Clement has been much displeased that Michelangelo has been paid 'certe centinara di ducati' and that he expects to be reimbursed; *Carteggio indiretto* I, p. 337, no. 224. For the ever increasing anti-Medicean feeling in Florence during Carducci's period as *gonfaloniere*, see Roth 1925, pp. 96–7, and Stephens 1983, pp. 234 and 240.

21 That the two-figure group was destined for Julius II's tomb has not escaped

question; see Vasari 1962, II, pp. 323ff. But the oak-leaves in the youth's hair point to the della Rovere context. Vasari's association of the group with the tomb, for which see Vasari 1987, VI, p. 28, is endorsed in a passage in Bocchi 1591, pp. 38–9, where, discussing the statues in the Sala del Consiglio of Palazzo Vecchio, he writes: 'Tramolte, che nella sepoltura di Papa Giulio Secondo si doveano collocare, fu quasi finite questa [the *Victory*] da Michelagnolo in Fiorenza'. Arguments for dating the group in the period from 1527 were advanced by Wilde; see his assessment of the artist's circumstances, Wilde 1954, pp. 13–14, now reprinted in Wallace 1995, III, pp. 437–58. More recently, the same date has been proposed by Hartt 1969, pp. 277ff., and Hatfield 2002, p. 130.

22   The events of the 'Tumulto di Venerdì' are most easily followed in Roth 1925, pp. 30ff., who did note Francesco Maria della Rovere's involvement, discussed most recently by Clough 2005, pp. 103ff.

23   There are excellent comments on this remarkable episode in Vasari 1962, IV, pp. 1565–6. Barocchi observed the connection between a *ricordo* of Antonio Mini, which describes the break in and dates it to the months prior to the start of the city's siege in September 1529, and a passage in Vasari's Life of Michelangelo of 1568 (Vasari 1987, VI, p. 82). Ammannati and Nanni di Baccio Bigio are there identified as those responsible. For Mini, see *Ricordi* 1970, pp. 371–2, no. CCCXIV. It seems that approximately fifty drawings, some for the Medici tombs, and a number of models in wax or clay, were stolen. Everything was ultimately returned.

24   For the text of the contract, see *Contratti*, no. LXXIII, p. 185.

25   *Carteggio* III, p. 183, no. DCCXXVI.

26   For the earlier project of Hercules and Antaeus, see pp. 217ff above.

27   For Vasari's account of Bandinelli and the *piazza* project, see Vasari 1987, V, pp. 247ff. For a highly dynamic earlier design of Bandinelli for *Hercules and Cacus*, see the model preserved in Berlin, reproduced in Poeschke 1996, fig. 77 on p. 170.

28   That the subject of Hercules fighting Cacus was retained when Michelangelo gained the commission is implicit in the wording of the contract of August 1528; reference is made to 'la imagine et figura di Cacco' and to 'una figura, usieme o congiunta con l'altra, secondo che et chomo parrà a Michelagniolo decto'; *Contratti*, p. 185. Vasari states that he relinquished the subject of Hercules and Cacus in favour of that of Samson and two Philistines in his Life of Bandinelli; see Vasari 1987, V, p. 251. The much-discussed two-figure clay model now in the Casa Buonarroti, for which see Poeschke 1996, pls 89–91, was probably made in preparation for the subject of Hercules and Cacus, although Springer 1883, II, p. 30, and Wilde 1954, pp. 18–19, proposed that it was for a pendant to the Victory group for Pope Julius's tomb. For excellent comments on this model, see O'Grody 2001, p. 41.

29 For Capponi's attempts to treat with Clement, see Varchi 1843, I, pp. 532–3, and Stephens 1983, pp. 244ff.

30 The treaty was signed on 29 May. For the terms, see Varchi 1843, I, pp. 590ff. It was pledged to restore the Medici family and its authority in Florence. Alessandro de' Medici was to marry Margaret, the illegitimate daughter of the emperor. News of the terms of the treaty reached Italy by July, and Florentine reactions of defiance were spelt out in a letter of the Dieci of the twentieth of the month; no step in resistance would be spared; see Gaye 1840, p. 197.

31 For the re-establishment of the Nove della Milizia, see Varchi 1843, I, p. 245.

32 Carteggio III, p. 262, no. DCCCLXXXI.

33 For the drawings, see Tolnay 1975–80, IV, nos. 563–83, many with designs on versos as well as rectos. The bibliography discussing them is now extensive. Apart from Tolnay's own entries, see Manetti 1980, pp. 47ff., and Wallace 1987a, pp. 119ff. Their dating in the summer of 1528 is supported by the following evidence: on the verso of Casa Buonarroti 14A Michelangelo wrote a ricordo of 23 July 1528, and on that of Casa Buonarroti 17 verso, another dated September 1528.

34 See Lamberini 1987, pp. 5ff. As she cogently points out, the skills required were modest, costs were low and the time required for construction was minimal.

35 See Busini 1860, Letter X, dated 31 January 1549, pp. 103ff. He writes of Capponi that, while he was gonfaloniere, he never wished to have San Miniato fortified: 'mai non volse che si fortificasse il monte di San Miniato; e Michelangelo che è uomo veritierissimo, dice che durò gran fatica a persuaderlo agli altri principali, ma a Niccolò mai potette persuaderlo ... e quando fu fatto de'Nove lo mandorno dua o tre volte fuora, e sempre quando tornava, trovava il Monte sfornito'. See also Letter XI, pp. 115–16. For a profile of Busini, see C. Pincin in DBI, XV, pp. 534–7.

36 See Machiavelli 2001, p. 664, and for comments on the dispute, Manetti 1980, pp. 21ff.

37 See Contratti, pp. 186–7.

38 Condivi 1998, p. 40.

39 These contracts, preserved in the Archivio Buonarroti, have recently been published for the first time in Contratti, nos. LXXV–LXXXI, pp. 188–94. Michelangelo had characteristically called upon men with whom he had worked at San Lorenzo.

40 See the letter of Capello in Albèri 1839–55, XI, pp. 238–9, dated 29 October 1529. He refers to no less than 1,800 balls of wool used to protect the campanile, which prevented damage from the artillery fire of the enemy batteries. According to Condivi 1998, p. 40, mattresses were employed; these may have been substituted for the protection described by Capello. For their adoption at a later date, see a payment of the Dieci di Balia of 28 May 1530, published in Falletti-Fossati

1883, I, p. 189, note 2, who disbursed 4 florins to an Antonio detto Capannino and companions 'per sua fatica di havere con 3 compagni fasciato di materassi el campanile di S. Miniato'. The enemy batteries were stationed only a little south of San Miniato at Giramonte; for their proximity, see Cropper 1997, fig. 33 (p. 76), and Vasari's rendering of the situation in his later fresco in Palazzo Vecchio, ibid., fig. 17 (p. 36). For the Florentine guns positioned on the *campanile*, see Vasari 1962, III, pp. 1076–7.

41   See the anonymous text published in Vasari-Milanesi 1878–85, VII, pp. 367–8. The criticism was picked up by Varchi 1843, II, p. 213.

42   For Giannotti's remarks, see Giannotti 1974, pp. 346–7: 'Michelangelo Buonarroti, uomo come nella pittura e scultura, così nella architettura singularissimo, aveva fortificato il Monte, instaurato il bastione di San Giorgio, e fatto il riparo alla porta alla Giustizia, le quali erano le principali e più importanti alla Città'. He considered the work that Malatesta Baglione carried out as either redundant or ill-executed.

43   Michelangelo was paid for the trip by the Dieci di Balia: 'per vedere e'danni che Arno faceva alla cittadella e altrove'. The money was collected by Stefano Lunetti, who accompanied him; see *Ricordi* 1970, pp. 251–2, no. CCXXVI. And for further documentation, see Gaye 1840, pp. 194–5. The commissioner in Pisa, Ceccotto Tosinghi, was put out by the artist's refusal to accept his hospitality: 'Per la presente mi occurre dira a Vostra Signoria chome hiersera [4 June] arrivò qui Michelangelo Buonaroti, che mi fu facto intendere era aloggiato al hostaria; mandai per levarlo che venisse a stare meco, che paseva si convenisse per honor suo et mio, il che non hebbi forza'. A similar episode would occur on the artist's visit to Ferrara.

44   The text of this ill-fated *condotta* was published by Varchi in his *Storia fiorentina*: Varchi 1843, I, pp. 500–02. For the procrastination of the Ferrarese, see Wallace 2001, especially pp. 489ff.

45   For the letter from the Signoria, see Gaye 1840, pp. 197–8, reprinted in Vasari 1962, III, pp. 931–2. The artist is described in laudatory terms as 'chiarissimo' and 'rarissimo', and the duke's collaboration in showing him everything required is warmly requested. For the letter from the Dieci, see Gaye 1840, p. 198, and Vasari 1962, III, pp. 931–2. They write: 'Sarà di questa apportatore Michelangiolo Buonarroti, il quale è mandato costì dai Nove della Milizia per vedere cotesti modi di fortificare che ha tenuti la Eccellentia del Duca'. These letters scarcely substantiate the argument of Wallace 2001, p. 496, that Michelangelo went to Ferrara as 'diplomat' as well as artist and military engineer. Florence had already looked to Ferrarese expertise in fortification in the previous autumn, when a small team headed by a military engineer had travelled to Florence to proffer advice; see Wallace 2001, p. 491, note 66. It should be added that ever since his succession to his father Ercole in 1504, Alfonso had devoted much attention to the fortification of Ferrara, in order to protect the city from Julius II. He was

also a notable expert in the manufacture of artillery. Not for nothing had he been portrayed with a cannon as accessory in a now lost Titian portrait, recorded in a copy. It was probably carried out by Titian only very shortly before Michelangelo's visit. For the copy and for the date of the original, see Hope 1980, pp. 66–7.

46 Giugni's public service was confined to his role in the last republic. He was devoted to the anti-Medicean regime and would be expelled from Ferrara by Duke Alfonso in 1530, when the latter adopted a more conciliatory attitude to Clement VII. He was sent into exile and his property confiscated after the re-establishment of Medicean rule in 1530. After attempting to solicit the support of Charles V in the following years, he would die in Rome in straitened conditions. For a review of his life, see V. Arrighi in *DBI*, LVI, pp. 696–700.

47 Gaye 1840, pp. 198–9; Vasari 1962, III, p. 932. Giugni writes of the artist's rejection of his hospitality and Alfonso's welcome as follows: 'Bene mi è dolsuto che non l'ho possuto gravar tanto che sia volsuto restar mechio, sì per l'onor suo e mio, sì ancora per amor di Vostra Signoria'. He added an important postscript on the following morning: 'Appresso post scripta. Questa mattina, che siamo alli 4, sono stato con Michelagnolo intorno a questa ciptà a vedere la muraglia; satisfalli assai. Dipoi siamo stati con la Excellentia del Duca, quale ne ha visto el prefato Michelagnolo tanto volentieri, quanto dir si possa; et è rimasto andar seco in persona per mostrarli tucto'. It is important to note that Vasari's account of Michelangelo at Ferrara is gravely confused. He assigns this visit and the duke's hospitality to the second journey of Michelangelo from Florence, his flight to Venice in September. For the passage, see Vasari 1987, VI, pp. 59–62. The flight is discussed below.

48 Condivi 1998, pp. 42–3. He writes that Alfonso showed the artist everything, 'tanto di bastioni quanto d'artigliere. Anzi gli aprì tutta la sua salvarola, di sua mano mostrandogli ogni cosa, massimamente alcune opera di pittura, e ritratti dei suoi vecchi. . . . Ma dovendosi Michelangnolo partire, il duca motteggiando gli disse: "Michelagnolo, voi siate mio prigione. Se volete ch'io vi lasci libero, voglio che voi mi promettiate di farmi qualche cosa di vostra mano, come ben vi viene, sia quel che si voglia, scultura o pittura".' There seems no good reason to dismiss the story. But even without it, the extensive argument of Wallace 2001, pp. 473–99, that Michelangelo was acting as a diplomat of the Signoria, is not borne out by the interesting and extensive documentation that he publishes. None of the letters that he quotes refers to the project of the painting. And there could be no greater contrast, in this respect, with the history of the bronze *David*, which, as seen earlier, was indeed a political gift and repeatedly referred to in government correspondence. Wilde 1957, pp. 270–71, suggested that, in accepting the project, the artist may have hoped to secure more support for the Florentine cause, a more plausible scenario.

49 For the earliest surviving reference to Alfonso's wish to acquire a painting

by Raphael, see Shearman 2003, I, pp. 190–91. His later efforts to obtain one were protracted but unsuccessful; see Shearman 2003, I, pp. 296ff. For a general survey of the supply of paintings for the *camerino*, see Shearman 1987, passim.

50   For the suggestion that a drawing in the Louvre could have been made with a painting for Alfonso in mind, see Joannides 2003, no. 21, pp. 123–6.

51   See Wallace 2001, p. 485, where he writes that, had it been delivered, Michelangelo's painting 'would have fitted perfectly into the greatest ensemble of mythological paintings in Italy'. However, the assumption that the *Leda*, a project settled on only in 1529, was made for the *camerino* of Alfonso is widespread in the bibliography.

52   Condivi emphasizes the great scale of the *Leda*, no doubt following the artist's information; he describes it as 'un quadrone da casa'; see Condivi 1998, p. 43. The cartoon now in the Royal Academy in London, a copy probably made from the painting in France, measures approximately 170 by 248 centimetres, much larger than, for example, Titian's paintings for the *camerino*.

53   See Hope 1987, pp. 25ff.

54   See Mini's letter to Michelangelo from France, dated 23 December 1531, in *Carteggio* III, p. 361, no. DCCCXLI, where he refers to the work as 'la tavolla della Leda'. Alfonso had actually sent a canvas from Ferrara to Titian in Venice in April 1518; see Hope 1971, p. 715.

55   Arezzo would fall to the imperial forces only days later.

56   For this extraordinary text, see *Carteggio* III, pp. 280–81, no. DCCXCVIII.

57   For Battista della Palla, see the study by Elam 1993, with many observations on his ties with France and his role as exporter of works of art. It was to him that Filippo Strozzi had presented the *Hercules* in the spring of 1529; see Elam 1993, pp. 58–61, and for the artist's own disapprobation of the event, p. 102, Document 13. Further evidence that Michelangelo's idea of moving to France was a real one is referred to below.

58   Going beyond Venice would have meant traversing threatening 'terra tesdesca'. Prior to this encounter, he had resolutely determined to stay on until the end of the war. Of the event itself he writes: 'Ma martedì mactina, a dì ventuno di sectembre, veun'uno fuori della porta a San Nicolò, dov'io ero a bastioni, e nell'occhio mi disse che è non era da star più, a voler camper la vita; e venue meco a chasa equivi desinò, e choudussemi chavalcature, e non mi lasciò mai che e'mi cavo di Firenze....O fio o'l diavolo, quello che si sia stato io non loso.' The precipitancy of the flight, however, as evoked in this letter to della Palla, is suspect. There survives a list of moneys that Michelangelo gave to his servant Caterina, to be passed on to his niece Francesca, living in the convent of Boldrone, suggesting that thoughtful provision for some needs was made before he left. The list, written by the artist's brother, Gismondo, is dated 24

September. For this note, and another *ricordo* concerning the money, see *Ricordi* 1970, pp. 263–4, nos. CCXXXII and CCXXXIII.

59 See Busini 1860, pp. 104–5; the letter is dated 31 January 1549. The passage, not always readily accessible, reads: 'Ho domandato Michelangnolo qual fu la cagione della sua partita. Dice cosi: che essendo de'Nove, e venute dentro le genti fiorentine e Malatesta e il signor Mario Orsino e altri caporali, i Dieci disposono i soldati per le mura e per i bastioni, ed a ciascuno capitano consegnorno il luogo suo, e dettono vettovaglie loro e munizioni, e fra gli altri dettono otto pezzi d'artiglieria a Malatesta che le guardasse e difendesse una parte de'bastioni del Monte; il quale le pose non dentro, ma sotto i bastioni, senza guardia alcuna; ed il contrario fece Mario. Onde Michelagnolo che come magistrato e architetto rivedeva quell luogo del Monte, domandò il signor Mario, onde nasceva che Malatesta teneva cosi straccuratamente l'artiglierie sua. A che e'disse: Sappi che costui e d'una casa, che tutti sono stati traditori, ed egli ancora tradirà questa città. Onde gli venne tanta paura, che bisognò parlirsi, mosso dalla paura, che la città non capitassi male, ed egli conseguentemente. Cosi risoluto, trovò Rinaldo Corsini, al quale disse il suo pensiero; e Rinaldo come leggieri disse: Io voglio venir con esso voi. Cosi montati a cavallo con qualche soma di danari, andorno alla Porta alla Giustizia, dove non volevano le guardie lasciargli andare; chè cosi si faceva a tutte le porte; onde vi debbe ricordare dello stupore alla Porta al Prato. In questo non so da chi si levò una voce: Lasciatelo andare, che egli è de'Nove, ed è Michelangelo; e cosi uscirno tre a cavallo, egli, Rinaldo, e quel suo che mai lo staccava'.

60 Capello, in Albèri 1839–55, XI, p. 218. Most subsequent historians, including Vardin, held the belief that Baglione had decided to betray the city from the time of his appointment in April 1529, a conclusion rightly rejected by Falletti-Fossati 1883, pp. 94ff., who dated the formation of the intention not earlier than May 1530.

61 Capello, in Albèri 1839–55, XI, pp. 221–2. Writing in graphic terms of the fact that even fourteen-year olds had been enrolled to work on the city's defences, he goes on to describe the fears that had gripped the city; already six days earlier, on, that is, 18 September, 'tutta la città era in soma trepidazione, ed attendevano con la fuga a salvarsi'.

62 *Carteggio* III, pp. 286–7, no. DCCCI. He writes: 'Ho inteso da Santi Quatro che voi vi siati partito da Fiorenza per fugire el fastidio et ancora la mola fortuna della guerra del paese'. He now urges Michelangelo to leave Florence again and stay with him, an indication of how little he knew current circumstances. The bibliography on the flight is extensive; it became a favoured topic of nineteenth-century commentators; see Vasari 1962, III, pp. 1096ff. It has been proposed that the artist fled, fearful that Niccolò Capponi would make a secret peace with Pope Clement; see Cropper 1997, p. 38. But the flight took place five months

after Capponi had lost the office of *gonfaloniere* and had been succeeded by the
utterly intransigent Francesco Carducci. Leonardo da Vinci's recommendations
of flight were appropriately quoted in the present context by Dorez 1918, p. 210,
note 5. He quotes no less than three; the first runs: 'Paura over timore è prol-
ungamento di vita'.

63   *Carteggio* III, pp. 323–4, no. DCCCXXIV.

64   Varchi 1843, II, p. 193. In both editions of the Michelangelo *Vita*, Vasari refers
to the money but gives no details. In both editions, he includes Piloto in the
party of fugitives: Vasari 1987, V, p. 160. For Piloto and Venice, see below,
pp. 239–40.

65   See Corti 1964, p. 29. Figiovanni refers to the artist as 'fuggendo da pericolo
el suo tesoro minacciato dal popolo nel bisogno della guerra'.

66   Busini records the detail that Corsini had gone to see the ailing Niccolò Capponi
in the Mugello but that Michelangelo had refused to accompany him, another
indication of his abiding dislike of the ex-*gonfaloniere*. Capponi would die only
a few weeks later.

67   The text of the *bando* was published in Gotti 1875, II, pp. 64–5, and reprinted
in Vasari 1962, III, pp. 1067–8.

68   See Gotti 1875, I, p. 193.

69   *Carteggio* III, pp. 282–3, no. DCCXCIX, and pp. 284–5, no. DCCC. Della Palla,
familiar with Lucca, where he seems to have engaged in searching for works
for Francis I, was anxious to arrange to meet the artist there; see Elam 1993,
p. 61.

70   There is an outline of Brucioli's career by R. N. Lear in *DBI*, XIV, pp. 480–85.
For a fine assessment of his career, see Spini 1940, especially pp. 63ff. for the
period that here concerns us. He points out that the grounds for Brucioli's
banishment were not made public by the Carducci regime. For an assessment
of the issue, see the excellent comments in Polizzotto 1994, pp. 358–9. While
his Lutheran sympathies may have been the ostensible cause of his sentence, it
was probably his attacks on the Savonarolans, ever more dominant in the regime,
that led to it. A reference to Brucioli is made in Condivi's Life that remains a
mystery: the statement that Brucioli was chosen by the Venetian government
to travel to Rome to invite Michelangelo to live in Venice; see Condivi 1998,
p. 54. Panciatichi had probably been exiled because of the family's Medicean
sympathies. Curiously, decades later, he would become sympathetic to Huguenot
circles when in France; see Passerini 1858, pp. 68ff.

71   This explanation, a totally convincing one, was advanced by Falletti-Fossati
1883, I, pp. 159ff. It discredits the theory of an earlier secret mission to Venice
that he himself had accepted in a previous publication, Fossati 1876. Unfortunately, his later book has been frequently overlooked, appearing neither in Vasari
1962 nor in the 1970 edition of the *Ricordi*, pp. 262–3. In his analysis of the
ricordo in 1883, he argued that it was made near the end of the artist's stay in

Venice, 'un conto fatto da Michelangelo sul punto di partire da Venezia'. Symonds 1899, I, pp. 424–5, unaware of Falleti-Fossati's conclusion, independently threw doubt on the theory of two visits.

72 Piloto was in Venice in January 1526, when he wrote to Michelangelo; see *Carteggio* III, pp. 200–01, no. DCCXXXV. Complaining of the bitter weather and lack of work, he nevertheless refers to the commission of an altarpiece, which would comprise figures in bronze and silver. This reference is striking. For one year later, Lorenzo Lotto, in Venice, would refer in two letters to an altarpiece destined for Bergamo and mentions two sculptors. One is Jacopo Sansovino. The other he describes as 'giovane e molto valente, unico et solo discipulo di Michelangelo, quale ha molto bene quelli andamenti del suo maestro'. This letter, of 5 August 1527, was followed by another written a week later in which he refers to the project again. He mentions Sansovino and the other as 'alevato di Micheagnolo et giovinato'. For the letters, see Lotto-Zampetti 1969, pp. 275–7. It is extremely likely, in view of what Piloto had written earlier, that it is he who is the 'discipulo'. Piloto's ties with Venice seem to have continued, for on 2 November 1528 the Florentine Otto di Guardia would grant him permission to go to Venice; see Florence, Archivio di Stato, Otto di Guardia, 203, fol. 71 verso.

73 Dorez 1918, pp. 211–12. He writes: 'pour vous faire scavoir que j'ay esté adverty que Michael Angelo excellent paintre, veoyant le dangier de Florence, s'est retiré en ceste ville et ne monstre point. Car il n'y venet faire sa demeure; et croy fermement que si l'on luy offre quelque bon party en vostre nom, il seroit pour l'accepter'.

74 Dorez 1918, p. 212.

75 Dorez 1918, p. 212: 'Sire, je vous avoys escript de Michael Angello paintre pour le vous faire recouvrer, mais depuys les Florentins l'ont remendé et pardonné le vice de trop grand crainte et timidité, et s'en est retourné audict Florence'.

76 Dorez 1918, pp. 212–13. For a more recent publication of the correspondence, see Cox-Rearick 1995, pp. 283–5. She points out that the annual sum promised Michelangelo was in line with the salaries paid to artists in Francis I's court. The letters of Baïf are in Paris, Bibliothèque Nationale, MS françaises no. 3941. How urgently Francis wanted Michelangelo's services is difficult to judge from Baïf's letters; the French side of the correspondence appears to be lost. However, it is appropriate to recall here that a letter had been addressed to the artist as early as January 1519, reporting on the arrival of paintings by Raphael in Paris and going on to record Francis's esteem for Michelangelo and his wish to own a work by him. See *Carteggio* II, pp. 151–2, no. CDI. The king's desire to have copies of works by the artist dates from the mid-1540s and has been alluded to above, p. 175.

77 Condivi 1998, p. 52.

78 Vasari 1987, VI, pp. 61–2. Varchi laid particular emphasis on Michelangelo's choice of isolation in the city. He writes: 'per fuggir le vicite e le cirimonie, delle quail egli era nimicissimo, e per vivere solitario, secondo l'usanza sua, e rimoti dale conversazioni, si ritirò solanamente nella Giudecco, dove la signoria, non si potendo celare la venuta d'un tel uomo in tanta città, mandò due de'primi gentiluomini suoi a vicitarlo in nome di lei, e ad offerirgli amore volmente tutte quelle cose, le quali o a lui proprio o ad alcuno di sua compagnia bisognassono'; Varchi 1843, II, pp. 194–5.

79 For the text of the safe conduct, see Vasari-Milanesi 1878–85, VII, p. 375, and Vasari 1962, III, pp. 1068–9. The artist is assured that he can freely return to Florence; the permission extends through November, 'non obstante che lui sia cascato in bando di rubella del Comune di Firenze'.

80 *Ricordi* 1970, pp. 264–5, no. CCXXXIV.

81 *Ricordi* 1970, pp. 265–6, no. CCXXXV. For Varchi, see Varchi 1843, II, p. 195.

82 See Giugni's letter to the Dieci di Balia of 9 November, first published in Gaye 1840, p. 312. He had already written a protective letter about the artist as early as 13 October; ibid., pp. 209–10.

83 For Alfonso's safe conduct, see Gotti 1875, II, p. 74, and Vasari 1962, III, p. 1070.

84 In this context, it is worth noting that Wilde 1957, pp. 270–71, proposed that it was only on this renewed visit to Ferrara, 'that Michelangelo made up his mind to comply with Alfonso's wish'.

85 For the text of the decision to lift the *bando*, see Gaye 1840, p. 214. The step was left open to be reviewed.

86 For successive payments relating to this forced loan, see *Ricordi* 1970, pp. 256ff., no. CCXXIX. It emerges that Michelangelo was one of forty citizens subjected to the loan; see *Ricordi* 1970, p. 259. Michelangelo would later press for reimbursement through the offices of Pope Clement, following the Medicean restoration in Florence. The issue can be followed in letters from Sebastiano del Piombo in Rome. One of these, dated 2 August 1533 (*Carteggio* IV, pp. 38–9, no. CMXXV), describes the pope's fury with the Florentine ambassador at the Curia. As Symonds 1899, II, pp. 463–4, saw, the issue certainly contributed to the bad relations between the artist and Duke Alessandro de' Medici. For the episode, see Vasari 1962, III, pp. 1045–6. In the last months of the republic, Michelangelo, along with other Florentines, would be compelled to hand over silver objects to the financially crippled government; see *Ricordi* 1970, p. 259. The items included seven forks and two spoons.

87 For this and much else about the genesis of the *Leda*, see Wilde 1957, pp. 270ff., a text now reprinted in Wallace 1995, III, pp. 418–36. For the antique relief of Leda, now lost but which survived in Rome until the late sixteenth century,

which inspired both the Medici Chapel *Night* and the *Leda*, see Wilde 1957, pl. 22, and Bober and Rubinstein 1986, no. 5, pp. 53–4.

88 That his duties to the government continued, however, is shown by an episode in February 1530, when the authorities at the cathedral granted him permission to ascend the cupola. For the document, see Guasti 1857, p. 130. The incident undoubtedly arose from the need to survey the dispositions of the besieging forces.

89 For Ovid's brief reference, see *Metamorphoses*, Book VI, pp. 108–9, and for a review of the sources, Dalli Regoli, Nanni and Natali 2001, pp. 82–3. The reference to Ariosto was first raised in Rosenberg 2000, p. 98, note 19, and for further comments on the subject, see Wallace 2001, p. 485. The two most dependable engravings after Michelangelo's painting, by Cornelius Bos and Nicolas Beatrizet, unlike the many painted copies record the detail of the newly born offspring of the union, Castor and Pollux. They are also referred to by Condivi.

90 For Alfonso's letter, see *Carteggio* III, p. 290, no. DCCCIII. There are other cases where the patron left the issue of payment to the artist: Cardinal Domenico Grimani had acted in the same way over a work he was seeking for his study; see *Carteggio* II, p. 376, no. DLXXIX.

91 Condivi 1998, p. 43. Campori established that Pisanello's real name was Jacopo Lachi and published the cameral payment for his journey from Ferrara to Florence, dated 4 November 1530. For the material, see Vasari 1962, III, p. 1103. Vasari nowhere refers to the *Leda* in his Life of Michelangelo of 1550 and adds little in his account of 1568, save the statement, which is difficult to credit, that the artist painted the *Leda* in tempera; see Vasari 1987, VI, p. 63. Vasari's silence about the work in his first edition is particularly strange, since he painted copies of Michelangelo's *Leda*, referred to below.

92 For the interest shown by Clement, see *Carteggio* III, p. 349, no. DCCCXXXIV, where della Volpaia writes: 'E anchora mi domandò partiqualarmente della Leda di pictura, che di costà [Florence] n'à "intenso assai" '.

93 It has been proposed that Leda is, in fact, represented asleep: see Tolnay 1948, p. 106, a suggestion adopted by a number of writers. But the artist's head studies, for which see Tolnay 1975–80, II, no. 301 recto, and Hirst 1988b, p. 92, no. 38, first recognized as preparatory for the *Leda* by Wilde, show that the artist's intention was to represent the eyes half-closed, expressing her rapture. Papini 1949, p. 299, evocatively wrote of Leda 'con gli occhi socchiusi, con espressione languorosa di voluttà'.

94 For the relief, see Bober and Rubinstein 1986, no. 5, and no. 5b for the cameo.

95 Aretino-Procaccioli 1998, p. 20, no. 5. The letter, addressed to Duke Guidobaldo della Rovere, may have been prompted by the arrival in Venice of copies of both the *Leda* and the *Venus and Cupid* by Vasari, dispatched from Florence in the autumn of 1541; see Vasari 1927, pp. 36–7.

96 For a brief but useful survey of Mini's activity, see Pini-Milanesi 1869–76 (unpaginated), the pages accompanying pl. 117. He seems to have been placed with Michelangelo by his uncle Giovan Battista Mini. This seems to have occurred not in 1522, as often proposed, but in 1523; see the letter of Michelangelo's good friend Piero Gondi, of December 1523, in which the latter reports favourably on his interview with Mini: 'lui è contento di fare tucto quello che voi vorrete … e dimostra d'averne piacere assai e vuole disegnare'; see *Carteggio* III, p. 3, no. DXCI. Mini's drawings require a separate study. For a discussion of those in the British Museum, see Wilde 1953, no. 31, pp. 62–4 and 67–8.

97 See *Ricordi* 1970, pp. 371–2, no. CCCXIV. An important book of *ricordi* is written entirely in Mini's hand; see *Ricordi* 1970, pp. 254–62, no. CCXXIX.

98 Writing from Rome in March 1526, Leonardo Sellaio sends his greetings to Mini and a recommendation that he should work hard from no less than Pope Clement himself: 'Salutate Antonio, e ditegli gli chomando per parte del Papa che studi'; see *Carteggio* III, p. 215, no. DCCXLIII. The injunction to study is matched by Michelangelo's written inscription on a sheet of drawing in the British Museum: Wilde 1953, no. 31 recto, p. 62: 'Disegnia antonio disegnia antonio/ disegnia e no[n] p[er]der te[m]po'.

99 The course of Mini's move to France, and the repeated setbacks he encountered there, can be followed in a whole series of letters. For a detailed account of Mini's troubles, see Cox-Rearick 1995, pp. 237–40; for the purchase of the *Leda* by Francis I and its much later destruction on the grounds of indecency, ibid., p. 241. The documentation, especially the contents of Mini's letters, show that the painting was repeatedly copied. Vasari states that Michelangelo's own preparatory cartoon came back to Florence, but unfortunately gives no details of how and when this happened; see Vasari 1987, IV, p. 64. He himself was familiar with the design by no later than 1542, as already noted. For a valuable attempt to identify some of the drawings that Mini took with him, see Joannides 1994, pp. 15–35.

100 Capello reported the fact in a letter to the Venetian senate of 31 May 1530, adding that, by late February, there were sixty to seventy deaths a day from the appalling conditions prevailing in the city; see Capello, in Albèri 1839–55, XI, p. 295, and for the death rate, p. 276.

CHAPTER TEN

1 Varchi 1843, II, pp. 453ff., describes the despairing attitude over the condition of the city held by Malatesta Baglione.

2 This is the figure given in Roth 1925, p. 320.

3 See Varchi 1843, II, p. 518, for the clause exonerating those who had served the republic; the text describes a 'generale remissione di tutte le pene in che

fossono incorsi per conto di disubbidienza dell'essere stati al servizio della città di Firenze nella presente guerra'.

4 For Clement's disregard of the agreed terms, see Varchi 1843, II, p. 519. He writes: 'Di tutte queste convenzioni non solo non ne fu osservata nessuna per la parte di Clemente ma di ciascuna ... fu fatto il contrario'. For an outstanding record of those who suffered on account of their previous role in the republic, see ibid., pp. 557ff. Varchi's description of the excesses of the new regime is the more remarkable when it is recalled that his *Storia fiorentina* had been commissioned by Duke Cosimo de' Medici during 1546–7. For an assessment of Varchi, see Albertini 1970, pp. 339–46.

5 For Battista della Palla's fate, see Varchi 1843, II, p. 558, and Elam 1993, p. 71. For a discussion of Giannotti, later to be a close friend of Michelangelo in Rome, see Albertini 1970, pp. 145–65.

6 See Condivi 1998, p. 40. He writes: 'Ma essendo poi per accordo entrati i nemici dentro, e molti cittadini presi e uccisi, fu mandata la corte a casa di Michelagnolo per pigliarlo, e furon le stanze e tutte le casse aperte, per in fin al camino e'l necessario. Ma Michelagnolo, temendo di quell che seguì, se n'era fuggito in casa d'un suo grande amico, dove molti giorni stando nascosto, non sapendo nessuno ch'egli in casa fusse, eccetto che l'amico, si salvò'. Condivi does not explain which property was involved, but it seems likely that it was the house that he had rented in 1529 on what is now the Via di Mezzo and where he was still living in 1530. For Vasari's remarks about the episode, totally dependent on Condivi, see Vasari 1987, VI, p. 63.

7 The story of the concealment in the *campanile* seems to have originated with an eighteenth-century member of the Buonarroti family, Senator Filippo, who passed on the information to Giovanni Bottari; see Gotti 1875, I, p. 199.

8 Frey seems to have been the first to propose that it was the Quaratesi family who sheltered him. The family's connections with San Niccolò went back to 1421; see Paatz and Paatz 1952, pp. 375ff. For a fine discussion of the family and of the artist's wonderful portrait drawing of Andrea Quaratesi, see Wilde 1953, pp. 97–8. The sheet is reproduced to scale in Tolnay 1975–80, II, no. 329, recto.

9 Figiovanni writes: 'Et facto la pace victorioso el papa, Michelangnolo conparse. Bartolommeo Valori commissario cercò farlo morire da Alexandro Corsini strumento del papa, per molte offensione facte alla casa de' Medici. Io lo canpai [i.e., campai] dalla morte et salva'li la roba: addomandonmi mille volte perdono'; see Corti 1964, p. 29.

10 For the episode of Corsini's public depiction as a traitor, see Varchi 1843, II, p. 244. The work was carried out by Andrea del Sarto; see Shearman 1965, II, p. 321.

11 Varchi 1843, I, p. 441. After recording the behaviour of the Bolognese, he

writes: 'Ma perchè da molti ancora oggi si crede, questo essere stato prima consiglio di Michelagnolo Simoni de'Buonarroti, il quale aveva detto, dicono, che rovinata quella casa, si dovesse della via fare una piazza, la quale la piazza de'Muli si chiamase'. Varchi continues that he never found the source for the story, but says of the words 'che apposte gli furono, come disse allora, e ancora dice egli stesso'.

12   Varchi 1843, II, p. 562: 'Michelagnolo per lo essere stato egli un de'nove della milizia, per lo aver bastionato il monte, e armato il campanile di San Miniato, e, quello che dispiaceva più, perchè di lui s'era detto (benchè falsamente, come si scrisse ne'libri precedenti) lui aver messo innanzi, che spiantato e spianato il palazzo de'Medici, nel quale egli era fin da fanciullo stato tanto onorato da Lorenzo Vecchio e da Piero de'Medici suo figliuolo, infino alle tavole loro, si dovesse fare dell'aia la piazza de'Muli, temendo l'ira di Clemente, era stato negli ultimi giorni dell'assedio sempre sfuggiasco, e fatto l'accordo si racchiuse nascosamente, senzachè altri il sapesse, in casa d'un suo amicissimo. Andò la famiglia degli otto e quella del bargello, e cercarono tutte le stanze della sua casa minutissimamente più volte'.

13   See Busini's letter to Varchi of 30 March 1549, in Busini 1860, Letter XVI, p. 164. The Venetian ambassador, Carlo Capello, wrote in a letter of 9 November 1529 that threats were being made to destroy all buildings associated with the Medici but for the most part these were being protected; see Albèri 1839–55, XI, p. 244. But destruction did take place, including Jacopo Salviati's villa at Montughi; see Nerli 1728, pp. 203ff. Salviati was himself declared a rebel in October 1529.

14   The Venetian envoy described Clement as wearing the long beard he had grown in Castel Sant'Angelo and refers to his deep depression: 'Sta sempre maninconico'; see Sanudo 1879–1903, XLVIII, col. 226. For an account of Clement in Orvieto, see Reynolds 2005, pp. 143ff.; he had arrived there on 8 December. He would leave for Viterbo at the end of April, arriving there on 1 June.

15   *Carteggio* III, p. 255, no. DCCLXXIV. The letter sheds light on Clement's anxiety that work at San Lorenzo should not come to an end. His offer of money is the more remarkable in the light of the dire financial state of the court at Orvieto; one Venetian witness would report that it was bankrupt, 'senza un carlino'; see Reynolds 2005, p. 155, note 67, quoting Sanudo 1879–1903, XLVI, col. 488.

16   Fragmentary passages from these letters of Marzi survive in the Archivio di Stato, Florence, in the form of copies: see ASF, *Carte Strozzianeane*, II series, no. 149. They were known in the nineteenth century; see Gaye 1840, no. CLXIII, pp. 221–2, who published parts of them in an unsystematic way. They are described as 'Estratto alfabetico di lettere scritte per ordine di Clemente VII da monsignor Piero Paolo a monsignore suo fratello l'anno 1530'. The passages selected by the copyist, however, are from nine letters to Figiovanni, who is

addressed as 'Figi', and two to Michelangelo himself. In this letter of 20 October, omitted by Gaye and apparently addressed to Figiovanni, we find the following information on fol. 37 verso: 'Et che al bancho de'Pitti et Lanfredini si è ordinato costì in Firenze li danari da paghare ogni mese Michelagnolo sculptore et a ogni sua requisitione gli anumerravanno facendo loro la fede del ricevuto'. I am greatly indebted to Dr Gabriella Battista for locating and transcribing these excerpts.

17   The sum is specified in two further extracts, one of which records a letter addressed to Michelangelo himself, dated 11 December; ASF, *Carte Strozzianeane*, II series, no. 149, fol. 86 verso: 'Michel Agnolo, Nostro Signore ha grandissimo piacere dell lavorare che 'l fa et vuole li sia dato la sua solita provisione che debbe essere cinquanta scudi il mese'. See Figiovanni's *ricordo* in *Ricordi* 1970, p. 267. At one point in the autumn, Clement had been seized by the fear that the artist had been overpaid; see ASF, *Carte Strozzianeane*, as above, fol. 40 recto, and a letter of Pier Polo Marzi to his brother in *Carteggio indiretto* I, p. 337, no. 224. Figiovanni had sent the accounts to Rome and his clarification acknowledged in a letter of 6 December; ASF, *Carte Strozzianeane*, fol. 40 recto. The fact confirms that he was once more *proveditore*, in charge of the finances at San Lorenzo.

18   ASF, *Carte Strozzianeane*, fol. 38 recto.

19   ASF, *Carte Strozzianeane*, fol. 40 recto.

20   *Carteggio* III, p. 291, no. DCCCIV. Cibo, like Giovanni Salviati, was one of the four Florentine cardinals most deeply trusted by Clement. A year later, he would be soliciting a tomb design from Michelangelo; see *Carteggio* III, p. 353, no. DCCCXXXVII.

21   For details of Figiovanni's career, see Corti 1964, pp. 24ff., and the biographical profile by V. Arrighi in *DBI*, XLVII, pp. 557–8.

22   Borromeo's letter was published in Luzio 1913, p. 249. He describes the artist as working night and day. The work is such that he doubts it will ever be finished: 'la quale è tanta che dubito non basterà la sua vita al fine'. Condivi would later write that the artist resumed work 'spinto più dalla paura che dall'amore'; see Condivi 1998, p. 41. The fragment of a sonnet, datable to this time, expressed Michelangelo's despair. He writes that if it is permitted to kill oneself in this world, believing that one may return to heaven through death, it would surely be justified for one who lives in such faithful service, wretched and unhappy. For these lines, see Girardi 1960, no. 52, p. 26, and Saslow 1991, no. 52, p. 138.

23   Gaye 1840, p. 227, and Luzio 1913, pp. 249–50.

24   Published only in part by Luzio 1913, p. 250. This extraordinary letter can be found in Pastor-Mercati 1944–63, IV, 2, pp. 340–41, Appendix 135. Clement is reported as saying: 'essendo lui occupato in la scolptura, come è et è per essere molto tempo, non può avere la mano disposta al dipingere, se non interpassare

per un tempo lo exercito del scarpello, per essere totalmente diversa l'una cosa da l'altra'.

25   *Carteggio* III, p. 301, no. DCCCXII.

26   *Carteggio* III, p. 328, no. DCCCXXVII.

27   *Carteggio* III, p. 340, no. DCCCXXXII.

28   For a study of the project undertaken for Vittoria Colonna, see Hirst 2004a, pp. 5–29.

29   Valori had been declared a rebel in the same *bando* as Michelangelo, of 30 September 1529. By December he had entered papal service and a price was put on his head and his palace subjected to a breach of three yards wide from the roof to the ground, a traditional punishment for treachery. Nerli 1728, p. 206, writes: 'oltre alla taglia data a Bartolommeo Valori di scudi mille d'oro achi lo desse prigione, e scudi cinquecento a chi l'ammazzase, gli fu per determinazione e sentenza della Guarantìa sdrucita la casa dal tetto a'fondamenti'. For similar information, see Varchi 1843, II, p. 192, and for documentation, Roth 1925, p. 205, note 117. Valori would be beheaded by Duke Cosimo in 1537 after allying himself with the anti-Medicean exiles defeated in battle at Montemurlo.

30   See Vasari 1987, VI, pp. 62–3. Repeated attempts to date the inception of the *Apollo* in the later 1520s woefully ignore the evidence. No preparatory material for the *Apollo* now survives. A drawing doubtfully ascribed to Rosso has been adduced for evidence of an earlier date; see Carrol 1987, no. 49, pp. 146–8. If by Rosso, it could have been made from preparatory drawings or models taken by Antonio Mini to France.

31   *Carteggio* III, pp. 386–7, no. DCCCLVI. It may be added that Valori would exploit his enhanced authority in this period to have his portrait painted in Rome by Sebastiano, who refers to his intention to carry it out in a letter to Michelangelo of November 1531; see *Carteggio* III, p. 344, no. DCCCXXXIII. For the painting, see Hirst 1981b, p. 113 and pls 146–7. Like the *Apollo*, the picture was sequestered by Duke Cosimo in 1537.

32   For Francesco del Lucchesino, see Wallace 1994, pp. 81–2 and 180. Michelangelo's renewed confidence in him, after earlier discord, is shown by his subsequently contracting with him and colleagues to carve the two doors and the staircase for the library at San Lorenzo; see *Contratti*, no. LXXXVIII, pp. 209–10.

33   The attribution of the windows to Michelangelo was first proposed by Howard Burns in a number of lectures in 1977.

34   *Carteggio* III, p. 305, no. DCCCXIII. Shrugging off reports that had reached him at the time of the siege, Clement has declared that he has never done Michelangelo an injury.

35   *Carteggio* III, p. 308–9, no. DCCCXV.

36   *Carteggio* III, p. 312, no. DCCCXVII.

37   *Carteggio* III, pp. 329–30, appended to no. DCCCXXVII; the text was first published by Gaye 1840, pp. 228ff. In the early 1530s Michelangelo was helping Bugiardini

with drawings for an altarpiece for Santa Maria Novella; see Wilde 1953, pp. 86–7.

38 Mini's description of the work in progress in the sacristy is unparalleled in its informality. He implies that one of the tombs still awaits assembling. In the coming winter 'si potrebe murare e'lavorare del quadro de le sepolture e chominciare a metervi sù le figure finite'. As long ago as June 1526 Michelangelo had reported that one tomb had been constructed and that he hoped to turn to the other; see *Carteggio* III, pp. 227–8, no. DCCLII. But from Mini's remarks, it would appear that this had never happened. There is a fair degree of unanimity in the literature that it was Duke Giuliano's tomb that was still awaiting installation at this time. Wallace 1994, p. 230, note 7, noted signs of haste in its construction.

39 *Contratti*, no. LXXXIV, p. 198. The brief was first published in Bottari 1759–73, VI, no. XV, who, however, misunderstood its meaning. 'Sepultura' can, in the context of 1531, refer only to Julius II's tomb, as Thode 1902–12, I, p. 416, correctly saw. The use of the second person singular would be adopted again in a brief of Paul III of 1535; see *Contratti*, no. LXXXIX, p. 211.

40 *Carteggio* III, pp. 348–9, no. DCCCXXXIV. For Bernardo della Volpaia, see Pagliara in *DBI*, XXXVII, pp. 795–7. The letter reveals many sides of Clement's character, including his humour when he suggests that, to satisfy demands, Michelangelo should stick a paintbrush between his toes and carry out four friezes. He has warned the artist not to provoke Duke Alessandro and made comments on Bandinelli, on close terms with the Curia at this time and once more given the project of carving the pendant to the giant *David*.

41 Clement is reported to have said that he will deal with Bartolommeo Valori. Gotti 1875, I, p. 211, noted the reference to the *Apollo*.

42 The general belief that Lodovico died in 1534 was first exposed as an error by Wilde in Popham and Wilde 1949, p. 249; he showed that he must have died in early 1531. More recently, Ristori has established that his death occurred before 23 March 1531; see *Carteggio indiretto* I, p. XXVIII, and p. 345, note 4.

43 *Carteggio indiretto* I, p. 313, no. 203.

44 *Carteggio indiretto* I, p. 314, no. 204. Lodovico writes: 'Io sono rovinato tutto, l'anima e'l chorpo e la roba e l'onore'.

45 *Carteggio indiretto* I, p. 315, no. 205.

46 *Carteggio indiretto* I, p. 323, no. 212.

47 *Carteggio indiretto* I, p. 328, no. 217.

48 *Ricordi* 1970, p. 273, no. CCXLVI. The entries extend from late 1530 to 1531. In one of them, Michelangelo notes that he has spent 25 ducats for funeral and burial expenses, which, as Wilde realized, must relate to his father's death.

49 *Carteggio* III, p. 431, no. DCCCLXXXIX. The letter dates from the late summer of 1532 after he had returned from a long absence in Pisa.

50 For the practice of the widow leaving the deceased husband's home, see Klapisch-Zuber 1985, especially pp. 120ff.

51   See *Ricordi* 1970, no. CCLI, pp. 276–7.

52   These facts were established by Ristori; see *Carteggio indiretto* I, p. 229, note 4.

53   *Carteggio* III, p. 297, no. DCCCIX.

54   For the poem, see Girardi 1960, no. 86, pp. 49–51, and Saslow 1991, no. 86, pp. 203–7. Michelangelo refers to a deeper grief for his more recently deceased father. While memory still paints his brother for him, it sculpts his father within his heart as if still alive: 'La memoria 'l fratel pur mi dipigne/ e te sculpisce vivo in mezzo il core'.

55   *Carteggio* IV, p. 63, no. CMXXXVIII. The artist insists that Giovan Simone take her in, 'perché mio padre alla morte me la rachomandò, non la abandonerò mai'. The words are telling evidence of Michelangelo's care for those who served his family and himself, a trait not always acknowledged. Florentine social history affords many examples of such solicitude for servants.

56   See his letter of 13 November 1540 to his nephew Leonardo in Florence; *Carteggio* IV, p. 114, no. CMLXXVII.

57   *Carteggio* III, pp. 299–300, no. DCCCXI. He writes: 'Hora, compar mio, che siamo passati per aqua et per fuoco ...Ancora non mi par esser quel Bastiano che io era inanti el sacco; non posso tornor in cervello ancora'. Evidence suggests that Sebastiano had been among those who, like Pope Clement himself, had taken refuge in Castel Sant'Angelo; see Hirst 1981b, p. 89.

58   For the letter of 16 June 1531, see *Carteggio* III, pp. 308–10, no. DCCCXV. Writing of the damage to the tomb, he informs Michelangelo that 'l'opera de quadro è precipitato sotto terra'. Damage is still visible on those parts of the tomb in San Pietro in Vincoli carried out in the earlier period. This was the second of two floods to strike Rome. For Cambi, *Istorie*, in *Delizie*, XXII, pp. 78ff., it was an evil omen for Pope Clement. Giovio 1555, p. 304, included the flood – in reality the second of two – in his list of disasters that had overtaken Rome; he refers to 'la prodiogiosa piena del Thebro, moltiplicando sciagure l'una sopra l'altra'.

59   *Carteggio* III, pp. 303–6, no. DCCCXIII. See also the letter of the pope's secretary, Pier Polo Marzi, of June; *Carteggio* III, pp. 312–13, no. DCCCXVIII, who refers to the need to rescue the artist from 'questo fastidio, molestia et fa[n]tasia'.

60   *Carteggio* III, pp. 316–19, no. DCCCXX.

61   *Carteggio* III, pp. 323–4, no. DCCCXXIV. The thought of finding the money is, nevertheless, an unpleasant one, and the artist's deep reluctance to part with any is emphasized by his extraordinary reference to his earlier financial setback, when he had had to pay the forced loan to the republican government in the autumn of 1529. His obsessive concern to reclaim the money would promote future problems with the restored Medicean regime in Florence.

62   *Carteggio* III, pp. 342–7, no. DCCCXXXIII. For the letters of della Porta and Staccoli, and the duke's replies, see Vasari 1962, III, pp. 1171ff., where most of the texts are

republished. Many first appeared in G. Vasari, *Le Vite* . . . , ed. V. Marchese, C. Pini and G. Milanesi, XII, 1856, pp. 157–311. Further ones were added in Gronau 1906, pp. 1–7. The correspondence can be found in Florence, Archivio di Stato, *Carteggio dei Duchi d'Urbino*.

63　In a much later letter of 1542, Michelangelo, close to breakdown, would accuse the dead pope Clement of having deceived him; see *Carteggio* IV, pp. 150–55, no. MI.

64　*Contratti*, nos. LXXXV–LXXXVI, pp. 199–207. The duke was represented by della Porta and Staccoli. Cardinals Antonio del Monte and Ercole Gonzaga, together with the dead Julius's daughter, Felice della Rovere Orsini, were the other parties who undertook to see to the completion of the agreement. In a letter of the following day, della Porta reported that Clement was present.

65　For an excellent account of the contract of 1532 and subsequent events, see Echinger-Maurach 1991, pp. 361–85. She points out that the decision to accept a simple wall tomb reflected the negotiations that had preceded the sack of 1527, which had envisaged a modest project modelled on the wall tombs of Pius II and Pius III.

66　The letter is republished in Vasari 1962, III, p. 1182. Reporting on the issue of the site, della Porta writes: 'Non si potendo mettere in San Pietro, come non si può, ad ognuno parebe convenientissimo che si mettesse in San Pietro in Vincula, come loco proprio della casa, che fu titolo di Xisto [Sixtus IV] ancora, e la chiesa fabricata da Giulio, che vi condusse gli frati che vi stano . . . Al popolo sarebbe stata bene, come in loco più frequentato; ma non v'è loco capace nè lume al proposito, secondo Michelangelo'. When created a cardinal in 1471, the future Julius II had taken the title of San Pietro in Vincoli and had subsequently carried out extensive building there; see Ippoliti 1999, passim. Even after his election in 1503, he would retire there for periods of repose and, as noted earlier, he chose the church for the formal submission of the Bolognese in 1512.

67　See Vasari 1962, III, p. 1184. Della Porta again refers to the benefit that Santa Maria del Popolo would bring because it is more visited, but goes on to repeat Michelangelo's objections: 'ma si comme altre volte n'era stato parlato e con Michelangelo medesimo in presenza di Sua Santità nel giorno del contratto, la chiesa del Popolo non havea nè lumi nè loco atto a questa opera . . . ; ma Michelangelo vi fu a vederla e disse non si potere accomodare altrovi che a S.P. in Vincula, contetandosi però Nostro Signore si come si contentò, che l'altare delle Catene si levasse et si trasportasse all'altare maggiore'. For the earlier history of the Cappella delle Catene, see, most recently, Satzinger 2001, p. 191, note 66.

68　*Carteggio* III, pp. 417–18, no. DCCCLXXX. He has sent the duke's ratification of the contract to the artist.

69　These comments were conveyed in a letter of Sebastiano's of 15 July; see *Carteggio*

III, pp. 419–20, no. DCCCLXXXI. Health concerns had been strengthened by the unexpected death of Michelangelo's recent host, Benvenuto della Volpaia, in late June.

70   *Carteggio* III, p. 426, no. DCCCLXXXV.

71   While still in Florence, Michelangelo was alerted by Figiovanni to a projected visit to the sacristy on the part of Duke Alessandro and Don Pedro da Toledo to see the statues. They had been compelled to gain access through a window, perhaps one of those in the lunettes; entrance at floor level was probably impeded by the scaffolding erected to allow Giovanni da Udine to begin decoration of the cupola. For the visit, see *Carteggio* III, p. 428, no. DCCCLXXXVI. A subsequent letter would describe this scaffolding as a fortress, 'una fortezza'; *Carteggio* III, p. 438, no. DCCCXCIII.

72   See *Carteggio* III, p. 436, no. DCCCXCII, and following letters. The relics, finally dispatched from Rome in accordance with Clement's long-standing wish, would reach Florence in early December. For the reliquary tribune, see Mussolin 2007, passim.

73   Girardi 1960 concluded that at least fourteen sonnets were definitely addressed and others probably addressed to Cavalieri. They include his numbers 58–61, 76–80, 82–4, 87–90 and 95. For translations of the poems, and many interesting comments on their nature and the artist's debts to Dante and Petrarch, see Saslow 1991, who retains Girardi's numbering. Other verses, including madrigals, were also dedicated to Cavalieri.

74   See *Carteggio* III, pp. 53–4, no. CMXXXV. Many of the letters that Angiolini sent to Michelangelo in Florence reveal a lively and humorous intelligence; he had known him for twenty years. Just after Michelangelo's leave-taking, he writes that the cats at Macel de' Corvi are missing him: 'le gatte molto si lamentano'; *Carteggio* III, p. 13, no. CMVII.

75   For the deeply subjective nature of these poems, see Cambon 1985, p. 48, who sees it as a consistent feature of the love poetry, be the recipient Febo di Poggio, Gherardo Perini, Tommaso de' Cavalieri, Vittoria Colonna or the unknown 'donna bella e crudele'. He never portrays the object of the poem; he portrays their effect on himself.

76   For Cecchini, see Frommel 1979, pp. 14–15. For his part in preparing the Rome house, see Sebastiano's letter of July 1532; *Carteggio* III, pp. 419–20, no. DCCCLXXXI.

77   Frommel 1979, pp. 69–70. For the collection, see Steinmann and Pogatscher 1906, pp. 502–4.

78   Documentary evidence for the date of Cavalieri's birth has not been found. Frommel 1979, p. 72, proposed one of a little after 1511. The suggestion of Panofsky-Soergel 1984, pp. 399ff., that he was born as late as 1519–20, is based on a serious misinterpretation of a document. Cavalieri's statement in this letter

that he is a youth scarcely born into the world is self-deprecating modesty over his attainments.

79 For Michelangelo's letter, see *Carteggio* III, pp. 443–4, no. DCCCXCVII. Cavalieri's reply is the following letter, pp. 445–6, no. DCCCXCVIII. It is in this letter that he refers to drawings of his own that he has shown to Michelangelo.

80 Vasari 1987, VI, pp. 109–10. For the original *Ganymede*, see Hirst 1975, pp. 166. For the *Tityus*, see Tolnay 1975–80, II, no. 345; for the Windsor *Phaeton*, the version Vasari refers to, no. 343, and for the *Bacchanal*, no. 238.

81 Vasari 1987, IV, p. 405.

82 The letter was published by Steinmann and Pogatscher 1906, pp. 504–5; it is reprinted in Vasari 1962, IV, pp. 1890–91. Cavalieri writes: 'La eccellenza vostra non si è punto ingannata nel promettersi di me, et per seggno di ciò mando questo diseggno a me tanto caro, ch'io reputo privarmi di uno de miei figliuli'. He adds that many Roman patrons had coveted the drawing without success. For the recto of the *Cleopatra*, see Tolnay 1975–80, II, no. 327. The sheet was lifted in 1988 and another sketch, of a frightened Cleopatra, was revealed on the verso.

83 See Steinmann and Pogatscher 1906, p. 505.

84 Tolnay 1975–80, II, no. 340, and Wilde 1953, no. 55, pp. 91–3.

85 For the relief, see Bober and Rubinstein 1986, no. 27, p. 70.

86 For the inscription, see Wilde 1953, no. 55, p. 91. The message provides us with the earliest evidence that Francesco d'Amadore, referred to as Urbino, had entered the artist's service. He would be a devoted assistant until his death in 1556.

87 For a survey of the drawings that Michelangelo made as presents, see Hirst 1988a, pp. 105–18, and for an analysis of the three *Phaeton* sheets, Hirst 1988b, pp. 107–12. That the Windsor *Archers Shooting at a Herm* was made for Cavalieri is rendered unlikely on grounds of provenance. In several of his poems addressed to Cavalieri, however, the artist likens himself to a target and refers to Cavalieri as the 'cruel archer'. His inspiration for the image was Petrarch's Sonnet no. CXXXIII: 'Amor m'à posto come segno a strale'.

88 Vasari 1987, VI, p. 110: 'Ritrasse Michelagnolo messer Tommaso in un cartone grande, di naturale, che né prima né poi di nessuno fece il ritratto'.

89 Steinmann and Pogatscher 1906, p. 506. The passage is reprinted in Wilde 1953, p. 97, and in Vasari 1962, IV, p. 1905. However, a description of the portrait drawing was written by the noted Spaniard Pablo de Céspedes at an earlier date. For his description, see Vasari 1962, IV, p. 1905. Both sources refer to the fact that Cavalieri is depicted holding a medal.

90 The Bayonne drawing was first published in Bean 1960, no. 73, there catalogued as School of Michelangelo with a question mark. Joannides 1995, pp. 3ff., attributed the drawing to Michelangelo, dating it about 1530. He did not at that

point advance the identification of the subject as Cavalieri, despite the sheet's close parallels with the written descriptions. More recently, he proposed the identification: Joannides 2003, p. 253. The one feature arguably at odds is the statement in the Corsini description that Cavalieri is clad 'al antico'. But this is not an objection if it is recalled that the note was written about a hundred years after the drawing was made. The original drawing appears in an inventory of Palazzo Farnese of 1644. Unfortunately, the description does not give its size, which, given the exceptional scale of the Bayonne sheet, could have been decisive. For the inventory, see Jestaz 1994, no. 4347, p. 173.

91   For Marzi's letter, see *Carteggio* III, pp. 312–13, no. DCCXVII. He writes of the pope's concern lest the intensity of work should damage the artist's health. Michelangelo should not work 'con tanta vostra extrema fatica, ma in modo et di sorte che vi haviate a mantenere sano et gagliardo, et vivo et non morto'.

92   *Carteggio* III, pp. 324–31. Mini suggests that Michelangelo should work elsewhere (i.e., not in the New Sacristy) and proceed with work on the *Virgin and Child* and the statue of Duke Lorenzo. He goes on to propose that the finished figures could be put in place. Of Michelangelo's ill health, he writes that his worries over the tomb of Pope Julius and the Duke of Urbino are affecting his heart: 'A quelo male del quore, è quanto a la chosa che gli à chol. duca d'Urbino'.

93   For documentation relating to Bandinelli's group, see Waldman 2004, p. 120, nos. 218 and 219. It would be unveiled on 1 May, 1534; ibid., pp. 133–4, nos. 236–7.

94   For Valori's letter, see *Carteggio* III, pp. 386–7, no. DCCCLVI. He writes: 'Vi ricordo bene che a satisfatione dell'animo mio non ho cosa che io desideri più che questa'.

95   The statue is recorded in the apartment of Duke Cosimo in Palazzo Vecchio in an inventory of 1553 (ASF, Guardaroba Medicea 28, Appendice n. 1). It is described as representing David and 'del Buonarroto imperfetto'. Vasari, however, clearly familiar with the statue, seems to have been in no doubt that it represents Apollo taking an arrow from his quiver, and it is so described in his first edition of the *Le Vite* of 1550: 'una figuretta d'uno Apollo che cavava del turcasso una freccia'.

96   See Nerli 1728, p. 206. He writes that in December 1529 Valori was among those condemned as a rebel and that the Florentine magistrate of the Quaranta ordered the destruction of his palace: 'oltre alla taglia data a Bartolommeo Valori di scudi mille d'oro a chi lo desse prigione, e scudi cinquecento a chi l'ammazzase, gli fu per determinazione e stentenza della Quarantià sdrucito la casa del tetto a fondamenti, con proibizione, che tale sdrucito non si potesse più in perpetuo rimurare'.

97   For Valori's letter to Michelangelo, which indicated that he was consulted over the new palace, see *Carteggio* III, pp. 386–7, no. DCCCLVII. It cannot be excluded that, as Howard Burns suggested (see n. 33 above), Michelangelo had some part

in the design of the window tabernacles. On Valori, see the judgement of Varchi 1843, II, p. 539ff., where he writes: 'E di vero Baccio era, se non più pietoso, meno crudele degli altri palleschi'.

98   For a discussion of Michelangelo's final departure from Florence and his break with Febo di Poggio, see the comments of Ramsden 1963, I, Appendix 25, pp. 302–4. It should not be overlooked that the artist faced serious financial problems following his return to Florence in 1531 and that Pope Clement had been forced to intervene to reimburse him for money he had been compelled to give to the anti-Medicean regime. For the issue, see Vasari 1962, III, pp. 1178ff.

BIBLIOGRAPHY

Ackerman 1961
J. S. Ackerman, *The Architecture of Michelangelo*, 2 vols, London, 1961

Ackerman 1974
—, 'Notes on Bramante's Bad Reputation', in *Studi bramanteschi. Atti del congresso internazionale*, Rome, 1974, 339–49

Agosti and Hirst 1996
G. Agosti and M. Hirst, 'Michelangelo, Piero d'Argenta and the "Stigmatisation of St Francis" ', *Burlington Magazine*, CXXXVIII (1996), 683–4

Agosti and Isella 2004
— and D. Isella, eds, *Antiquarie prospetiche romane*, Parma, 2004

Albèri 1839–55
E. Albèri, *Le relazioni degli Ambasciatori Veneti al Senato durante il secolo decimo sesto*, 3rd series, 12 vols, Florence, 1839–55

Alberti 1980
L. B. Alberti, *I Libri della famiglia*, ed. R. Romano and A. Tenenti, Turin, 1980

Albertini 1510
F. Albertini, *Memoriale di Molte Statue et Picture di Florentia* [Florence, 1510]; in P. Murray, *Five Early Guides to Rome and Florence*, Farnborough, 1972

Albertini 1970
R. von Albertini, *Firenze dalla repubblica al principato*, Turin, 1970

Aldrovandi 1556
U. Aldrovandi, 'Delle statue antiche, che per tutta Roma, in diversi luoghi

e case si veggano', in L. Mauro, *Le antichità de la città di Roma*, Venice, 1556

Amy 2000
M. Amy, 'The Dating of Michelangelo's "St Matthew" ', *Burlington Magazine*, CXLII (2000), 493–6

Androsov and Baldini 2000
S. Androsov and U. Baldini, eds, *L' 'Adolescente' dell'Ermitage e la Sagrestia Nuova di Michelangelo*, Florence, 2000

Anselmi, Pezzarossa and Avellini 1980
G. M. Anselmi, F. Pezzarossa and L. Avellini, *La 'memoria' dei mercatores: tendenze ideologiche, ricordanza, artigianato in versi nella Firenze del Quattrocento*, Bologna, 1980

Apollonj Ghetti 1968
F. M. Apollonj Ghetti, 'Le case di Michelangelo in via dei Fornari in Roma', *L'urbe*, XXI (1968), 13–25

Aretino-Procaccioli 1998
P. Aretino, *Lettere*, II, ed. P. Procaccioli, Rome, 1998

Argan and Contardi 1990
G. C. Argan and B. Contardi, *Michelangelo architetto*, Milan, 1990

Aschoff 1967
W. Aschoff, 'Studien zu Nicolò Tribolo', Ph.D. thesis, Frankfurt-am-Mein, 1967

Baldini 1999
N. Baldini, 'Il primo soggiorno di Michelangelo a Roma: fonti cinquecenteschi e testimonianze documentarie', in Weil-Garris Brandt et al. 1999, 149–52

Baldini and Giulietti 1999
— and R. Giulietti, eds, *Andrea Sansovino: i documenti*, Florence, 1999

Baldini, Lodico and Piras 1999
—, D. Lodico and A. M. Piras, 'Michelangelo a Roma: i rapporti con la famiglia Galli e con Baldassarre del Milanese', in Weil-Garris Brandt et al. 1999, 149–62

Baldriga 2000

I. Baldriga, 'The First Version of Michelangelo's *Christ* for Santa Maria sopra Minerva', *Burlington Magazine*, CXLII (2000), 740–45

Bambach 1999

C. C. Bambach, *Drawing and Painting in the Italian Renaissance Workshop: Theory and Practice, 1300–1600*, Cambridge, MA, 1999

Barbieri and Puppi 1964

F. Barbieri and L. Puppi, 'Catalogo delle opere di Michelangelo', in *Michelangelo architetto*, ed. P. Portoghesi and B. Zevi, 3 vols, Turin, 1964, 813–973

Bardeschi Ciulich 1989

L. Bardeschi Ciulich, *Costanza ed evoluzione nella scrittura di Michelangelo*, Florence, 1989

Bardeschi Ciulich 1993

—, 'Michelangelo e il Banco Salviati di Pisa', *Annali della Scuola Normale Superiore di Pisa, Classe di Lettere e Filosofia*, series III, XXIII (1993), 1041–128

Bardeschi Ciulich 1994

—, 'I marmi di Michelangelo', in *La difficile eredità: architettura a Firenze dalla Repubblica all'Assedio*, ed. M. Dezzi Bardeschi, Florence, 1994, 100–05

Bardeschi Ciulich and Raggionieri 2001

— and P. Raggionieri, eds, *Vita di Michelangelo*, Florence, 2001

Barocchi 1971

P. Barocchi, ed., *Scritti d'arte del Cinquecento*, I, Milan and Naples, 1971

Barocchi 1992

—, ed., *Il Giardino di San Marco: maestri e compagni del giovane Michelangelo*, Milan, 1992

Barolsky and Wallace 1993

P. Barolsky and W. Wallace, 'The Myth of Michelangelo and il Magnifico', *Source*, XII/3 (1993), 16–21

Battaglia 1961–2002

G. S. Bataglia, *Il Grande Dictionario della lingua italiana*, 21 vols, Turin 1961–2002

Battisti 1966

E. Battisti, 'I "coperchi" delle tombe medicee', in G. Mansuelli (ed.), *Arte in Europa: Scritti di storia dell'arte in onore di Edoardo Arslan*, Milan, 1966, 517–30

Bean 1960

J. Bean, *Les Dessins italiens de la collection Bonnat*, Bayonne: Musée Bonnat, 1960

Beck 1990

J. H. Beck, 'Cardinal Alidosi, Michelangelo and the Sistine Ceiling', *Artibus et historiae*, XI (1990), 63–77

Bensi 1980

P. Bensi, 'Gli arnese dell'arte: I Gesuati di San Giusto alle Mura e la pittura del rinascimento a Firenze', *Studi di storia delle arti*, III (1980), 33–47

Biering and von Hesberg 1987

R. Biering and H. von Hesberg, 'Zu Bau- und Kultgeschichte von St Andreas apud S. Petrum', *Römischer Quartalschrift für christliche Altertumskunde und Kirchengeschichte*, LXXXII (1987), 145–82

Bizocchi 1995

R. Bizocchi, *Genealogie incredibili: scritti di storia nell'Europa moderna*, Bologna, 1995

Bober and Rubinstein 1986

P. P. Bober and R. Rubinstein, *Renaissance Artists and Antique Sculpture*, Oxford, 1986

Bocchi 1591

F. Bocchi, *Le Bellezze della città di Fiorenza*, Florence, 1591

Bode 1925

W. von Bode, *Bertoldo und Lorenzo dei Medici: Die Kunstpolitik des Lorenzo il Magnifico im Spiegel der Werke seines Lieblingskünstlers Bertoldo do Giovanni*, Freiburg, 1925

Böninger and Boschetto 2005

L. Böninger and L. Boschetto, 'Bertoldo di Giovanni: nuovi documenti sulla sua famiglia e i suoi primi anni Fiorentini', *Mitteilungen des Kunsthistorischen Institutes in Florenz*, XLIX (2005), 233–68

Bonora 1875

T. Bonora, *L'arca di San Domenico e Michelangelo Buonarroti: ricerche storico-artistiche*, Bologna, 1875

Borghini 1964

V. Borghini, 'Esequie del Divino Michelangelo Buonarroti', in *The Divine Michelangelo*, ed. R. Wittkower and M. Wittkower, London, 1964, 49–133

Borsi 1985

S. Borsi, *Giuliano da Sangallo: i disegni di architettura e dell'antico*, Rome, 1985

Borsook 1980

E. Borsook, *The Mural Painters of Tuscany from Cimabue to Andrea del Sarto*, Oxford, 1980

Bottari 1759–73

G. G. Bottari, ed., *Raccolta di lettere sulla pittura, scultura ed architettura*, 7 vols, Rome, 1754–73

Botto 1932

C. Botto, 'L'edificazione della chiesa di Santo Spirito in Firenze', *Rivista d'arte*, XIV (1932), 24–53

Boucher 1991

B. Boucher, *The Sculpture of Jacopo Sansovino*, 2 vols, New Haven and London, 1991

Branca 1986

V. Branca, ed., *Mercanti scrittori ricordi nella Firenze tra Medioevo e Rinascimento: Paolo da Certaldo, Giovanni Morelli, Bonaccorso Pitti . . .* , Milan, 1986

Brockhaus 1909

H. Brockhaus, *Michelangelo und die Medici-Kapelle*, Leipzig, 1909

Bullard 1980

M. Bullard, *Filippo Strozzi and the Medici: Favor and Finance in Sixteenth-century Florence and Rome*, Cambridge, 1980

Bulst 1990

W. A. Bulst, 'Uso e trasformazione del Palazzo mediceo fino ai Riccardi', in *Il Palazzo Medici Riccardi di Firenze*, ed. G. Cherubini and G. Fanelli, Florence, 1990, 98–124

Burchard 1907–42

J. Burchard, *Liber notarum: ab anno MCCCCLXXXIII usque ad annum MDVI*, 2 vols in 12, ed. E. Celani, in Rerum Italicarum Scriptores, new edn, 32, Città di Castello, 1907–42

Burns 1979

H. Burns, 'San Lorenzo in Florence before the Building of the New Sacristy: An Early Plan', *Mitteilungen des Kunsthistorischen Institutes in Florenz*, XXIII (1979), 145–54

Busini 1860

G. Busini, *Lettere di Giambattista Busini a Benedetto Varchi sopra l'assedio di Firenze*, ed. G. Milanesi, Florence, 1860

Butters 1985

H. C. Butters, *Governors and Government in Early Sixteenth-century Florence, 1502–1519*, Oxford, 1985

Butzek 1978

M. Butzek, *Die Kommunalen Repräsentationsstatuen der Päpste des 16. Jahrhunderts in Bologna, Perugia und Rom*, Bad Honnef, 1978

Cadogan 1993

J. D. Cadogan, 'Michelangelo in the Workshop of Domenico Ghirlandaio', *Burlington Magazine*, CXXXV (1993), 30–31

Cadogan 2000

—, *Domenico Ghirlandaio: Artist and Artisan*, New Haven and London, 2000

Caglioti 1993

F. Caglioti, 'Una conferma per Andrea dall'Aquila scultore: la "Madonna" di casa Caffarelli', *Prospettiva*, LXIX (1993), 2–27

Caglioti 1996

—, 'Il *David* bronzeo di Michelangelo (e Benedetto da Rovezzano): il problema dei pagamenti', in *Ad Alessandro Conti, 1946–1994*, Quaderni del Seminario di storia della critica d'arte, VI, Pisa, 1996, 85–132

Caglioti 2000a

—, *Donatello e i Medici: storia del David e della Giuditta*, 2 vols, Florence, 2000

Caglioti 2000b

—, 'Gli ambienti accessori', in *La Basilica di San Pietro in Vaticano*, ed. A. Pinelli, Modena, 2000, 828–9

Caglioti 2005

—, 'La capella Piccolomini nel Duomo di Siena da Andrea Bregno e Michelangelo', in *Pio II e le arti: la riscoperta dell'antico da Federighi a Michelangelo*, ed. A. Angelini, Siena, 2005, 387–482

Calì 1967

M. Calì, 'La "Madonna della Scale" di Michelangelo: il Savonarola e la crisi dell'Umanesimo', *Bolletino d'arte*, ser. V, LII (1967), 152–66

Cambi, *Istorie*

G. Cambi, *Istorie*, 4 vols, in *Delizie degli eruditi toscani*, ed. I. di San Luigi, XX–XXIII, Florence, 1785–6

Cambon 1985

M. Cambon, *Michelangelo's Poetry: Fury of Form*, Princeton, 1985

Campori 1855

G. Campori, *Gli artisti italiani e stranieri negli stati estensi*, Modena, 1855

Campori 1881

—, 'Michelangelo Buonarroti e Alfonso d'Este', in *Atti e memorie delle R. R. Deputazioni di storia patria per le provincie dell'Emilia*, n.s. VI, I, Modena, 1881, 127–40

Carl 1999

D. Carl, 'Eine unbekannte antike Bronze aus der Sammlung des Kardinals Raffael Riario', in *Mosaics of Friendship: Studies in Art and History for Eve Borsook*, ed. O. Francisci Osti, Florence, 1999, 338–9

Carl 2006

—, *Benedetto da Maiano*, 2 vols, Regensburg, 2006

Carrol 1987

E. A. Carrol, *Rosso Fiorentino: Drawings, Prints and Decorative Arts*, Washington, DC, 1987

Carteggio I

Il Carteggio di Michelangelo, I, ed. G. Poggi, P. Barocchi and R. Ristori, Florence, 1965

Carteggio II

—, II, ed. P. Barocchi and R. Ristori, Florence, 1967

Carteggio III

—, III, ed. P. Barocchi and R. Ristori, Florence, 1973

Carteggio IV
—, IV, ed. P. Barocchi and R. Ristori, Florence, 1979

Carteggio V
—, V, ed. P. Barocchi and R. Ristori, Florence, 1983

Carteggio indiretto I
Il Carteggio indiretto di Michelangelo, I, ed. P. Barocchi, K. L. Bramante and
R. Ristori, Florence, 1988

Carteggio indiretto II
—, II, ed. P. Barocchi, K. L. Bramante and R. Ristori, Florence, 1995

Castiglione-Serassi 1769–71
B. Castiglione, *Lettere del conte Baldessar Castiglione ora per la prima volta date in
luce e con annotazioni storiche illustrate dall'abate Pierantonio Serassi*, 2 vols,
Padua, 1769–71

Cecchi 1984
A. Cecchi, 'Raffaello fra Firenze, Urbino e Perugia, 1504–1508', in *Raffaello
a Firenze*, exh. cat., Florence, Palazzo Pitti, 1984, 37–46

Cecchi 1987
—, 'Agnolo e Maddalena Doni, committenti di Raffaello', in *Studi su Raffaello*,
ed. M. Sambucco Hamoud and M. L. Strocchi, I, Urbino, 1987, 429–39

Cecchi 1996a
—, 'Niccolò Machiavelli o Marcello Virgilio Adriani? Sul programma e
l'assetto compositivo delle "Battaglie" di Leonardo e Michelangelo per la
Sala del Maggiore Consiglio in Palazzo Vecchio', *Prospettiva*, LXXXIII–LXXXIV
(1996), 102–15

Cecchi 1996b
—, review of Rubinstein 1995, in *Burlington Magazine*, CXXXVIII (1996),
330–31

Cecchi 2005
—, *Botticelli*, Milan, 2005

Cerretani 1993
B. Cerretani, *Ricordi*, ed. G. Berti, Florence, 1993

Chambers 1992
D. S. Chambers, *A Renaissance Cardinal and his Worldly Goods: The Will and
Inventory of Francesco Gonzaga (1444–1483)*, London, 1992

Chastel 1959

A. Chastel, *Art et humanisme à Florence au temps de Laurent le Magnifique*, Paris, 1959

Chastel 1983

—, *The Sack of Rome, 1527*, Princeton, 1983

Ciammitti 1999

L. Ciammitti, 'Note biografiche su Giovan Francesco Aldrovandi', in Weil-Garris Brandt et al. 1999, 139–41

Ciapelli 2000

G. Ciapelli, 'Family Memory: Functions, Evolution, Recurrencies', in *Art, Memory and Family in Renaissance Florence*, ed. G. Ciapelli and P. L. Rubin, Cambridge, 2000, pp. 25–38

Ciapelli and Rubin 2000

G. Ciapelli and P. L. Rubin, eds, *Art, Memory and Family in Renaissance Florence*, Cambridge, 2000

Ciseri 1990

I. Ciseri, *L'Ingresso trionfale di Leone X in Firenze nel 1515*, Florence, 1990

Cittadella 1868

L. N. Cittadella, *Notizie relative a Ferrara per la maggior parte inedite ricavate da documenti*, Ferrara, 1868

Clough 2005

C. H. Clough, 'Clement VII and Francesco Maria della Rovere, Duke of Urbino', in *The Pontificate of Clement VII: History, Politics, Culture*, ed. K. Gouwens and S. E. Reiss, Aldershot, 2005, 75–108

Colalucci 1994

G. Colalucci, 'La tipologia dei cartoni e la tecnica esecutiva della volta della Cappella Sistina', in *Michelangelo: la Cappella Sistina*, ed. K. Weil-Garris Brandt, Novara, 1994, 77–82

Collareta 1978

M. Collareta, 'Un'ipotesi Michelangiolesca: "Il mio segno" ', *Annali della Scuola Normale Superiore di Pisa, Classe di Lettere e Filosofia*, ser. III, VIII (1978), 167–85

Colnaghi 1928
D. E. Colnaghi, *A Dictionary of Florentine Painters from the 13th to the 17th Centuries*, London, 1928

Colonna 1892
Vittoria Colonna, Marchesa di Pesara: Carteggio, ed. E. Ferrero and G. Müller, 2nd edition, Turin, 1892

Condivi 1553
A. Condivi, *Vita di Michelangelo Buonarroti raccolta per Ascanio Condivi da la Ripa*, Rome, 1553

Condivi 1998
—, *Vita di Michelangelo Buonarroti*, ed. G. Nencioni, Florence, 1998

Condivi-Gori 1746
—, *Vita di Michelangelo Buonarroti pittore scultore architetto e gentiluomo fiorentino pubblicata mentre viveva dal suo scolare Ascanio Condivi, seconda edizione corretta ed accresciuta*, ed. A. F. Gori, Florence, 1746

Conti 1984
E. Conti, *L'imposta diretta a Firenze nel Quattrocento, 1427–1494*, Rome, 1984

Contratti
I Contratti di Michelangelo, ed. L. Bardeschi Ciulich, Florence, 2005

Corti 1964
G. Corti, 'Una ricordanza di Giovan Battista Figiovanni', *Paragone*, CLXXV (1964), 24–31

Cox-Rearick 1995
J. Cox-Rearick, *The Collection of Francis II: Royal Treasures*, New York, 1995

Cropper 1997
E. Cropper, *Pontormo: Portrait of a Halberdier*, Los Angeles, 1997

Cummings 1992
A. Cummings, *The Politicized Muse*, Princeton, 1992

Dalli Regoli, Nanni and Natali 2001
G. Dalli Regoli, R. Nanni and A. Natali, eds, *Leonardo e il mito di Leda: modelli, memorie e metamorfosi di un'invenzione*, Cinisello Balsamo, 2001

Daly Davis 1989
M. Daly Davis, ' "Opus isodomum" at the Palazzo della Cancelleria: Vitru-
vian Studies and Archeological and Antiquarian Interests at the Court of
Raffael Riario', in *Roma centro ideale della cultura dell'antico nei secoli XV e
XVI*, ed. S. Danesi Squarzina, Milan, 1989, 442–57

Danti 1996
C. Danti, 'Osservazioni sulla tecnica degli affreschi della Cappella Tornabuoni', in *Domenico Ghirlandaio, 1449–1494. Atti del convegno internazionale*,
ed. W. Prinz and M. Seidel, Florence, 1996, 141–8

Danesi Squarzina 2000
S. Danesi Squarzina, 'The Bassano "Christ the Redeemer" in the Giustiniani
Collection', *Burlington Magazine*, CXLII (2000), 746–51

DBI
Dizionario biografico degli italiani, vols I–LXXIII, Rome, 1960–2009

Devonshire Jones 1972
R. Devonshire Jones, *Francesco Vettori: Florentine Citizen and Medici Servant*,
London, 1972

Dodsworth 1995
B. W. Dodsworth, *The Arca di San Domenico*, New York, 1995

Dolce 1557
L. Dolce, *Dialogo della Pittura di M. Lodovico Dolce, Intitolato L'Aretino*, Venice,
1557

Doni 1552–3
A. F. Doni, *I Marmi del Doni*, Venice, 1552–3

Dorez 1918
L. Dorez, *Nouvelles recherches sur Michel-Ange et son entourage*, Paris, 1918

Dovizi 1955–65
B. Dovizi da Bibbiena, *Epistolario di Bernardo Dovizi da Bibbiena*, ed. G. L.
Moncallero, 2 vols, Florence, 1955–65

Draper 1992
J. D. Draper, *Bertoldo di Giovanni, Sculptor of the Medici Household*, Columbia,
MO, 1992

Ducrot 1963
A. Ducrot, 'Histoire de la Cappella Giulia au xvie siècle', *Mélanges d'archéologie et d'histoire*, LXXV (1963), 179–240, 467–559

Duppa 1807
R. Duppa, *The Life of Michelangelo Buonarroti, with his Poetry and Letters*, London, 1807

Echinger-Maurach 1991
C. Echinger-Maurach, *Studien zu Michelangelos Juliusgrabmal*, 2 vols, Hildesheim, 1991

Echinger-Maurach 2009
—, *Michelangelos Grabmak für Papst Julius II*, Munich, 2009

Elam 1979
C. Elam, 'The Site and Early Building History of Michelangelo's New Sacristy', *Mitteilungen des Kunsthistorischen Institutes in Florenz*, XXIII (1979), 155–86

Elam 1988
—, 'Art and Diplomacy in Renaissance Florence', *Journal of the Royal Society of Arts*, CXXXVI (1988), 813–26

Elam 1990
—, 'Il palazzo nel contesto della città: strategie urbanistiche dei Medici nel gonfalone del Leon d'Oro, 1415–1430', in *Il Palazzo Medici Riccardi di Firenze*, ed. G. Cherubini and G. Fanelli, Florence, 1990, 44–53

Elam 1992a
—, 'Drawings as Documents: The Problem of the San Lorenzo Façade', in *Michelangelo Drawings*, ed. C. H. Smyth, Washington, DC, 1992, 99–114

Elam 1992b
—, 'Il Giardino delle Sculture di Lorenzo de' Medici', in Barocchi 1992, 157–70

Elam 1992c
—, 'Lorenzo de' Medici's Sculpture Garden', *Mitteilungen des Kunsthistorischen Institutes in Florenz*, XXVI (1992), 41–84

Elam 1993
—, 'Art in the Service of Liberty: Battista della Palla, Art Agent for Francis I', *Tatti Studies*, V (1993), 33–109

Elam 2005a

—, ' "Tuscan Dispositions": Michelangelo's Florentine Architectural Vocabulary and its Reception', *Renaissance Studies*, XIX (2005), 48–82

Elam 2005b

—, 'Michelangelo and the Clementine Architectural Style', in *The Pontificate of Clement VII: History, Politics, Culture*, ed. K. Gouwens and S. E. Reiss, Aldershot, 2005, 199–225

Erasmus 1906

D. Erasmus, *Opus Epistolarum*, II, Oxford, 1906

Ettlinger 1972

L. D. Ettlinger, 'Hercules Florentinus', *Mitteilungen des Kunsthistorischen Institutes in Florenz*, XVI (1972), 119–42

Eubel 1923

C. Eubel, *Hierarchia catholica medii aevi sive Summorum Pontificum, III: Saeculum XVI ab anno 1503*, Kallenberg, 1923

Falletti-Fossati 1883

P. C. Falletti-Fossati, *L'Assedio di Firenze*, 2 vols, Palermo, 1883

Ferrai 1891

L. A. Ferrai, *Lorenzino de' Medici e la società cortigiana del Cinquecento*, Milan, 1891

Fossati 1876

C. Fossati, *La fuga di Michelangelo Buonarroti da Firenze nel 1529*, Sassari, 1876

Franklin 1994

D. Franklin, *Rosso in Italy: The Italian Career of Rosso Fiorentino*, New Haven and London, 1994

Frediani 1875

C. Frediani, *Ragionamento storico su le diverse gite che fece a Carrara Michelangiolo Buonarroti*, 2nd edition, Siena, 1875

Frey 1885

K. Frey, 'Denunzia dei beni della famiglia de' Buonarruoti', *Jahrbuch der Königlich Preussischen Kunstsammlungen*, VI (1885), 189–201

Frey 1892

—, ed., *Il Codice Magliabechiano contenente notizie sopra l'arte degli antichi e quella de' Fiorentini da Cimabue a Michelangelo Buonarroti ... scritte da Anonimo Fiorentino*, Berlin, 1892

Frey 1897
—, *Die Dichtungen des Michelagniolo Buonarroti*, Berlin, 1897

Frey 1899
—, *Sammlung ausgewählter Briefe an Michelagniolo Buonarroti*, Berlin, 1899

Frey 1907a
—, *Michelagniolo Buonarroti: Quellen und Forschungen zu Geschichte und Kunst; Michelagniolos Jugendjahre*, Berlin, 1907

Frey 1907b
—, *Michelagniolo Buonarroti: Sein Leben und seine Werke, I: Michelagniolos Jugendjahre*, Berlin, 1907

Frey 1909
—, 'Studien zu Michelagniolo Buonarroti und zur Kunst seine Zeit', *Jahrbuch der Königlich Preussischen Kunstsammlungen*, xx (1909), supplement, 103–80

Frey 1910
—, 'Zu Baugeschichte des St Peter: Mitteilungen aus der Reverendissima Fabbrica di S. Pietro', *Jahrbuch der Königlich Preussischen Kunstsammlungen*, xxxi (1910), supplement, 1–95

Frey and Frey 1930
— and H.-W. Frey, *Der Literarische Nachlass Giorgio Vasaris*, ii, Munich, 1930; reprinted Hildesheim and New York, 1982

Frommel 1961
C. L. Frommel, *Der Farnesina und Peruzzis Architektonisches Früwerk*, Berlin, 1961

Frommel 1976
—, 'Die peterskirche unter Papst Julius ii: Im Licht neuer Dokumente', *Römisches Jahrbuch für Kunstgeschichte*, xvi (1976), 59–136

Frommel 1977
—, ' "Capella Julia": Die Grabkapelle Papst Julius ii in Neu-St Peter', *Zeitschrift für Kunstgeschichte*, xl (1977), 26–62

Frommel 1979
—, *Michelangelo und Tommaso dei Cavalieri*, Amsterdam, 1979

Frommel 1989

—, 'Il Cardinal Raffaele Riario ed il Palazzo della Cancellaria', in *Sisto IV e Giulio II, mecenate e promotori di cultura. Atti di convegno internazionale di studi: Savona, 1985*, ed. S. Bottaro, A. Dagnino and G. R. Terminiello, Savona, 1989, 73–85

Frommel 1992

—, 'Jacobo Gallo als Förderer der Künste: das Grabmal seines Vaters in S. Lorenzo in Damaso und Michelangelos erste römische Jahre', in *Kotinos: Festschrift für E. Simon*, ed. H. Froning, T. Hölscher and H. Mielsch, Mainz am Rhein, 1992, 450–60

Frommel 1995

—, 'Raffaelo Riario, commitente della Cancellaria', in *Economia a Roma e nelle corti del Rinascimento, 1420–1530*, ed. A. Esch and C. L. Frommel, Turin, 1995, 198–211

Frommel 1996

—, ' "In pristinam formem": Die Erneurung von S. Maria in Navicella durch Leo x', in *Antiken Spolieri in der Architektur des Mittelalters und der Renaissance*, ed. J. Poeschke, Munich, 1996, 309–20

Frommel 1999

—, 'Raffaele Riario, la Cancellaria, il teatro e il Bacco di Michelangelo', in Weil-Garris Brandt et al. 1999, 143–8

Fusco and Corti 1992

L. Fusco and G. Corti, 'Lorenzo de' Medici, on the Sforza Monument', in Achademia Leonardo Vinci, *Journal of Leonardo Studies and Bibliography of Vinciana* V (1992), 11–32

Fusco and Corti 2006

L. Fusco and G. Corti, *Lorenzo de' Medici, Collector and Antiquarian*, Cambridge, 2006

Gamba 1948

C. Gamba, *La pittura di Michelangelo*, Novara, 1948

Gatteschi 1993

R. Gatteschi, *Baccio da Montelupo: scultore e architetto del Cinquecento*, Florence, 1993

Gatti 1994

L. Gatti, ' "Delle cose de' pictori et sculptori si può mal promettere cosa certa": la diplomazia Fiorentina presso la corte del re di Francia e il *Davide* bronzeo di Michelangelo Buonarroti', *Mélanges de l'Ecole Française de Rome*, CVI (1994), 433–72

Gaye 1840

G. Gaye, *Carteggio inedito d'artisti dei secoli xiv. xv. xvi.*, II: *1506–1557*, Florence, 1840

Giannotti 1974

D. Giannotti, *Opere politiche*, ed. F. Diaz, Milan, 1974

Gilbert 1971

C. E. Gilbert, 'Texts and Contexts of the Medici Chapel', *Art Quarterly*, XXXIV (1971), 391–410

Gilbert 1980

F. Gilbert, *The Pope, his Banker and Venice*, Cambridge, MA, 1980

Giovio 1555

P. Giovio, *Dialogo dell'Imprese militari et amorose*, Rome, 1555

Girardi 1960

E. N. Girardi, ed., *Michelangelo Buonarroti: Rime*, Bari, 1960

Gnoli 1923–4

U. Gnoli, 'Piermatteo da Amelia', *Bollettino d'arte*, series 2, III (1923–4), 391–415

Gnoli 1935

—, 'Appunti d'archivio: documenti senza casa', *Rivista d'arte*, XVII (1935), 213–19

Godman 1998

P. Godman, *From Poliziano to Machiavelli: Florentine Humanism in the High Renaissance*, Princeton, 1998

Goldthwaite 1968

R. Goldthwaite, *Private Wealth in Renaissance Florence: A Study of Four Families*, Princeton, 1968

Gombrich 1966

E. H. Gombrich, 'The Early Medici as Patrons of Art', in *Norm and Form*, London, 1966, 35–57

Gotti 1876
A. Gotti, *Vita di Michelangelo Buonarroti narrate con l'aiuto di nuovi documenti*, 2 vols, Florence, 1876

Grassi 1886
P. Grassi, *Le due spedizioni militari di Giulio II: tratte dal diario di Paride Grassi Bolognese ... con documenti e note di Luigi Frati*, Bologna, 1886

Gronau 1906
G. Gronau, 'Die Kunstbestrebungen der Herzöge von Urbino, II–III', *Jahrbuch der Preussischen Kunstsammlungen*, XXVII (1906), supplement, 1–11, 12–44

Gronau 1911
—, 'Dokumente zur Entstehungsgeschichte der neuen Sakristei und der Bibliothek von S. Lorenzo in Florenz', *Jahrbuch der Königlich Preussischen Kunstsammlungen*, XXXII (1911), supplement, 62–81

Guasti 1857
C. Guasti, *La cupola di Santa Maria del Fiore: illustrata con i documenti dell'Archivio dell'Opera Secolare; saggio di una compiuta illustrazione dell'Opera Secolare e del Tempio di Santa Maria del Fiore*, Florence, 1857

Guasti 1864
—, ed., *Le rime di Michelangelo Buonarroti pittore, scultore e architetto, cavate dagli autografi e pubblicate da Cesare Guasti*, Florence, 1864

Guasti 1880
—, *Il sacco di Prato e il ritorno de' Medici in Firenze*, Bologna, 1880

Guicciardini 1857–67
F. Guicciardini, *Opere inedite*, ed. G. Canestrini, 10 vols, Florence, 1857–67

Guicciardini 1931
—, *Storie fiorentine dal 1378–1509*, ed. R. Palmarocchi, Bari, 1931

Guicciardini 1962
—, *Carteggi*, ed. G. Ricci, Rome, 1962

Guicciardini 1971
—, *Storia d'Italia*, 4 vols, Turin, 1971

Haines 1996
M. Haines, 'L'Arte della Lana e l'opera del Duomo a Firenze, con un accenno a Ghiberti tra due istituzioni', in *Opera: carattere e ruolo delle fabbriche cittadine*

fino all'inizio dell'Età Moderna, ed. M. Haines and L. Riccetti, Florence, 1996, 267–94

Hartt 1969
F. Hartt, *Michelangelo: The Complete Sculpture*, London, 1969

Hartt 1971
—, *The Drawings of Michelangelo*, London, 1971

Hatfield 2002
R. Hatfield, *The Wealth of Michelangelo*, Rome, 2002

Hayum 1981–2
A. Hayum, 'Michelangelo's Doni Tondo: Holy Family and Family Myth', *Studies in Iconography*, VII–VIII (1981–2), 209–51

Herlihy and Klapisch-Zuber 1985
D. Herlihy and C. Klapisch-Zuber, *Tuscans and their Families: A Study of the Florentine Catasto of 1427*, New Haven and London, 1985

Hirst 1961
M. Hirst, 'The Chigi Chapel in S. Maria della Pace', *Journal of the Warburg and Courtauld Institutes*, XXIV (1961), 161–85

Hirst 1969
—, review of M. Weinberger, *Michelangelo: The Sculptor* [London, 1967], *Burlington Magazine*, CXI (1969), 762–4

Hirst 1973
—, review of H. R. Mancusi-Ungaro, *Michelangelo, the Bruges Madonna and the Piccolomini Altar*, in *Italian Studies* XXVIII (1973), 120–21

Hirst 1975
—, 'A Drawing of the *Rape of Ganymede* by Michelangelo', *Burlington Magazine*, CXVII (1975), 166

Hirst 1981a
—, 'Michelangelo in Rome: An Altarpiece and the "Bacchus" ', *Burlington Magazine*, CXXIII (1981), 581–93

Hirst 1981b
—, *Sebastiano del Piombo*, Oxford, 1981

Hirst 1985
—, 'Michelangelo, Carrara and the Marble for the Cardinal's *Pietà*', *Burlington Magazine*, CXXVII (1985), 154–9

Hirst 1986a
—, 'I disegni di Michelangelo per la Battaglia di Cascina', in *Tecnica e stile*, ed. E. Borsook and F. Superbi Gioffredi, 2 vols, Milan, 1986, 43–58

Hirst 1986b
—, '"Il modo delle attitudini": il taccuino di Oxford per la volta della Sistina', in *La Cappella Sistina: i primi restauri; la scoperta del colore*, Novara, 1986, 208–17

Hirst 1988a
—, *Michelangelo and his Drawings*, London and New Haven, 1988

Hirst 1988b
—, ed., *Michelangelo Draftsman*, Milan, 1988

Hirst 1991
—, 'Michelangelo in 1505', *Burlington Magazine*, CXXXII (1991), 760–66

Hirst 1997
—, 'Michelangelo and his First Biographers', *Proceedings of the British Academy: Lectures and Memoirs,* XCIV (1997), 63–84

Hirst 2000a
—, 'Michelangelo Buonarroti, *Pietà*', in *La Basilica di San Pietro in Vaticano*, ed. A. Pinelli, 3 vols, Modena, 2000, 731–6

Hirst 2000b
—, 'Michelangelo in Florence: "David" in 1503 and "Hercules" in 1506', *Burlington Magazine*, CXXXXII (2000), 487–92

Hirst 2000c
—, 'A Portrait of Lorenzo Pucci by Parmigianino', *Apollo*, CLI (2000), 43–7

Hirst 2004a
—, *Tre saggi su Michelangelo*, Florence, 2004

Hirst 2004b
—, 'Two Notes on Michelangelo in Florence: The Façade of San Lorenzo and the "Kneeling" Windows of Palazzo Medici', *Apollo*, CLIX (2004), 39–43

Hirst 2005
—, 'The Marble for Michelangelo's Taddei Tondo', *Burlington Magazine*, CXLVII (2005), 548–9

Hirst and Dunkerton 1994
— and J. Dunkerton, *The Young Michelangelo: The Artist in Rome, 1496–1501*, London, 1994

Holst 1974
C. von Holst, *Francesco Granacci*, Munich, 1974

Hope 1971
C. Hope, 'The "Camerini d'Alabastro" of Alfonso d'Este, I and II', *Burlington Magazine*, CXIII (1971), 641–50, 712–21

Hope 1980
—, *Titian*, London, 1980

Hope 1987
—, 'The Camerino d'Alabastro: A Reconsideration of the Evidence', in *Bacchanals by Titian and Rubens*, ed. G. Cavalli-Björkman, Stockholm, 1987

Hughes 1981
A. Hughes, 'A Lost Poem by Michelangelo?', *Journal of the Warburg and Courtauld Institutes*, XLIV (1981), 202–6

Hurtubise 1985
P. Hurtubise, *Une Famille-Témoin: Les Salviati*, Vatican City, 1985

Ippoliti 1999
A. Ippoliti, *Il complesso di San Pietro in Vincoli e la committenza della Rovere (1467–1520)*, Rome, 1999

Jestaz 1994
B. Jestaz, 'L'Inventaire du Palais et des Proprietés Farnèse à Rome en 1644', in *Les Palais Farnèse*, III, 3, Ecole Française de Rome, Rome, 1994

Joannides 1994
P. Joannides, 'A propos d'une sanguine nouvellement attribuée a Michel-Ange: la connaissance des dessins de l'artiste en France au XVIe siècle', *Revue du Louvre*, XLIV (1994), 15–29

Joannides 2000
—, in Androsov and Baldini 2000, 105–31

Joannides 2003
—, *Michelangelo*, Paris and Milan, 2003

Jŭren 1974
V. Jŭren, 'Feci faciebat', *Revue de l'art*, XXVI (1974), 27–30

Jŭren 1975
—, 'Politien et la théorie des arts figuratifs', *Bibliothèque d'Humanisme et Renaissance*, XXVII (1975), 131–40

Justi 1900
C. Justi, *Michelangelo: Beiträge zue Erklärung der Werke und des Menschen*, Leipzig, 1900

Kemp 1992
M. Kemp, ed., *Leonardo da Vinci: The Mystery of the Madonna of the Yarnwinder*, Edinburgh, 1992

Kent 1977
F. W. Kent, *Household and Lineage in Renaissance Florence: The Family Life of the Capponi, Ginori and Rucellai*, Princeton, 1977

Kent 1991
—, 'La famiglia patrizia fiorentina nel Quattrocento: nuovi orientamenti nella storiografia recente', in *Palazzo Strozzi: metà millennio, 1489–1984. Atti del convegno di studi*, ed. D. Lamberini, Rome, 1991, 70–91

Kent 2004
—, *Lorenzo de' Medici and the Art of Magnificence*, Baltimore and London, 2004

Klaczko 1902
J. Klaczko, *Jules II*, 2nd edition, Paris, 1902

Klapisch-Zuber 1969
C. Klapisch-Zuber, *Les Maîtres su marbre: Carrara, 1300–1600*, Paris, 1969

Klapisch-Zuber 1985
—, *Women, Family and Ritual in Renaissance Italy*, Chicago and London, 1985

Kristellar 1956
P. O. Kristellar, *Studies in Renaissance Thought and Letters*, Rome, 1956; reprinted 1984

Kuehn 1982
T. Kuehn, *Emancipation in Late Medieval Florence*, New Brunswick, 1982

Lamberini 1987
D. Lamberini, 'Practice and Theory in Sixteenth Century Fortifications', *Fort: The International Journal of Fortification and Military Architecture*, xv (1987), 5–20

Lanckoronska 1932–3
K. Lanckoronska, 'Appunti sulla interpretazione del "Giudizio Universale: di Michelangelo', *Annales institutorum*, v (Rome, 1932–3), 122–30

Lanciani 1902
R. Lanciani, *Storia degli scavi di Roma e notizie intorno le collezioni romane di antichità*, 4 vols, Rome, 1902

Landucci 1883/1969
L. Landucci, *Diario fiorentino del 1450 al 1516*, ed. I. del Badia, Florence, 1883; reprinted 1969

Lapini 1900
A. Lapini, *Diario fiorentino del 252 al 1596*, ed. G. O. Corazzini, Florence, 1900

Lascaris-Meschini 1976
G. Lascaris, *Epigrammi greci*, ed. A. Meschini, Padua, 1976

Lavin 1965
I. Lavin, review of J. Pope-Hennessy, *Italian High Renaissance and Baroque Sculpture*, in *Art Bulletin*, LXXXIX (1969), 22–31

Lavin 1993
—, *Past–Present: Essays on Historicism in Art from Donatello to Picasso*, Berkeley, Los Angeles and Oxford, 1993

Lightbown 1969
R. W. Lightbown, 'Michelangelo's Great Tondo: Its Origins and Setting', *Apollo*, LXXXIX (1969), 22–31

Lillie 1993
A. Lillie, 'Giovanni di Cosimo and the Villa Medici at Fiesole', in *Piero de' Medici 'il Gottoso', 1416–1469: Kunst im Dienster der Mediceer*, ed. A. Beyer and B. Boucher, Berlin, 1993, 189–205

Lippincott 1989
K. Lippincott, 'When was Michelangelo Born', *Journal of the Warburg and Courtauld Institutes*, LII (1989), 228–32

Lisner 1958
M. Lisner, 'Zu Benedetto da Majano und Michelangelo', *Zeitschrift für Kunstwissenschaft*, XII (1958), 141–56

Lisner 1966
—, 'Il Crocifisso di Santo Spirito', in *Atti del Convegno di Studi Michelangioleschi*, Rome, 1966, 295–316

Lisner 1980
—, 'Form und Sinngehalt vor Michelangelos Kentaurenschlat', *Mitteilungen des Kunsthistorischen Institutes in Florenz*, XXIV (1980), 299–344

Lodico 1999
D. Lodico, 'Le case della famiglia Galli in via dei Leutari', in Weil-Garris Brandt et al. 1999, 149–62

Lotto-Zampetti 1969
L. Lotto, *Il Libro di spese diverse: con aggiunta di lettere e d'altri documenti*, ed. P. Zampetti, Venice and Rome, 1969

Lotz 1965
W. Lotz, 'Zu Michelangelos Christus in S. Maria sopra Minerva', in *Festschrift für Herbert von Einem zum 16. Februar 1965*, ed. G. von der Osten and G. Kauffmann, Berlin, 1965, 143–50

Lowe 1993
K. J. P. Lowe, *Church and Politics in Renaissance Italy: The Life and Career of Cardinal Francesco Soderini, 1453–1524*, Cambridge, 1993

Luschino 2002
B. Luschino, *Vulnera Diligentis*, ed. S. Dall'Aglio, Florence, 2002

Luzio 1886
A. Luzio, 'Federico Gonzaga ostaggio alla corte di Giulio II', *Archivio della R. Società Romana di Storia Patria*, IX (1886), 509–82

Luzio 1909
—, 'Isabella d'Este e Giulio II', *Rivista d'Italia*, XII (1909), 837–76

Luzio 1912

—, *Isabella d'Este di fronte a Giulio II negli ultimi tre anni del suo pontificato*, Milan, 1912

Luzio 1913
—, *La Galleria dei Gonzaga venduta all'Inghilterra nel 1627–28*, Milan, 1913

Luzio and Renier 1893
—and R. Renier, *Mantova e Urbino: Isabella d'Este ed Elisabetta Gonzaga nelle relazioni famigliare e nelle vicende politiche*, Turin, 1893

McManamon 1991
J. M. McManamon 'Marketing a Medici Regime: The Funeral Oration of Marcello Virgilio Adriano for Giuliano de' Medici (1516)', *Renaissance Quarterly*, XLIV (1991), 1–41

Machiavelli 1964
N. Machiavelli, *Legazioni e commissarie*, ed. S. Bertelli, 3 vols, Milan, 1964

Machiavelli 1984
—, *Opere di Niccolò Machiavelli*, III: *Lettere*, ed. F. Gaeta, Turin, 1984

Machiavelli 2001
—, *l'arte della guerra e scritti politici minori*, ed. J. J. Marchand, D. Fachard and G. Masi, Rome, 2001

Maffei 1506
Raffaello Maffei, *Commentariorum Urbanorum libri XXXVIII*, Rome, 1506

Magister 1999
S. Magister, 'Censimento delle collezioni di antichità a Roma, 1471–1503', *Xenia antiqua*, VIII (1999), 129–204

Magister 2002
—, 'Censimento delle collezioni di antichità a Roma, 1471–1503: addenda', *Xenia antiqua*, X [2001] (2002), 113–54

Mancinelli 1982
F. Mancinelli, 'Il ponte di Michelangelo per la Cappella Sistina', *Rassegna dell'Accademia Nazionale di San Luca*, XII (1982), 1–6

Mancinelli 1986
—, *Michelangelo at Work: The Painting of the Ceiling in the Sistine Chapel: Michelangelo Rediscovered*, London, 1986

Mancinelli 1992

—, 'La progettazione della volta della Cappella Sistina di Michelangelo', in *Michelangelo Drawings*, ed. C. H. Smyth, Washington, DC, 1992, pp. 43–55

Mancinelli 1994a

—, 'Il Ponteggio di Michelangelo per la Cappella Sistina e i problemi cronologica della volta', in *Michelangelo, La Cappella Sistina, III. Atti del convegno internazionali di studi*, ed. K. Weil-Garris Brandt, Novara, 1994, 43–9

Mancinelli 1994b

—, 'Il Problema degli aiuti di Michelangelo', in *Michelangelo, La Cappella Sistina, III. Atti del convegno internazionali di studi*, ed. K. Weil-Garris Brandt, Novara, 1994, 107–14

Mancinelli 1994c

—, 'Tecnica e metodologia operative di Michelangelo sulla volta della Cappella Sistina', in *Michelangelo, La Cappella Sistina, II: rapporto sul restauro della volta*, ed. F. Mancinelli, Novara, 1994, 9–22

Mancusi-Ungaro 1971

H. R. Mancusi-Ungaro Jr, *Michelangelo: The Bruges Madonna and the Piccolomini Altar*, New Haven and London, 1971

Manetti 1980

R. Manetti, *Michelangelo: le fortificazione per l'assedio di Firenze*, Florence, 1980

Marchini 1977

G. Marchini, 'Il balatoio della cupola di Santa Maria del Fiore', *Antichità viva*, XVI (1977), 36–48

Marucci et al. 1983

V. Marucci, A. Marzo and A. Romano, *Pasquinate romane del Cinquecento*, 2 vols, Rome, 1983

Masi 1906

Ricordanze di Bartolomeo Masi, calderaio fiorentino dal 1478 al 1526, ed. G. O. Corazzini, Florence, 1906

Maurer 1999–2000

G. Maurer, 'Michelangelos Projekt für den Tambour von Santa Maria del Fiore', *Romisches Jahrbuch der Bibliotheca Herziana*, XXXIII (1999–2000), 85–100

Merisalo 1999
O. Merisalo, ed., *Le collezioni medicee nel 1495: deliberazioni degli ufficiali dei ribelli*, Florence, 1999

Milanesi 1875
G. Milanesi, *Le lettere di Michelangelo Buonarroti*, Florence, 1875

Millon and Magnago Lampugnani 1994
H. A. Millon and V. Magnago Lampugnani, eds, *Rinascimento da Brunelleschi a Michelangelo: la rappresentazione dell'architettura*, Milan, 1994

Millon and Smyth 1988
— and C. H. Smyth, *Michelangelo architetto: la facciata di San Lorenzo e la cupola di San Pietro*, Milan, 1988

Molho 1994
A. Molho, *Marriage Alliance in Late Medieval Florence*, Cambridge, MA, and London, 1994

Moncallero 1953
G. L. Moncallero, *Il Cardinale Bernardo Dovizi da Bibbiena, umanista e diplomatico, 1470–1520*, Florence, 1953

Moreni 1816
D. Moreni, *Continuazione delle memorie istoriche dell'Ambrosiana Imperiale Basilica di S. Lorenzo di Firenze*, I, Florence, 1816

Morozzi 1988–9
L. Morozzi, 'La "Battaglia di Cascina" di Michelangelo: nuova ipotesi sulla data di commissione', *Prospettiva*, LII (1988–9), 320–24

Mussolin 2007
M. Mussolin, 'La Tribuna delle Reliquie di Michelangelo e la controfacciata di San Lorenze a Firenze', in *Michelangelo architetto a San Lorenzo: quattro problemi aperti*, ed. P. Ruschi, Florence, 2007, 183–99

Nardi 1838–41
J. Nardi, *Istoria della città di Firenze*, ed. L. Arbib, 2 vols, Florence, 1838–41

Nash 1968
E. Nash, *Pictorial Dictionary of Ancient Rome*, 2 vols, London, 1968

Neri di Bicci 1976
Neri di Bicci, *Le ricordanze, 10 March 1453–24 April 1475*, ed. B. Santi, Pisa, 1976

Nerli 1728
F. Nerli, *Commentari de' fatti civili occorsi dentro la città di Firenze dall'Anno MCCXV al MDXXXVIII*, Augsburg, 1728

Newbigin 2002
N. Newbigin, 'Ser Giusto Giusti d'Anghiari (1437–1482)', *Letteratura italiana antica*, III (2002), 41–246

Nitti 1892
F. Nitti, *Leone X e la sua politica, secondo documenti e carteggi inediti*, Florence, 1892

O'Gorman 1972
J. F. O'Gorman, *The Architecture of the Monastic Library in Italy, 1300–1600*, New York, 1972

O'Grody 2001
J. A. O'Grody, 'Michelangelo: The Master Modeler', in *Earth and Fire: Italian Terracotta Sculpture from Donatello to Canova*, ed. Bruce Boucher, New Haven, 2001, 34–42

Orlandi 1964
S. Orlandi, 'Michelangelo Buonarroti e i domenicani', *Memorie domenicane*, N.S. XL (1964), 195–221

Ovid, *Metamorphoses*
Ovid, *Metamorphoses*, Books I–VIII, Cambridge, MA, and London, 1994

Paatz and Paatz 1952
W. Paatz and E. Paatz, *Die Kirchen von Florenz*, IV, Florence, 1952

Panofsky 1964
G. S. Panofsky, ' The Mouse that Michelangelo Failed to Carve', in *Essays in Memory of Karl Lehmann*, ed. L. Freeman Sandler, New York, 1964, 242–51

Panofsky 1991
—, *Michelangelos Christus und sein römischer Auftraggeber*, Worms, 1991

Panofsky-Soergel 1984
G. Panofsky-Soergel, 'Postscriptum to Tommaso Cavalieri', in *Scritti di storia dell'arte in onore di Roberto Salvini*, ed. C. de Benedictis, Florence, 1984, 399–405

Papini 1949
G. Papini, *Vita di Michelangiolo nella vita del suo tempo*, Milan, 1949

Parenti 1994

P. di M. Parenti, *Storia fiorentina*, I, ed. A. Matucci, Florence, 1994

Passerini 1858

L. Passerini, *Genealogia e storia della famiglia Panciatichi*, Florence, 1858

Pastor-Mercati 1944–63

L. B. von Pastor, *Storia dei papi: dalla fine del medio evo compilato col sussidio dell'Archivio Segreto Pontificio e di molti altri archivi. Nuova versione italiana di Angelo Mercati*, Rome, 1944–63

Pesman 2002

R. Pesman, *Pier Soderini and the Ruling Class in Renaissance Florence*, Goldbach, 2002

Piccolomini 1874–5

Enea Piccolomini, 'Intorno alle condizioni ed alle vicende della Libreria Medicea privata', *Archivio Storico Italiano*, series 3, XIX–XXI (1874–5), 101–29, and 254–81.

Picotti 1955

G. B. Picotti, *Ricerche umanistiche*, Florence, 1955

Pini-Milanesi 1869–76

C. Pini and G. Milanesi, *La scrittura di artisti italiani, secoli XIV–XVII*, 12 fasc., Florence, 1869–76

Podestà 1868

B. Podestà, 'Notizie intorno alle due statue erette in Bologna a Giulio II distrutte nei tumulti del 1511', *Atti e memorie della R. Deputazione della storia patria nelle provinca di Romagna*, VII (1868), 107–30

Poeschke 1990

J. Poeschke, *Die Skulptur der Renaissance in Italien: Donatello und seine Zeit*, Munich, 1990

Poeschke 1996

—, *Michelangelo and his World*, New York, 1996

Poggi 1906

G. Poggi, 'Della prima partenza di Michelangiolo Buonarroti da Firenze', *Rivista d'arte*, IV (1906), 33–7

Poggi 1909 / 1988
—, *Il Duomo di Firenze: documenti sulla decorazione della chiesa e del campanile tratti dall'Archivio dell'Opera*, 2 vols, Berlin, 1909; reprint ed. M. Haines, Florence, 1988

Poggi 1942
—, 'Note Michelangiolesche', in *Michelangelo Buonarroti nel iv centenario del 'Giudizio Universale'*, Florence, 1942, 112–32

Polizzotto 1994
L. Polizzotto, *The Elect Nation: The Savonarolan Movement in Florence, 1494–1545*, Oxford and New York, 1994

Popham and Wilde 1949
A. E. Popham and J. Wilde, *The Italian Drawings of the XI and XVI Centuries in the Collection of His Majesty the King at Windsor Castle*, London, 1949

Popp 1927
A. E. Popp, 'Unbeachtete Projekte Michelangelos', *Münchner Jahrbuch der bildenden Kunst*, IV (1927), 390–476

Portoghesi 1966
P. Portoghesi, 'Le architetture fiorentine di Michelangelo', in *Atti del convegno di studi michelangioleschi*, Rome, 1966, 201–27

Portoghesi and Zevi 1964
—and B. Zevi, eds, *Michelangiolo architetto*, Turin, 1964

Prater 1979
A. Prater, *Michelangelos Medici-Kapelle: 'ordine composto' als Gestaltungsprinzip von Architektur und Ornament*, Waldsassen, 1979

Procacci 1965
U. Procacci, *La Casa Buonarroti a Firenze*, Milan, 1965

Ramsden 1963
E. H. Ramsden, ed., *The Letters of Michelangelo*, 2 vols, London, 1963

Rapetti 2001
C. Rapetti, *Michelangelo, Carrara e i maestri di cavar marmi*, Florence, 2001

Reiss 1992
S. E. Reiss, *Cardinal Giulio de' Medici as Patron of Art, 1513–1523*, Ann Arbor, 1992

Reiss 1993

—, 'The Ginori Corridor of San Lorenzo and the Building History of the New Sacristy', *Journal of the Society of Architectural Historians*, LII (1993), 339–43

Reiss and Wilkins 2001

S. E. Reiss and D. G. Wilkins, eds, *Beyond Isabella: Secular Women Patrons of Art in Renaissance Italy*, Kirksville, MO, 2001

Reynolds 2005

A. Reynolds, 'The Papal Court in Exile: Clement VII in Orvieto, 1527–28', in *The Pontificate of Clement VII: History, Politics, Culture*, ed. K. Gouwens and S. E. Reiss, Aldershot, 2005, 143–61

Ricordi 1970

I Ricordi di Michelangelo, ed. L. Bardeschi Ciulich and P. Barocchi, Florence, 1970

Ristori 1986

R. Ristori, 'L'Aretino, il David di Michelangelo e la "modestia fiorentina"', *Rinascimento*, series II, XXVI (1986), 77–97

Roscoe-Bossi 1816–17

W. Roscoe, *Vita e pontificato di Leone X*, ed. L. Bossi, 12 vols, Milan, 1816–17

Rosenberg 2000

C. Rosenberg, 'Alfonso d'Este, Michelangelo and the Man who sold Pigs', in *Revaluing the Renaissance*, ed. R. Shepherd and G. Neher, London, 2000, 89–100

Rota 1937

A. Rota, 'Michelangelo e il Monte della Fede', *Archivi d'Italia*, VI (1937), 27–60

Roth 1925

C. Roth, *The Last Florentine Republic*, London, 1925

Rubinstein 1995

N. Rubinstein, *The Palazzo Vecchio, 1298–1532*, Oxford, 1995

Saalman 1975

H. Saalman, 'Michelangelo: S. Maria del Fiore and St Peter's', *Art Bulletin*, LVII (1975), 374–409

Saalman 1985
—, 'The New Sacristy of San Lorenzo before Michelangelo', *Art Bulletin*, LXVII (1985), 199–228

Salmon 1990
F. Salmon, 'The Site of Michelangelo's Laurentian Library', *Journal of the Society of Architectural Historians*, XLIX (1990), 407–29

Salvini 1782
S. Salvini, *Catologo cronologico de' canonici della chiesa metropolitana fiorentina*, Florence, 1782

Samaran 1921
C. Samaran, *Jean de Bilhères-Lagraulas, Cardinel de Sant-Denis, un diplomate français sous Louis XI et Charles XIII*, Paris, 1921

Sanudo 1879–1903
I diarii di Martino Sanuto, ed. R. Fulin et al., 58 vols, Venice, 1879–1903

Sarre 1909
F. Sarre, 'Michelangelo und der türkische Hof', *Repertorium für Kunstwissenschaft*, XXII (1909), 61–6

Saslow 1991
J. M. Saslow, trans., *The Poetry of Michelangelo*, New Haven and London, 1991

Satzinger 2001
G. Satzinger, 'Michelangelos Grabmal Julius II. in S. Pietro in Vincoli', *Zeitschrift für Kunstgeschichte*, LXIV (2001), 177–222

Sauer 1912
H. Sauer, 'Neue Beiträge zur Kunstgeschichte der Renaissance', *Quellen und Forschungen aus italienischen Archiven und Bibliotheken*, XV (1912), 146–58

Savonarola 1956
G. Savonarola, *Prediche sopra l'Esodo*, ed. P. G. Ricci, 2 vols, Rome, 1956

Schiavo 1964
A. Schiavo, *Il Palazzo della Cancelleria*, Rome, 1964

Schottmüller 1928
F. Schottmüller, 'Michelangelo und das Ornament', *Jahrbuch der Kunsthistorischen Sammlungen in Wien*, n.s. XI (1928), 219–32

Schreurs 2000
A. Schreurs, *Antikenbild und Kunstanschauungen des neapolitanischen Malers, Architekten und Antiquars Pirro Ligorio, 1513–1583*, Cologne, 2000

Schulte 1904
A. Schulte, *Die Fugger in Rom, 1495–1523*, 2 vols, Leipzig, 1904

Schulz 1962
J. Schulz, 'Pinturicchio and the Revival of Antiquity', *Journal of the Warburg and Courtauld Institutes*, XXV (1962), 35–55

Settesoldi 1994
E. Settesoldi, 'Regesto documentario', in *La difficile eredità: architettura a Firenze dalla Repubblica all'Assedio*, ed. M. Dezzi Bardeschi, Florence, 1994, 130–39

Settis 1999
S. Settis, *Laocoonte: fama e stile*, Rome, 1999

Shaw 1993
C. Shaw, *Julius II: The Warrior Pope*, Oxford, 1993

Shearman 1965
J. Shearman, *Andrea del Sarto*, 2 vols, Oxford, 1965

Shearman 1972
—, *Raphael's Cartoons in the Collection of Her Majesty the Queen and the Tapestries for the Sistine Chapel*, London, 1972

Shearman 1975a
—, 'The Collections of the Younger Branch of the Medici', *Burlington Magazine*, CXVII (1975), 12–27

Shearman 1975b
—, 'The Florentine Entrata of Leo X, 1515', *Journal of the Warburg and Courtauld Institutes*, XXVIII (1975), 136–54

Shearman 1987
—, 'Alfonso d'Este's Camerino', in *Il se rendit en Italie: études offertes à André Chastel*, Rome and Paris, 1987, 209–30

Shearman 1994
—, 'Un nota sul progetto di Papa Giulio', in *Michelangelo, La Cappella Sistina*, ed. K. Weil-Garris Brandt, Novara, 1994, 29–36

Shearman 1995
—, 'Il mecenatismo di Giulio II e Leone X', in *Arte, committenza ed economia a Roma e nelle corti del Rinascimento, 1450–1530*, Turin, 1995, 213–42

Shearman 2003
—, *Raphael in Early Modern Sources, 1483–1602*, 2 vols, New Haven and London, 2003

Simeoni 1934–5
L. Simeoni, 'L'Ufficio dei Forestieri a Bologna dal secolo XIV al XVI', in *Atti e memorie della R. Deputazione di Storia Patria per le Provincie di Romagna*, series IV, XXV (1934–5), 71–95

Spallanzani and Bertelà 1992
M. Spallanzani and G. G. Bertelà, eds, *Libro d'inventario dei beni di Lorenzo il Magnifico*, Florence, 1992

Spini 1940
G. Spini, *Tra rinascimento e riforma: Antonio Brucioli*, Florence, 1940

Spini 1991
—, *Michelangelo: politico e altri studi sul Rinascimento fiorentino*, Milan, 1991

Springer 1883
A. Springer, *Raffael und Michelangelo*, 2 vols, Leipzig, 1883

Steinmann 1905
E. Steinmann, *Die Sixtinische Kapelle, II: Michelangelo*, Munich, 1905

Steinmann 1930
—, *Michelangelo im Spiegel seiner Zeit*, Leipzig, 1930

Steinmann and Pogatscher 1906
— and H. Pogatscher, 'Dokumente und Forschungen zu Michelangelo', *Repertorium für Kunstwissenschaft*, XXIV (1906), 387–486

Steinmann and Wittkower 1927
— and R. Wittkower, *Michelangelo Bibliographie, 1510–1926*, Leipzig, 1927

Stephens 1983
J. N. Stephens, *The Fall of the Florentine Republic, 1512–1530*, Oxford, 1983

Symonds 1899
J. A. Symonds, *The Life of Michelangelo Buonarroti* [1893], 2 vols, London, 1899

Tampieri 1997
R. Tampieri, ed., *La Biblioteca dell'Istituto Nazionale di Studi sul Rinascimento*, Florence, 1997

Tempieri 1997
R. Tempieri, ed., *Carte Poggi*, Florence, 1997

Thode 1902–12
H. Thode, *Michelangelo und das Endeder Renaissance*, 3 vols, Berlin, 1902–12

Thode 1908–13
—, *Michelangelo: Kritische Untersuchungen über seine Werk*, 3 vols, Berlin, 1908–13

Thomas 1995
A. Thomas, *The Painter's Practise in Renaissance Tuscany*, Cambridge, 1995

Tolnay 1943
C. de Tolnay, *The Youth of Michelangelo*, Princeton, 1943

Tolnay 1948
—, *Michelangelo: The Medici Chapel*, Princeton, 1948

Tolnay 1954
—, *Michelangelo: The Tomb of Julius II*, Princeton, 1954; reprinted 1970

Tolnay 1960
, *Michelangelo: The Final Period*, Princeton, 1960

Tolnay 1975–80, *Corpus dei disegni di Michelangelo*, 4 vols, Novara, 1975–80

Trexler 1974
R. C. Trexler, *The Spiritual Power: Republican Florence under Interdict*, Leiden, 1974

Trexler 1978
—, *The Libro Cerimoniale of the Florentine Republic by Francesco Filarete and Angelo Manfidi: Introduction and Text*, Geneva, 1978

Trexler and Lewis 1981
— and M. Lewis, 'Two Captains and Three Kings: New Light on the Medici Chapel', *Studies in Medieval and Renaissance History*, n.s. IV (1981), 93–177

Ulivi 2002
E. Ulivi, *Benedetto da Firenze (1429–1475): un maestro d'abaco del XV secolo*, Pisa, 2002

Ullman and Stadter 1972
B. L. Ullmann and P. A. Stadter, *The Public Library of Renaissance Florence: Niccolò Niccoli, Cosimo de' Medici and the Library of San Marco*, Padua, 1972

Varchi 1564
B. Varchi, *Orazione funerale di M. Benedetto Varchi fatta, e ricitata da Lui pubblicamente nell'essequie di Michelagnolo Buonarroti in Firenze, nella chiesa di San Lorenzo*, Florence, 1564

Varchi 1843
—, *Storia fiorentina*, ed. L. Arbib, 3 vols, Florence, 1843

Vasari 1568
G. Vasari, *Le vite de' più eccellenti architetti, pittori, e scultori italiani*, Florence, 1568

Vasari 1927
—, *Il Libro delle Ricordanze di Giorgio Vasari*, ed. A. del Vita, Arezzo, 1927

Vasari 1962
—, *La vita di Michelangelo nelle redazioni del 1550 e del 1568*, ed. P. Barocchi, 5 vols, Milan and Naples, 1962

Vasari 1987
—, *Le vite de' più eccellente Pittori, Scultori ed Architettori nelle redazioni del 1550 e 1568*, ed. R. Bettarini and P. Barocchi, Florence, 1987

Vasari-Milanesi 1878–85
—, *Le vite de' più eccellente Pittori, Scultori ed Architettori*, ed. G. Milanesi, 9 vols, Florence, 1878–85

Vecce 1998
C. Vecce, *Leonardo*, Rome, 1998

Verde 1973
A. F. Verde, *Lo studio fiorentino, 1473–1503: ricerche e documenti*, II, Florence, 1973

Vettori 1972
F. Vettori, *Scritti storici e politici*, ed. E. Niccolini, Bari, 1972

Villari 1898
P. Villari, *La Storia di Girolamo Savonarola e de' suoi tempi*, 2 vols, Florence, 1898

Villata 1999

Leonardo da Vinci: i documenti e le testimonianza contemporanee, ed. E. Villata, Milan, 1999

Voci 2001

A. M. Voci, *Il figlio prediletto del Papa: Alessandro VI, il Duca di Gandia e la Pietà di Michelangelo in Vaticano*, Rome, 2001

Waldman 2004

L. A. Waldman, *Baccio Bandinelli and Art at the Medici Court: A Corpus of Early Modern Sources*, Philadelphia, 2004

Wallace 1987a

W. E. Wallace, 'Michelangelo's Assistants in the Sistine Chapel', *Gazette des Beaux-Arts*, CX (1987), 203–16

Wallace 1987b

—, '"Dal disegno allo spazio": Michelangelo's Drawings for the Fortifications of Florence, *Journal of the Society of Architectural Historians*, XLVI (1987), 119–34

Wallace 1989

—, 'Michelangelo at Work: Bernardino Basso, Friend, Scoundrel and Capomaestro', *I Tatti Studies*, III (1989), 235–77

Wallace 1992a

—, 'Bank Records Relating to Michelangelo's Medici Commissions at San Lorenzo, 1520–1533', *Rivista d'Arte*, XLIV (1992), 3–27

Wallace 1992b

—, 'How Did Michelangelo Become a Sculptor?', in *The Genius of the Sculptor in Michelangelo's Work*, ed. D. L. Bissonnette, Montreal, 1992, 151–67

Wallace 1994

—, *Michelangelo at San Lorenzo: The Genius as Entrepreneur*, Cambridge, 1994

Wallace 1995

—, ed., *Michelangelo: Selected Scholarship in English*, 5 vols, New York and London, 1995

Wallace 1999

—, 'Friends and Relics at San Silvestro in Capite', *Sixteenth Century Journal*, XXX (1999), 2, 419–39

Wallace 2001

—, 'Michelangelo's *Leda*: The Diplomatic Context', *Renaissance Studies*, xv (2001), 473–99

Weil-Garris Brandt 1987

K. Weil-Garris Brandt, 'Michelangelo's "Pietà" for the Cappella del Re di Francia', in *Il se rendit en Italie: études offertes à André Chastel*, Rome and Paris, 1987, 77–108

Weil-Garris Brandt 1992

—, 'Michelangelo's Early Projects for the Sistine Ceiling: Their Practical and Artistic Consequences', in *Michelangelo Drawings*, ed. C. H. Smyth, Washington, DC, 1992, 57–87

Weil-Garris Brandt 1996

—, 'A Marble in Manhattan: The Case for Michelangelo', *Burlington Magazine*, CXXXVIII (1996), 644–59

Weil-Garris Brandt et al. 1999

— et al., eds, *Giovinezza di Michelangelo*, Florence, 1999

Wilde 1932

J. Wilde, 'Eine Studie Michelangelos nach der Antike', *Mitteilungen des Kunsthistorischen Institutes in Florenz*, XIV (1932), 41–64

Wilde 1944

—, 'The Hall of the Great Council of Florence', *Journal of the Warburg and Courtauld Institutes*, VII (1944), 65–81

Wilde 1953

—, *Italian Drawings in the Department of Prints and Drawings in the British Museum: Michelangelo and his Studio*, London, 1953

Wilde 1954

—, *Michelangelo's Victory*, Oxford, 1954

Wilde 1955

—, 'Michelangelo's Designs for the Medici Tombs', *Journal of the Warburg and Courtauld Institutes*, XVIII (1955), 54–66

Wilde 1957

—, 'Notes on the Genesis of Michelangelo's *Leda*', in *Fritz Saxl: Memorial Essays*, London, 1957, 270–80

Wilde 1978

—, *Michelangelo: Six Lectures*, ed. M. Hirst and J. Shearman, Oxford, 1978

Wilson 1876

C. H. Wilson, *Life and Works of Michelangelo Buonarroti*, London, 1876

Wind 2000

E. Wind, *The Religious Symbolism of Michelangelo: The Sistine Chapel*, ed. E. Sears, Oxford, 2000

Wittkower 1934

R. Wittkower, 'Michelangelo's Biblioteca Laurenziana', *Art Bulletin*, XVI (1934), 123–218

Wright 1994

A. Wright, 'The Myth of Hercules', in *Lorenzo il Magnifico e il suo mondo*, ed. G. C. Garfagnini, Florence, 1994, 323–39

Wright 2005

—, *The Pollaiuolo Brothers: The Arts of Florence and Rome*, New Haven and London, 2005

INDEX

PHOTOGRAPH CREDITS

Illustrative material has been provided by the respective owners or custodians of the works. Additional credits are as follows, by plate number:

Antonio Quattrone: 2
Casa Buonarroti, Florence: 3
Alinari, Florence: 4
Conway Library, Courtauld Institute of Art, London: 5, 13, 31, 37, 38, 39, 40, 43

Réunion des musées nationaux, Agence Photographiques: 12, 29, 30
© The Trustees of the British Museum: 23, 45
Photo: Allan Macintyre © President and Fellows of Harvard College: 47
The Royal Collection © 2011 Her Majesty Queen Elizabeth II: 48, 51

peri mdice Eb muole a chora
o sei di erò auêdo a far chomto
lo p andar secho dapisa e poi
mezo Eb io tardero qua usino
pagnio dadrea ducati dieci
hari chare uoi spaciate fa
j pisa
erò passati qu
ça e poi ue
so o stretto
hora chome
marzi Eb io mi part
mamotes auisato dafranc
no scieuo dischiò ui ringratio
ui uedo questo p papa Eb a
puoi

. Vostro r

A di uenti sei di dic bre J fu

1518